A Management System for the Information Business

A Management System for the Information Business: Organizational Analysis

EDWARD A. VAN SCHAIK
Information Systems Management Institute
International Business Machines Corporation
Dallas, Texas

Prentice-Hall, Inc., Englewood Cliffs, New Jersey 07632

Library of Congress Cataloging in Publication Data

Van Schaik, Edward A., 1934–
A management system for the information business.

Bibliography: p.
Includes index.
1. Management information systems—Management.
I. Title.
T58.64.V36 1985 001.64'068 84-26606
ISBN 0-13-549965-8

Editorial/production supervision and
interior design: David Ershun / Barbara Palumbo
Cover design: Joseph Curcio
Manufacturing buyer: Gordon Osbourne

Printed in the United States of America

10 9 8 7 6 5 4 3 2 1

ISBN 0-13-549965-8 01

Prentice-Hall International, Inc., *London*
Prentice-Hall of Australia Pty. Limited, *Sydney*
Editora Prentice-Hall do Brasil, Ltda., *Rio de Janeiro*
Prentice-Hall Canada Inc., *Toronto*
Prentice-Hall Hispanoamericana, S.A., *Mexico*
Prentice-Hall of India Private Limited, *New Delhi*
Prentice-Hall of Japan, Inc., *Tokyo*
Prentice-Hall of Southeast Asia Pte. Ltd., *Singapore*
Whitehall Books Limited, *Wellington, New Zealand*

Contents

Preface

Many books have been written over the years focusing on subject areas such as "management information systems," "managing the data processing resource," "information resource management," and "effective information systems management." Information systems (I/S) managers have searched and experimented with techniques to organize and manage their function better. Consultants are hired to study and recommend how to make I/S function better.

This book focuses on how to take the things that I/S, user, and corporate management would like I/S to do, and make them happen. As a friend of mine once said: "Planning must degenerate into work." My objective is to provide a vehicle, a rational model of the I/S function, and enable the wish list of desired things to degenerate into work done—*the delivery of quality I/S service to the enterprise.*

This book will use three windows to examine the organization and management of the I/S function.

1. The IBM Corporation's rational model, called the Information Systems Management Architecture, will be the primary window. Any rational model must consider the most important ingredient, people operating in a high-quality manner. In this context, the architecture can be used as one standard to measure the quality of the organization.
2. The phases of growth concept will be used as the second window. This concept will examine the evolution of the architecture model over time.
3. The McKinsey and Company's 7-S organization concept will be used as the third window. This concept brings a business perspective to the other two windows.

Many people have studied each of these concepts, but have rarely considered their relationship. This book attempts to explain my perspective of those relationships and to show how the combination can be used for organization analysis. Clearly, this is not the only perspective that could be taken. I encourage the reader to examine alternative views.

The newest of the three windows is the IBM Corporation's Information Systems Management Architecture. Since this architecture is one of the three cornerstones of this book, I would like to review briefly the IBM research effort that produced the concept. For those already exposed to the concept, the title of this book could be: *Beyond the Architecture.*

BACKGROUND ON THE ARCHITECTURE RESEARCH

The research on the Information Systems Management Architecture began in 1972 using the Business Systems Planning (BSP) methodology. Several enterprises, including Phillips Petroleum in Bartlesville, Oklahoma, conducted BSP studies for their enterprises. Those studies examined numerous business groups and divisions, and produced long-range information systems plans. In all studies, the last phase included an analysis of the I/S organization and its ability to carry out that plan.

In 1978 it became apparent that in many cases a more in-depth study of I/S would be required. Robert Gruel, the I/S planning manager at Phillips Petroleum (now retired), explored the possibility of using the same BSP methodology on I/S itself. That early effort proved that the idea was indeed sound but would require more resources.

In 1979 the IBM Corporation began research on this BSP approach for studying information systems management. A selected group of I/S specialists with various disciplines participated in the first study at Research Triangle Park, North Carolina. Those disciplines included planning, communications, distributed processing, data base, marketing, service support, operations, and programming.

That study effort produced an Information Systems Management Architecture which defined generic business processes for I/S. The results of that study were published in 1980 as Volume I of the IBM management series entitled "A Management System for the Information Business." Those results were explored with many users of data processing equipment in 1980–1981.

In 1981 IBM expanded that research by forming a second study team with representatives from the United States; Paris, France; and La Hulpe, Belgium. The study team worked to refine the concept further and make it usable throughout the world. Japan and many other countries began using those results. This updated work was published in the second version of Volume I released in 1981. The more detailed Volumes II, III, and IV were released in 1983.

Many people working for IBM contributed to the Information Systems Management Architecture research and supporting documentation. Besides myself, the other key persons were:

1. J. M. (Mike) Daniels of IBM United Kingdom
2. Gerry Jacobs of the Market Support Center in Raleigh, North Carolina
3. Pierre Leipold of IBM France
4. Curt Marc of the National Accounts Division Systems Center in Gaithersburg, Maryland
5. Marshall Mason of the Field Engineering Division Systems Center in Gaithersburg, Maryland
6. Jim Roark of the Field Engineering Division in Raleigh, North Carolina

Ron Swift, Dave Heim, and Bob Hunnius of the Dallas Information Systems Management Institute provided sample reports and reviewed the original documentation. Elaine Schapker, IBM Technical Editor, did the hard work of editing Volumes II, III, and IV.

The Architecture research was also supported by the Guide International User Group in its project MA-279. They examined the architecture model and its documentation. The Guide input was very valuable in improving the usability and accuracy of the model.

ACKNOWLEDGMENTS

The research to extend the Architecture concept into an organization analysis methodology was conducted at the Information Systems Management Institute in Dallas, Texas. In 1983 IBM began offering a course, "Organizing the Information Systems Business," which presented the results of that research. This book is consistent with that research and course. Besides myself, the key IBM people who worked on that effort were:

1. R. E. (Cotton) Ellis of the Dallas Information Systems Management Institute, who created the fictitious Brazwell case study.
2. Josef Lucic of IBM Brazil, who developed several course modules.
3. Al Kawamoto of the Dallas Information Systems Management Institute, who provided key research on the enterprise perspective of I/S.

Don Larimer, Systems Engineer in the IBM National Accounts Division, developed many of the management planning survey techniques and the system of personal computer programs used in this book.

I would like especially to recognize several people who supported this book by providing valuable and constructive criticism on its content and flow:

1. Nancy Abraham, Assistant Commissioner, Department of Administration, State of Minnesota, St. Paul, Minnesota
2. Eugene W. Lieb, Senior Vice-President, Information System, Century Companies of America, Waverly, Iowa

3. Curt Marc, Consulting Systems Engineer, IBM Internal Branch Office, Harrison, New York
4. Marshall Mason, Senior System Center Representative, IBM Field Engineering System Center, Gaithersburg, Maryland
5. Donald E. Stehr, Manager of the IBM Information Systems Management Institute, Dallas, Texas
6. Theodore P. VonFeldt, System Center Representative, IBM Field Engineering System Center, Irving, Texas

I would also like to thank my wife, Martha, for her patience and help through both the research and the writing of this book.

1

Executive Perspective

In the decade of the 1970s, American managers began to feel the pressure to manage their enterprises better. The pressure is increasing in the 1980s. In the private sector, we found worldwide competition literally destroying the very fabric of our industrial might—auto, steel, electronics, shipbuilding. We fought back desperately, often copying our competitors. In the public sector, we found that the citizens no longer accepted unlimited government spending. Taxpayer revolts such as Proposition 13 in California have made it clear that citizens are demanding a greater return on their taxes and less taxes.

We have a mandate in the public sector and a need in the private sector to better manage the American enterprise. The basis for all management decisions is information. Information allows the enterprise to achieve the enterprise mission and objectives through its business processes (decisions and activities). The accuracy and timeliness of that information greatly influence the profitability of the enterprise and the productivity of its employees.

Therefore, enterprises must allocate a share of their resources (people, computers, and facilities) to focus on the quality of that information. Since the share of the enterprise revenues devoted to information management ranges from 1 to 30%, effective management is imperative. One survey places the average at 2.4% of the enterprise revenues. For simplicity, I will round the average to 2%, and suggest that you determine the real percentage for your enterprise.

It is generally assumed throughout the book that the information systems (I/S) function is part of a profit-making organization. To make certain parts of the text applicable to non-profit-making organizations, such as government agencies, the profit objective must be replaced by appropriate productivity criteria.

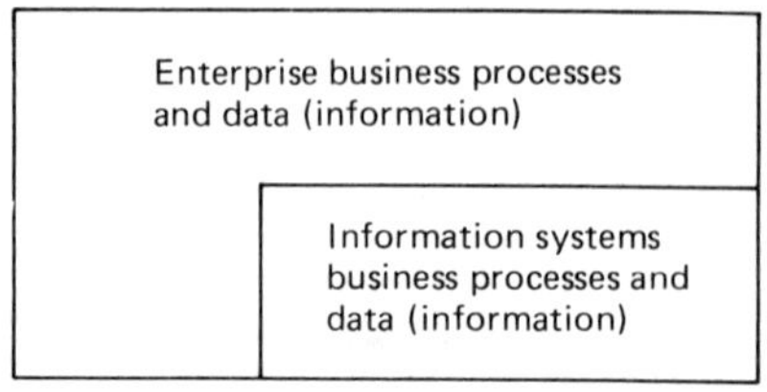

Figure 1-1 A business within a business.

THE INFORMATION BUSINESS

This book will take the perspective that I/S is a business within the enterprise business, and that I/S can be managed like any other business (Fig. 1-1). With this approach, the I/S organization can deal with the enterprise in a businesslike manner, or the I/S functions could be totally integrated within the enterprise organization.

Peter Drucker, in his book *Management: Tasks, Responsibilities, Practices* [1], suggested that the basic difference between a service institution and a business is the way they are paid. A service institution is paid out of a budget allocation. Businesses are paid to satisfy customers. Therefore, the assumption that I/S is a business requires a careful examination of the enterprise perspective of I/S.

Cost Center

Most I/S organizations are viewed by the enterprise as a cost center that should be managed with high *efficiency*. Costs are charged to users of the services based on the amount of resources consumed. Charging rules are set by the basic accounting practices of the enterprise. Those costs are charged either directly through some elaborate charge-back algorithm or indirectly as overhead expenses. For those that do not charge, there is no such thing as a free lunch. The accounting function takes over and charges are based on the department's share of the budget rather than its use of I/S resources. In fact, some business departments may be getting a significant subsidy through this accounting practice.

This focus on resource accounting generally is accompanied with an overall attitude of "How cheaply can we do the function?" That attitude puts I/S in a no-win situation. The users are dependent on the service and want more of it. The "budget slasher" is constantly trying to cut the amount being spent on this overhead function.

This environment is often reflected in the I/S executive's performance appraisal. If the executive does everything right and manages this resource shortage with high efficiency, the resulting appraisal is "meets minimum requirements." No one is happy, but you got the job done. If anything goes wrong (and it will), there are insufficient resources to correct the situation. Users are unhappy that their work does not get done, and the I/S executive receives an "unsatisfactory" appraisal. The "budget slasher" may be the only person who can correct the situation.

Service Center

As a business, the I/S organization should be providing a *high-quality service* to a *customer* at a *fair price.* Quality as defined by Philip Crosby [2] is conformance to a requirement or a standard. I/S can be viewed as an investment opportunity with a measurable return on investment. Since I/S on the average is only 2% of the enterprise resources focusing on information to make the other 98% more effective, it has the potential of a 49:1 leverage.

A simple example illustrates the fundamental difference between the cost and service centers. A major I/S organization had debated spending $100,000 for an application conversion from one generation of technology to another. This organization was heavily cost center oriented and chose to run the application on a technology emulator rather than incur the cost of conversion. A later business study discovered that this application was critical to the success of a $2.5 billion enterprise group. The failure to convert was jeopardizing that business unit.

The study also discovered that the enterprise could invest $1,000,000 in an on-line application replacement and show a $13,000,000 return on that investment over a three-year period. The benefits resulted from improved decision making in that enterprise. With a 13:1 return on investment, I/S was given an immediate approval for the replacement application.

The following conclusions can be drawn from the example.

1. As a cost center, the I/S organization used cost as the only consideration to make its decision. The impact on the client was not considered since I/S efficiency was the measurement of success.
2. As a service center, the I/S organization looked for business opportunities to support the enterprise.

When I/S is run as a business, all services are priced based on the value of that service to the customer and the costs incurred in its delivery. In any business, the price can be equal, less than, or more than cost. A new service could be offered at a reduced price to encourage a new customer or a marketplace. The price could be higher than cost to provide money for research, a major change, or to discourage the use of an obsolete service. All the marketing techniques used in any business can be applied by I/S.

Profit Center

There is a danger in extending this business concept into I/S being a profit center. In one example, a savings institution set up an independent I/S business unit to service the affiliated institutions. The I/S executive found that he could make a profit by selling those services to nonaffiliated savings institutions. However, he failed to recognize that this sets conflicting objectives, namely, external profit versus the productivity of the affiliated institutions. In this case, the profit incentive was achieved at the expense of the affiliated banks. Service was so bad that the executive was eventually replaced.

There are other examples where the I/S executive was able to achieve this difficult balance of profit and service. In most cases, a I/S business does not need to make a profit in order to be successful. The information business only needs to serve the enterprise in a businesslike manner.

SCOPE OF THE INFORMATION BUSINESS

Many enterprises have divided their information business into separate organizations based on each new technology or technology-related idea. Among the current groupings are:

- Data processing
- Office systems
- Information centers
- Personal computers
- Advanced technologies such as voice/data integration and local area networks

Each new concept is viewed as having new organization and management issues requiring a separate organizational unit reporting to the I/S executive. Many enterprises get organizational whiplash from the rapidly changing technology. Before we examine a more businesslike management of I/S, let us examine the issues and concerns in each of these areas.

Data Processing

In the early days of electronic computing, many non-data processing (DP) managers believed that data processing was unmanageable. The reason for this belief can perhaps be attributed to the general mystique surrounding data processing at that time. But there were other reasons, too. Electronic computing was a completely new field, and few people not directly employed in its use knew very much about it. Also, the data processing function was usually headed by a data processing specialist with little knowledge of general management principles. As a result, budget was often imposed rather loosely, almost as an afterthought. The emphasis in data processing was placed more in technical excellence and developing new uses for the computer.

Gradually, as computer operations claimed an ever-increasing share of the company's financial resources, this attitude changed. Senior management understandably became more and more concerned about the return on their data processing investment and began putting pressure on data processing management to manage their operational efficiency.

Increasingly, the growth and profitability of the enterprise became more dependent on data processing. Users within the enterprise gained a better insight into the nature of data processing, and many data processing organizations came to be headed by managers with previous experience in the administration of other business operations. Today, hardly anyone still believes, or is prepared to accept, that data processing is unmanageable.

Yet management problems still exist in the data processing organization and indeed sometimes seem to be getting more acute than ever. Money is spent on applications that prove to be either unprofitable or of minimal real value to the company. Application development projects slip schedules and overrun their budgets, often by several times the original estimate. And computing centers' commitments on user service levels are not met. This is causing a deterioration in the relations of many data processing organizations with their users and with senior management. In effect, data processing is failing to demonstrate that it contributes to the business results of the company in proportion to the costs of the resources allocated for it.

I believe that the solution to this "image" problem lies in the disciplined application to data processing of the same general management principles that have been used successfully for many years in the management of other similar business operations, for example, manufacturing and processing industries. In other words, a management system needs to be established that provides a sound basis for control of the data processing operation, provides a proper mechanism for effective communication among all parties concerned with data processing, and encourages a businesslike attitude in the people involved.

Office Systems

The office systems technology allows professionals not in data processing to create and distribute information within the enterprise. This technology started with secretaries producing letters, and has grown to have a remarkable similarity with data processing technology. There is little fundamental difference between a computing technology which processes text and a text processing technology which can compute.

Organizationally, this part of the information business has often been placed under separate enterprise control. This forms a second information business whose budget often does not appear in the 2% previously described. In many cases, these information businesses compete with each other to support the enterprise.

Information Centers

Enterprise managers and other business professionals have chosen to enter the information business with a concept called the information center. Fundamentally, this concept allows the business professional to convert data processing data into useful information with "user-friendly" languages. It also allows the business professional to create and distribute information to other business professionals.

The technology used for this third part of the information business looks remarkably like that for the other two businesses. In some cases, it is the same data processing equipment. In other cases, the information center equipment is placed under direct control of the user organization. The boundary between I/S and the enterprise is not precise when viewed from a technology perspective.

Personal Computers

The word "personal" implies that anyone within the enterprise could establish his or her own small information business. In fact, the technology used in today's personal computer is equivalent in power to the largest technology used in data processing 25 years ago. The cost and size have decreased, making it generally available to any business unit.

Personal computer uses

The personal computer is being used for a wide variety of applications, including a traditional office systems application, word processing. In other cases, the users are developing traditional data processing applications such as billing and collecting, inventory control, and accounts receivable, usually on a small departmental basis. These applications might not have been feasible for centralized application development by I/S.

Many users are also developing decision support applications, such as financial planning and forecasting. These often use one of the several spread-sheet software packages available on the market. With the introduction of high-resolution color monitors on the personal computer, business graphics applications become feasible. The user gets excellent response time, compared with many such host-based applications. It becomes feasible to use this personal computer capability extensively, both for data analysis and data presentation.

Increasingly, the personal computer is being used for direct personal support. This covers a wide range of activities, such as calendaring, messages, and electronic bulletin boards. We also see many personal applications developed of a record-keeping nature. The personal computer is ideal for tracking travel expenses and reimbursements, the inventory of physical equipment, and departmental budget line items. In a sense, the personal computer becomes the "electronic desk" for the professional.

An important consideration is the potential of the personal computer to unlock the door to the executive suite. For the very reasons we have just enumerated, the personal computer is an ideal vehicle for introducing the executive to end-user computing. It is flexible, simple, and nonthreatening. There is a growing number of corporations where several of the senior executives have started using the personal computer directly. The applications range from personal support (calendar, address book) to financial reporting and "what if . . .?" planning models. Organizations need to capitalize on this opportunity to ensure that the top executives understand the phenomenon of end-user computing.

Personal computer organizational approaches

The concept of a major enterprise having 8000 to 10,000 information businesses creates organization and management issues that are difficult to imagine. Loss of enterprise information control is not only possible, but highly probable. Some auditors fear that they may be unable to close corporate books because of an inability to verify data.

There are many suggested organizational approaches for the personal computer. The two extreme cases are called the "ostrich" approach and the "company store" approach. In the ostrich approach, data processing management takes the position that if the personal computer does not connect to their network, it is not their problem. Whose problem is it, that of the chief executive officer? In the company store approach, the data processing management, the information center management, or both make personal computers available as a service of the I/S business. They provide consultation on personal computer use, and establish policies required to make them effective.

Future Technologies

The trends of the last 25 years will continue over the foreseeable future. Local area networks, graphic displays, and voice/data integration will compound the management of the enterprise information business. In particular, the following facts are clear:

1. I/S is and will continue to be much larger than data processing.
2. Data processing has lost its monopoly on information processing.
3. The I/S executive must become a business manager for the information business.
4. Organizational units under the I/S executive must be organized around business functions, not just technology types.
5. Each business unit will be required to manage multiple technologies, for example, personal computers and office systems.
6. The examination and introduction of new technologies will require a new entrepreneurial dimension to the I/S organization.

THE INFORMATION CONSUMER

Historically, there has been an organizational and skill separation between the enterprise and I/S. I/S produced the information and the enterprise consumed it. In many cases, the consumer of information had little understanding of I/S and almost feared it. With the advent of the personal computer, the role of the information consumer and producer has changed. A simple example can illustrate this point.

On Friday night, the chief executive officer (CEO) buys a personal computer at the local shopping center and gives it to his 13-year-old son. From Friday until Sunday, the son programs the family income on the personal computer, including a color graphical display. On Sunday evening, the son shows the results of his weekend to dad. Dad is obviously impressed. On Monday morning, the CEO informs the data processing manager that he would like to have the same program for the financial status of the enterprise. The CEO is astounded to hear that it will take nine months and large increases in technology to accomplish the same result. The CEO's

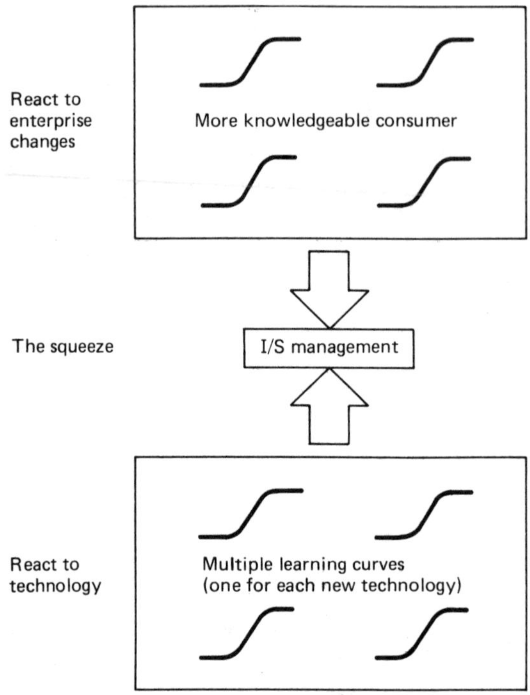

Figure 1-2 Learning curves for I/S and users.

first reaction is to hire his son and make him responsible for data processing. Clearly, a perception problem exists about the difficulty to produce the results.

This perception problem can be illustrated as a set of learning curves (Fig. 1-2). The consumer of information views television commercials and reads airline travel magazines which indicate that information processing is simple and readily available. Many of those consumers have their own personal computer at home. They no longer fear the computer world. On the other side, data processing professionals are constantly struggling to keep current with rapidly changing technical solutions. They no longer have a monopoly on the information business and could easily lose control.

I/S management is in a squeeze. Centralization of the data processing organization is giving way to many decentralized information businesses. Centralization based on the hardware economy of scale is giving way to centralization based on the productivity of people. It is even possible that the I/S resources will be fully integrated into the enterprise without a clear protective organization called Data Processing or Information Systems. Nothing seems to be stable.

BUSINESS MANAGEMENT OF I/S

Peter Drucker writes in his book *The Effective Executive* [3]: "An organization is not, like an animal, an end in itself, and successful by the mere act of perpetuating the species. An organization is an organ of society and fulfills itself by the contribution it makes to the outside environment.'' This is no less true for I/S than for any other organization.

Since technology is not a stable base for organizing and managing I/S, we must search for an alternative. As was stated earlier, this book assumes that if we really understand the information business, we can manage *any* technology. With this understanding, many business management concepts apply to the I/S subset.

One methodology that has been successful for 15 years to study enterprises and their information needs is Business Systems Planning (BSP). If that methodology works for enterprises, it should work for the I/S business subset. The ''1000-pound marshmallow'' called I/S can be divided into a finite number of business processes and data classes. Those business processes and data classes can be combined with people to make a management system. The result is a management system model for the information business.

Management System Overview

Effectiveness in the I/S business can be achieved only by setting its objectives within the overall objectives of the company it serves and by constantly seeking the real business opportunities. This in turn can be accomplished only if senior management and users take an active part in the decisions concerned with the direction and use of the I/S business, and if people in the I/S organization continually ask for the advice and cooperation of senior management and users.

Control in the I/S business is not possible unless I/S personnel submit themselves to the same disciplined working methods as people do elsewhere in the business community. Only then will committed objectives, schedules, and costs be met in application system development. Only then will agreed-upon service levels be met in terms of quality and timeliness of output from computer operations.

Efficiency in the I/S business, finally, can be achieved only if all staff members take a businesslike attitude toward their own work, measure their own performance or the performance of the area of their responsibility against established goals or standards, and try to improve productivity by constantly looking for more cost-effective ways of doing business.

Mission of the I/S business

Generally speaking, the three primary missions of the I/S business are:

1. Provision of service to the end user, including the collecting, storing, processing, and distributing of data
2. Development of new services and applications for other departments in the enterprise
3. Consultation with other departments on the need for and use of information

The service mission relates closely to the I/S organizational unit called ''operations.'' Similarly, the development mission relates to I/S organizational units called "applications development" and "systems programming." In most I/S organizations, the consultation mission does not have an organizational counterpart. However, many I/S executives are experimenting with the information center as an initial consultation organization.

These missions are also analogous to organizational units in other parts of the enterprise; for example, service is manufacturing, development is engineering, and consultation is marketing. Equating consultation to marketing is not an easy concept to accept. We will revisit that idea several times in this book.

In nearly every company, the I/S business has become an important factor in the performance of the total enterprise, and its importance is increasing. Establishment of meaningful objectives is an important part of the management process, for without them there is no basis for proper control, and effective management becomes impossible. As a result, many people are involved in setting objectives for the I/S business: The user departments set expectations on the quality of the services they receive, senior management in relation to corporate goals, and I/S management in reconciling these demands with operational efficiency.

The user view

At the operational level of the company, I/S is generally seen as a tool for improving work efficiency. Users view the I/S organization as a service function in much the same way as they view the payroll department, the messenger service, and so on. Each user group has its own expectations of service type and level, often without due regard to the budget, and usually without consideration of the needs of other user groups.

The senior management view

Senior management, however, take a broader view of the I/S business. The I/S function represents a large and probably growing investment in service. They are concerned primarily with maximizing the return on this investment. They therefore expect I/S resources to be allocated where they give maximum benefit to the company, and the I/S organization to operate economically and to control its costs.

The I/S management view

Essentially, the main goals for the I/S organization are the same as those of any service department: to combine adequate service to users with operational economy. The problem is to strike a balance, since user service can almost always be improved at the expense of operational economy, and vice versa.

What this means, in effect, is that the service provided by the I/S organization should maximize the difference between the benefits of the service to the users and the cost of providing it. A key factor in this trade-off will always be quantification: Users and I/S management must work together in quantifying, not only the costs, but also the benefits of the I/S service. This is not easy, because of the inherent difficulty of quantifying benefits. Difficulty in quantification is, however, not an acceptable reason for avoiding the requirement. Indeed, the more difficult the expected benefits are to quantify, the more careful management should be in quantification before incurring the costs.

The I/S manager's job is to control the various work activities in the organization so as to achieve these goals in the most efficient and effective way. Quantification is the key to this control. Objectives must be specified in concrete terms (for example, in terms of terminal response times, job turnaround times, schedule deadlines, and costs) and results must be measured in the same terms in order to make control comparisons and evaluations meaningful.

The starting point for effective management is the establishment of a management system for the I/S organization. A management system can be defined as the methods by which an *organization,* making use of available resources (people, equipment, materials, and information), directs and controls its *processes* (*activities and decisions*) to meet established objectives [4]. Separating people (organization) from what people do (processes) is a key concept of business systems planning. The advantage of this separation will become apparent in later chapters.

Components of a Management System

Organization and processes are two of the management system components (Fig. 1–3). The third component is the data resource required to run the information business. That data resource is used by the organization for management reporting and by the processes for planning and control. This planning and control loop will be called the Information Systems Management Architecture.

To support management planning and control, we will add the fourth component, systems/tools. This component includes any applications, hardware, and software to run I/S itself.

We will use the following formal definitions for these components:

- *Business processes:* groups of logically related decisions or activities required to manage the business resources
- *Data classes:* categories of logically related information required to accomplish the business processes
- *Organization:* logical groupings of people and responsibility to accomplish the business processes
- *Systems/tools:* logical groupings of computer hardware and software functions required to support the business processes

With this businesslike approach, the information business is manageable. The next few chapters provide an overview of some fundamental management principles and suggest how these can be applied to the information business. I hope in this way to inspire I/S management with new ideas on how to manage their operation more effectively and thus achieve what should always be of foremost concern: improved customer satisfaction.

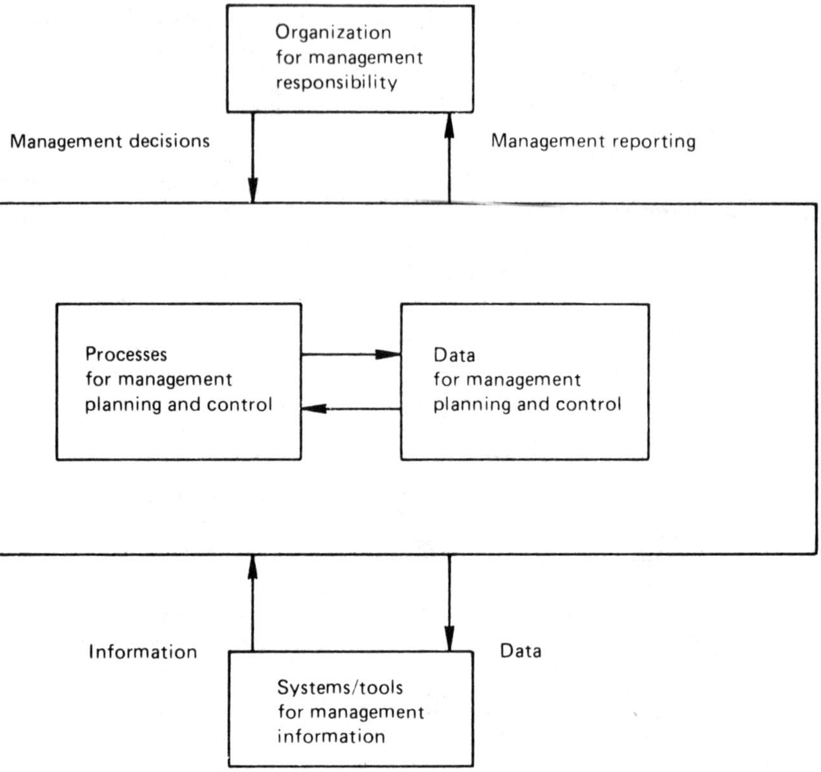

Figure 1–3 Components of a management system.

2

Phases of Growth for I/S Processes

In Chapter 1 we explored the learning curve of the information consumer and the I/S technician (Fig. 1-2). This chapter focuses on the corresponding learning experience for the I/S manager. As you read this chapter you should review your progress through these learning experiences.

An experienced I/S manager will gain insight into why the previous experiences happened and how the bad situations could have been prevented. You should especially focus your attention on the processes required to move your organization forward toward maturity.

For a student or new manager, you will find that this chapter is your career path to becoming an I/S executive. Each phase poses challenges and obstacles that you must overcome. Each year or two you might review this chapter to study your progress, or lack of it, in management learning.

OVERVIEW

Originally, Richard Nolan of the Harvard Business School defined four stages to the I/S phases of growth: initiation, contagion, control, and integration [5]. Nolan examined the organizing, controlling, and planning tasks required in each phase. Since a high percentage of large I/S organizations were in stage III, he was particularly interested in the relationship of stages III and IV. The fourth-stage integration included a rethinking of the role of the computer resource in respect to organizational goal achievements.

Nolan later hypothesized that the fourth stage was the end of one learning experience on computers and the start of a new learning experience on data [6]. This concept has six stages of growth: initiation, contagion, control, integration, data administration, and maturity. His study examined the applications portfolio, DP organization, DP planning and control, and user awareness for each phase. A transition point or discontinuity was experienced in switching the management focus from computers to data administration. This concept has added much to the understanding of organizational growth.

However, many I/S organizations are still locked in late stage II or stage III. The larger I/S organizations have taken 15 to 20 years to reach this transition point, and have failed to cross into stage IV. Newer I/S organizations are reaching the transition point in 18 to 24 months without making the transition. Perhaps we need a further explanation of that critical growth point.

A NEW PERSPECTIVE

There is clearly a discontinuity in the learning experience, but is it related to a switch in technology? Possibly, it is related to the skills required by managers in the I/S organization, and the management processes they are required to manage.

To simplify our discussion, we will assume a five-phase learning curve rather than the six stages (Fig. 2–1). The integration and data administration stages are combined in phase IV (planning). The fifth phase (strategic planning) has many of the same characteristics of stage VI, maturity. The relationship between these five phases and the Nolan six stages will be explored further in Chapter 4.

The associated basic issues at each phase are:

- *Phase I:* startup of the management system
- *Phase II:* growth of the management system to keep up with the growth of technology
- *Phase III:* control to bring the management system and technology growth into agreement
- *Phase IV:* planning to maintain both growth rates
- *Phase V:* strategic planning to allow the I/S management system to respond to enterprise environment changes

As we examine the management system growth in each phase, we must constantly consider the view of the user and senior management. Both groups can have a significant impact on this learning experience. This phase of growth discussion also assumes the following definitions:

- *Development:* engineering and building new resources (hardware, applications, system software, and facilities)
- *Upgrade:* adding new functions to existing resources
- *Maintenance:* repairing broken resources

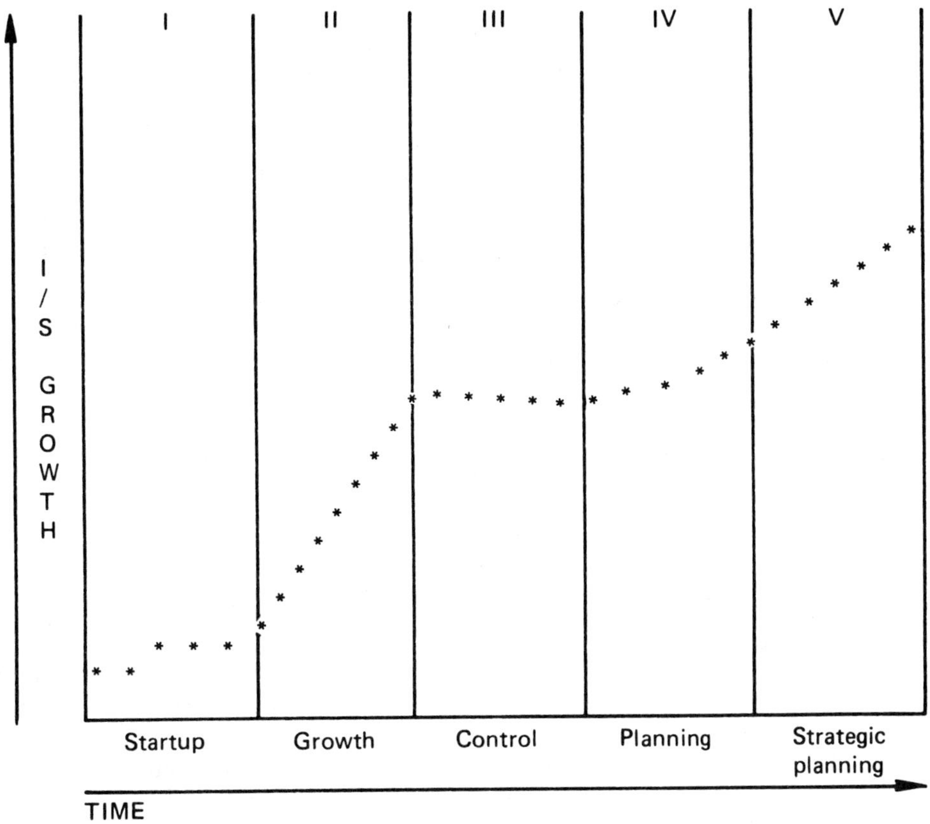

Figure 2–1 Phases of growth.

These terms will be defined further in Chapter 6. Also, the concepts introduced in this section will be detailed in later chapters; for example, service agreement details are presented in Chapter 7 under the process called "service evaluating."

Phase I: Startup*

The key word in phase I must be "simple," both in the management system and the technical solution we are attempting to manage. Historically, the technical solution has been restricted to batch-oriented applications, concentrating on end-user clerical replacement or other laborsaving uses. Often a single user or user department owned both the technical solution and the clerical function. The I/S management system was closely aligned with the user management system. In today's environment, the initial entry into the I/S business can be far more complex.

*The following discussion of the five phases is reprinted from the IBM publication *A Management System for the Information Business,* Vol. I: *Management Overview,* GE20-0662-1, by permission of the IBM Corporation.

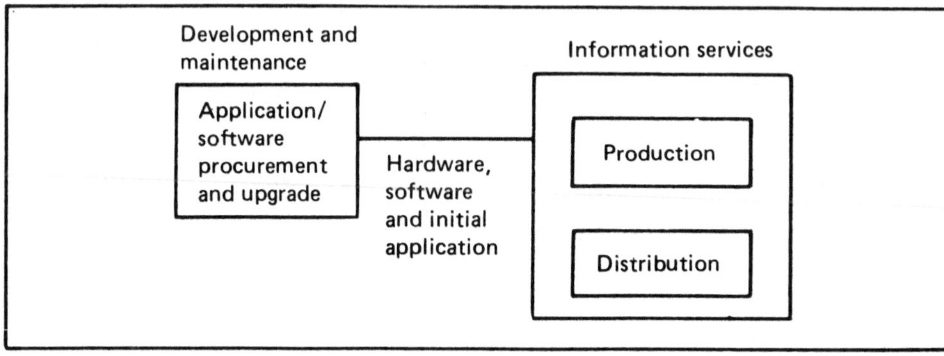

Figure 2–2 Startup phase processes.

Since we are learning the new technology at the same time we are learning how to manage it, the processes (Fig. 2–2) will generally require the first management attention.

Information services: production

A computing center can be likened to the production units of a manufacturing plant. In processing scheduled, recurring, batch-oriented applications, a computing center is like a manufacturing job shop. Resources (people and machines) must be scheduled, inventories of operating supplies maintained, orders received and made ready for production, equipment operated, and finished products inspected and sent out to the customers. In providing computing power for demand usage (for example, unscheduled batch jobs of all kinds, interactive programming, real-time update, and on-line data entry and inquiry), it is similar to a processing facility, such as an electric power plant, a gasworks, or a telephone service.

However, a computing center is unique in that it can be, and often is, both a job shop and a processing facility at the same time. Most information systems installations handle both scheduled and unscheduled work and process both batch-oriented and on-line work, sometimes simultaneously, often in the same processing unit. Therefore, the operations function must be managed to satisfy both kinds of demand with minimum impact on performance and schedules, and with the most economical use of personnel and equipment.

It may look as if the importance of a smooth flow of work has diminished with the introduction of remote job entry and output, and on-line and real-time processing, since many local workstations are then bypassed. In practice, however, local batch work can seldom be completely eliminated; on the contrary, many installations that have added on-line applications to their workload still find they are processing the same amount of local batch work as before—sometimes even more than before. Also, it is not unusual that local batch work is initiated from remote terminals. All that has happened, in effect, is that new—now remote—workstations have been added to the computing center, introducing a new dimension to the management of the work flow.

Information services: distribution

From a business perspective, information distribution is similar to the movement of products to and from the manufacturing or processing plant in the enterprise. For example, an extensive pipeline network is used in any petroleum business to move crude from the wellhead to the refinery or refined products to the consumer. In the petroleum business, the management of this function is separate and distinct from the refinery operation.

In the I/S business, the distribution of batch-produced information is generally managed as part of the production operation and does not require special attention. With the evolution to on-line applications, the distribution network requires specialized skills and organizational philosophy to adequately service the information needs of the enterprise. At this point, the distribution process, like the petroleum business example, becomes a separate and distinct part of the I/S business.

With the emergence of on-line information systems comes the requirement to adopt a network perspective in managing all application system resources. Of particular concern here is the management of the data distributed from the user to a computing resource and the information provided in response to user requests. This is the information distribution process of an on-line system, an area of I/S that is broader than the management of the communication equipment.

To manage the information distribution process, it is necessary to make a functional (not physical) distinction between the network and the central sites. A functional distinction enables the system to more easily adapt to a changing environment and allows new technology, hardware, and software to be readily implemented. A functional differentiation provides a clear, logical boundary that makes it easier to manage the network, since responsibilities and performance can be more sharply defined.

In today's I/S environment, the movement of information and the production of information are of at least equal importance. In some situations, such as "word processing" or "electronic mail," the distribution process has predominance over the production process.

Maintenance and development

To reduce the management system concerns in phase I, the development and maintenance processes can be supported by organizations outside I/S. Since the initial application may have significant business impact, it can be procured from a vendor or outside supplier. This minimizes the application staff required in this phase. Also, the initial hardware/software often comes in some preconfigured arrangement supplied by the vendor or selectable from the vendor options. It is possible to enter the I/S business with a reasonably sophisticated computer, including terminals.

Phase I summary

If we examine the Information Services process group, the startup phase ends with the user submitting jobs and getting information back. The user likes this environ-

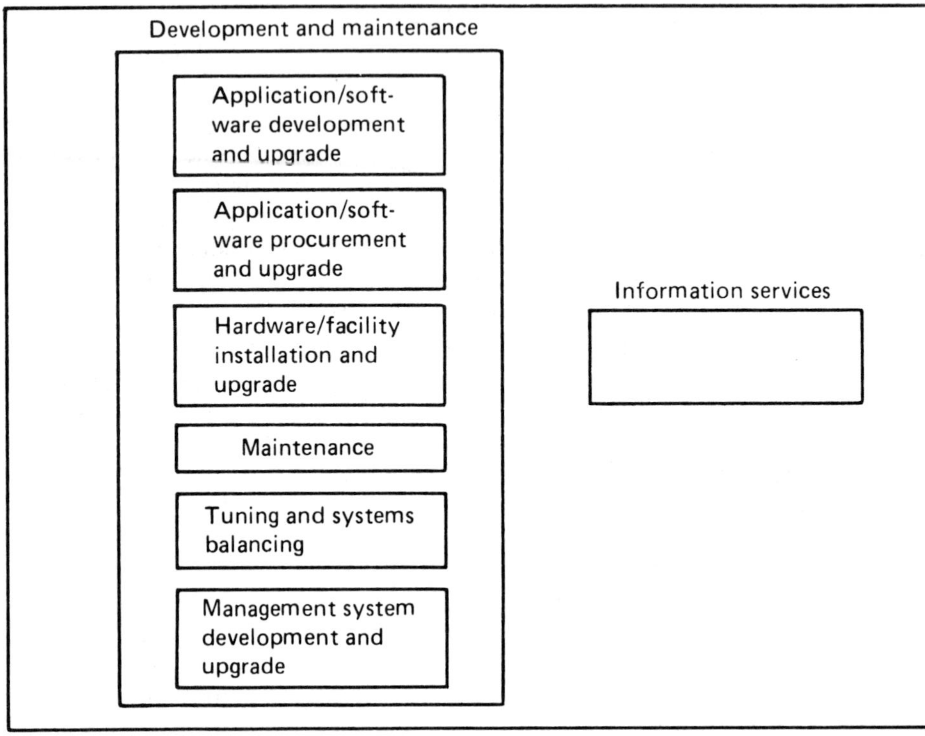

Figure 2–3 Growth phase processes.

ment, mainly because there are single applications, users, and resources. Therefore, the interactions are minimal—thus the complexity has not arisen.

Phase II: Growth

At the end of phase I, we have answered one basic question: We like the information business and want it to grow. Phase II must carry out that growth. However, a new question will arise: Can our management system grow fast enough to stay up with the growth of technology?

To guide this technological growth, the process group, development and maintenance, must be greatly expanded to provide the engineering required for new applications, hardware, software, facilities, and management procedures. This second major interface to the user is shown in Figure 2–3.

Development and maintenance

Almost every project-oriented undertaking, be it the construction of a bridge, the building of a house, or the development of a new type of aircraft, follows a certain pattern that recurs again and again for every project of a particular type. The same is true for information systems development and maintenance projects. They occur as a structured series of activities that are much the same for every application, software, or other resource. Within I/S, projects can be divided into the following categories:

- Application/software development and upgrade
- Application/software procurement and upgrade
- Hardware/facility installation and upgrade
- Maintenance
- Tuning and systems balancing
- Management systems development and upgrade

Each of these begins with the definition of requirements for the project and ends with testing and installation. The intermediate steps vary slightly with the type of project but follow the same pattern.

Every one of these major activities (or development phases) can be broken down further into smaller tasks; and again each of these tasks occurs almost invariably in every development and maintenance project.

Every information systems organization should develop such a standard project structure and apply it to all new development and maintenance projects. It probably does not matter very much what the details of the structure look like, as long as the list of activities and tasks is reasonably complete and each task is well defined.

Thus, each phase is a self-contained, manageable piece of work. A project cannot proceed to the next phase of development until it has successfully completed the present one. If problems occur in a phase, work can be restarted in that phase without returning to previous phases.

Information services

With these new project deliverables, the first user interface, Information Services, greatly expands with more users and resources. Some operational planning is required because of schedule conflicts. Project management and standards are added to reduce the operational impact of change. However, these controls are often informal and unenforceable. In an environment where growth requirements far exceed the time to grow, management is reluctant to delay projects that do not meet specifications or divert operations personnel to track problem situations. The management system growth quickly falls behind the technical growth.

Phase II summary

The users are submitting more jobs and are receiving more information. Information Services is operating but not at a level satisfactory to the user. The new work causes outages, jobs take longer, response is poorer even though the resources are much larger. Schedules are conflicting more and more. The user, who has now become dependent on the I/S business, becomes more concerned.

The user community, who forced this high rate of growth, now realizes that I/S can absorb only a rate of change determined by the ability of the I/S management system to control it. When the rate of change increases and the stability suffers, the users become seriously impacted. This inability to absorb changes and the resulting user dissatisfaction signal that the management system is out of control. Senior management now becomes involved.

Phase III: Control

Phase III is a critical and difficult phase. The key issues which formed late in phase II include:

1. The users are experiencing widely varying service levels.
2. The system/network capacity has become difficult to gauge.
3. Growth has caused significant dislocation, system outages, and user complaints.
4. Users are reluctant to commit additional resources to expand usage of an already unstable system.
5. The application backlog has greatly increased and is not responding to business growth.
6. I/S expenditures are growing at a rate exceeding annual sales growth.
7. Expenditures for outside I/S service is increasing rapidly.

This situation can best be viewed from the perspective of the senior executive who has major responsibility for I/S. On Thursday afternoon, the executive signed the I/S budget, which, for the second year in a row, is at an annual growth rate of 35%. On Friday, the executive attends a meeting with user department vice-presidents. The ensuing confrontation about the poor service from I/S includes: "I can't get my applications written." "Response time is poor." "Turnaround time is poor." "They don't seem to understand my needs." And so on.

This obvious user community revolt greatly disturbs the senior executive. On Monday morning, the direction of I/S is reevaluated. In many cases, this takes the form of a new I/S manager with a good history as a professional manager (with or without I/S background). The new I/S manager is given directives that are somewhat dichotomous. Put strong management controls in place to:

- Reduce cost
- Improve service to the user

These are conflicting objectives that are very difficult to implement, especially if we remember the phase II issues that caused the revolt. Phase II has implemented significant on-line applications that change the user departments' way of doing business. Any disruptions affect the user departments' ability to get their jobs done. Any severe impact finally erupts in a user revolt.

The user reaction is interesting. Since the I/S organization is not responsive to the requirements of the users and the new controls are tending to make them even less responsive, they look for alternatives.

There is a migration or a movement within the user community to install "simple" phase I types of solutions. This further erodes the I/S control. Even with the reduced I/S expenses, the overall enterprise expenditures for I/S continue to grow at a fast rate.

The users' move toward minicomputers provides only a temporary solution. In time, any or all of these installations will tend to grow with multiple users and services leading to many phase III environments. We now have several management systems out of control in a far more complex environment.

Figure 2–4 shows the phase III evolution required to correct this situation. Information Services is operating. Users submit jobs/data to the information service function and return with information. The development and maintenance processes are the source of all changes to information services. As we grow, Information Services is being disrupted at an ever-increasing rate. We must put a series of controls into place to regain the stability of Information Services.

First, we must formalize the control of projects to place more discipline on the "changers." This mechanism is called Development and Maintenance Control. Second, we must control the gating of resources and resource changes into Information Services. This is called Resource Control.

Third, we must control Information Services itself with Service Control. Service Control monitors the ongoing delivery of service and takes corrective action to ensure service availability. On interruptions, it must initiate defined bypass procedures to keep the service available. Similarly, performance problems affecting service quality must be detected and bypassed. On any of these detected problems, it forwards the problem to Development and Maintenance Control to have a solution constructed. This solution, constructed with the processes in Development and Maintenance, is placed into Information Services through the gate of Resource Control.

In addition, we must increase the financial accountability through better administration functions. The common approach is to bill users in computer terms, "EXCPs" and "page SWAPs." This sets the stage for the user to submit a job on Thursday and get billed $49. Submit exactly the same job with the same number of transactions on the following Thursday and get billed $75. This leads to further frustration on

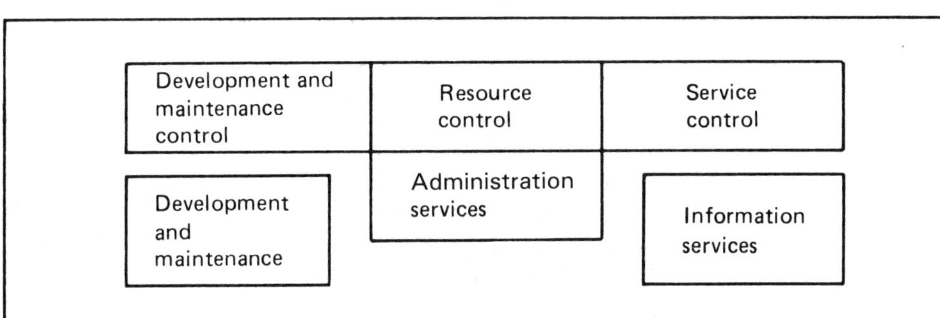

Figure 2–4 Control phase processes.

the part of the user. The fourth function, Administrative Services, has both a control and an administration role.

Development and maintenance control

As stated earlier, the vehicle for introducing change is a properly controlled project. A project can be defined as a mechanism to control the allocation of time and personnel to make a change in the resources available to deliver service to the end user.

Project size will vary from hours to repair a problem situation to hundreds of person-hours for the development of a major new application. The total project effort consumes from 60 to 75% of the personnel in a typical I/S installation.

It is no secret that information systems application development projects frequently slip their schedules, require more resources in terms of people and machine time than initially projected, and consequently exceed their budgets. Nor is it uncommon that an application system that finally emerges out of this disorganized development process fails to meet the expectations of both users and operations staff.

To solve this problem and produce quality deliverables in terms of function, ease of use, and/or performance, the following must be considered:

1. *Assigning the project.* Appropriate project leader and user sponsor must be assigned with sufficient scope to accomplish the project.
2. *Developing a detailed project plan.* A complete, detailed, and quantified project plan should be developed, which provides a firm basis for control of the development activities.
3. *Controlling a project.* An accounting and reporting system must be established, which allows the project manager to follow up on progress and recognize out-of-control situations.
4. *Reviewing progress.* Frequent checkpoints should be planned where management, users, operation staff, and outside technical experts review the progress of a project with the specific purpose of either approving it to proceed to the next checkpoint or terminating it if it is no longer attractive.
5. *Evaluating the project.* Compare the actual results with the planned results and identify the reasons for the deviation.

Service control

Installations that as standard practice draw up user service agreements have already taken a big step in establishing performance objectives for the operations function. In fact, these agreements represent the user-oriented performance criteria. User satisfaction with operations will normally depend on how well operations lives up to the terms and conditions of that agreement. If it turns out that a user has other expectations about the service to be rendered or the service cannot be delivered, the agreement should be renegotiated. While the individual user of computing resources is mainly interested in getting good service, operations management has to make sure that the resources of the computing center are being used economically. Improved service can almost always be obtained by adding more resources, but this always means higher cost, and may also mean poorer utilization of resources. The factors used to measure the economic performance of the operations department represent the operations-oriented performance criteria. The most important examples of such factors are workload, utilization of resources, and cost.

It is the task of operations management to strike a balance between the user-oriented performance objectives and the operations-oriented performance objectives. This can be done only by considering the two sets of objectives, not separately, but in conjunction with each other.

To provide good user service, the following factors must be considered:

1. *Scheduling the production and distribution of information.* Plan and schedule the current workload, monitor and modify schedule to optimize both production and distribution.
2. *Control performance.* Report systems performance by quantifying, measuring, correcting, and reporting system performance.
3. *Control problems.* Resolve problems detected in the I/S services by recognizing, tracking, and resolving abnormal situations.
4. *Evaluating service.* Evaluate performance against service agreements and identify the report variances.

Resource control

The "valve" that operates to control the flow of changes into the service environment is Change Control. No change is permitted to the operating environment without passing through this block. It controls the transfer of project deliverables into the production and distribution facilities and maintains control of changes to the I/S resources that result therefrom.

It should be emphasized at this point that there are six types of projects that can produce change. They are:

- Application/software development and upgrade
- Application/software procurement and upgrade
- Hardware/facility installation and upgrade
- Maintenance
- Tuning and systems balancing
- Management systems development and upgrade process

Once these deliverables have crossed this "valve," they become part of the systems inventory available to deliver service. In many installations, this systems inventory can exceed 100,000 unique items. The Resource and Data Inventory Control process is responsible for the definition, security, and location of these resources.

The identity and security of three other I/S resources (personnel, finances, and supplies) are entered directly through this process.

Administration services

The highly technical aspects of the I/S business often overshadow the processes required to administer finances and personnel in order to support them. This is surprising since the principal problem in many I/S functions is finding and retaining qualified people. Also the I/S budget often consists of over 60% personnel costs.

While most of these processes may be performed by a corporate function, two special areas of concern are education/training and I/S charge-out. As a minimum, the training and education plan should present a training program that will fulfill its objectives. It should include basic training of new hires, advanced training for people already on board, and training of user personnel utilizing the I/S business. In addition, it must provide for proper career paths aimed at improving job interest and job satisfaction. The education/training plan should therefore include the development of a skills inventory, job satisfaction surveys, and a career development program.

I/S often looks for some way to establish and control the relationship between I/S and the user. Financial charge-out for services is often implemented. Administration services handles the "record keeping" for these activities. There are several reasons that financial accountability is important:

1. Incentive is provided to use the I/S resources economically and effectively. Good investment decisions can be made only if those who realize the benefits also bear the costs.
2. Pressure is brought to bear on user management to live up to the committed savings due to the stated benefits of new services.
3. User involvement, which is essential to effective I/S services, is encouraged, since the users can control their costs only by controlling their I/S utilization.
4. Pressure is brought to bear on the I/S function to be more efficient.
5. The relations between users and the I/S function become more businesslike, since the type and level of service a user gets can be related to the cost for that service, and therefore negotiations can take place on equal terms.

Information services

In addition to providing for the production and distribution of I/S services, experience has shown that there are another set of processes to be performed in this area. These processes provide the user interface to help understand and guide their expectations, to obtain the services they need, and to keep them informed on how well the services are being performed.

The Customer Service process provides a focal point for the user within the I/S organization. Sometimes, I/S must provide services to the marketplace to satisfy user needs before there are enough users to completely utilize that service. A second process, Services Marketing, can be added to market these services in order to have them be a successful part of their offerings.

Phase III summary

In phase III we have concentrated on building discipline in the way the doers accomplish their work. Phase IV, planning, will attempt to ensure the doers have the right framework to do this disciplined work. This will require a shift from a reaction-driven to a plan-driven mode and necessitate the same disciplined approach by the managers.

Phase IV: Planning

The goal of tactical planning is to balance the demands for resources for the development of new projects and the demand for resources for ongoing services. This is shown in Figure 2–5.

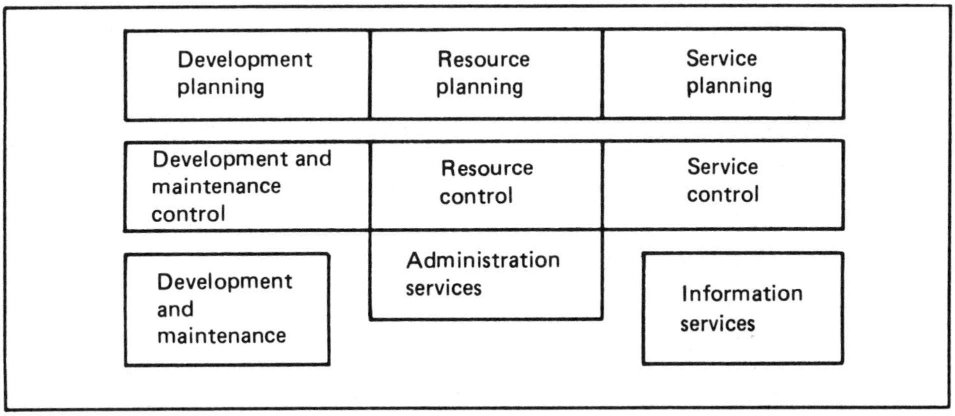

Figure 2–5 Planning phase processes.

Development planning

Development planning includes the processes that present the request for resources for the development of projects; it communicates these demands to service planning as well in order to determine the additional resources required for the operation of the services specified by the projects.

After these additional demands are combined with the needs already calculated for the operation of the ongoing services in service planning, the complete set of demands for resources is passed along to resource planning to do the final balancing, consulting the strategic plan, if necessary.

Service planning

For I/S to be a "business," service to the user must become the cornerstone of tactical planning. Batch service offerings provide a means of submitting the user application to the computer complex and receiving processed information. Quality of this service is often measured in terms of the application response, or "turnaround" time encountered, often leading to the addition of remote batch terminals in the user area. The quality and value of the product, information, is generally considered by only the end user. When a user has a problem, the computer center personnel usually provide some degree of immediate satisfaction. The relationship between the user and the provider of service is on a person-to-person basis.

Interactive or distributive service offerings require the user to interact with the "system" via a terminal. In this mode, the user is more aware of the system because of the contention factors associated with getting a terminal, getting a line, establishing a session, and receiving a service. In most cases, the value of this service rapidly diminishes with poor quality or response.

Service agreements can be negotiated to define the services available to the customer, measure that service, and record what transpired during the use of that service. Service agreements are key to adequate forecasts of demands for I/S services.

Like all other plans, the service plan goes through many iterations before an acceptable and approved version is obtained. Because I/S is basically a service function for the rest of the company, the initial phase of the service plan work requires the extensive involvement of user management in order to get up-to-date and accurate input regarding service objectives and needs for I/S services.

Resource planning

The resource plan is an essential part of the company operating plan and, as such, it is usually updated once a year. Some companies, however, use a concept of rolling plans, in which a new plan is prepared, for example, every quarter. During each planning cycle, the plan for the quarter just completed is omitted, the existing plans for the next three quarters are revised as and if necessary, and a new plan for the fourth quarter is added. In some cases, the plan must be updated as a result of major events or milestones, such as a disastrous fire, rather than only by a time cycle.

The final result of the resource plan work is the approved budget for I/S. This budget is supported by a set of activity-oriented plans, principally outlining all major projects and other activities that will take place in I/S during the planning period, and the resources needed to carry them out. All facets of the resource plan should generally support the approved long-range objectives.

One key process in resource planning, Tactical Plan Management, allows us to track the actual attainment over the planning period and handle variances that could arise. This control point is extremely critical in ensuring that the planning processes are truly guiding the environment required at the operating level.

Normally, this variance analysis occurs at a regular monthly meeting of I/S and user managers who have responsibility for the plan. Any of the following options are available to these managers:

1. Minor variances must be tracked to observe trends.
2. Resource variances may require replanning by the capacity, skills, or budget planning processes.
3. Objectives variances may require replanning by the development and service planning process groups.

This interface between the tactical level and the operational level will determine a true phase IV environment.

Phase IV summary

Essentially, the purpose of the I/S tactical plan is to provide the framework for the day-to-day activities of I/S during the period covered by the plan. The tactical plan can vary widely in size, scope, and level of detail. It is not an end in itself, but a tool to achieve a desired effect, namely, a definition of satisfactory (and obtainable) service objectives and a reliable statement of the programs, actions, procedures, and resources needed to accomplish the objective.

The phase IV plan will ensure that the doers at the operating level have the right framework to do their disciplined work. If this is successful, the managers can shift from a reaction-driven to a plan-driven mode.

Phase V: Strategic Planning

Just as the parent company must devote resources to strategic planning so that it can adjust its business to the changing conditions of the outside world, so must I/S invest resources in strategic planning so that it can respond to changes in its operating environment. In the I/S business, as in any other business activity, the requirements for personnel, equipment, materials, and processes all change with time; and the I/S manager must think ahead to cope with these changing requirements. Strategic planning for I/S is concerned with decisions about future directions (Fig. 2–6).

Establishing an I/S strategy begins with understanding the environment of I/S (the external environment, the business environment—especially objectives, strategy, key changes, major problems, and policies that will affect I/S—and the I/S environment itself). From this knowledge, it should be possible to define the responsibilities of I/S—goals, missions and scope, and objectives—and to obtain a commitment to them. Knowing these responsibilities, the necessary fundamental strategies for I/S can be established to "give direction" to what services will be delivered, how they will be delivered, and what resources will be employed (data, people, technology, and finance).

Using the I/S guidelines (a combination of the basic business guidelines and the additional ones necessary for I/S), the strategies can be converted into the key

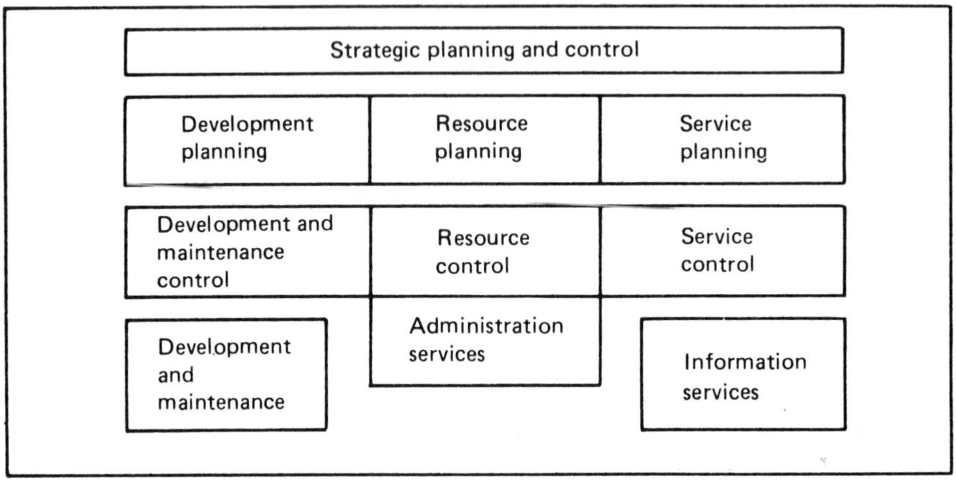

Figure 2–6 Strategic planning phase processes.

architectures (data, applications, and technology). These architectures begin with assessing the impact of the changes to be brought about by I/S. This permits a data architecture to be developed; the application architecture can then be defined and enacted by a technology architecture. As each architecture takes shape, it must "fit" correctly with the others.

The final step in creating the strategic plan is accomplished by establishing a time scale for the desired strategic moves and estimating the resources required, always keeping in mind the dependencies that are created thereby.

The strategic planning process ends with providing the plan thus established and gaining commitment to it.

Phase V summary

The successful implementation of phase V allows the I/S functions to be truly integrated into the overall enterprise. Any changes in the enterprise can be reflected in the information provided from I/S. Similarly, enterprise decisions can be made with a clear measure of the impact on the information that may be required to carry out that decision.

Summary of Growth Phases

The phase-of-growth concept is adequate to show the natural evolution of the management system through time, but must be modified with the facts in the real world. If each phase is slightly skewed, limited resources could be applied in the predecessor phase to install the planning and control processes required in the needed phase. For example, many of the problem and change techniques required for phase III could be installed in phase II.

This concept accomplishes the following:

1. It minimizes the time required for phase transition.
2. It allows each phase to start smoothly and finish sooner.
3. It maximizes the productivity of personnel installing the planning and control processes.

ENTERPRISE PHASES OF GROWTH

These I/S learning experiences can be altered by changes that occur within the enterprise itself. In any dynamic organization, executives and business managers are constantly adjusting to new opportunities and challenges. Significant business changes can force I/S to restart their learning experience, often at earlier phase levels.

This gives us the opportunity to introduce the fictitious Brazwell Home Electronics Corporation and its experiences with I/S. Although Brazwell does not really exist, it could easily symbolize the growth in your company.

Brazwell was founded 51 years ago by Norman Brazwell to manufacture his patent, a highly sophisticated superhetrodyne radio. In the first full year, it employed seven people and had a net profit after taxes of $16,821.17. From that humble beginning, it has grown in 50 short years to become a large manufacturer of home electronics, and ranks high in the Fortune 500 list.

The Brazwell Corporation has the following current characteristics:

- Four manufacturing plants in Austin, Texas
- Sales and service in 91 countries
- 11,000 employees worldwide
- Headquarters in Austin, Texas
- Net income of $696,000,000

The corporation had the following growth:

- Brazwell manufactured radios for seven years before he invented a unique radio and phonograph combination.
- Ten years later, Brazwell opened his first international sales office.
- Over the next 20 years, Brazwell acquired a number of companies in the electronics business, including the Ardmore Appliance Corporation and Morton Electronics.
- Ten years ago, the Brazwell Corporation entered a new market by inventing a revolutionary videotape machine.
- Four years ago, Brazwell moved into a new business area by acquiring the Justin Medical Equipment Company.
- Three years ago, Alex Brazwell, son of the founder, was elected the chief executive officer.

Alex spent his whole life working for his dad's company in various positions. Although his father was an electrical engineer, Alex chose to get his undergraduate degree in business administration, and a master's degree in finance. Alex was well prepared for his new position.

Alex strongly believed in the three principles of his father's company: quality products generate customer loyalty, fair treatment of employees generates personnel loyalty, and quick response generates a fair share of the marketplace. Alex strongly believes in information systems, but frankly admits that he does not understand the I/S people.

Two years ago, Brazwell acquired the Home Security System Corporation. Alex hired Ms. Nancy Allen as the I/S director and instructed her to merge the Home Security I/S staff of 65 with her 85 people. A consultant discovered that her organization had major service delivery problems associated with phase III. Home Security had major development problems associated with early phase II.

We might ask some interesting questions:

1. What organizational characteristics would you look for in each group?
2. Do you think there were any problems merging the two groups?
3. Is this Alex's last major challenge for Ms. Allen?

We examine answers to those questions in the next chapters.

3

Introduction to I/S Organization

This chapter presents an overview of the management concepts required to deliver the service quality desired by senior management. You should read this material with two perspectives in mind. First, it will tell you ways to manage the I/S functions in a more effective manner, hopefully making your job more enjoyable.

A fundamental conviction running through this book is that I/S can and should be managed by the same basic principles as those used for any other business unit. Established management theory may therefore be applied equally well to the I/S function as to, for instance, a manufacturing plant. Therefore, this chapter should be viewed as an opportunity to expand your management skills beyond the 2% of the enterprise dealing with the information resources. I/S managers can have a career path through any part of an enterprise if they develop sufficient management skills. In fact, the decentralized I/S organization of the future will require many managers to fill a business position and an I/S position simultaneously.

At this point in the book, you should have a solid understanding of learning curves or phases of growth. If you still have questions about that idea, I suggest that you review Chapter 2. This chapter will introduce organization, the second key concept required to analyze an I/S management system. The process model described in Chapter 2 does not come alive until you apply people as managers and doers of the processes. People operating in an organized manner is the purpose of this chapter.

Organization was previously defined as "a logical grouping of people and responsibility to accomplish the business processes." That definition is somewhat general and does not provide a clear framework for developing an I/S organizational model.

ORGANIZATION FACTORS*

In 1979, McKinsey and Company introduced a framework for understanding organizational change called the 7-S concept. This framework is less precise but gives a more inclusive perspective. The 7-S concept has seven factors, all beginning with the letter S. Those seven factors, defined in the book *The Art of Japanese Management* [7], are:

- *Strategy:* plan or course of action leading to the allocation of a firm's scarce resources, over time, to reach identified goals.
- *Structure:* characterization of the organization chart (that is, functional, decentralized, etc.).
- *Systems:* proceduralized reports and routinized processes such as meeting formats.
- *Staff:* "demographic" description of important personnel categories within the firm (that is, engineers, entrepreneurs, M.B.A.s, etc.). "Staff" is not meant in line–staff terms.
- *Style:* characterization of how key managers behave in achieving the organization's goals; also the cultural style of the organization.
- *Skills:* distinctive capabilities of key personnel or the firm as a whole.
- *Superordinate goals* (henceforth called *shared values* in this book): the significant meanings or guiding concepts that an organization imbues in its members.

This McKinsey and Company idea has been used to examine several critical management issues. In *The Art of Japanese Management* [7], Richard Pascale and Anthony Athos used the 7-S concept to examine the differences between American and Japanese management. In the book *In Search of Excellence* [8], Thomas Peters and Robert Waterman used the 7-S concept to examine why certain companies succeed and others fail.

We will use the 7-S concept to examine how the management of I/S differs from the management of the enterprise. Since the 7-S system factor is very global, it could be interpreted to include the Information Systems Management Architecture. The management system organizational component could be defined by the other six factors (shared values, strategy, structure, staff, skills, and style). This relationship of the 7-S's to the Information Systems Management Architecture will be used throughout the book.

Shared Values

In *The Art of Japanese Management* [7], the authors examined the importance of the enterprise shared values. One significant difference between the Japanese com-

*In this section, the list of 7–S definitions and the Matsushita business principles, employee creed, and spiritual values are reprinted from *The Art of Japanese Management* by permission of Simon & Schuster, Inc.; copyright 1981 by Richard Tanner Pascale and Anthony G. Athos.

pany Matsushita and the American company International Telegraph and Telephone related to the shared values initiated by the early executives. Matsushita had the following principles, creed, and spiritual values.

Basic business principles

- To recognize our responsibilities as industrialists
- To foster progress
- To promote the general welfare of society
- To devote ourselves to further development of world culture

Employee creed

"Progress and development can be realized only through the combined efforts and cooperation of each member of our company. Each of us, therefore, shall keep this idea constantly in mind as we devote ourselves to the continuous improvement of our company."

The seven "spiritual" values

- National service through industry
- Fairness
- Harmony and cooperation
- Struggle for betterment
- Courtesy and humility
- Adjustment and assimilation
- Gratitude

The American company, International Telegraph and Telephone (ITT), was managed for nearly two decades by Harold S. Geneen. Geneen relied heavily on style, systems, and structure. Therefore, he did not clearly document the ITT shared values.

As an I/S executive, our options also range from these two extreme cases. In comparing enterprise and I/S management, we must address two separate issues:

1. Are there well-defined enterprise shared values?
2. Does I/S management follow those shared values?

The authors of *In Search of Excellence* [8] found that most successful businesses have well-defined shared values. Although the book does not address the issue of I/S management for the same companies, one would assume that I/S follows the enterprise shared values.

In many I/S organizations, the computer industry shared values take precedence over the enterprise shared values. I/S personnel move from one company to another for more money or some special interest. The concept of a business within a business assumes that the enterprise and I/S shared values are in harmony. That cooperative relationship can reduce conflict and open new career paths for I/S management.

Strategy

Since the information business is in support of the enterprise, the I/S strategy must be in harmony with the enterprise business strategy. The strategic processes of Business Strategic Planning, Architecture Definition, and I/S Strategic Planning and Control will be discussed in Chapter 8. Two key factors developed by the first process are the I/S mission and policies.

Mission

The enterprise must decide whether I/S is to be a cost, service, or profit center. That decision cannot be made by I/S itself. Senior enterprise management through a steering committee or other organizational techniques must make that decision.

The actual implementation of the three I/S missions (service, development, and consultation) will vary for a cost, service, or profit center. This can be illustrated with the third mission, consultation. As a cost center, the consultation mission serves to perform the accounting and control of the I/S resources, and could be called Resource Management. This bookkeeping function is of low priority when compared to the other missions.

If I/S is an information business, this mission serves as the critical customer focus. Peters and Waterman (*In Search of Excellence* [8]) found that successful businesses never lose sight of their customers. The consultation mission becomes equal in importance to the other two missions.

Policies

The enterprise must establish the basic policies regarding the relationship of the information business to the individual business units, for example,

- Should there be one information business to serve the whole enterprise or should smaller information business units be integrated into groups and divisions?
- Even with varying degrees of integration, should there be an overall enterprise organization that guides planning, standards, communications, and data?
- What should be the data standards when data is shared between organizations?

Historically, the terms "centralization," "decentralization," and "distributed" have been more associated with the ownership of technology rather than managing business processes. In this book, a centralized organization will be based on a single I/S executive owning a major share of the Information Systems Management Architecture processes. A decentralized organization will have the processes either disbursed or distributed to several enterprise business units.

In all cases, the information business must optimize the productivity of the enterprise personnel supported by the Information Systems Management Architecture processes. This optimization will require an analysis of all seven of the organizational factors and their relationships.

Structure

Organizational structures require a different trade-off, such as:

- Focusing on efficiency, effectiveness, or both
- Grouping by skills, functions (processes), or both
- Maintaining continuity without destroying creativity
- Delegating responsibility and authority to the correct management level without building too much bureaucracy
- Maintaining career opportunities across the I/S organization and enterprise

Although structure is only one of the 7-S factors, it can have multiple dimensions itself (Fig. 3–1). The functional structure axis provides the formal continuity for the organization, the entrepreneurial structure axis provides the creativity, and the information flow axis ensures that all managers are kept informed about the status of the organization. Each of these axes is extremely complex and requires extensive study for any real comprehension. This section will introduce concepts dealing with each of the three axes.

Functional structures

The functional organizational structure, typically illustrated with a pyramid (Fig. 3–2), tends to focus on efficiency. Its characteristics include:

1. A single manager who gives unity of command, for example, the president

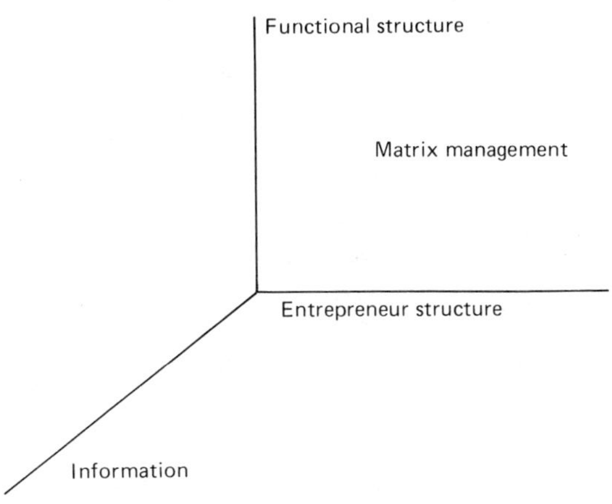

Figure 3–1 Organization structure.

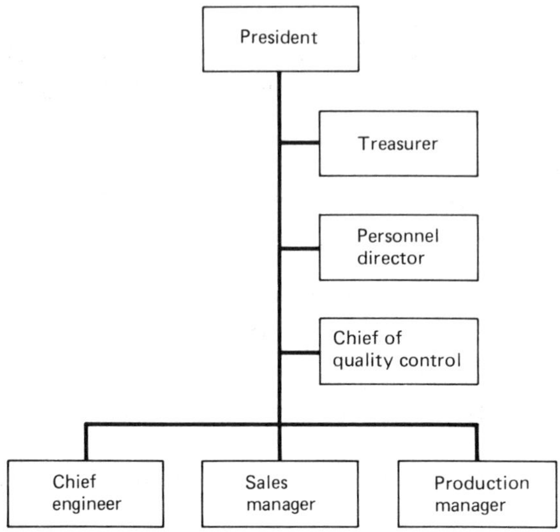

Figure 3–2 Manufacturing organizational model.

2. A delegation of authority and responsibility down the organization starting from the single manager
3. An understood power relationship where authority and responsibility are higher with a higher position in the organizational hierarchy
4. Resources that are dedicated to each manager

The manufacturing example (Fig. 3–2) can be used to ask three basic questions about traditional approaches to structuring I/S.

1. If I/S is truly a business, why does it not have a "sales manager"? The manufacturing sales manager focuses on customer needs, and serves as a balance between the engineering and production functions. Perhaps I/S needs a group with a customer focus.
2. Why do many I/S organizations not have a formal plans and controls group focusing on the critical resources of finances and personnel? Even small manufacturing businesses realize that survival depends upon accurate control of those two resources.
3. Why does I/S not install the quality control concepts used successfully by manufacturing businesses? Much documentation is available that could be easily applied to I/S, for example, a quality control program.

As pyramids are stacked on top of pyramids, organizations tend to lose their creative spirit. The efficiency begins to disappear. One approach to revitalize the organization is an entrepreneurial structure.

Entrepreneurial structures

Entrepreneurial structures tend to focus on effectiveness by using a temporary or alternate leader with a specific objective to accomplish. The most common entrepreneurial efforts are:

- *Project:* Accomplish the work within the time frame and resources.
- *Product:* Extend the product life and maximize return.
- *Program:* Direct the overall effort, for example, quality in I/S.
- *Location:* Coordinate the projects, products, and customers for a geographic area.
- *Account:* Focus on the needs of the customer and their use of our products.

These entrepreneurial efforts have three levels of formality and permanency.

1. A temporary overlay such as a project or task force has a short life and is replaced by other temporary efforts.
2. A permanent overlay such as a quality program complements the existing functional structure. It allows critical personnel to serve in creative roles regardless of their position in the hierarchy. The personnel involved in these overlays still work for their functional manager.
3. As people begin sharing more and more of their time, there is a need for more formal controls and responsibility reporting. Matrix management is an approach to formalizing those resource-sharing relationships.

In all three approaches, there is an opportunity for dynamic resource allocation. In the life cycle of a project, several organizations may be required to provide the resource needs for the project tasks. A product manager might have sufficient resources to do simple maintenance efforts, but be dependent on a project manager for major upgrades.

This flexibility allows the use of critical resources across the organization, and generally improves effectiveness. However, the use of both functional and entrepreneurial structures places new challenges on the manager and employee. This can be clearly illustrated by examining formal matrix management.

Matrix management

The term "matrix management" implies not only a matrix structure, but also a matrix environment consisting of processes, behavior, and culture. Formal matrix management is considered when the following three factors are present:

1. Outside pressure for dual focus (for example, functions, locations, products, services)

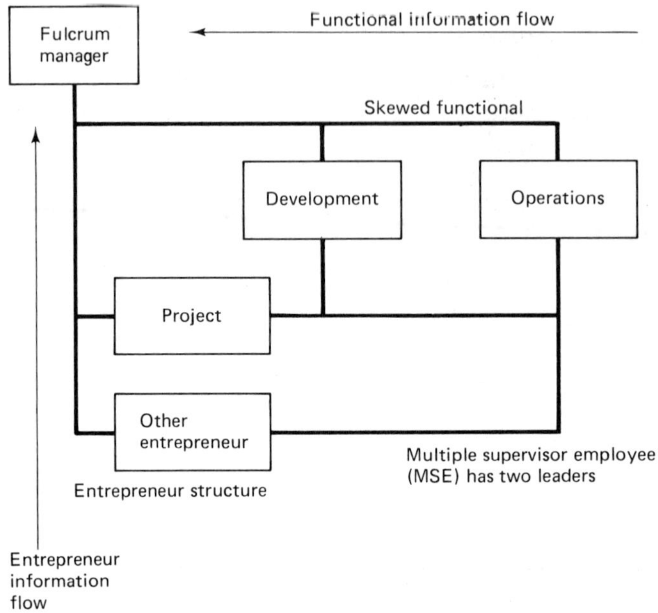

Figure 3–3 Matrix management organization chart.

2. Pressure for high information processing by managers
3. Pressure for shared resources (for example, data base designers)

A matrix organization chart (Fig. 3–3) represents this balancing of functional and entrepreneurial organizational advantages. The manager who must do this balancing could be called a *fulcrum manager.* Since there are multiple authority paths running from this fulcrum manager, the organizational chart takes on a different appearance. One convention is to show the major skewing on the traditional vertical axis, for example, the functional skewing in the example. The other skewing is shown in one or more horizontal axes.

Personnel who are shared by the multiple authority paths are called *multiple supervisor employees* (*MSEs*). It is beyond the scope of this document to address the problems of having multiple managers and being measured by more than one set of objectives. The solutions are difficult and require a different management behavior and culture. These solutions are well documented in Davis and Lawrence's book *Matrix* [9]. We will assume that matrix management is a feasible organizational alternative. In fact, matrix management has its greatest successes in high-technology businesses such as I/S.

Structure summary

You are probably asking: "What does this have to do with me and my I/S organization?" Quite simply, we live in a matrix world and must learn to deal with it. Every I/S organization must use projects, study teams, and other entrepreneurial structures to be effective. These form an overlay or de facto matrix across the I/S organization. The I/S executive has great flexibility to alter this informal structure, as needs arise.

The I/S executive can formalize any of these de facto matrices, if necessary. Several organizations have a formal I/S matrix across the enterprise. In most cases, the enterprise also uses matrix management itself.

Another important structure issue can be illustrated with the Brazwell example. Before the acquisition, the Home Security Corporation had a functional I/S structure supporting its information needs. We do not have sufficient data to determine the effectiveness of that organization. As the new I/S director, you have several options available to you.

1. You could merge the staff, skills, and management style into your functional structure, eliminating Home Security as an I/S identity.
2. You could retain the Home Security functional I/S organization, and manage both as separate entities.
3. You could centralize some resources, and leave other resources in the Home Security Division. This is a distributed organization approach.

The Brazwell I/S director chose the traditional option, a single functional structure of 150 people. The next 12 months was chaotic as each group sorted the 7-S factors (shared values, strategy, structure, systems, skills, staff, and style).

A feasible alternative would have been to understand each current organization before making any changes. A technique to do this is as follows. The Brazwell I/S, the Home Security I/S, and the Brazwell Enterprise structures can be placed on the vertical axis of the process-to-organization matrix (Fig. 3–4). Each of the Information Systems Management Architecture processes can be placed on the horizontal axis. For each process, the I/S director asks four key questions.

1. Who owns that process in each organization?
2. How effectively does each organization manage that process?
3. Where are there areas for improvement?
4. How many personnel resources are being used for that process by each organization?

	Brazwell I/S organization	Home Security I/S organization	Brazwell enterprise organization
Process 1			
Process 2			
Process n			

Figure 3–4 Process-to-organization matrix.

A more detailed discussion of this technique will be presented in Chapter 5. Two key messages are: Do not change the organization until you have enough facts; and structure is not organization.

Systems

In Chapter 2 we introduced one key system factor, business processes. As we group those processes into a functional, entrepreneurial, or matrix structure, we must examine the flow of information through the organization. Communication among managers will largely determine the success or failure of the structure. Later in this section we propose computer applications to automate that information flow.

Information flow in an organization

As a functional structure grows in size, significant changes occur in the flow of information within the organization. In a large organization, less than one-third of the information flows upward or downward along organizational lines. The other two-thirds crosses organizational bounds with one-third peer to peer and one-third peer to peer's manager. This communication problem is often characterized with comments such as "I can't communicate with management!", "Management does not understand!", or "My talents are being wasted!"

The multiple authority paths of matrix management serve as parallel information paths to the fulcrum manager (Fig. 3–3). Some organizations have implemented separate but related budgets and personnel systems for each of these paths. This complex information flow requires a clear definition of the processes, procedures, and reports which are the base for the structure. The Information Systems Management Architecture can be used as a framework in matrix or functional structures. This information flow consists of two report types.

Control reports deal with the present situation and have the following factors:

- They follow lines of organization and are structured to reflect the responsibilities of individual managers.
- They constitute an integrated structure in which the information supplied to successive levels of management is tied together and becomes more condensed as it reaches higher levels of management.
- They cover all the important controllable elements of performance that affect the organizational unit's contribution to the I/S business.
- They facilitate evaluation of what happened in the past by measuring actual performance against planned results.
- They cover relatively short periods of time and are issued soon enough to permit corrective action to be taken.

Planning reports deal with the future and have the following factors:

- They emphasize long-term trends of actual performance only and typically compare the results of the same organizational unit over this longer period. Reporting periods generally cover months, quarters, or even years with such factors as growth, unit costs, and productivity.

- They provide the basis for assessing where the I/S business stands, identifying new opportunities or performance improvements, and formulating new objectives or plans.

In both cases, the organizational structure has a large influence on the flow of reports. Often, control reports are used for the wrong purpose or the reports get misinterpreted. A poor structure can seriously restrict the flow of information to managers who need to make decisions. Any attempt to reorganize must consider the changes in this flow of information.

Applications for the information business

This information flow can be supported with a set of applications for I/S itself. However, I/S is exposed to the same data consistency problem as that being addressed for the enterprise. The following scenario written about enterprise application development applies equally to the I/S subset.

Any business must have consistent information throughout its organization. The keyword is consistency, both in the use of information by the processes and built into applications supporting the business. The traditional application growth to support the business has had problems in data consistency arising from the historical evolution of computer usage.

1. Isolated and independent application areas are selected and mechanized, typically to reduce operational costs.
2. The data files are defined as necessary to support the specific needs of each application without regard to one another or to future applications.
3. The data itself is converted from manual files located and maintained by the various organizations.
4. As computer applications are added, new data files are usually required since the combination data required for different applications are rarely the same. These are usually created from existing mechanized files and combined with additional data required for each unique business area.
5. Summary-type reports for higher management are the result of sorting and merging various existing data files together to create new ones. Rarely is any existing data file of the form or content required to provide newly requested information. Thus, new data files are born.
6. Data redundancies and file update requirements multiply.

With all these potential data inconsistencies, it is no wonder that reports frequently do not match between managers. This becomes a problem most often during interdepartmental decision making or at higher reporting levels where consolidation of multiple function activities is important.

Attempts to provide better data consistency usually result in existing applications being "systematized" or consolidated into larger applications with broader scope and expanded data definitions. This may yield a satisfactory system within the expanded scope, but will result in data inconsistencies between the larger systems. Efforts to "systematize" these larger applications may be extremely expensive and difficult to justify, let alone accomplish. Comments prevail such as "our systems cannot talk to one another."

What has been described is the classical "bottom-up" evolution of applications. In order to begin to address the data consistency problem, a different philosophy must be adopted relative to data management. This is commonly referred to as managing data as a resource.

Data as a resource

This concept suggests that data is of considerable overall value to an organization and should be managed accordingly. It should be potentially available to and shared by the total business on a consistent basis. It should not be controlled by an organizational segment but by a central coordinator, much like other corporate resources, such as cash and personnel. The management function would include formulating policies and procedures for consistent definition, sources, technical implication, use, and security of the data.

The data associated with the I/S business encounters the same fate as that described for the total enterprise. In many cases, the I/S data situation can be compared with the analogy of the mechanic who never fixes his car because he is too busy servicing others. The data classes described in this document illustrate the similarity of the data required for both the I/S and the enterprise businesses. In fact, the extension of the "data is a resource" concept to cover I/S allows the resolution of both problems simultaneously.

ORGANIZATION SUMMARY

Each of the 7-S factors (shared values, strategy, structure, systems, skills, staff, and style) has some degree of instability. Then, what is the most stable factor? I suggest that business processes within the system factor are the most stable.

Processes force us to think through the basic decisions and activities independent of organizational structure. The Information Systems Management Architecture provides a logical view and relationship of how processes occur within I/S. If we have the right processes, we can study the enterprise shared values and build an I/S strategy. We can plan the skills and staff to meet that strategy. We can plan and build several structural solutions.

We can even define processes to build and monitor the management system itself. In the next chapter we examine the Information Systems Management Architecture.

4

*Information Systems Management Architecture**

We have discussed two key windows for analyzing an I/S management system: the phases of growth and the 7-S organization factors. The first window allows you to observe the growth of your management system through time. The second window allows you to superimpose the 7-S organization factors on that growth. Together, the two windows provide a powerful management tool. In this chapter we add the third window for observing your I/S management system, the Information Systems Management (ISM) Architecture. The ISM Architecture provides a generic representation of the processes and data that must be managed by the I/S organization.

You already have seen a bottom-up perspective of the ISM Architecture in the phase of growth discussion. This chapter will give you the perspective of a senior I/S executive who must manage a large, mature organization with data processing, office systems, personal computers, and other technologies. It might be called a top-down perspective that is independent of growth and organization.

Several key management concepts are presented in a condensed form. Even with prior management training and experience, you will have to study each concept carefully.

PLANNING AND CONTROL CONCEPTS

A business process defines the decisions and/or activities that must be accomplished by the personnel in the organization. If we combine those processes with data, we

*Parts of this chapter are reproduced from the IBM publication *A Management System for the Information Business*, Vol. I: *Management Overview*, GE20-0662-1, by permission of the IBM Corporation.

form a planning and control loop. That planning and control loop is called the Information Systems Management Architecture. It shows the logical sequence of I/S decisions and the data flow from process to process. Before we examine the individual processes and data classes in the architecture, let us review basic planning and control concepts.

Basic Planning and Control Loop

The management system processes contain planning, execution, measurement, and control activities (and/or decisions). Sound processes are based on an understanding of the fundamental activities of the decision maker. Although these activities have a complex relationship and are usually carried out concurrently rather than consecutively, they are nevertheless distinct enough to be considered separately. The activities and their interrelationship are shown in Figure 4–1 and described below.

- Setting objectives involves the definition of the goals and success factors to be obtained.
- Planning involves developing what is going to be done, by whom, with what resources, and within what period of time. It also involves obtaining and combining the human and physical resources needed for the work activities to be performed in order to meet the objectives.
- Execution involves the performance of work activities in the plan.
- Measurement is the gathering of data about the progress or actual results of these work activities.
- Control consists of comparing progress against the plans to see whether the desired goals are being met, and if the results have deviated from the plans, taking appropriate corrective action.

Thus, a "closed-loop" relationship between planning and control is established. Under normal conditions, the control functions verify that the work activities are

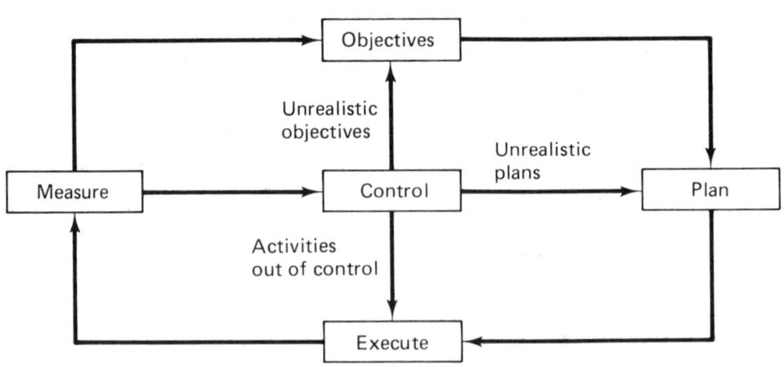

Figure 4–1 The planning and control process activities.

accomplishing the desired plan. If the comparison shows a discrepancy between the plans and the results of the work activities, a decision must be made as to which of them is at fault, and what is to be done. Reassignment of resources may bring the work activities in line with the plan. Replanning may be required if external factors have changed. The original objectives may no longer be feasible.

Planning and Control Levels

The planning and control level concept was presented by Robert Anthony of the Harvard Business School in 1965 [10]. His work considered the time to make business decisions and relationships of those decisions.

When developing management systems for an organization, it must be appreciated that the planning and control processes take place at different levels, the management activities at each level covering a specific time span and having a specific purpose. Three levels are considered (Fig. 4–2).

- Strategic level (covering a five-year period, or longer)
- Tactical level (covering a one- to two-year period)
- Operational level (on a daily, weekly, or monthly basis)

In practice, there are variable degrees of overlap between the various planning and control levels. The strategic level can be considered as what to do or doing the right things, and operational level as how to do it or doing things right. Tactical level is a mixture of both. In more specific terms:

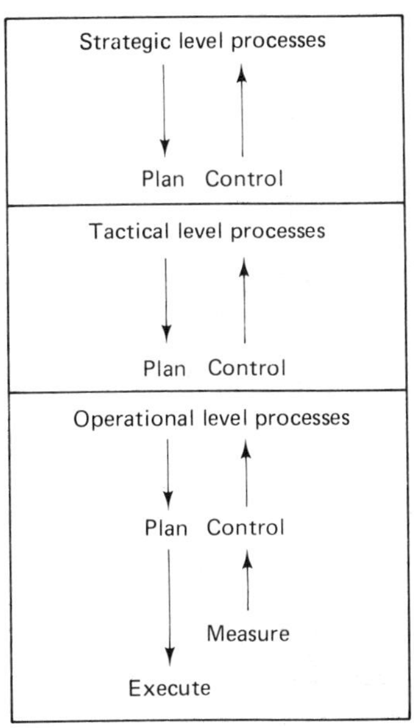

Figure 4–2 Planning and control levels.

1. The strategic level is concerned with adjusting the business over time according to the ever-changing conditions and requirements of the environment, the environment being, for example, society, the market, and advances in technology. It involves the direction setting of long-range objectives, the establishment of overall priorities, and the selection of the strategies (that is, the approaches and methods) to be used to meet the objectives.
2. The tactical level concerns the planning and control of resource management within the framework of the established strategic objectives. In many organizations this often requires considerable effort. It involves breaking down the long-range objectives into shorter-range objectives, determining the resources needed, setting up and implementing specific plans to reach the objectives, and ensuring that the resources are brought in and used by the organization in the best possible way.

   The tactical-level processes are performed in many parts of an organization: for example, personnel planning, purchasing planning, and production planning. Budgeting and other financial organizations play a key role at this level, because they provide information about the combined financial effects of other tactical decisions in the company.
3. The operational level is directed toward the planning and control of individual activities and tasks within the framework of given resources. It is primarily responsible for seeing that assigned tasks are carried out in the best possible manner and that resources are used efficiently. Planning the work to be done next week, following up the work accomplished last week, and detailed scheduling are examples of management activities in this category.

PROCESS GROUPS AND FLOW

Before we continue our discussion, let us summarize several key points:

1. A planning and control loop consists of objectives setting, planning, execution, measurement, and control.
2. Three separate planning and control loops are required to manage the organization direction (strategic), resource allocation (tactical), and task execution (operational). Each loop operates over different time horizons and time increments.
3. These three planning and control loops are required to accomplish the three missions (service, development, and consultation).
4. Information, including objectives and plans, must flow through the planning and control loops. Information content and resolution change at the boundary of each level.

These four critical concepts are basic to understanding the remainder of this chapter. You might review these concepts before proceeding.

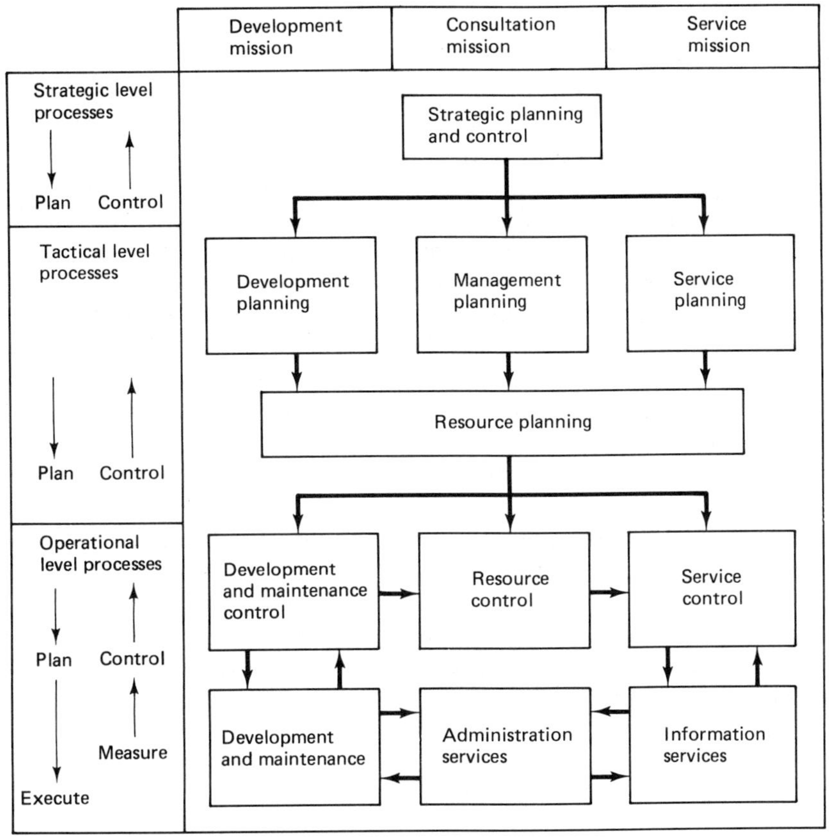

Figure 4–3 ISM process groups.

Top-Down Overview

We can combine the three I/S missions with the planning and control level concept to illustrate the Information Systems Management (ISM) Architecture (Fig. 4–3). This illustration is a grid with the missions forming the vertical axis and the planning and control levels forming the horizontal axis. Superimposed on this grid are the 11 process groups of the ISM Architecture. Each process group is placed in the mission and time frame which it supports; for example, the Development Planning process group supports the development mission in the tactical time frame.

The processes are combined into 11 process groups, each with multiple processes, to simplify a general understanding of the information business. The flow of information between process groups generally illustrates the relationship of these processes.

The basic explanation of the ISM Architecture begins with setting strategic objectives (Strategic Planning and Control). These objectives are then translated into tactical objectives for the operation of ongoing services (Service Planning) and the creation of new services (Development Planning).

These two sets of objectives are consolidated and integrated into a plan to achieve them (Resource Planning). Following this plan at the operational level means managing the ongoing services (Service Control) while new projects are being developed (Development and Maintenance Control) and introduced into the operations side through a transfer process (Resource Control). The actual "doing" processes of Service Control are carried out in Information Services; similarly, the actual "doing" processes of Development and Maintenance Control are described in Development and Maintenance. An additional block of processes, Administration Services, includes all the processes necessary to support the activities already described.

Finally, there is the need to continue to inspect and upgrade this management system and so another block of processes (Management Planning) is included. This tactical process group sets the objectives or rules under which I/S will operate. These I/S internal needs are balanced with the enterprise needs as part of the consolidated resource plan. The actual "doing" processes for building the management system are shared with the normal development and maintenance processes.

In the next section we examine each of these 11 process groups in more detail. We will again present the 10 process groups that form the "content" of the management system before we discuss the process group that guides the building of the management system.

Strategic Planning and Control

This process group stemming from the strategic planning needs of the total enterprise defines the more specific needs of the "information business." The Business Strategic Planning process establishes the I/S mission and policies, and defines the information framework for the enterprise. That framework consists of the enterprise business processes, the enterprise information flow, and the I/S subset defined in this chapter as the Information Systems Management Architecture. Those frameworks are used to define the enterprise information requirements to be supported by I/S.

The Architecture Definition process builds three additional frameworks under which I/S must operate: the Application, Data, and Technology Architectures. The Technology Architecture includes hardware, software, and facilities. These architectures form the base necessary to build information systems.

The I/S Strategic Planning and Control process defines the long-range plan for the I/S organization. It monitors the execution of the long-range plan and makes appropriate corrections.

Development Planning

From the strategic requirements, previously discussed, a set of shorter-term requirements are selected, a time schedule assigned, and resources calculated. The purpose of Development Planning is to define an implementable subset of the strategic plan to be executed over the tactical time horizon. In order to do this, it must select an appropriate subset of applications from the basic architecture, verify that the necessary changes to data bases can be made in order to implement the applications, and verify that they are technologically achievable within the basic technology architecture already established.

The integration of these plans for applications, data, and technology defines projects and specifies the requirements for both the development and the operation of these projects. A project can be defined as a mechanism to control the allocation of time and manpower to make a change in the resources available to deliver service to the end user.

Service Planning

The purpose of the parallel process group, Service Planning, is to define the requirements for providing I/S services: both ongoing and those required as a result of the new projects defined in Development Planning. To do this means understanding the complete set of services, inspecting them for requirements of service levels required, recovery procedures, security procedures, and audit procedures, and as a result, defining the requirements to "run" all the services.

Resource Planning

The purpose of Resource Planning is to receive the requirements from Development Planning and Service Planning and to resolve them into a sensible, achievable, and coordinated plan for the total I/S function. During these processes it will compare the available and alternative resources against identified resource requirements (both projects and services) over the planning horizon or at major milestones, identify imbalances, recommend corrective action, and publish a tactical plan.

This tactical plan, within the budget established, will define the system capacity required, the skills and education necessary, and provide for the management of the plan during its lifetime. Once the tactical plan has been established, it is enacted by Service Control, Development and Maintenance Control, and Resource Control.

Service Control

The purpose of Service Control is to maintain the satisfactory production and distribution of I/S services. In order to do this, it must translate the planned service levels into operation schedule, measure against that schedule, and report variances. It must also recognize, track, and ensure resolution of problems resulting therefrom.

Development and Maintenance Control

Similarly, the purpose of Development and Maintenance Control is to maintain the satisfactory development of projects. In order to do this, it must manage project objectives, define the specific tasks for each phase, assign resources, track schedule progress, resolve development problems via project review, and inform all levels of management.

Resource Control

During the life of the plan, the deliverables from projects must be transferred into the production and distribution facilities with a minimum of disruption and providing a more stable environment for the user. One purpose of Resource Control is to provide a "valve" through which all project deliverables flow and to maintain control of the changes to the I/S resources resulting therefrom.

Once the deliverable had cleared this "valve," it becomes part of the inventory available to the service environment. This inventory, sometimes called the systems inventory, defines and controls the resources used to deliver the production and distribution services. Control of the systems inventory is perhaps one of the most critical points in the management system.

Development and Maintenance

The purpose of Development and Maintenance is to develop and implement a project according to the procedures defined by Development and Maintenance Control. Basically, projects can be of the following types:

- Application/software develolpment and upgrade
- Application/software procurement and upgrade
- Hardware/facility installation and upgrade
- Maintenance
- Tuning and system balancing
- Management systems development and upgrade

Several such projects may be combined into a larger project. But they should all be developed as specified by Development and Maintenance Control.

Information Services

The purpose of Information Services is to provide the I/S services under the control of Service Control. These processes include both the production of information (that part of the operation directly under control of an operating system) and the distribution (all the rest of the activities required to obtain or deliver data to and from end users). This flow can be from user to user (message switching), user to production (normal input), production to user (normal output), or production to production (networking). To produce and deliver the appropriate information successfully requires an understanding of the services needed, and provision for a satisfactory customer interface when delivering them.

Administration Services

The purpose of Administration Services is to administer all the financial and personnel services required for the I/S business. Because these functions must fit closely with similar functions in the total enterprise, they are considered separately here rather than as part of the other I/S processes which they support.

Management Planning

I/S has a management system under which it operates at all three levels: strategic, tactical, and operational. Analysis of I/S performance under this system is an ongoing activity. The presence of unsatisfactory performance can result in two actions: either changing the performance or changing the management system by which it is measured.

The tactical-level process group, Management Planning, is devoted to the creation, measurement, and modification of the management system for I/S. It consists of two processes, Management Systems Planning and Management Systems Monitoring. The first process is required to plan the management system under which I/S will operate and integrate it with the other key management systems (especially finance and personnel) which function for the enterprise as a whole. The second process monitors the execution of the management plan and takes corrective action when required.

The full generic process model to be planned and monitored by this group is illustrated in Appendix A (Chart A-1). It has 42 separate I/S business processes. I suggest that you reference this chart as you read the remainder of this book.

DATA GROUPS AND FLOW

The data that flows from process to process can be grouped into five different data groups. Each data group consists of data classes and elements. Overall, there are 38 data classes in the ISM Architecture (see Appendix B).

The five data groups are defined as follows:

1. *Environment Group:* the data classes required to define the overall structure of applications, data, systems, processes, and enterprise information flow
2. *Resource Group:* the data classes required to define the basic resources used in the I/S business, including applications, data, software, hardware, networks, facilities, supplies, personnel, finances, and standards
3. *Administration Group:* the data classes required to define the organization, users, customers, and vendors
4. *Plans Group:* the data classes required to plan the I/S business, including applications, data, system, service, management, and capacity plans
5. *Controls Group:* the data classes required to control the I/S business, including problems, changes and requirements

These data groups, classes, and elements must be converted into useful information for the I/S organization. In the next section we examine the ISM Architecture from a data or information perspective.

Architecture Data Flow

From the definition of a management system given earlier, we can conclude that the purpose of an I/S management system is to give the manager a means of directing and controlling the work activities within the information business so as to establish objectives. Since the I/S business should serve the overall enterprise, it follows that the I/S objectives should support the corporate objectives.

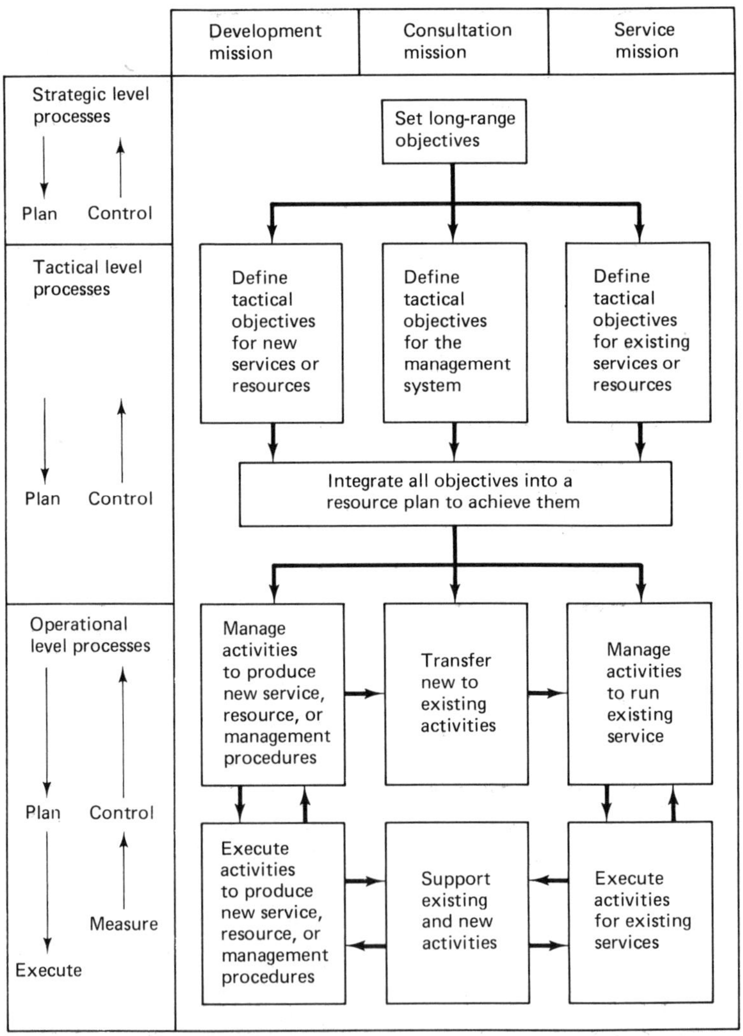

Figure 4–4 Setting the I/S objectives.

Normally, the data required to manage I/S objectives conforms to the planning and control hierarchy. This data includes:

- The strategic I/S level sets objectives using data originating outside the I/S business and summary data from the tactical level.
- The tactical I/S level sets objectives using summary data from both the tactical and operational levels. It also uses data defining the status of resources.
- The operational I/S level sets objectives and executes using detailed data about resources and the use of resources.

This information flow becomes more complicated as we separate the three missions (Fig. 4–4). The actual execution of tasks to meet the I/S strategic objectives occurs only at the lowest levels of the hierarchy. The other levels are concerned with planning and control at sequentially greater levels of detail. This hierarchy also follows a time sequence in that the plans become more detailed as one comes closer in time to the actual execution of tasks. This flow includes the following:

- The development mission defines the tactical objectives for new services or resources, including applications, systems, data bases, and facilities. It also includes project management activities to meet those objectives.
- The service mission sets tactical service objectives and manages resources to deliver the existing services.
- The consultation mission sets tactical resource objectives and manages the resources used in both the service and development missions. Two of those critical resources are information and data.

This information flow is detailed in Appendix A (Chart A–2).

ISM ARCHITECTURE SUMMARY

In this chapter we have identified the process and data groups in the ISM Architecture. It is important to recognize that this architecture evolves to match the changing I/S and enterprise environment. Therefore, these processes and data are only implemented when they are actually needed.

In the next chapter we will use all three windows to analyze the Brazwell Corporation and its I/S management system. Before we proceed, I would like to summarize several key points:

1. We will assume that the I/S management system will be planned from the top down, but will be built from the bottom up. "Top down" is the executive perspective presented in this chapter, and starts with the strategic level. "Bottom up" is the phase of growth perspective presented in Chapter 2, and starts with the operational level.

2. This top-down planning/bottom-up implementation concept was used to derive the five phases of growth introduced in Chapter 2. The Nolan six stages of growth show the bottom-up growth or learning experience of I/S (Fig. 4-5). The discontinuity or transition occurs between the two learning curves.
3. We can superimpose the top-down planning (Anthony planning and control levels) on that learning experience.

A conclusion can be drawn that the initial learning experience is heavily operational planning and control oriented. Later learning deals with the tactical and strategic

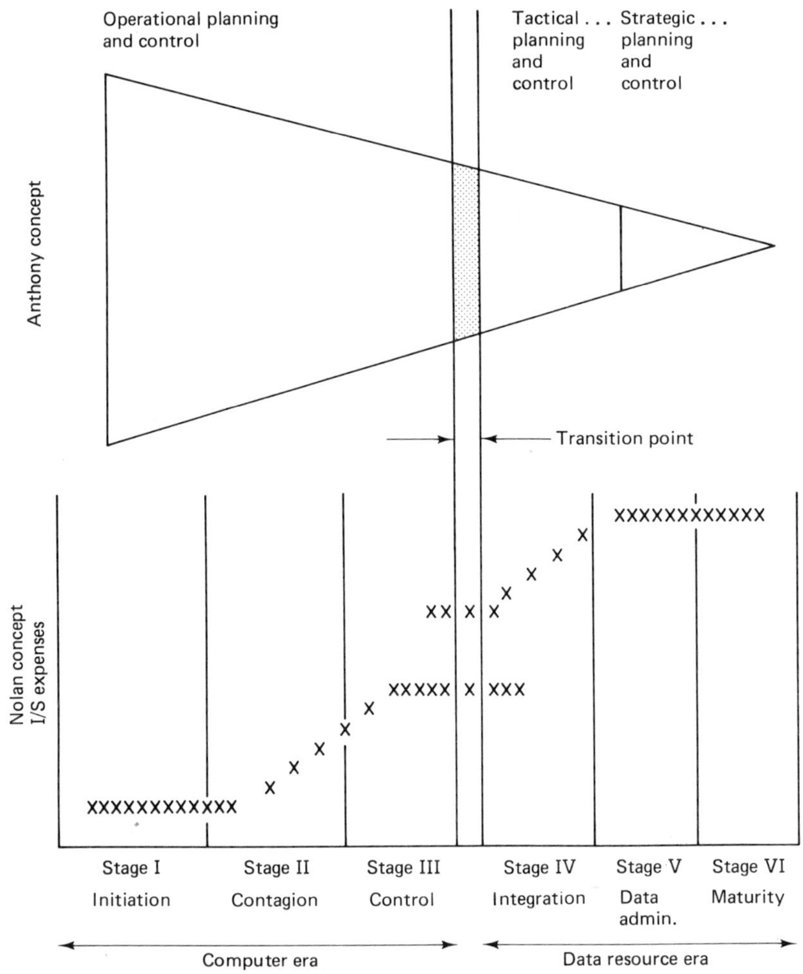

Figure 4-5 Anthony/Nolan concept overlay. Reprinted by permission of the Harvard Business Review. An exhibit from "Managing the Crises in Data Processing" by Richard L. Nolan (March/April 1979). Copyright © 1979 by the President and Fellows of Harvard College; all rights reserved.

levels. The discontinuity arises from the switch required for operational task management to tactical resource management skills. If we assume data management is a logical subset of resource management, then Nolan's six-stage observation agrees with this conclusion.

We can illustrate these points by updating the status of the Brazwell Corporation. I/S growth has been dramatic since the acquisition of Home Security. We now have 213 people in the service organization supporting a massive on-line terminal and personal computer network. However, very little top-down planning has been done. Brazwell I/S continues to struggle with phase III issues, and a deteriorating service quality. Ms. Allen has two separate problems to solve:

1. What combination of 7-S factors and/or ISM Architecture processes will solve the phase III crisis?
2. How do we achieve the planned growth of phases IV and V?

Ms. Allen has been told by a consultant that a System/Network Control Center will solve the first problem. Before we take any action, let us hear an overview of the consultant's recommendation.

SYSTEM/NETWORK CONTROL CENTER OVERVIEW

The System/Network Control Center is often recommended as a phase III organizational structure to manage the service mission (Fig. 4-6). Briefly, the System/Network Control Center concept considers the functional separation of the Production

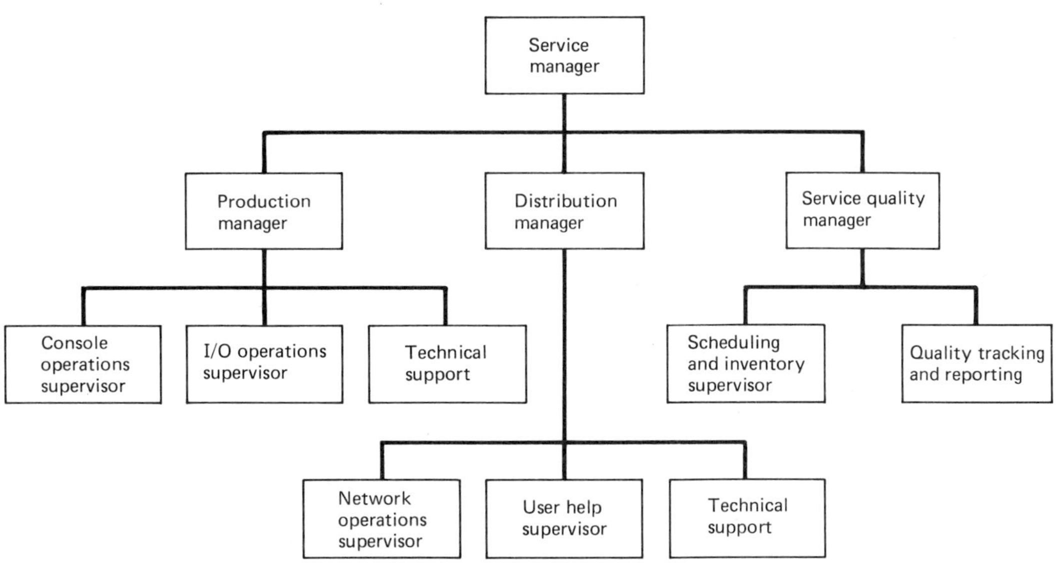

Figure 4-6 System/network control center.

and Distribution processes, the addition of the Customer Service process as a user help desk, and a service quality focus.

The need for the production and distribution separation can be illustrated with a simple manufacturing analogy. Often, a manufacturing facility will paint a yellow line through the receiving area for management control. All parts on one side of the line belong to shipping or receiving. Everything on the other side of the line belongs to manufacturing or production. This simple physical control is adequate until the company opens a second plant or begins building warehouses. The physical control is replaced with organizational control, for example, a distribution department.

If I/S has a single facility, the "yellow line" appears as a glass wall between the central complex and the network control center. This simple physical control is eventually replaced with organizational separation. Interestingly, this change usually occurs when I/S opens multiple sites or installs distributed processing.

Production Manager

There is a production manager for every major computer facility in the organization. Their responsibilities would include:

- Console operations
- I/O operations, including disk, tapes, and printers
- Technical support for that production complex

Under this concept, any major office system location and each personal computer would be considered to be a production facility, with or without a production manager.

Some organizations are exploiting the independence phenomenon of these technologies. In one instance, I/S is systematically introducing personal computers to off-load the host-based time-sharing activity. The rationale is, in part, that many of the applications that the users have developed do not require the power of the host-based tools. However, this approach may be the same illusion that many organizations envisioned for distributed processing.

A more realistic approach is to consider the personal computer as a service delivery facility that can enhance the service to the end user. With this service focus, the personal computer can be viewed as a means to deliver intelligence and data consistent with structure and geography. The goal is to achieve a higher level of service, not just off-load work from the host. These users can connect through communication devices if they require access to host-based data bases for some of their more complex applications.

Distribution Manager

There is one distribution manager for each major network in the enterprise. Many corporations use the concept of a single network for the whole enterprise. In that situation, there should be a single distribution manager whose duties would include:

User help desk

The user help desk is the focal point for all end users with problems: operational, procedural, or administrative. Since this customer service function should be placed as close to the user as possible, it can be organized under the distribution manager.

People staffing the user help desk should be skilled in telephone communications and understand the needs of the end user. They should be able to determine through information sources the status of the system and the problems and changes that have occurred, and be able to assist in problem determination using this information.

The size and staffing of this function are dependent on the service level requirements of end users, the volume of calls expected, and the complexity of the system. Experience has shown that this function can be done with a single person in a small installation or by a staff of 15 or more people in a large network.

Network operations

This function is responsible for controlling resources of the network, both hardware and software components. This group should be able to add or remove components from the system with no impact on related devices. This capability would be useful in bypassing out-of-service components. By modifying transaction load processed by an individual component, network operations could balance loads to improve service. The group could alter the configuration of components, for example, altering transaction priority or giving precedence to output transmission over input transmissions.

Another function of network operations would be to monitor the status of various applications, checking against standards established during the development phase. System performance monitoring is another function that could be supported by the group. This group supports the Problem Control process by recording any problem detected during network operations, isolating problems to a specific component, and bypassing the difficulty until the problem can be resolved.

Technical support

All personnel in the Systems/Network Control Center should focus on the delivery of quality service, not developing new systems or applications. Therefore, the system programming function should be assigned to another organizational unit, for example, a Technical or Development Manager.

Since the technical experts have been removed from the service organization, it is important to have specialized personnel act as a bridge between operations and the technical experts. These technical support personnel will have a lower skill level, and will be much more dependent on documented procedures and tools. They serve as the next level of problem determination after the help desk and the network operators. History has shown that 90 to 95% of the user problems can be solved through these multiple levels of support, minimizing the impact on the highly skilled in-short-supply technical staff.

The technical support group must also work closely with the education function to ensure that the user understands the procedures and can communicate with the service organization. They also interface with the Development and Technical Managers to ensure that adequate procedures are available for I/S and the user.

The placement of technical support personnel for both the production and distribution centers will be determined by the physical location of the equipment. If both are in one location, only a single support staff would be required. As the equipment becomes geographically distributed, a separate support staff would be required at each major location. All these support staffs would have the central Technical Manager's expertise for detailed problem determination and problem resolution.

Service Quality Manager

The Service Quality Manager is the focal point for service quality. Production and distribution scheduling would be formalized and possibly automated. Network operations and the user help desk would provide data about problems and resource utilization. This Service Quality group must translate that data into useful information about the service being provided to the user. This includes the following processes and reports:

- Resource and Data Performance Control provides availability and performance reporting.
- Problem Control tracks and reports problems.
- Change Control coordinates and reports changes.
- Service Evaluating tracks and reports service attainment.

Any difficulties must be reported to the service manager and the I/S executive for corrective action.

INSTALLING A SYSTEM/NETWORK CONTROL CENTER

Planning, building, and installing a System/Network Control Center requires many processes in the Information Systems Management Architecture. A simplified flow includes the following steps and processes (Fig. 4–7).

1. *Decide.* Someone must start the planning cycle for the System/Network Control Center. That decision could have originated in the I/S Strategic Planning and Control process, or it could have worked its way up from an operational process such as Service Evaluating.
2. *Measure.* The Management Systems Monitoring process would measure the current service delivery organization for effectiveness and efficiency. Techniques to perform that analysis are discussed in Chapter 5. Results of that analysis would be passed to the Management Systems Planning process.

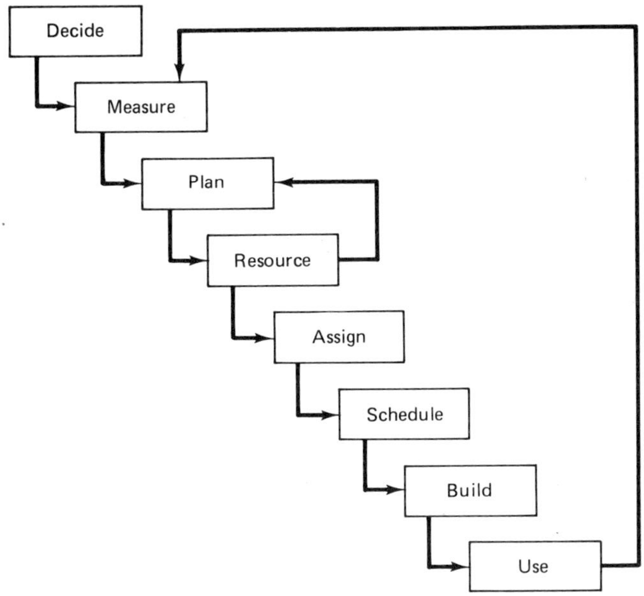

Figure 4–7 Planning a system/network control center.

3. *Plan.* Using this data as input, the Management Systems Planning process would determine the need, feasibility, and possible sequence of implementation. For example, an installation might install the help desk as a first step, followed by the installation of the Service Quality Organization, and later splitting the Production and Distribution processes. Another installation might reverse that sequence. With the acceptance of a sequence, this Management Systems Planning process would define and justify a project plan for that work effort.
4. *Resource.* This development project for the System/Network Control Center would be considered with all other resource demands in the Resource Planning Process Group. The capacity, skills, and funding would be weighed against the other possible uses of the resources. If resources are not available for the implementation and/or operation, the project would be returned to the Management Systems Planning process for further analysis and justification. If resources are available, the project would be released to project management for assignment and scheduling.
5. *Schedule.* Scheduling the implementation of a System/Network Control Center would use the same project management methodologies as application development projects.
6. *Build.* Many of the 7-S factors are affected by the proposed project. Organization structures must be changed, requiring new titles and position codes. Personnel must be retrained. Staffing levels must be determined for the help desk. A new participative management style must be considered. Implementation of the project to improve the management system can take several months of

concentrated effort. In fact, many organizations choose to break the System/Network Control Center implementation into multiple projects for better control.

7. *Use.* After implementation, the Management Systems Monitoring process must complete the planning and control loop, looking for variance and recommending improvements. The loop never stops.

In the next chapter we will study these consultant recommendations.

5

Management Planning

You should understand all three key management concepts by this time:

1. Management planning and control levels, especially as they relate to the Information Systems Management Architecture
2. Learning curves or phases of growth
3. The 7-S organization concept

If so, you are now ready to apply these concepts and analyze your I/S management system. This chapter is designed to give you step-by-step procedures for that analysis using the three concepts.

OVERVIEW

The Management Planning process group is unique in that it builds and monitors the I/S management system, yet it is also part of the management system. This concept can be confusing without a simple analogy. The management system can be viewed as a container consisting of qualified managers, structure, and procedures (Fig. 5–1). Once the container is built, the contents (objectives, data, information, and resources) flow through the container as it performs to the designed management specifications. The processes built into the container control this flow and regularly report the content status.

The initial container must be designed and built according to some enterprise requirements. Additional status information is required to measure the effectiveness and strength of the container itself. This information could be used to alter the con-

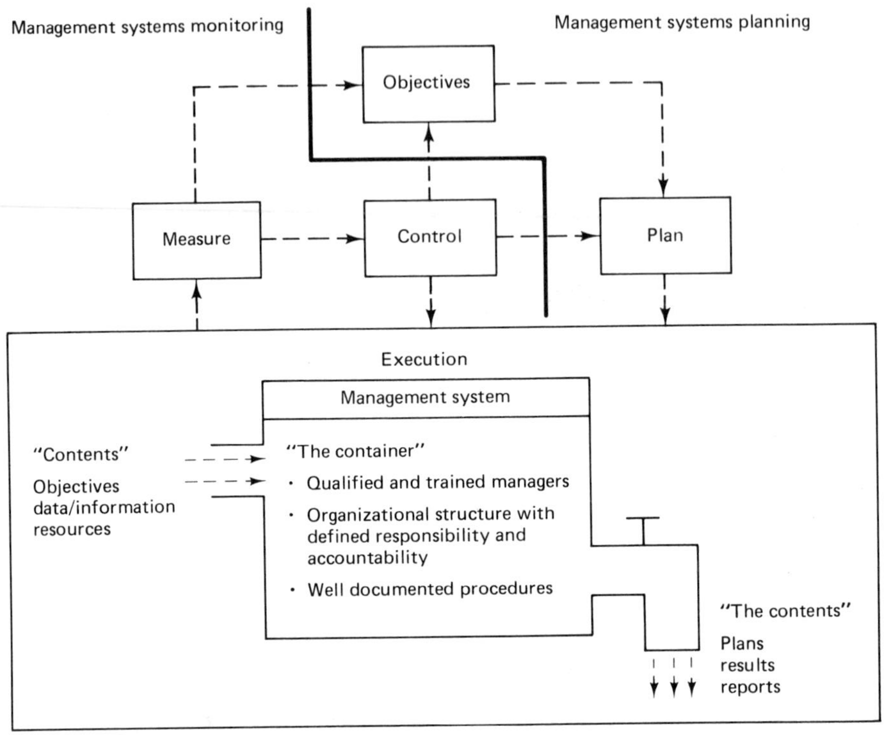

Figure 5–1 Management system planning and control.

tainer design, possibly affecting the flow of contents through the container. If these design and monitoring functions are built into the container, it becomes self-correcting and self-tuning.

The two processes in the Management Planning group are Management Systems Monitoring and Management Systems Planning. Their interrelationship (Fig. 5–1) forms a tactical-level planning and control loop.

- *Management Systems Planning.* Using the strategic plan as input, the Management Systems Planning process must set the I/S management objectives to be accomplished over the tactical time period. With those objectives, a management plan must be developed containing a specific organization, assigned responsibilities, and management system development projects.
- *Management Systems Monitoring.* This process compares the organizational performance against those management factors to determine if and how the management system should be modified. Corrections can be made to the execution, plan, or objectives. These corrections can adjust the currently installed processes or become a recommendation for modifying the management system itself.

In the next two sections we examine these two processes in more detail. The topics covered include an explanation of each process, illustrated by representative reports. The processes are discussed using the following input–process–output approach:

- The process definition and description of the elements (decision or activities) are repeated from Appendix A.
- The data input and output of the process are defined using the data classes in Appendix B.
- Each process element is documented under a separate subheading.

The remainder of this book provides in-depth techniques for analyzing your I/S management system. The executive or nontechnical reader will still find this material useful. I will guide you around the more technical sections. We will assume that you have a management system installed and want to improve its effectiveness. Therefore, we will start with the Management Systems Monitoring process.

MANAGEMENT SYSTEMS MONITORING

DEFINITION:

Using feedback from all the I/S processes, this process assesses the effectiveness of the management system and makes sure that it will be enhanced, if necessary.

DESCRIPTION:

The elements of Management Systems Monitoring are:

1. Collect and summarize organization performance data.
2. Compare to the organizational objectives and standards.
3. Diagnose deviation or substandard performance.
4. Initiate effectiveness/efficiency improvements in the organization standards, procedures, or methods.

DATA CLASSES REQUIRED:

Data input to process (data class)	Data output of process (data class)
C1 Service	C8 Management systems performance
C3 Change	
C4 Problem	

Data input to process (data class)	Data output of process (data class)
C5 Requirements	
C4 Problem	
C8 Management systems performance	
C9 Tactical plan	
A2 Customer/user/group	
A3 Organization	
R10 Standards/procedures/methods	

Collect and Summarize Organization Performance Data

Since Management Systems Monitoring is a tactical-level control process, it should be assigned to the I/S executive in smaller organizations, or to the Plans and Controls Manager in larger organizations. This functional organization can be supplemented with an entrepreneur study team.

Management planning study techniques

Often, we need a more extensive technique to make a thorough analysis of the management system. This Management Planning technique is based on the business systems planning methodology. Business systems planning has been used to study an enterprise business system and make management recommendations. It uses an entrepreneur study team structure staffed with representatives of all organizations involved in the business area to be examined. It normally takes 6 to 12 weeks to complete. The results are normally implemented by the functional structure.

The management planning study team can define the I/S process model, relate it to the organization, and interview the managers about their issues, concerns, and problems. With this assessment, the study team can answer the following questions:

1. Do we have the right processes in place for our maturity in the phases of growth?
2. Is our organizational responsibility and structure adequate to control those processes?
3. Do we have an adequate set of information system applications to support the I/S business?
4. Do we have adequate management reporting based on an understanding of the I/S data classes?

The entrepreneur study team could recommend improvements in any of the I/S management systems components: organization, processes, systems, or data.

The sponsor of the management planning study should be the I/S executive or the executive who owns the I/S organization. Without this direct involvement of senior management, the study team recommendations will be difficult (if not impossible) to implement. The study team leader should be the I/S executive or someone well respected within the I/S functional organization. That person might be the future candidate for the position of Plans and Controls Manager.

The four to six study team members should be managers who have an interest in improving the effectiveness of I/S. They need to be available over 50% of their time for the study. Other people will participate in the study through the interview and/or questionnaire techniques.

The study normally takes 6 to 12 weeks as follows:

1. The first two weeks of the study should be devoted to understanding how the current I/S management system works, and to gathering organizational performance data. To gather that data, we will use a survey form to get a combined management perception of where key process responsibilities reside, where resources are assigned, and how effectively the individual processes are being carried out.
2. The second two weeks should be devoted to conducting interviews with key people who participate or have major interest in the I/S management system. Fifteen to twenty interviews are recommended.
3. The last two weeks should be devoted to analyzing the results and making recommendations.

The data-gathering procedures will be discussed in the remainder of this process element. The interviews and analysis will be discussed in later process elements.

Gathering performance data

In this book we assume that the organizational performance data can be gathered by either the entrepreneur study team or the I/S functional management. We will gather data/information about the Brazwell Home Electronics Company, but analyze only the service mission. Brazwell is a fictitious company, and any similarity to a real company is purely coincidental. The Brazwell I/S organization chart is shown in Figure 5-2.

Before the survey is conducted, the participants must be educated on the various processes in the ISM Architecture. Normally, a half-day training session is sufficient. During the data gathering, each manager surveyed is required to complete the survey form (Fig. 5-3) for the entire I/S organization. The procedures for completing this form are:

1. The process definitions are shown in Appendix A. Before you respond for each process, refer to the appendix to gain a basic understanding of what key elements and activities are contained in the process.
2. In each column of organization, indicate that organization's responsibility regarding the process; code an "X" for a major decision maker, a "/" for those with major involvement, and an "#" for those with minor involvement. Leave it blank if the organization has no involvement in the management of the process.

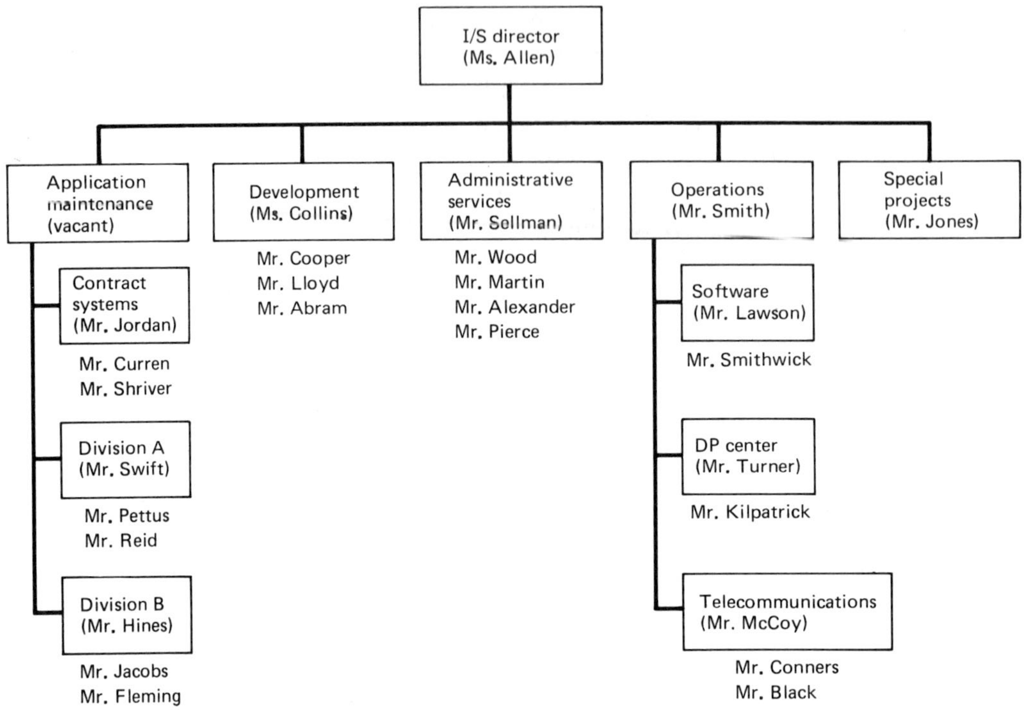

Figure 5-2 Brazwell organizational chart.

3. Indicate your assessment of the process effectiveness in the column marked "EFF"; use a scale from 1 to 9, with 9 being the highest possible effectiveness and 1 the lowest. A blank or "0" response is permissible if you truly have no knowledge of the process or of how effective it is. The following guidelines may be used:
   - 0 No response
   - 1 Process not in place
   - 3 Process in place but not effective
   - 6 Process in place but not fully effective
   - 9 Process in place and effective

   These rating values are only examples. The managers surveyed can use any number from 0 to 9 to complete the survey.
4. Indicate your assessment of the priority that should be given to the improvement of this process in the column marked "PRI"; use a scale of 1 to 9, with 9 being the highest possible priority. Use these guidelines:
   - 0 No response
   - 1 No improvement necessary
   - 3 Some improvement desirable

Brazwell Inc. Feb. 19, 19XX

Organization:

Process:	Allen	Jones	Smith	Turner	Kilpatrick	Black	McCoy	Lawson	Smithwick	Conners	Collins	Cooper	Abram	Lloyd	Jordan	Shriver	Curren	Fleming	Hines	Jacobs	Swift	Pettus	Reid	Sellman	Wood	Martin	Alexander	Pierce	EFF	PRI	FTE
Service Market Planning																															
Service Level Planning																															
Recovery Planning																															
Security Planning																															
Audit Planning																															
Production/Distr. Sched.																															
Resource/Data Perf. Ctl.																															
Problem Control																															
Service Evaluating																															
Production																															
Distribution																															
Customer Service																															
Service Marketing																															
Application Planning																															
Data Planning																															
System Planning																															
Project Planning																															
Project Assignment																															
Project Scheduling																															
Project Controlling																															
Project Req'ts. Control																															
Project Evaluating																															
Applic./Software Devel.																															
Applic./Software Procur.																															
Hardware Facilit's. Inst.																															
Maintenance																															
Tuning/System Balancing																															
Mgt. System Development																															
Business Strategic Plng.																															
Architecture Definition																															
I/S Strategic Planning																															
Management System Plng.																															
Management System Monit.																															
Capacity Planning																															
Skills Planning																															
Budget Planning																															
Tactical Plan Management																															
Change Control																															
R/D Inventory Control																															
Financial Administration																															
Education and Training																															
Staff Performance																															

Figure 5–3 ISM process to organization matrix: survey response form.

- 6 Significant improvement needed
- 9 Must improve as soon as possible

5. Indicate your estimate of the number of "full-time-equivalent" persons in your area of responsibility who perform this process. This number need only be an approximation. The total for all processes will normally be about equal to the number of persons in your span of control. It is most important to remember that this is full-time-equivalent persons and not a head count; 6 persons each working about 15% of their time on a process would yield a full-time-equivalent value of 0.9, or more reasonably, 1. Put this response in the column marked "FTE."
6. Feel free to make comments on a separate sheet of paper regarding each process or explaining your responses in more detail. This input is often as valuable as your specific responses.

Each manager should fill out this questionnaire separately to record his or her perspective of the I/S organization. *This survey should indicate how the current organization works, not how the managers wish it would work.* Later surveys could be used to obtain that input. This survey will be combined statistically with all other surveys to provide a relative rating of the organization. All the ratings, including average effectiveness, should not be considered as absolute.

Compare to Organizational Objectives and Standards

The survey results are used to perform three analyses about the organization.

1. Is the responsibility for the processes correct? Questions that need to be answered include:
   a. Are there owners for every process?
   b. Are there multiple owners?
   c. Are they owned by a manager who has too wide a span of control?
   d. Are they owned by a manager involved in too many time frames?
   e. Are they owned by a manager involved in multiple missions?
2. Which processes are most or least effective? Questions that need to be answered include:
   a. Which process groups are most or least effective?
   b. Are the processes installed in the organization consistent with the phases of growth?
   c. Do we have the process installed and working?
   d. Which specific processes need improvement?
3. What data is required to run our processes? Questions that need to be answered include:

a. Does a process receive data from another process? Is it high-quality data?
b. What management reports are required?

The executive or nontechnical reader might skip to the section entitled "Diagnose Deviations or Substandard Performance."

Responsibility analysis

The responsibility analysis examines the ownership and involvement in the various processes. The analysis requires several process-to-organization matrix reports. The summary matrix (Fig. 5–4) shows the total "X" responses to the survey. A second matrix (Fig. 5–5) makes the survey results more understandable by using a threshold mask. The mask specifies the number of people surveyed who must concur on the responsibility rating before that rating is included in the responsibility analysis. In the example, the report masks any X responsibility if fewer than 10 surveys agreed on the designation. The mask value would be determined by the size of the survey sample. The 13 processes in the service mission are at the top of both matrix charts.

These reports show much about the service mission, especially the Service Planning process group. All 28 managers were perceived to own one or more of the five processes. With a survey mask of 10, none of the processes has a clear owner (Fig. 5–5). Many of the processes in the Service Control and Information Services groups have another organizational problem, multiple owners. For example, the Customer Services process with seven decision makers would be extremely difficult to manage. Since this process provides the end-user help function for the System/Network Control Center, it could also be a major source of user dissatisfaction.

In general, an examination of the responsibility of various organizations includes:

1. Is responsibility for attaining process objectives throughout the organization assigned to a single accountable manager?
2. Does this manager have the decision-making authority or escalation capability required to ensure that process objectives are met?
3. Are cross-organizational responsibilities for the process elements explicitly defined, documented, and understood throughout the organization?

The analysis must ensure that the survey includes input from key I/S managers. These reports also serve to define the managers who are likely candidates for follow-up interviews.

Process analysis

Using the process summary report (Fig. 5–6), we can evaluate the process performance from several perspectives, including:

- By process groups

Organization:

Process:	Allen	Jones	Smith	Turner	Kilpatrick	Black	McCoy	Lawson	Smithwick	Conners	Collins	Cooper	Abram	Lloyd	Jordan	Shriver	Curren	Fleming	Hines	Jacobs	Swift	Pettus	Reid	Sellman	Wood	Martin	Alexander	Pierce
Service Market Planning	4	2	4	4	2	1	5	2	4	7	7	3	3	3	6	4	4	2	6	4	7	4	4	5	5	4	3	3
Service Level Planning	2	—	3	7	3	1	3	—	5	5	—	—	—	—	4	3	3	1	1	4	2	3	2	2	4	3	—	2
Recovery Planning	—	—	2	6	8	1	2	—	8	4	1	2	3	—	—	1	1	—	—	1	—	1	1	3	4	5	—	—
Security Planning	1	—	3	3	6	1	2	1	1	1	1	—	1	—	1	—	—	—	1	—	1	—	—	8	8	9	—	—
Audit Planning	1	—	3	1	1	1	—	2	—	—	1	—	—	—	1	—	—	—	1	—	1	—	—	3	6	6	—	—
Production/Distr. Sched.	—	—	—	1	21	4	9	—	6	5	—	4	4	4	—	10	10	1	1	9	1	9	9	—	2	2	2	6
Resource/Data Perf. Ctl.	—	—	—	1	15	5	7	2	18	7	—	2	2	2	—	3	3	1	—	3	1	4	4	—	3	3	2	4
Problem Control	—	—	—	2	19	7	6	1	10	3	—	2	2	2	—	4	4	1	—	4	—	4	4	1	4	2	2	3
Service Evaluating	—	—	—	—	7	4	3	—	7	4	—	2	2	2	2	6	6	1	2	6	2	6	5	—	7	5	1	3
Production	—	—	1	4	24	5	5	—	2	3	—	2	2	2	—	3	4	—	—	3	—	3	3	—	1	—	1	4
Distribution	—	—	—	2	21	4	6	—	2	4	—	2	2	2	—	2	2	—	—	2	—	2	2	—	1	—	1	9
Customer Service	—	—	1	1	12	8	13	1	4	6	1	4	4	3	3	16	16	2	4	16	4	16	16	1	4	2	2	4
Service Marketing	2	—	1	1	4	4	8	—	2	6	7	5	5	5	8	11	10	3	6	10	7	11	10	1	1	1	—	2
Application Planning	6	2	5	5	1	1	1	4	1	3	14	6	3	3	8	4	3	3	9	4	9	4	4	9	4	4	1	1
Data Planning	2	1	2	2	1	1	4	2	2	2	3	3	3	3	3	2	2	2	3	2	3	2	2	2	2	1	1	1
System Planning	1	2	9	5	3	1	2	8	14	8	6	3	2	3	4	2	2	1	2	1	2	1	2	3	4	2	1	1
Project Planning	3	1	2	1	5	2	4	1	4	5	10	14	13	12	4	8	8	3	4	8	4	8	8	4	8	7	3	3
Project Assignment	3	1	5	2	5	2	7	5	6	7	14	16	16	15	7	14	12	4	7	14	7	14	14	6	8	8	3	3
Project Scheduling	2	1	1	1	6	3	9	1	8	7	5	22	22	21	1	18	16	4	1	18	1	18	18	2	10	11	7	5
Project Controlling	1	1	2	1	5	3	9	1	7	6	4	19	19	19	1	16	14	2	1	16	1	16	16	1	10	11	4	4
Project Req'ts Control	2	1	3	2	5	3	9	3	8	7	5	21	21	20	3	17	15	4	3	17	3	17	18	2	9	10	5	5
Project Evaluating	1	2	1	1	5	4	5	1	6	5	4	15	16	15	2	10	7	2	2	10	2	10	10	2	9	10	3	4
Applic./Software Devel.	—	—	1	1	2	1	9	2	16	4	3	21	21	21	1	16	15	2	1	16	2	16	16	—	2	2	1	1
Applic./Software Procur.	1	—	5	3	2	2	6	5	17	8	5	17	16	16	2	9	8	1	2	10	2	9	10	—	1	1	—	—
Hardware Facilit's. Inst	1	—	6	9	17	5	2	3	14	15	3	5	5	4	1	4	4	1	—	3	—	3	4	1	—	—	—	—
Maintenance	—	—	—	2	14	5	9	4	16	11	—	7	7	7	1	16	16	1	1	17	1	17	17	—	1	1	—	1
Tuning/System Balancing	—	—	—	—	6	2	8	2	18	10	—	7	6	6	1	9	10	—	—	9	1	9	9	—	—	—	1	1
Mgt. System Development	1	—	1	—	4	1	10	—	2	3	—	4	4	3	—	2	2	—	—	2	—	2	2	4	11	9	2	—
Business Strategic Plng.	22	1	7	2	—	—	—	2	—	—	6	—	—	—	2	—	—	—	3	—	3	—	—	8	1	1	—	—
Architecture Definition	9	1	6	4	—	—	1	5	1	1	7	—	—	—	3	—	—	—	3	—	3	—	—	4	1	1	—	—
I/S Strategic Planning	13	1	7	4	1	—	—	4	1	2	7	1	1	1	4	1	1	1	3	1	3	1	1	8	2	2	—	—
Management System Plng.	9	1	6	4	2	1	2	3	3	3	5	2	2	2	4	2	2	1	4	2	3	2	2	11	7	6	4	1
Management System Monit.	4	1	2	2	2	—	2	1	3	2	2	1	1	1	1	1	1	—	1	1	1	1	1	8	7	5	1	—
Capacity Planning	—	—	4	2	2	1	1	5	20	11	—	—	—	—	—	—	—	—	—	—	—	—	—	—	—	—	2	5
Skills Planning	—	—	2	2	5	2	4	2	4	5	2	5	5	5	3	3	4	2	2	4	2	4	3	9	6	5	17	4
Budget Planning	2	—	2	—	4	2	4	1	4	4	1	4	4	3	—	4	4	1	—	4	—	4	4	9	21	14	2	3
Tactical Plan Management	6	—	2	2	1	—	2	—	4	2	2	1	1	1	2	—	1	1	1	1	1	1	1	13	15	13	5	2
Change Control	—	—	—	—	5	1	2	—	4	3	1	1	1	1	1	7	7	1	1	7	1	7	6	2	4	4	3	2
R/D Inventory Control	—	—	—	2	8	2	5	—	5	2	1	2	2	2	—	4	4	1	—	4	—	4	4	4	13	11	11	7
Financial Administration	1	2	4	9	8	2	1	2	5	7	—	—	—	—	—	—	—	—	—	—	—	—	—	5	20	10	1	5
Education and Training	—	—	—	1	1	—	1	1	—	—	1	—	—	—	1	—	—	—	1	—	1	—	—	3	—	—	21	—
Staff Performance	2	1	2	2	7	5	5	3	5	3	2	5	5	5	3	5	5	2	2	5	2	5	5	4	8	9	18	17

Figure 5-4 ISM process to organization matrix: summary of "X" responses.

Organization:

Process:	Allen	Jones	Smith	Turner	Kilpatrick	Black	McCoy	Lawson	Smithwick	Conners	Collins	Cooper	Abram	Lloyd	Jordan	Shriver	Curren	Fleming	Hines	Jacabs	Swift	Pettus	Reid	Sellman	Wold	Martin	Alexander	Pierce
Service Market Planning	-	-	-	-	-	-	-	-	-	-	-	-	-	-	-	-	-	-	-	-	-	-	-	-	-	-	-	-
Service Level Planning	-	-	-	-	-	-	-	-	-	-	-	-	-	-	-	-	-	-	-	-	-	-	-	-	-	-	-	-
Recovery Planning	-	-	-	-	-	-	-	-	-	-	-	-	-	-	-	-	-	-	-	-	-	-	-	-	-	-	-	-
Security Planning	-	-	-	-	-	-	-	-	-	-	-	-	-	-	-	-	-	-	-	-	-	-	-	-	-	-	-	-
Audit Planning	-	-	-	-	-	-	-	-	-	-	-	-	-	-	-	-	-	-	-	-	-	-	-	-	-	-	-	-
Production/Distr. Sched.	-	-	-	-	X	-	-	-	-	-	-	-	-	-	-	X	X	-	-	-	-	-	-	-	-	-	-	-
Resource/Data Perf. Ctl.	-	-	-	-	X	-	-	-	X	-	-	-	-	-	-	-	-	-	-	-	-	-	-	-	-	-	-	-
Problem Control	-	-	-	-	X	-	-	-	X	-	-	-	-	-	-	-	-	-	-	-	-	-	-	-	-	-	-	-
Service Evaluating	-	-	-	-	-	-	-	-	-	-	-	-	-	-	-	-	-	-	-	-	-	-	-	-	-	-	-	-
Production	-	-	-	-	X	-	-	-	-	-	-	-	-	-	-	-	-	-	-	-	-	-	-	-	-	-	-	-
Distribution	-	-	-	-	X	-	-	-	-	-	-	-	-	-	-	-	-	-	-	-	-	-	-	-	-	-	-	-
Customer Service	-	-	-	-	X	-	X	-	-	-	-	-	-	-	-	X	X	-	-	X	-	X	X	-	-	-	-	-
Service Marketing	-	-	-	-	-	-	-	-	-	-	-	-	-	-	-	X	X	-	-	X	-	X	X	-	-	-	-	-
Application Planning	-	-	-	-	-	-	-	-	-	-	X	-	-	-	-	-	-	-	-	-	-	-	-	-	-	-	-	-
Data Planning	-	-	-	-	-	-	-	-	-	-	-	-	-	-	-	-	-	-	-	-	-	-	-	-	-	-	-	-
System Planning	-	-	-	-	-	-	-	-	X	-	-	-	-	-	-	-	-	-	-	-	-	-	-	-	-	-	-	-
Project Planning	-	-	-	-	-	-	-	-	-	-	X	X	X	X	-	-	-	-	-	-	-	-	-	-	-	-	-	-
Project Assignment	-	-	-	-	-	-	-	-	-	-	X	X	X	X	-	X	X	-	-	X	-	X	X	-	-	-	-	-
Project Scheduling	-	-	-	-	-	-	-	-	-	-	-	X	X	X	-	X	X	-	-	X	-	X	X	-	X	X	-	-
Project Controlling	-	-	-	-	-	-	-	-	-	-	-	X	X	X	-	X	X	-	-	X	-	X	X	-	X	X	-	-
Project Req'ts. Control	-	-	-	-	-	-	-	-	-	-	-	X	X	X	-	X	X	-	-	X	-	X	X	-	-	X	-	-
Project Evaluating	-	-	-	-	-	-	-	-	-	-	-	X	X	X	-	X	-	-	-	X	-	X	X	-	-	X	-	-
Applic./Software Devel.	-	-	-	-	-	-	-	-	X	-	-	X	X	X	-	X	X	-	-	X	-	X	X	-	-	-	-	-
Applic./Software Procur.	-	-	-	-	-	-	-	-	X	-	-	X	X	X	-	-	-	-	-	X	-	-	X	-	-	-	-	-
Hardware Facilit's. Inst	-	-	-	-	X	-	-	-	X	X	-	-	-	-	-	-	-	-	-	-	-	-	-	-	-	-	-	-
Maintenance	-	-	-	-	X	-	-	-	X	X	-	-	-	-	-	X	X	-	-	X	-	X	X	-	-	-	-	-
Tuning/System Balancing	-	-	-	-	-	-	-	-	X	X	-	-	-	-	-	-	X	-	-	-	-	-	-	-	-	-	-	-
Mgt. System Development	-	-	-	-	-	-	X	-	-	-	-	-	-	-	-	-	-	-	-	-	-	-	-	-	X	-	-	-
Business Strategic Plng.	X	-	-	-	-	-	-	-	-	-	-	-	-	-	-	-	-	-	-	-	-	-	-	-	-	-	-	-
Architecture Definition	-	-	-	-	-	-	-	-	-	-	-	-	-	-	-	-	-	-	-	-	-	-	-	-	-	-	-	-
I/S Strategic Planning	X	-	-	-	-	-	-	-	-	-	-	-	-	-	-	-	-	-	-	-	-	-	-	-	-	-	-	-
Management System Plng.	-	-	-	-	-	-	-	-	-	-	-	-	-	-	-	-	-	-	-	-	-	-	-	X	-	-	-	-
Management System Monit.	-	-	-	-	-	-	-	-	-	-	-	-	-	-	-	-	-	-	-	-	-	-	-	-	-	-	-	-
Capacity Planning	-	-	-	-	-	-	-	-	X	X	-	-	-	-	-	-	-	-	-	-	-	-	-	-	-	-	-	-
Skills Planning	-	-	-	-	-	-	-	-	-	-	-	-	-	-	-	-	-	-	-	-	-	-	-	-	-	-	X	-
Budget Planning	-	-	-	-	-	-	-	-	-	-	-	-	-	-	-	-	-	-	-	-	-	-	-	-	X	X	-	-
Tactical Plan Management	-	-	-	-	-	-	-	-	-	-	-	-	-	-	-	-	-	-	-	-	-	-	-	X	X	X	-	-
Change Control	-	-	-	-	-	-	-	-	-	-	-	-	-	-	-	-	-	-	-	-	-	-	-	-	-	-	-	-
R/D Inventory Control	-	-	-	-	-	-	-	-	-	-	-	-	-	-	-	-	-	-	-	-	-	-	-	-	X	X	X	-
Financial Administration	-	-	-	-	-	-	-	-	-	-	-	-	-	-	-	-	-	-	-	-	-	-	-	-	X	X	-	-
Education and Training	-	-	-	-	-	-	-	-	-	-	-	-	-	-	-	-	-	-	-	-	-	-	-	-	-	-	X	-
Staff Performance	-	-	-	-	-	-	-	-	-	-	-	-	-	-	-	-	-	-	-	-	-	-	-	-	-	-	X	X

Figure 5-5 ISM process to organization matrix: processes and owners; number of X's > = threshold value: 10.

Brazwell Inc. Feb. 19, 19xx

	Effectiveness			Priority			FTE personnel			No. owners		
	Hi	Lo	Avg	Hi	Lo	Avg	Hi	Lo	Tot	Hi	Lo	Avg
Process Group:												
Service Planning	4.0	2.3	3.4	6.4	4.5	5.7	4	0	9	0.0	0.0	0.0
Service Control	6.6	4.7	6.0	5.4	4.3	4.8	20	5	47	3.0	0.0	1.8
Information Services	7.6	5.0	6.6	5.6	3.5	4.4	89	9	157	7.0	1.0	3.5
Development Planning	6.3	2.8	5.3	6.0	4.9	5.5	6	0	12	4.0	0.0	1.5
Devel/Maint Control	7.6	5.5	7.0	4.7	3.4	3.8	28	10	109	10.0	8.0	9.2
Development and Maintenance	7.7	6.1	7.0	4.7	3.4	4.0	127	4	238	9.0	2.0	5.2
Strategic Planning and Ctl.	5.3	4.4	4.9	6.6	6.4	6.5	1	0	1	1.0	0.0	0.7
Resource Planning	7.2	6.1	6.7	5.2	4.3	4.8	7	3	17	3.0	1.0	2.0
Resource Control	5.3	5.0	5.2	6.2	5.5	5.9	5	4	9	3.0	0.0	1.5
Administration Services	7.3	6.3	6.8	5.0	3.7	4.3	13	7	30	2.0	1.0	1.7
Planning Level:												
Strategic Level Processes	5.3	4.4	4.9	6.6	6.4	6.5	1	0	1	1.0	0.0	0.7
Tactical Level Processes	7.2	2.3	5.1	6.4	4.3	5.4	14	0	51	4.0	0.0	1.0
Operational Level Processes	7.7	4.7	6.6	6.2	3.4	4.4	127	4	588	10.0	0.0	4.4
Mission:												
Service Processes	7.6	2.3	5.2	6.4	3.5	5.0	89	0	213	7.0	0.0	1.6
Development Processes	7.7	2.8	6.5	6.0	3.4	4.4	127	0	358	10.0	0.0	5.5
Consultation Processes	7.3	4.4	6.0	6.6	3.7	5.3	14	0	69	3.0	0.0	1.4
Growth Phase:												
Phase I Processes	7.6	6.8	7.1	4.3	3.5	4.0	89	22	157	6.0	1.0	2.7
Phase II Processes	7.7	5.0	6.7	5.6	3.4	4.3	127	4	237	9.0	2.0	5.3
Phase III Processes	7.6	4.7	6.4	6.2	3.4	4.5	28	4	194	10.0	0.0	4.4
Phase IV Processes	7.2	2.3	5.1	6.4	4.3	5.4	14	0	51	4.0	0.0	1.0
Phase V Processes	5.3	4.4	4.9	6.6	6.4	6.5	1	0	1	1.0	0.0	0.7
Overall:												
All Processes	7.7	2.3	5.9	6.6	3.4	4.9	127	0	641	10.0	0.0	2.9

Figure 5-6 Process summary report.

- By planning levels
- By mission
- By growth phase
- Overall

In the example, the Service Planning process group has a 3.4 average effectiveness, the poorest of all process groups. The poor performance could be explained by the limited 9 full-time-equivalent resources being applied or the lack of ownership. If we expand our perspective to the whole service mission, we find a 5.2 average effectiveness and 213 full-time-equivalent resources being applied. The Service Planning performance is clearly impacting the overall service results.

Since the Service Planning processes are critical to phase IV, we can observe that our service organization is somewhere between phase III and phase IV. This can

Brazwell Inc. Feb. 19, 19xx

Process:	Avg. eff.	Eff. qrtl.	Avg. pri.	Pri. qrtl.	Tot. FTE	FTE qrtl.	No. own's.	Own qrtl.	Growth phase
→ Audit Planning	2.3	*	5.7	····	0	-	0	=	4
Data Planning	2.8	*	6.0	····	0	-	0	=	4
→ Security Planning	3.4	*	6.3	····	2	-	0	=	4
→ Recovery Planning	3.5	*	6.4	····	1	-	0	=	4
→ Service Level Planning	3.8	*	5.8	····	4	--	0	=	4
→ Service Market Planning	4.0	*	4.5	··	2	-	0	=	4
Architecture Definition	4.4	*	6.6	····	0	-	0	=	5
→ Service Evaluating	4.7	*	5.4	···	5	--	0	=	3
I/S Strategic Planning	4.9	*	6.4	····	1	-	1	=	5
Change Control	5.0	*	6.2	····	4	--	0	=	3
Service Marketing	5.0	*	5.6	···	9	---	5	====	2
R/D Inventory Control	5.3	**	5.5	···	5	--	3	===	3
Business Strategic Plng.	5.3	**	6.4	····	0	-	1	=	5
Project Evaluating	5.5	**	4.7	··	22	----	8	====	3
Application Planning	5.7	**	5.9	····	6	--	1	=	4
Management System Monit.	5.8	**	5.1	···	0	-	0	=	4
Management System Plng.	5.8	**	5.3	···	14	---	1	=	4
Tactical Plan Management	6.1	**	4.7	··	4	--	3	===	4
Mgt. System Development	6.1	**	4.7	··	4	--	2	==	2
Project Planning	6.2	**	5.3	···	4	--	4	===	4
Financial Administration	6.3	**	5.0	···	7	--	2	==	3
System Planning	6.3	**	4.9	···	1	-	1	=	4
Resource/Data Perf. Ctl.	6.3	**	4.3	·	9	---	2	==	3
Tuning/System Balancing	6.4	***	4.4	··	7	---	3	===	2
Problem Control	6.4	***	4.8	···	14	---	2	==	3
Skills Planning	6.6	***	5.0	···	3	--	1	=	4
Production/Distr. Sched.	6.6	***	4.7	··	20	---	3	===	3
Staff Performance	6.7	***	4.3	·	10	---	2	==	3
Capacity Planning	6.7	***	5.2	···	3	-	2	==	4
Applic./Software Procur.	6.8	***	4.3	·	47	----	6	====	1
Customer Service	6.8	***	4.4	··	37	----	7	====	2
Distribution	6.9	***	4.1	·	22	----	1	=	1
Budget Planning	7.2	****	4.3	·	7	---	2	==	4
Hardware Facilit's. Inst	7.2	****	4.0	·	8	---	3	===	2
Project Req'ts. Control	7.2	****	4.0	·	24	----	9	====	3
Education and Training	7.3	****	3.7	·	13	---	1	=	3
Project Assignment	7.4	****	3.5	·	10	---	9	====	3
Project Controlling	7.5	****	3.5	·	28	----	10	====	3
Project Scheduling	7.6	****	3.4	·	26	----	10	====	3
Production	7.6	****	3.5	·	89	----	1	=	1
Maintenance	7.7	****	3.4	·	44	----	8	====	2
Applic./Software Devel.	7.7	****	3.4	·	127	----	9	====	2

Figure 5-7 Sorted process report: sorted by effectiveness.

be substantiated by comparing the service mission rating of 5.2 against the phase III rating of 6.4 and the phase IV rating of 5.1.

We can examine the service mission in more detail with the process report sorted in effectiveness sequence (Fig. 5-7). The five processes in the Service Planning group (Service Marketing Planning, Service Level Planning, Recovery Planning, Security

Planning, and Audit Planning) have five of the six worst performance ratings. None of the five has a defined owner.

However, the poor service performance is not limited to the Service Planning process group. Service Evaluating, a critical process in the Service Control group, has no owner and a 4.7 effectiveness. The Service Evaluating process measures the actual service attainment, and reports that attainment to users and management. Poor performance of this process should be a major concern.

The following are considerations for determining effectiveness of the processes:

1. Are the objectives of the process defined in quantifiable terms? Are they documented? Are they related to the mission and objectives of the I/S business?
2. Is the attainment of process objectives measured and monitored by management?
3. Does this manager have sufficient resources to attain the process objectives?
4. Are process objectives, organizational responsibilities, procedures, standards, and measurements periodically assessed to ensure process effectiveness and staff productivity?
5. Are procedures and standards relating to this process explicitly defined, documented, and understood throughout this organization?
6. Is the functioning of this process under constant criticism within the I/S organization or by end-user departments?
7. Are meetings frequently required to resolve procedural or operational issues for this process?

These questions are not intended to be rigid guidelines but to serve as thought provokers. Clearly, the person who completed the survey could have misunderstood the process, or disagreed with how the process occurs in his or her organization. Chapters 6 to 8 provide detailed discussions of the generic processes and the data/information required to manage that process. These chapters can be used to resolve any misunderstanding of the processes.

Data analysis

We now know who owns each process, and how effective we are at accomplishing that process. The data analysis can be used to expand the understanding of an individual process or the relationship of the processes. A generic matrix of the process-to-data relationships is shown in Figure 5–8. This process-to-data matrix shows the data input to each process and the data created by each process.

To accomplish the data analysis, we will use that matrix and the previous process analysis (Fig. 5–7). The process analysis of the Service Evaluating process shows the results summarized in Figure 5–9:

- Effectiveness = 4.7
- Priority = 5.4

Data classes:

Processes:	Enterprise	IS Businss	IS Indust.	Appl Plan	Data Plan	System Pln	Person Pln	Financ Pln	MgtSyst Pln	Service Pln	Project Pln	Capacity Pl	Applicatns	Data	Software	Hardware	Network	Facilities	Supplies	Personnel	Financial	Std/Proc/M	Test Data	Service	Project	Change	Problem	Requiremts	Syst Perf	P/D Sched.	MgtSys Perf	Vendor	Cust/User	Organizatn
Service Market Planning	_	A	_	_	_	_	_	_	_	C	A	_	_	_	_	_	_	_	_	_	_	A	_	C	_	_	_	A	_	_	_	A	A	_
Service Level Planning	_	_	_	_	_	U	_	_	U	U	A	_	_	_	_	_	_	_	_	_	_	A	_	C	_	C	_	_	A	_	_	A	A	_
Recovery Planning	_	_	_	_	_	_	_	_	_	C	_	_	_	_	_	_	_	_	_	_	_	A	_	A	_	_	_	_	_	_	_	_	A	_
Security Planning	_	_	_	_	_	_	_	_	_	C	_	_	_	_	_	_	_	_	_	_	_	A	_	A	_	_	_	_	_	_	_	_	A	_
Audit Planning	_	_	_	_	_	_	_	_	_	C	_	_	_	_	_	_	_	_	_	_	_	A	_	A	_	_	_	_	_	_	_	_	A	_
Production/Distr. Sched.	_	A	_	_	_	A	_	_	_	_	_	A	A	A	A	A	A	A	A	A	_	A	_	_	_	C	A	_	C	C	_	_	A	_
Resource/Data Perf. Ctl.	_	_	_	_	_	_	_	_	_	_	_	_	_	_	_	_	_	_	_	_	_	A	_	_	_	_	C	C	C	C	_	_	_	_
Problem Control	_	_	_	_	_	_	_	_	_	_	_	_	A	A	A	A	A	A	A	A	_	A	A	_	_	A	C	_	_	A	_	_	A	_
Service Evaluating	_	_	_	_	_	_	_	_	_	_	_	_	_	_	_	_	_	_	_	_	_	A	_	C	_	C	U	_	A	A	_	_	A	_
Production	_	_	_	_	_	_	_	_	_	_	_	_	A	A	A	A	A	A	A	_	_	A	A	_	_	C	_	_	C	U	_	_	_	_
Distribution	_	_	_	_	_	_	_	_	_	_	_	_	_	A	A	A	A	A	U	_	_	A	A	_	_	_	_	_	C	A	_	_	A	_
Customer Service	_	_	_	_	_	_	_	_	_	_	_	_	_	_	_	_	_	_	_	_	_	A	_	U	_	C	C	C	_	A	_	_	A	A
Service Marketing	_	_	_	_	_	_	_	_	_	A	_	_	_	_	_	_	_	_	_	_	_	A	_	C	_	_	_	C	_	_	_	_	A	_
Application Planning	_	A	A	C	_	_	_	_	_	_	_	_	A	_	_	_	_	_	_	_	_	A	_	_	_	_	_	A	_	_	_	A	A	_
Data Planning	_	A	A	U	C	_	_	_	_	_	_	_	_	A	_	_	_	_	_	_	_	A	_	_	_	_	_	A	_	_	_	A	A	_
System Planning	_	A	A	U	U	C	_	_	_	_	_	_	_	_	A	A	A	A	_	_	_	A	_	_	_	_	_	A	_	_	_	A	A	_
Project Planning	_	_	_	A	A	A	_	_	_	_	C	_	_	_	_	_	_	_	_	_	_	A	_	_	_	_	_	_	_	_	_	_	_	_
Project Assignment	_	_	_	_	_	_	_	_	_	_	A	_	_	_	_	_	_	_	_	A	_	A	_	_	C	_	A	_	_	_	_	A	A	_
Project Scheduling	_	_	_	_	_	_	_	_	_	_	A	_	A	A	A	A	A	A	A	A	_	A	A	_	C	_	_	_	_	_	_	A	A	_
Project Controlling	_	_	_	_	_	_	_	_	_	_	_	_	A	A	A	A	A	A	A	_	_	A	A	_	C	C	_	A	_	_	_	A	A	_
Project Req'ts. Control	_	_	_	_	_	_	_	_	_	_	_	_	_	_	_	_	_	_	_	_	_	A	_	_	U	_	U	U	_	_	_	_	_	_
Project Evaluating	_	_	_	_	_	_	_	_	_	_	_	_	_	_	_	_	_	_	_	_	_	A	_	_	C	A	U	_	_	_	_	_	_	_
Applic./Software Devel.	_	_	_	A	A	A	_	_	_	_	_	_	C	C	C	_	_	_	_	_	_	C	C	_	U	_	_	C	_	_	_	_	_	_
Applic./Software Procur.	_	_	_	A	A	A	_	_	_	_	_	_	C	C	C	_	_	_	_	_	A	C	C	_	U	_	_	C	_	_	_	A	_	_
Hardware Facilit's. Inst	_	_	_	_	_	A	_	_	_	_	_	_	_	_	_	C	C	C	_	_	A	C	C	_	U	_	_	C	_	_	_	A	_	_
Maintenance	_	_	_	_	_	_	_	_	_	_	_	_	U	U	U	U	U	U	_	_	_	U	U	_	U	_	A	C	_	_	_	A	_	_
Tuning/System Balancing	_	_	_	_	_	_	_	_	_	_	_	_	U	U	U	U	U	U	_	_	_	U	U	_	U	_	A	C	_	_	_	A	_	_
Mgt. System Development	_	_	_	_	_	_	_	_	A	_	_	_	_	_	_	_	_	_	_	_	_	C	_	_	U	_	_	C	_	_	_	_	_	A
Business Strategic Plng.	C	C	A	_	_	_	_	_	_	_	_	_	_	_	_	_	_	_	_	_	_	A	_	_	_	_	_	_	_	_	A	_	_	_
Architecture Definition	A	C	_	_	_	_	_	_	_	_	_	_	_	_	_	_	_	_	_	_	_	A	_	_	_	_	_	_	_	_	_	_	_	_
I/S Strategic Planning	A	C	A	_	_	_	_	_	_	_	_	_	_	_	_	_	_	_	_	_	_	A	_	_	_	_	_	_	_	_	A	_	_	_
Management System Plng.	_	A	A	_	_	_	_	_	C	_	U	_	_	_	_	_	_	_	_	_	_	A	_	_	_	_	_	A	_	_	A	A	A	A
Management System Monit.	_	A	_	_	_	_	_	_	U	_	_	_	_	_	_	_	_	_	_	_	_	A	_	_	_	A	A	A	_	_	C	_	A	A
Capacity Planning	_	_	_	_	_	A	_	_	_	A	_	C	_	A	A	A	A	A	A	_	_	A	A	_	_	_	_	_	C	_	_	_	_	_
Skills Planning	_	_	A	_	_	_	C	_	_	A	A	A	_	_	_	_	_	_	_	A	_	A	_	_	_	_	_	_	_	_	_	A	_	A
Budget Planning	_	A	_	_	_	A	A	C	_	A	A	A	_	_	_	_	_	_	_	_	A	A	_	_	_	_	_	_	_	_	_	_	_	A
Tactical Plan Management	A	C	_	U	U	U	U	U	U	U	U	U	_	_	_	_	_	_	_	A	A	A	_	A	A	_	_	_	A	A	A	_	_	_
Change Control	_	_	_	_	_	_	_	_	_	_	_	_	_	_	_	_	_	_	_	_	_	A	_	_	A	C	U	_	A	A	_	_	_	_
R/D Inventory Control	A	A	_	_	_	_	_	_	_	_	_	_	C	C	C	C	C	C	C	C	C	C	C	C	A	A	_	_	_	A	_	C	C	C
Financial Administration	_	_	_	_	_	_	_	_	_	_	_	_	_	_	_	_	_	_	_	_	A	A	_	U	_	C	_	_	_	_	_	A	A	_
Education and Training	_	_	C	_	_	_	A	_	_	_	_	_	_	_	_	_	_	_	_	A	_	A	_	_	_	C	_	C	_	_	_	A	A	_
Staff Performance	_	_	_	_	_	_	U	_	_	_	_	_	_	_	_	_	_	_	_	A	_	A	_	_	_	C	_	_	_	_	_	_	_	_

C = Creates data U = Updates data A = Accesses data

Figure 5-8 Generic process to data matrix.

PROCESS NUMBER	PROCESS NAME	EFF	PRI	OWN	FTE
9	Service Evaluating	4.7	5.4	0.0	5.0

The following data classes are used by that process:

DATA CLASSES USED BY PROCESSES YOU SELECTED	PROCESS NUMBERS THAT CREATE OR UPDATE THE DATA									
R10 Std/prc/md	23	24	25	26	27	28	39			
C1 Service	1	2	9	12	13	39	40			
C3 Change	2	6	9	10	12	20	38	40	41	42
C4 Problem	7	8	9	12	21	22	38			
C6 System performance	6	7	10	11	34					
C7 Prod/Dist. Schedule	6	7	10							
A2 Customer/user	39									

In addition to the processes selected, the data classes are created or updated by this group of processes. You should examine these for improvement:

NO	ADDITIONAL PROCESSES	EFF	PRI	OWN	FTE
1	Service Market Planning	4.0	4.5	0.0	1.8
2	Service Level Planning	3.8	5.8	0.0	4.2
13	Service Marketing	5.0	5.6	5.0	9.1
22	Project Evaluating	5.5	4.7	8.0	21.7
38	Change Control	5.0	6.2	0.0	3.5
39	R/D Inventory Control	5.3	5.5	3.0	5.0

Figure 5–9 Process-to-data analysis.

- Ownership = none
- Full-time resources = 5.0

The data classes required for the Service Evaluating process can be obtained by reading the process-to-data matrix from left to right. Those seven data classes listed in Figure 5–9 are Standards/Procedures/Methods, Service, Change, Problem, System Performance, Production and Distribution Schedule, and Customer/User. The poor performance of this process could be the result of inadequate data associated with any of these seven data classes.

Each of these data classes has one or more processes that create, update, or use that data. In total, 24 different processes interact directly or indirectly with the Service Evaluating process. We can filter that analysis by examining only processes with a poor effectiveness rating, for example, below 6.0. For each of those selected processes, we can examine the effectiveness, priority, ownership, and full-time equivalent. For example, process 38, Change Control, has only a 5.0 effectiveness and no ownership. Failure of Change Control could be having a major impact on the Service Evaluating process.

What if the generic process-to-data matrix does not depict the actual information flow in your organization? The create, update, and use relationships could be changed based on your actual flow. However, major changes could invalidate the Information Systems Management Architecture model.

This information flow can be used to examine the management reports used throughout the management system. In general, the reporting mechanism should include the following properties:

- Detailed information is important only for the operational processes dealing with the direct delivery of services or the development of projects. To climinate irrelevant details and preserve relevant processes, it is almost always necessary to condense the information before it is used. This summary information must flow to processes at the higher planning and control levels.
- Interpreting information requires that it be evaluated in relation to some objective, critical success factor, standard, or past result. The user of the data should not be required to look at several reports simultaneously to understand this comparison. Whenever possible, the comparison data should be next to the measurement.
- The exception principle should be used whenever possible to report only the variations from the expected condition. An exception is considered to have occurred when an actual deviates from the objective by more than a predefined limit or threshold value.
- Use of spontaneous inquiries should supplement normal reporting. A periodic report is normally based on the expected or recurring needs of several people. It often contains much information that is irrelevant to a specific user at a given point in time. An inquiry-reporting mechanism provides reports tailored to each specific need for information, or details needed to explain a higher-level summary.
- Reporting formats should be reasonably consistent to improve human factors considerations in using reports. Fixed headings, columns, page numbers, labels, and other presentation formats are important. Avoiding unnecessary precision in numeric data combined with graphs provides clear, easy-to-understand reports.

Representative reports for many processes are provided in Chapters 6 to 8.

Diagnose Deviations or Substandard Performance

The previous process, organization, and data analysis determined what was wrong and why it was occurring. Before we recommend changes in the management system, we should evaluate the impact of those weaknesses on senior management, users, and I/S itself. Structured interviews are one technique to gather that type of information. The number of interviews will vary with the size of the organization, but normally 15 to 20 interviews are adequate. Each interview should be scheduled for a 1- to $1\frac{1}{2}$-hour session.

The following are a sample list of questions,* the associated charts (or subjects), and the reason for asking them [11]. If an interview response does not provide the information desired, it may mean that the wording of the question should be altered.

Objectives

- Briefly, what is your area of responsibility?
- What are its basic objectives?
- What major changes are anticipated in your area in the next year? In three years?

The interviewer asks the executives what their responsibilities are because conclusions drawn from the organization matrix may not be correct. Also, the objectives that executives set for themselves in performing their functions have a large bearing on their information needs.

The question on anticipated changes is important because the development cycle for major applications can take two to five years to complete. Recommendations for development could be affected by plans to centralize, decentralize, change the organization, or introduce new products.

Factors critical to success

- What factors are critical to success in your area of responsibility?
- How are you and your subordinates measured against the factors critical to success?
- What other types of measurements are you expected to make?
- What types of decisions are you expected to make?

The questions concerning factors critical to success and measurements are intended to disclose how the effectiveness of resource allocation and use is measured. A major factor in attaining business goals is efficient use of resources, especially in areas critical to business success.

The question as to what decisions are made is intended to disclose whether executives receive adequate information on which to base them.

Problems

- What are the greatest problems that you have met in trying to achieve your objectives within the last year?
- What has prevented your solving these problems?
- What is needed to solve them?
- What value (in person-hours saved, dollars saved, or programs enhanced) would better information have in these areas?

*These questions are extracted from the IBM publication *Business Systems Planning: Information Systems Planning Guide,* GE20-0527-3.

When asking about problems, the interviewer should be sure that the executives do not indicate only their latest problems. Sometimes people overlook more serious problems that occurred months before.

Process/organization/data matrix

- In which of the processes could the greatest improvements be realized, given the needed information support?
- What would be the value of these improvements in person-hours saved, dollars saved, or program enhanced?
- How would you rate your information support with respect to adequacy, validity, timeliness, consistency, cost, and volume?
- What is the most useful information that you receive?

These questions should focus on information requirements and costs that may be incurred from inaccurate and late information. The value of any additional information desired should also be determined. The person analyzing the results must determine where the current information support is inadequate so that these benefits are retained.

Summary

The interviews probably substantiated our concerns about the service mission. Without the Service Evaluating process, users are unable to quantify the service quality. I/S does not have a service standard at an agreed-to price. Everyone operates much like the high jumper who has no cross-bar on the uprights. No one is sure whether the jump was successful.

The lack of Service Planning processes indicates that I/S operates in a crisis or reaction mode. Recovery, security, and auditing of services are probably weak and subject to rapid changes in emphasis. Service objectives are not clearly defined or reviewed. Improvement is required.

Initiate Effectiveness/Efficiency Improvements

The organizational recommendation could involve any of the 7-S factors or their relationships. In our Brazwell example, we will assume that quality has become one of our major shared values and that our strategy is to deliver quality service through a centralized I/S organization. The remainder of this section focuses on the other factors.

Structure

At first glance, the Brazwell I/S service organization under Mr. Smith (Fig. 5–2) resembles the System/Network Control Center discussed in Chapter 4. One major difference is the inclusion of a software development group under Mr. Lawson. The System/Network Control Center concept recommends that the service mission be functionally separated from the development mission. This could be accomplished by transferring Mr. Lawson and his responsibility to the Ms. Collins's development group or Mr. Jones's special projects group. We might suggest that Mr. Jones's title be changed to Customer Support Manager.

To achieve the three key features of the System/Network Control Center, we could:

1. Separate the Production and Distribution processes between Mr. Turner and Mr. McCoy. Mr. McCoy has the title Telecommunications Manager, but does not have the distribution responsibility (Fig. 5–5).
2. Assign the Customer Service process to Mr. Conners or Mr. Black. Our surveys indicated that Mr. McCoy is the decision maker.
3. Promote Mr. Smithwick to the Service Quality Manager position. He already has most of the assigned processes.

However, those recommendations will not solve our problems in the tactical-level Service Planning. An examination of Figure 5–4 indicates confusion between the service organization under Mr. Smith and the planning organization under Mr. Sellman. Both groups are major decision makers for the Service Planning processes. Our recommendation in this case does not require a structural change, only a clarification of which group owns the processes.

Systems

We can use the survey form to map our proposed organization against the various processes. Those recommendations could be reviewed by various managers before submitting the final proposal. We could also recommend that the Application, Data, and Systems Planning processes review the support for the information business. We could also recommend a management systems development project to review the reports used for Service Evaluating.

Skills and staffing

We cannot achieve these strategy, structure, and systems changes without some reevaluation of personnel resources. Of the 641 FTE resources, we have allocated 9 to Service Planning and 47 to Service Control.

Our recommendation could include the assignment of those resources to the responsible organization. This would focus the productivity of those persons. A later recommendation might increase or decrease those staffing levels. The survey forms can be used to track those FTE levels.

Style

Throughout this analysis, we have not evaluated the style of each manager. That analysis is extremely important but also very sensitive. Our recommendation should address the qualifications for the position. The I/S executive or senior managers should make the decision about persons who best fit those qualifications.

Summary

These recommendations should be submitted to the Management Systems Planning process. Once a management plan is defined and accepted, the Management Systems Monitoring process can be used to track the management systems development project or the performance of the System/Network Control Center.

This chapter has focused on the service mission to illustrate the techniques. Clearly, the technique would apply equally to the development and consultation missions.

MANAGEMENT SYSTEMS PLANNING

DEFINITION:

Using strategic guidance and an assessment of the existing management system, this process defines a prioritized management plan to improve the management system through a project approach.

DESCRIPTION:

The elements of Management Systems Planning are:

1. Relate this I/S process model to the local situation.
2. Define I/S organization and its objectives.
3. Relate organizational responsibility to the I/S processes.
4. Define the requirements for standards, procedures, and methodology to enhance the management system and thus increase the effectiveness and efficiency of the I/S processes (including financial and personnel performance/productivity improvements). Document the benefits, priorities, preliminary cost estimates, and planned usage.
5. Define technically feasible and manageable projects to support the management system.
6. Define project resources and time.
7. Justify and prioritize the projects for the management systems plan.

DATA CLASSES REQUIRED:

Data input to process (data class)	Data output of process (data class)
E2 I/S business	P6 Management systems plan
E3 I/S industry	P8 Project plan
P6 Management systems plan	T1 Inventory
P7 Service plan	
P8 Project plan	

Data input to process (data class)	Data output of process (data class)
C5 Requirements	
C8 Management systems performance	
A1 Vendor	
A2 Customer/user/group	
A3 Organization	
R10 Standards/procedures/methods	

Relate This I/S Process Model to the Local Situation

Throughout the Management Systems Monitoring discussion, the generic or ideal process was used to simplify the understanding of the technique. However, no real I/S organization will have processes exactly like those of the generic model. This process element must translate the ideal process and data models into a representation of your organization.

Many installations will use terminology that differs from Appendix A of this book. The initial translation step should alter the wording of the process definitions to more truly reflect this terminology difference. With the examination of the currently installed processes and the translated model, management must decide which process to use for the remainder of the planning. One approach is to consider the generic model as a target, and migrate the currently installed process toward that target.

Define I/S Organization and Its Objectives

In Chapter 2 we explored the processes that evolve in each phase of growth. To select an organization, we must expand that phasing to encompass the other factors (shared values, strategy, structure, systems, skills, staff, and style).

Phase I: startup

In this phase management should emphasize the old ''keep it simple'' principle. Functional structures with clear lines of responsibilities and authority are highly recommended. Focus should be on the two primary missions, service and development. The consultation mission can be divided across the other two missions.

Phase II: growth

In this phase growth must be managed to maintain a reasonable quality standard. One suggested structure is shown in Figure 5–10.

- *Service Mission.* Critical to this phase is the delivery of high-quality service to the consumer. A Service Quality Manager can provide that key management

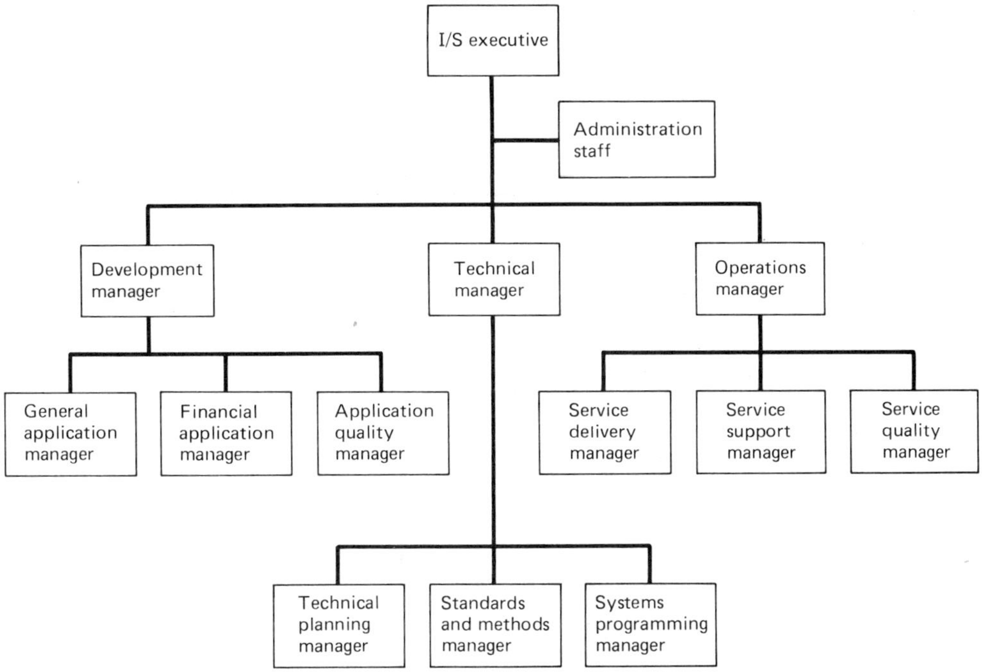

Figure 5-10 I/S organizational model—Phase II.

focus through processes such as Problem Control, Change Control, and Resource and Data Performance Control.

- *Development Mission.* This phase should see the emergence of the first serious use of entrepreneurial structures with project management. Since projects are key to growth, this mechanism can provide the control to meet schedules on time and in budget.
- *Consultation Mission.* This phase should also see the emergence of the consultation mission as a major means to maximize the use of the ever-increasing number of resources. This resource management organization has three subunits: technical planning, standards and methods, and systems programming.

Phase III: controls

In this phase the pressures for decentralization begin to occur and should signal a switch from a cost center focus into a customer-oriented information business. One phase III structure is shown in Figure 5-11.

- *Service Mission.* This phase includes a reexamination of the skills and staffing required for a larger service organization. The System/Network Control Center organization separates the Production and Distribution processes and installs a Customer Service process under the Distribution Manager.

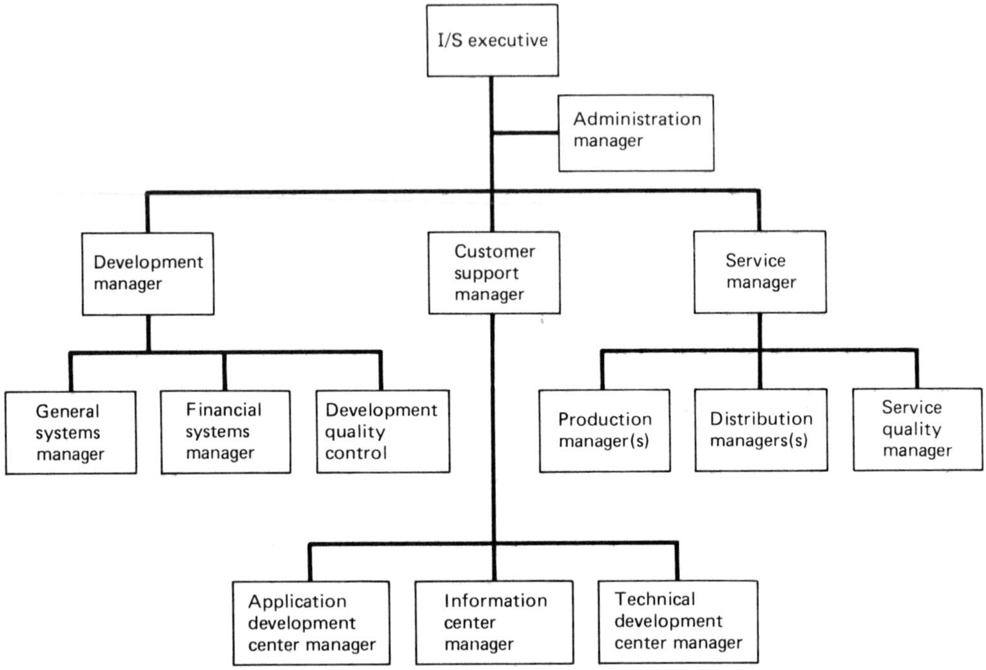

Figure 5–11 Centralized organizational model—Phase III.

- *Development Mission.* The grouping of individual applications into application systems is emphasized by changing the manager's title from Application Manager to Application System Manager.
- *Consultation Mission.* The customer orientation of the consultation mission appears in this phase. The Customer Support Manager includes the following:

    The Application Development Center focuses on improving the productivity of the development staff.

    The Technical Development Center provides technical competence for both the service and development missions. This organization is an increased role for the phase II Technical Manager.

    The Information Center provides support for the casual programmer and overall marketing of information.

Phase IV: planning for centralized strategy

One phase IV structure is shown in Figure 5–12.

- *Service Mission.* The System/Network Control Center remains essentially unchanged, except that it must support several thousand personal computers and office systems. These technologies can be considered as specialized cases of the production facility.

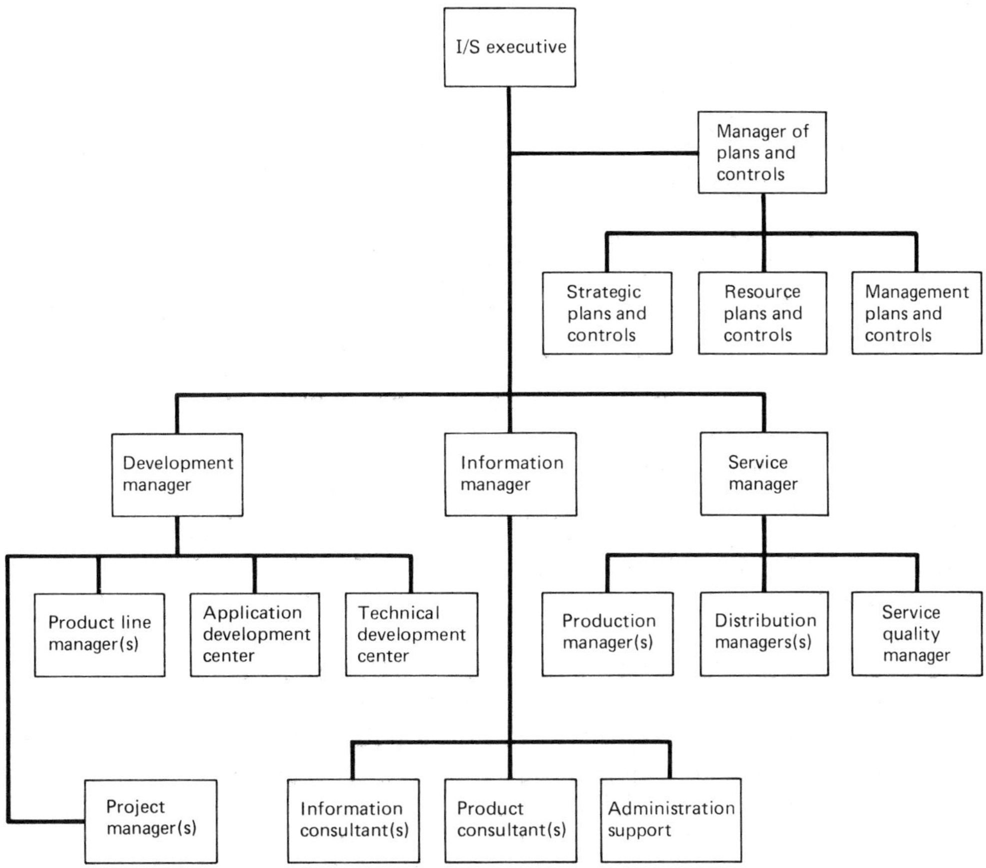

Figure 5-12 Centralized organizational model—Phase IV.

- *Development Mission.* To simplify management control, the Application and Technical Development Centers are realigned in a matrix within the development organization. These centers were previously placed under the Customer Support Manager to protect the resources until the function could be established.

  The Application System Managers can be organized along business or enterprise product lines: for example, life insurance, casualty insurance. This can be reflected in manager titles that are more product oriented, such as Manager of Life Insurance Information Systems.
- *Consultation Mission.* After the Application and Technical Development Centers have been removed, the Information Center is increased in level and focuses as the marketing organization for I/S. In this phase, a Plans and Controls organization should formalize many of the Strategic, Management, and Resource Planning processes. At a minimum, that organization should focus on increasing the quality of I/S services. This can be achieved through a quality

council using concepts similar to those presented in the book *Quality Is Free,* by Philip Crosby [2]. The Management Plans and Controls Manager would chair the quality council.

Serious consideration could be given to doing a full management planning study of the I/S organization with heavy end-user participation. This would serve several purposes:

1. It could clearly establish I/S as a business within the business.
2. It could examine the centralization versus decentralization issues in a more businesslike manner.
3. It could allow users to better understand what I/S could do in their business area.
4. It allows a natural evolution to phase V.

Phase IV: planning for decentralized strategy

In a large I/S organization, the Service, Development, and Consultation Missions could be vertically integrated into the enterprise business units (Fig. 5–13). The central I/S organization supports planning, standards, communications, and information across the enterprise.

Phase V: strategic planning

In this phase the entrepreneur study team becomes a way of life for developing long-range plans. Combining these studies with a steering committee allows I/S to be creative while providing continuity. In many cases, decentralization will be a standard mode by this phase. Some consideration should be given to formal matrix management. Some consideration should be given to allocating personnel within each mission to supplement overall planning.

Summary

These phase considerations are given only as one possible scenario. You must select and guide your own direction.

Relate Organizational Responsibility to the I/S Processes

The process-to-organization matrix has been used for two different purposes. The Management Systems Monitoring process used it to gather information about the current management system (Fig. 5–3). A similar matrix was used in the Management Systems Planning process to analyze alternative recommendations. Before we select a structure and assign responsibility, it might be helpful to clarify the analysis that can be done with this matrix.

Span of manager control

Each vertical column shows the span of control for each manager or unique organizational unit. Special consideration should be given to the number of decision points

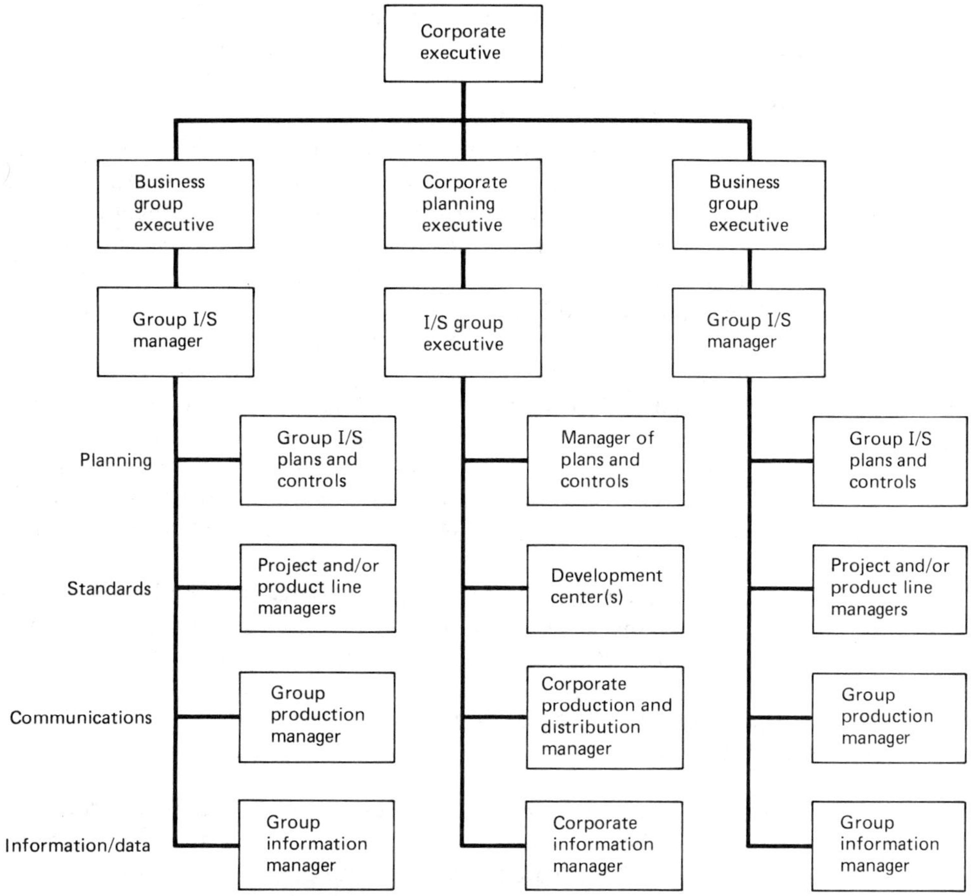

Figure 5–13 Decentralized organizational model.

shown by an X under the control of that manager. Too many could indicate the need for grouping some functions with other managers; for example, Mr. Kilpatrick has many of the key service mission processes and may not be able to support them (Fig. 5–5).

Careful consideration should be given to the time horizon spanned by each manager. Executives would normally focus on strategic processes with some responsibility at the tactical level. Middle managers would focus on tactical process with some responsibility at the strategic and operational levels. Operational managers would normally focus largely on the operational processes.

Generally, it is better to separate the various missions by function. The management techniques used for the service mission differ from those used in the development mission. Any manager who manages processes in both missions must be aware of that difference, for example, Mr. Smithwick is responsible for processes in all three missions, and both the tactical and operational time frames (Fig. 5–5). This span of control is rather large and could be the source of difficulty.

Span of information

An analysis of a horizontal row indicates the span of involvement in a process and the need for management information. A process with many decision makers or involved organizations will require careful analysis of the management reports required. Too many decision makers for any one process could indicate the need for reorganization or reassignment of responsibility. A process without a single assigned manager could also be a source of difficulty.

Multiple involvement in a single process could indicate the need for a committee or entrepreneurial program overlay, for example, the Customer Services process might be supported with a quality council chaired by one of the decision makers. Each of the other six decision makers would have active participation.

Even with all this analysis and planning, there is no "right" answer for the I/S organization. Someone must make a decision on the structure and assign the responsibilities. Those decisions are part of a management plan spanning the tactical time horizon with planned increments of change.

If the Management Systems Monitoring process has been installed properly and is functioning, progress on the management plan would be reviewed on a regular basis, and corrections could be made to control the plan.

Define the Requirements for Standards, Procedures, and Methodology

What is the correct documentation level for standards, procedures, and methodologies? If they are too general, they are not useful in the execution of the management system. If they are too detailed, no one will read them. What will work for one organization will not work for another. Each organization must learn through experience what is an acceptable level.

If the Management Planning processes are ongoing, the level of detail can be adjusted based on the need, experience level, and results. I was once asked whether it was better to spend one year building a complete management plan, or doing an incomplete plan in six to eight weeks. Assuming we have a monitoring process that incorporates improvements, the second alternative is always best. In any dynamic organization, too many things would have to be changed in the one year required to generate the plan. It would have been obsolete on the day it was published.

I/S manager's manual

The documentation provided in this book is designed as the starting point for an I/S Manager's Manual. In this context, the Information Systems Management Architecture becomes a manager's "vocabulary" to communicate with other managers. When one manager talks about managing service, service has the same definition for both managers. The need for a management language arises as an organization grows in size and complexity, people are geographically separated, or people become more specialized in their tasks. They lose the overall perspective of I/S.

An organization could add sample reports to Chapters 6 to 8 and use the resulting manual to educate new managers. The process and data definitions offer a framework for that education. This framework could also be supported with organizational guidelines or practices on the other 7–S factors (shared values, strategy, structure, staff, skills, and style).

Detailed documentation

This framework can be supported with how-to-do documents on each methodology or management technique. It is at that level of detail that organizations have significant differences. One organization might purchase a project management methodology from a vendor, another might develop its own. The two methods might use different reports and input documents. However, the basic framework would be the same.

Define Technically Feasible and Manageable Projects

To implement or alter the management system, we can use the same project management techniques designed for application development, but with a separate life cycle. Those project management techniques discussed in Chapter 8 use a Project Objectives Document for Project Planning [12]. That document for the System/Network Control Center might indicate the following:*

BRAZWELL HOME ELECTRONICS SYSTEM/NETWORK CONTROL CENTER PROJECT 075 OBJECTIVES

Executive summary

The growth of Brazwell Home Electronics during the last several years has put considerable strain on our ability to provide quality I/S service. The acquisition of the Home Security Systems Corporation merged two highly incompatible I/S organizations. It took 14 months to resolve defects in the Home Security Order Entry System and to merge the two I/S staffs. Throughout that period, the vice-president of marketing constantly complained about inventory shortages, incomplete orders, and competitors luring away old, faithful dealerships.

We have recently acquired the Marco Systems Corporation, a manufacturer of residential telephones. Marco has a chain of 300 retail stores operating on a small profit margin. The acquisition assumed that an expanded communication network,

*The format of this project objectives document is extracted from the IBM publication *Managing the Application Development Process,* Part 2. SR20-7246-1.

Relationships X = Decision maker / = Major involvement * = Minor involvement						
Processes	I/S executive Ms. Allen	Service manager Mr. Smith	Service planning Mr. Kilpatrick	Production mgr. Mr. Turner	Distribution mgr. Mr. McCoy	Service quality Mr. Smithwick
Service Planning						
Service marketing plan	/	X	/	*	*	*
Service level planning	/	X	/	*	*	*
Recovery planning	/	X	/	*	*	*
Security planning	/	X	/	*	*	*
Audit planning	/	X	/	*	*	*
Service Control						
P/D scheduling		*		/	/	X
R/D performance control		*		/	/	X
Problem control		*		/	/	X
Service evaluating		*		/	/	X
Information services						
Production		/		X	/	*
Distribution		/		/	X	*
Customer services		*	/	/	X	*
Services marketing		*		/	/	

Figure 5–14 Service process-to-organization matrix.

point-of-sale terminals, and tight inventory control could make Marco more profitable.

Three months after the acquisition, our major competitor, International Electronics Incorporated, began an intense drive to establish its own retail stores. For that reason, Information Systems and the Marketing Division are jointly proposing the development of a new order entry system and the establishment of a System/Network Control Center. The order entry applications will be developed under project 075A.

The objectives of the System/Network Control Center are:

1. The point-of-sale network will be managed as a single information network.
2. Regional Customer Service Centers will provide outlet store help assistance.
3. Service Quality will be tracked and reported.

The System/Network Control Center will be constructed in three major phases over a 20-month period. First, the I/S organization will be realigned to focus responsibility for the new environment (Fig. 5–14). That effort will be completed by December 1.

Starting in January, a study team chaired by the Service Quality Manager will design a service measurement and reporting system. At the same time, a second study team is to design a customer assistance system. The designs for both systems are to be submitted by June 1. The total design cost is estimated to be $100,000, which is primarily labor costs for I/S and Marketing.

The actual costs of implementation are estimated to be around $150,000 over the next 12 months. Although these costs are only approximations, a better estimate will be available when the final design is submitted. Using these cost figures, it is estimated that the payback for the system will occur in the fourth year.

The benefits for the System/Network Control Center project are included in the order entry project proposal. Both projects are key to the profitability of the Marco Division.

System overview

The business processes of the Marketing Order Entry System are included for reference:

- Order Processing: functions included
  - Remote entry of customer identification
  - Remote entry of customer orders by title and number
  - Orders extended and discounts applied
  - Inventory status checked for in-stock and out-of-stock items
  - Inventory status records reflect order amounts
  - Order acknowledgments printed remotely for sales personnel
  - Orders printed at warehouse location for picking and shipping
- Order Processing: functions not included
  - Alphabetical search look-up of customer information from name only
  - Returns processing
  - Automatic back-order status reporting
- Inventory Control: functions included
  - Master inventory file reflects balances at the three distribution center locations
  - Shipments from printing plant update inventory records
  - Shipments from distribution center to customer cause flagged inventory records to be updated
  - Billing information passed to the accounts receivable system (current system modification)
- Inventory Control: functions not included
  - Picking tags in warehouse location
  - Master list for annual inventory
- Customer Service: functions included
  - Credit status information obtained by telephone from district sales office
  - Order status information obtained by telephone from district sales office

Order confirmation sheets sent automatically after order entry
Customer master file maintenance on batch basis

- Customer Service: functions not included
  - On-line changes to back-order status records
  - Remote addition of new ship-to locations
  - On-line inquiry to fulfilled orders

The I/S business processes of the Systems/Network Control Center are:

- Service Control
  - Production and Distribution Scheduling
  - Resource and Data Performance Control
  - Problem Control
  - Service Evaluating
- Information Services
  - Production
  - Distribution
  - Customer Services
  - Services Marketing

To support the System/Network Control Center, the Service Manager will add staff for the Service Planning processes:

- Service Marketing Planning
- Service-Level Planning
- Recovery Planning
- Security Planning
- Audit Planning

Operation environment

It is anticipated that the System/Network Control Center will operate as follows (see Chapter 4).

System development approach

The System/Network Control Center will be planned and developed in phases. The design phase will produce the following:

- A Systems Requirements Report
- A Systems Design Report containing:
  - The external design
  - The internal design

- An Implementation Plan

This documentation will be produced according to Brazwell I/S guidelines for such products, dated xx/xx/xx. Top-down development principles will be followed, and the functional documentation will be produced according to the same guidelines.

Products and completion criteria

The Systems Requirements Report will be delivered in draft form for review by the Marketing department. Approved changes will be incorporated, and Marketing will approve the final document. The document will serve as the basis for system design (see estimated schedule of draft document availability).

The systems design functions will be approved by Marketing as they are developed. Draft sections of the external design documentation will be reviewed for approval. Final reviews and user walk-throughs of the system will be held over a four-week period (see schedule). The approved external systems design will be used as the design baseline for the internal design and the Implementation Plan.

The internal design will be reviewed by I/S systems assurance for completeness, quality, and adherence to our guidelines. The Implementation Plan will be reviewed and approved by the following groups:

- Marketing
- I/S
- Controller's office
- Corporate Planning

Approval of the Systems Requirements Report, Systems Design Report, and Implementation Plan constitutes completion of the design phase of the System/Network Control Center project.

Project team major tasks

Project Team Major Tasks

1.0 Project Management.
1.1 Develop detailed project plans.
1.2 Conduct team orientation and team assignments.
1.3 Track and evaluate progress.
1.4 Administer the project change control plan.
1.5 Conduct monthly management status meetings.
2.0 Management Systems Development Requirements Tasks.
2.1 Interview users.
2.2 Prepare a draft Systems Requirements Report.
2.3 Conduct user reviews and obtain approvals.

2.4 Produce final Systems Requirements Report.
3.0 Management Systems Development Design Tasks.
3.1 Develop external design.
3.2 Conduct user walk-through and obtain approvals.
3.3 Develop internal design.
3.4 Develop Implementation Plan.
3.5 Produce final copy of Systems Design Report.

User Department Tasks

1.0 User Management will designate a Project Administrator.
1.1 Participate in interviews to document department requirements.
1.2 Review and prioritize requirements.
1.3 Review and approve the draft Systems Requirements Report.
1.4 Participate with I/S in developing the external design.
1.5 Participate in doing walk-throughs and approve systems functions.
1.6 Review and approve the Systems Design Report.
1.7 Attend monthly status meetings.

Key project assumptions

1. Users will be available and will participate according to attached schedule.
2. Hardware plan and configuration will be developed by the I/S Technical Development Center.
3. Secretarial support for documentation will be provided by the Application Development Center.
4. Project personnel will be available according to the attached staffing plan.
5. Key documents will be approved in seven working days.

Estimates and estimated schedule

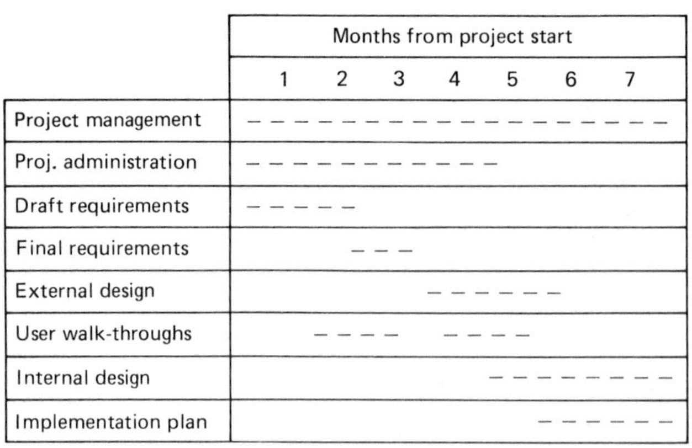

Figure 5-15 Project time estimates.

Define Project Resources and Time

A Management Systems Development project such as the Brazwell System/Network Control Center requiring 26 person-months of resources, over $250,000, and 20 elapsed months should be managed by an experienced project leader. However, many I/S organizations assign the project based on technical knowledge rather than management experience. The resulting service mission often has the latest technical hardware but fails to support the enterprise.

Unless the marketing organization recognizes the benefits of the project, they will be reluctant to spend the required 6-person-month effort. The Brazwell example interconnects the development of a major on-line application with the installation of the management support organization. This is a wise move for every I/S organization.

The staff for this type project would include personnel from nearly all I/S organizations, including operations, applications development, and systems programming. All of these resources are in short supply and under severe demand. Executives must be committed to the project and enforce its extreme importance.

Otherwise, the Management Systems Development project will always lose resources to application or software projects. If this happens, managing this understaffed project is much like the criminal who appeared before a judge in a Texas court. The judge sentenced the criminal to 10 years of hard labor in the Huntsville, Texas, prison. The criminal, looking bewildered, said: "Judge, I'm not sure I can do 10 years in Huntsville." The judge replied: "Sir, you go down there and do the best you can."

"Doing the best you can" could mean jeopardizing the $700,000,000 Brazwell Corporation and its customers with a poorly designed System/Network Control Center. This attitude is prevalent in late phase II and early phase III. Rather than address management issues as the organization grows in size, I/S management delays until a major crisis occurs. Then the Management Systems Development project must be accomplished in a panic mode without end-user cooperation. The results are unpredictable and usually unsatisfactory.

Justify and Prioritize the Projects

A $250,000 investment to protect the $700,000,000 Brazwell Corporation is a sound business decision. If I/S views itself as a business and uses sound business practices, the justification and prioritization of management system development projects are not difficult.

The required justification techniques are identical to those described in Chapter 8 for applications. The most significant benefits must include the increased productivity of the end user. A small improvement in I/S can have a significant impact on the Brazwell sales.

Any benefits derived within I/S can be used to reallocate resources to unsupported processes, for example, Service-Level Planning. Clearly defined service objectives allows I/S to plan the future rather than react to it. That is the fundamental difference between phases II and IV.

MANAGEMENT PLANNING SUMMARY

The Information Systems Management Architecture allows an understanding of the total management system to determine when to start the actual improvement. Thus we have tried to define the key groups of processes required in an I/S business. Although we have discussed them separately, they are, of course, related to each other; each set of processes directly affects most of the others.

Executives often ask which of the planning processes are critical in making the phase III to the phase IV transition. In a "top-down" planning mode, the answer must include the processes to plan the management system itself. Starting in phase I, the processes of the management system are defined and implemented without any clear plan. By phase III, many of these processes have become ineffective and inefficient.

The process Management Systems Planning is concerned with planning this "container" to allow the information business to work. This container includes the organizational structure, standards, procedures, and methodology to run the information business. With this starting point, the other planning process groups dealing with the contents of this container (that is, the plans to manage I/S) can be evaluated and assigned to the proper management organization.

6

Implementing a Management System

Development Mission Definition: Development of new services and applications for other departments in the enterprise.

Consultation Mission Definition: Consultation with other departments on the need and use of information.

CONTROLLING THE PROJECT

While we are awaiting approval of our System/Network Control Center project, we might think ahead to controlling and delivering that project. One key issue will be the project management methodology to be used. That management systems decision follows the same Information Systems Management Architecture flow described for the System/Network Control Center project. Hopefully, the decision would have been made in phase II. The flow for Brazwell was:

1. *Decide.* This effort was started in phase II as a result of our rapid growth in applications.
2. *Plan.* The Management Systems Planning process evaluated the possible solutions and made a management systems development project recommendation.
3. *Resource.* Resources were allocated by Resource Planning to schedule and install the project management methodology.
4. *Schedule and Build.* The management systems development team studied the general project management methodology requirements described in this chapter. The team also examined several vendor methodologies for function, com-

puter support, documentation, and educational support. A package was selected largely on its ease of use and educational support.

The first two sections discuss the project management controls and the various project types, respectively.

Controlling the project deliverables

Again, you looked ahead and found that your deliverables must interface with the Resource Control processes: Resource and Data Inventory Control and Change Control. Two sections describing those controls and the related Administration Services are included in this chapter. While you are reading this section, we will assume that the executives are reviewing our System/Network Control Center and Order Entry proposals.

DEVELOPMENT AND MAINTENANCE CONTROL*

Development and maintenance control process overview

This group of processes deals with the management of projects to be developed. Any change to the ongoing operations of I/S that cannot be handled within its daily operating schedule and by use of predefined, tested actions must result in a project.

The five processes in this group will be discussed in the following sequence:

1. Project Assignment
   - How are planned projects staffed to meet their objectives?
   - How are short-term maintenance, tuning, and system balancing projects defined?
2. Project Scheduling
   - What is required to deliver projects on time and within budget?
3. Project Controlling
   - How are resources assigned and controlled within a project?
   - How is the quality of the final deliverables controlled?
4. Project Requirements Control
   - How are changes to the original project controlled?
5. Project Evaluating
   - How are project postaudits conducted?

It is suggested that the reader refer periodically to the flow shown in the overview (Fig. 6–1).

*The remainder of this chapter (with the exception of the "Implementation Summary") is reproduced from the IBM publication *A Management System for the Information Business,* Volume III—*The I/S Development Mission,* GE20–0750–0, and Volume IV—*Managing the I/S Resources,* GE20–0751-0 by permission of the IBM Corporation.

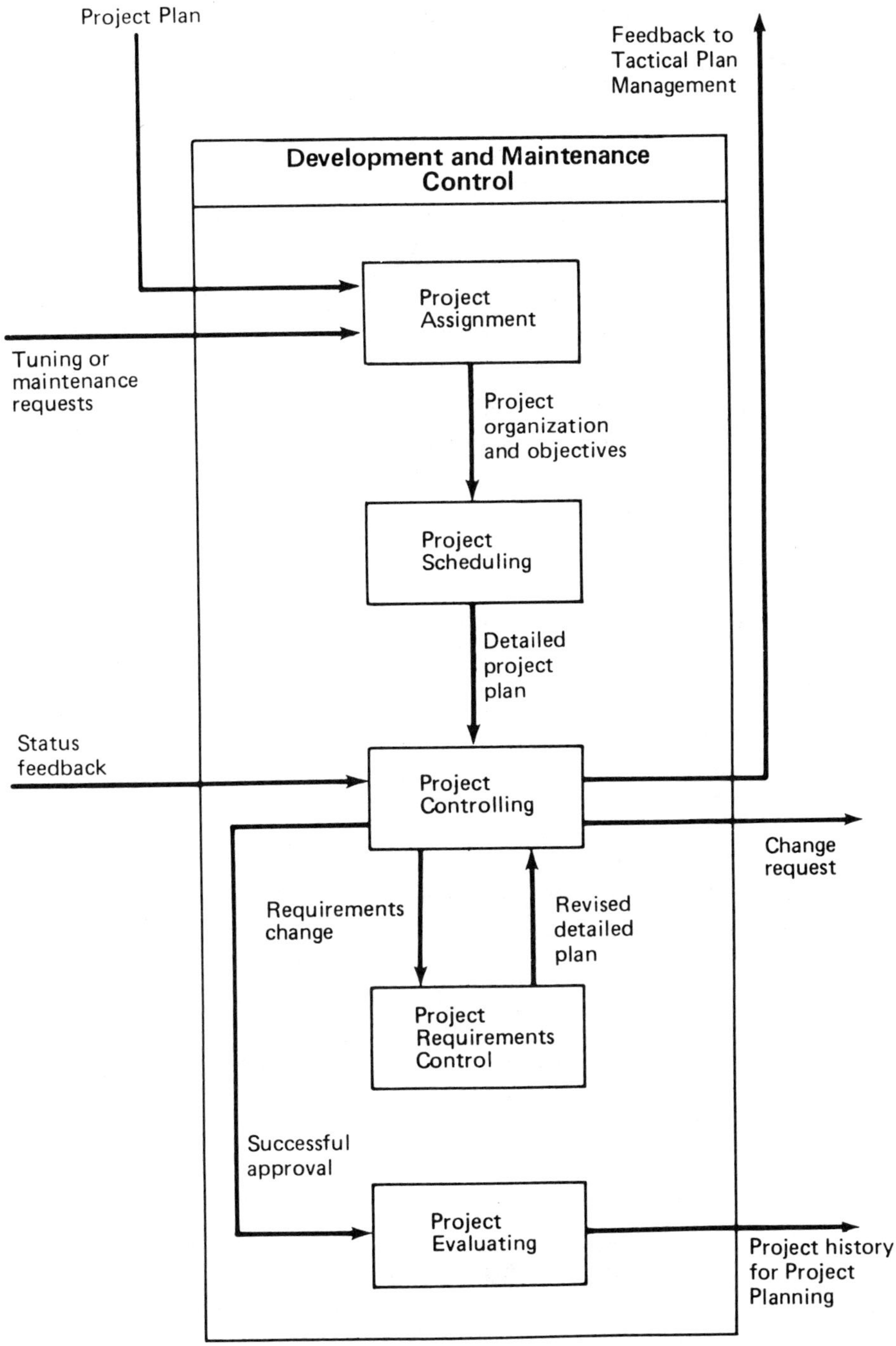

Figure 6–1 Development and maintenance control overview.

Assessing development and maintenance control

Questions that could be asked to measure the effectiveness and efficiency of the Development and Maintenance Control process group are:

- Are projects consistently late?
- Are projects always in crisis mode?
- Is extreme overtime required to finish the project cycle?
- Do projects require more resources than planned?
- Are only application projects tracked?
- Are projects evaluated at regular checkpoints?
- Do managers know early enough about schedule slippages?
- Are projects always "80%" complete for long periods of time?
- Are cost/benefit ratios consistent with forecasts?

Project Assignment

DEFINITION:

Using the project objectives document or problem statement, this process defines the project scope, leadership, and user involvement necessary to ensure successful accomplishment.

DESCRIPTION:

The elements of Project Assignment are:

1. Select project leader.
2. Define I/S and user involvement.
3. Obtain management commitment.

DATA CLASSES REQUIRED:

Data input to process (data class)	Data output of process (data class)
P8 Project plan	C2 Project
C2 Project	
C4 Problem	
A1 Vendor	
A2 Customer/user/group	
R8 Personnel	
R10 Standards/procedures/methods	

Select project leader

In order to select a project leader, it is important to understand basic project concepts. Almost every project-oriented undertaking, the construction of a bridge, building of a house, or the development of a new aircraft, follows a certain pattern that recurs again and again. The same is true for I/S application, data, and system projects. They occur as a structured series of activities that are very similar for every solution.

For example, the user application requirements must first be established and then transformed into system (external) functional specifications; the internal logic of the application system is then outlined, and program modules coded and tested. Manual procedures associated with the application must be developed, users trained, and so on, until the new application is finally accepted by the concerned parties and put into production. Every one of these major activities (or development phases) can be broken down further into smaller tasks; and again each of these tasks occurs almost invariably in every application development project.

A project could be defined as a mechanism to control the allocation of time and resources to change something about the existing environment. Clearly, the large projects associated with the development of new technologies consume more time and resources for each change, but many small maintenance problems can also consume considerable resources. In all cases, control of resources to make a change is a key management decision. Each change, regardless of size, can seriously disrupt the stability of the installation.

Project Assignment has the following data sources:

- The planned application, data, and systems projects (hardware, software, and facilities) are received from tactical planning. They have a committed objective, time, and resource level that must be verified by the assigned project leader.
- Problems requiring resolution (maintenance or tuning and system balancing) are received from Problem Control. These must be solved in some cases while the system is down, and the problem statement must be used as the initial project objectives statement until the situation is better defined. The estimate of resources must be done early in the project life cycle to allow management to make decisions on the importance of this fix over some other use of the resources.
- The status of all resources in the system inventory, including people, must be known. Project assignment must be aware of the project managers and technical personnel who could be assigned to this project.

In the remainder of this chapter it is assumed that the project control mechanism can handle both the planned projects and the projects required to resolve problems. Many system projects (for example, a major reconfiguration of the computing equipment) are as important to the success of the organization as development of applications; consequently they should be subjected to the same strict project planning and control practices. The variation in the actual project activities will be handled by separate life cycles for the Development and Maintenance project types.

To be successful, the project must be assigned to a trained and qualified project manager who can guide it through the many phases of activity. The selection of a leader early in the effort allows the project to capitalize on the talent of all the parties involved. Selecting a leader will vary with the type of project and available resources, but should follow a logical approach. Each potential candidate should be reviewed for strengths and weaknesses relative to each project.

A large project must have leaders designated from both the involved I/S and user organizations. This does not mean that projects are to be run by a committee of I/S and user personnel. The project manager, selected from I/S or the user area, is responsible for meeting the objectives and assigning tasks. Additional project administrator(s), selected in key user areas, are responsible for obtaining all the concurrences and approvals that will be required.

A small project to solve a problem actually places the applications or systems programmer in the project manager role with the same responsibility to meet the objectives with committed resources. These technical personnel should be formally trained in good project techniques to achieve satisfactory results.

Define I/S and user involvement

Even though the intended users may have originated the ideas on which a new application, data, or system is based, they are often not given sufficient opportunity to influence the evolving solution once the initial requirements have been established. After using the new solution, they often complain that it does not meet their expectations and is awkward and costly to run.

It is operations staff who have to live with the new application, not the development team; and they may have to live with it for as long as 5 to 10 years after its initial installation. They should therefore be brought into the development process at an early stage to review requirements and design considerations. In some cases, Operations can establish standards under which the new solution must operate before it is acceptable. In other projects, they may actually participate actively in the project until it is installed or running (for example, the installation of hardware).

The user involvement must be clearly specified during all phases of the project. In the scheduling process, user tasks need to be defined and user resources committed to those tasks (the reviews of input/output documents).

In this way, everyone concerned can begin to understand the nature of the project early in its development and be given ample opportunity to influence and determine its functions and behavior. To make sure that this happens, and to remove all grounds for complaint once the solution is in use, the finished product should be formally accepted by users and operations before it is put into production.

Obtain management commitment

Once the involvement of each party is clearly defined in terms of resources, skills, and names, it is mandatory to obtain the commitments of both I/S and user management. Many projects fail because user management is not aware of the impact on their resources and organization. Too often the resource commitment is fulfilled by assigning the new tasks to a busy individual. The ''business as usual'' tasks take priority and delay the project.

For projects that have been approved and funded, this element must ensure that the original commitment still exists. For problem solving projects (maintenance or tuning and system balancing), this management approval is required before proceeding. In many cases, approval is a by-product of the regular problem meeting. The responsible manager commits dates and resources to solve the outstanding problem; other managers either approve or reject this solution. Once approved, this constitutes a commitment for all involved managers.

Project Scheduling

DEFINITION:

Using the plans and documentation of the project, this process prepares a detailed project plan including objectives, resources, time scale, tasks, organization, and deliverables; it also obtains approval from the project team, sponsor, and I/S.

DESCRIPTION:

The elements of Project Scheduling are:

1. Define deliverables.
2. Define tasks.
3. Estimate project.
4. Schedule resources.
5. Finalize detailed project plan.

DATA CLASSES REQUIRED:

Data input to process (data class)		Data output of process (data class)
P8	Project plan	C2 Project
C2	Project	
A1	Vendor	
A2	Customer/user/group	
R1	Application	
R2	Data	
R3	Software	
R4	Hardware	
R5	Network	
R6	Facilities	

Data input to process (data class)	Data output of process (data class)
R7 Supplies	
R8 Personnel	
R10 Standards/procedures/methods	
R11 Test data	

Define deliverables

A project must have a finite set of products and completion criteria as a measure of the completion of each milestone and of the final project. Users should assist the definition of these deliverables and agree on the measurement criteria. The project leader must establish tasks to produce the deliverables and ensure checkpoints at the completion of each phase.

Some of the deliverables are:

- A system requirements report
- A system design report for both external and internal designs
- An implementation plan
- A prototype
- Coding specifications
- Programs
- System test plan
- System installation plan
- User training material
- User manuals
- Operator manuals
- Maintenance plan

The project team has the responsibility to ensure that these are defined and accepted by all parties involved in the project.

Define tasks

An estimate is a statement of the time and resources needed to produce an end product with certain capabilities and functions. For planned projects, the Project Planning process initially estimated the time, resources, and major milestones to be accomplished. These estimates will need further refinement in this element. Thus, estimating an application, data, or system project is concerned with three parameters (Fig. 6–2).

The scope of the project must be broken down into tasks that can be estimated and controlled. The scope of these tasks is locked into the resources and time required. If the scope, resources, or time changes, the estimate is no longer valid. If,

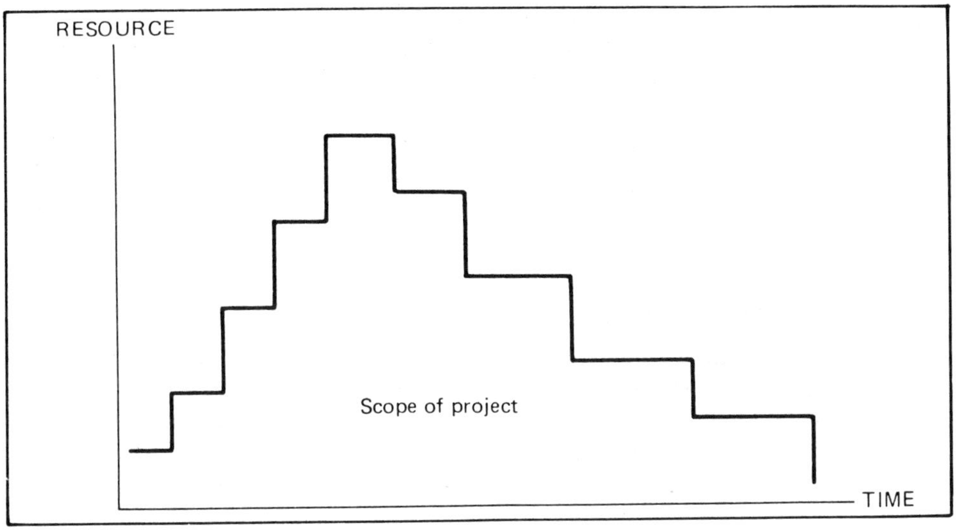

Figure 6–2 Parameters of an estimate—scope, resources, and time.

for example, the available resources are changed, the scope of the project must be changed, or the time span, or both.

Why does an estimate often turn out to be grossly inaccurate? The probable reason is the relationship between scope, time, and resources. Causes for incorrect estimates include the following:

- Tasks are not specified in sufficient detail; this almost inevitably leads to underestimation of the amount of work to be done. A rule of thumb is that tasks requiring more than one person-week of effort should be further subdivided into smaller units of work.
- Whole sets of activities are forgotten. These are often nonproject activities (holidays, vacation, and military service); and secondary project activities (education and training, report writing, project reviews, information meetings, and general administration).
- No allowances are made for mistakes or unexpected events; it is always assumed that everything will go well. Examples of such events are sickness, personnel leaving the project (which means that replacements must be brought in and trained), a design having to be partly redone, computing facilities going down, and organizational conflicts.
- The complexity of the project or the end product is not fully appreciated. This complexity may be real, inherent in the scope of the end product, or perhaps created due to bad design and/or bad project organization. For example, the maximum number of people that a project can effectively utilize depends on the number of independent tasks involved; those tasks depend very much on the design and on how interfaces between subsystems are specified.

- Technical people (designers and programmers) tend to overdo technical solutions to user problems so that the evolving computer application becomes unnecessarily rich in function. Unless strictly controlled, this tendency inevitably leads to schedule and resource problems. Rather than allowing the technical solutions to influence the time and resources needed to implement the system, the opposite approach should be used to let the allocated time and resources allocated determine (within reasonable limits) how rich in function the system can be.

Estimate projects

The precision in project estimating is improved by using data from past projects similar to the one being estimated. The use of historical data presupposes that a suitable tracking system has been in place for some time so that this data is readily available. A standard project structure also facilitates the use of historical data in estimating since it is easier to interpret the precise meaning of the collected data when tasks and activities are well defined.

The estimating process can be facilitated, and the estimates themselves made more accurate, by a detailed and comprehensive project plan. The project plan is also the basis for controlling all activities of a particular application development effort by showing what the results of the job should be, how the job will be done, when it will be done, and the resources required to do it. In fact, without the plan, there is no such thing as control.

Schedule resources

Taking into account the available resources, one technique for this scheduling is a precedence diagram showing all tasks and their dependencies. Preparation of the precedence diagram begins after information about the products has been assembled and the tasks necessary to develop the product have been individually defined on task sheets and estimates have been made.

The purpose of the precedence diagram is to illustrate the performance sequence of each task, to show task interdependencies, and to assist in calculating time required to do the job. Although the precedence diagram might look formidable, there are techniques to simplify its preparation.

In larger projects, this exercise can be automated with tools to allow the production of a large grid network with one or more subnetworks.

Finalize detailed project plan

With assigned personnel, defined tasks, estimated resources, and a detailed schedule, the project manager is ready to begin the implementation of the first phase. It is advisable to publish the final plan in written form and to obtain written concurrence before actually starting. With this management agreement, the tasks can be started.

Project scheduling summary

In larger projects, the above process elements would be repeated at the completion of each phase or major milestone. The next process, Project Controlling, will reactivate Project Scheduling when required.

Project Controlling

DEFINITION:

Using the detailed project plan, this process monitors the project through its phases, conducting reviews, resolving any development problems, and documenting its life. This also includes submitting the change request to move the deliverables to the system inventory.

DESCRIPTION:

The elements of Project Controlling are:

1. Track progress against plan.
2. Report status.
3. Conduct project reviews, resolve development problems, and review any make/buy decision.
4. Submit change request.

DATA CLASSES REQUIRED:

Data input to process (data class)	Data output of process (data class)
C2 Project	C2 Project
C5 Requirements	C3 Change
A1 Vendor	
A2 Customer/user/group	
R1 Application	
R2 Data	
R3 Software	
R4 Hardware	
R5 Network	
R6 Facilities	
R7 Supplies	
R8 Personnel	
R9 Financial	
R10 Standards/procedures/methods	
R11 Test data	

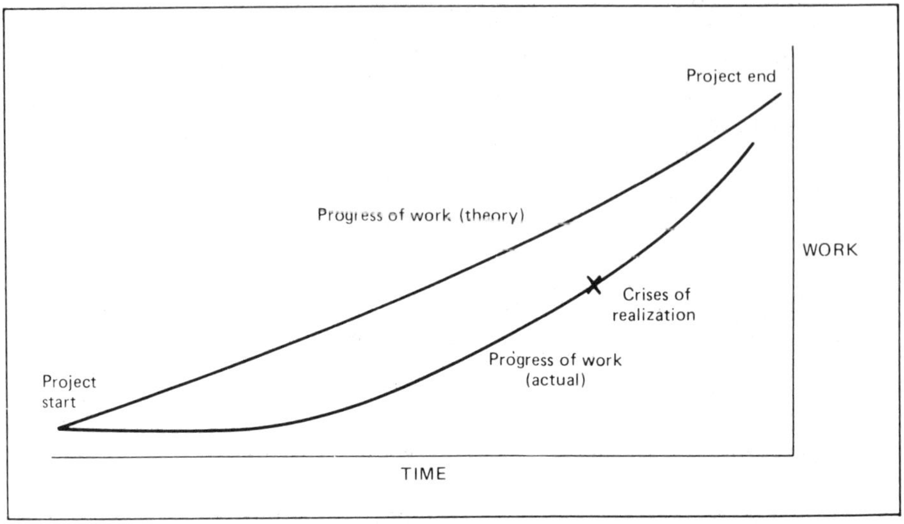

Figure 6–3 How people work on projects.

Track progress against plan

Project control consists essentially of balancing the three variables: scope, resources, and time. Even if a project is properly planned, there are many factors that can jeopardize its success and bring it out of control. Some of these factors, such as the occurrence of unexpected events, have been discussed. Another factor that can work against the successful completion of a project is human nature.

Instead of working steadily on a project from beginning to end, people tend to get involved in side activities and they put things off. The result is that rate of work follows a sagging line (Fig. 6–3) rather than a straight line between the beginning and the end of the project. Suddenly a point is reached where people realize they are behind schedule. As a result, they try to speed up their work in an all-out effort to achieve agreed objectives.

In a project with few or no intermediate phase reviews, the end result may not be achieved within the scheduled time. The situation can be rectified by breaking down the project into smaller phases and tasks (Fig. 6–4), each having its own stated end result and completion date. People will still go through the same process, but on a much smaller scale and within a much smaller time period. As a result, the problem of catching up with a schedule is not as serious, and it should be possible to maintain an almost steady level of work output from the project team.

The control methodology described has one major snag: How does the project manager really know where a particular activity stands at any time? The purposes of a project plan are to make estimates more accurate and to allow for the measurement of progress. Progress can only be measured with accuracy by comparing the actual, concrete result of an activity with the quantitatively expressed objectives of that activity as defined in the project plan. Ideally, this measurement process is a

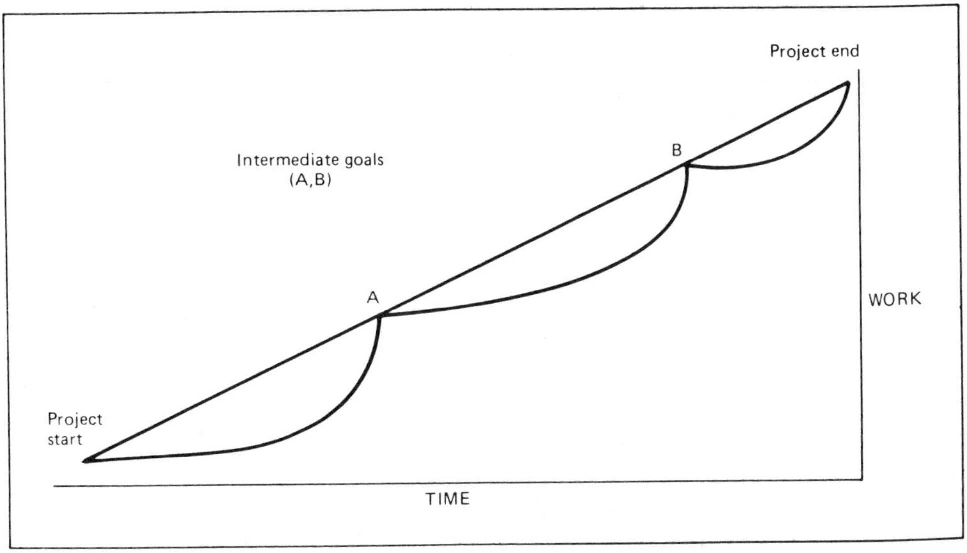

Figure 6–4 Breaking down a project into smaller tasks.

binary comparison: Does the actual result completely match the specifications, yes or no? For example, a program module is never 50% or 90% complete; it is either not completed (coding has not begun or the module is being coded), or it has successfully run against all appropriate unit test cases.

To allow this binary way of measuring progress, the development process must be broken down into a large number of small tasks. As was discussed earlier, a rule of thumb is that tasks requiring more than one person-week of effort should be subdivided into smaller units of work.

Report status

What specific means should the project manager use to follow up the project? Precedence diagrams and critical path techniques report the precedence constraints among activities. The results can be effectively reported using bar charts and simple variance reports which show items such as actual versus estimated person-hours and actual versus budget expenditures. It is probably more rewarding to develop, use, and enforce working methods aimed at preventing out-of-control situations, rather than to design and put in place elaborate procedures for the detection of such situations.

Conduct project reviews and resolve development problems

Project reviews at each major milestone determine the completion of one phase and the scheduling of the next phase. All involved managers, I/S and users, should attend the meeting conducted by the project manager. The possible decisions from this meeting include:

- If the project phase was completed as planned, the managers could agree to allow the start of the next phase.
- If resource consumption exceeded the plan, the project could be delayed pending a Project Planning process review of the impact on the tactical plan.
- If the variance was within tolerance, the managers could allow the project to proceed with restrictions.
- The project could be abandoned for any of the following:

  The original estimates were too low.

  The business conditions have changed.

  Another project with higher priority needs the resources.

  The project sponsor has retired or no longer supports the effort.
- The prior work phase requires rework (for example, the external specifications do not reflect the real user requirements or the user was not involved).

Other project meetings mostly with technical personnel need to measure the quality of the project deliverables. This could include structured walk-throughs.

Submit change request

The ultimate purpose of the project is to produce deliverables for use in the delivery of service. The change request allows the project manager to formally signal that a change review process should begin to anticipate this transfer in control of the deliverables. Once completed, these deliverables become part of the system inventory available to the service mission.

The change request must be submitted early enough to allow all potentially interested parties sufficient advance notification of a planned change. On small projects, the change request is submitted almost at the beginning of the effort.

Large, complex projects generally submit the change request during the programming phase when the deliverables are beginning to appear. At that point, the cut-over date has been estimated but testing has not started. Once the change request has been submitted, the resources or procedures to be altered are flagged as in-process in the system inventory. In developing the regular schedule, the Production and Distribution Scheduling process can examine these in-process items to anticipate their planned availability.

Project Requirements Control

DEFINITION:

This process accepts or rejects requests for changes and adjusts the detailed project plan to incorporate the approved ones. These changes result from modified objectives, new procedures, new technology, or errors in the original project scope.

DESCRIPTION:

1. Receive requests for requirements changes from users and other sources.
2. Analyze specification of a new request, including the impact on the project.
3. Accept or reject request.
4. Revise project plan (if necessary).

DATA CLASSES REQUIRED:

Data input to process (data class)	Data output of process (data class)
C2 Project	C2 Project
C5 Requirements	C5 Requirements
R10 Standards/procedures/methods	

Receive request for requirements changes

The term "change control" has multiple meanings in the I/S business. The use described earlier relating to the change request provides a mechanism to move the final deliverables from one control point (project) to another control point (inventory). A second use of change control refers to the containment of alterations in the project objectives, requirements, and deliverables during the development phases. To eliminate this redundancy, this section will call the latter term "project requirements control."

In the application or other project development, some change must be accommodated to handle reasonable alterations to the project. However, these changes must be evaluated and planned to ensure that the project meets the anticipated results within budget. Such a plan allows users and I/S to make cost and benefit trade-offs based on the analysis of the requested change. It also ensures that approved changes are implemented.

The requirements change request is normally a formal form with the associated procedures. At a minimum, it should contain:

- A description of the requested change, statement of the problem, or need to change a specification
- An indication of the priority or importance of the change, or the business or system impact
- The data requested or required for the incorporation of the change
- The name of the initiator of the request

All changes are reviewed by users and I/S for evaluation and comments.

Analyze specification of new request

After a brief analysis, the project manager and the team members must decide whether resources are available to evaluate fully the proposed change. In most cases, this is a difficult decision that may require higher management involvement.

If project resources are used to evaluate the change, the project may miss its deadlines. However, the change could seriously alter the user requirements and require a complete rethinking of the project. The project team must make this trade-off.

Accept or reject the request

Even with this evaluation, the decision to reject or accept a change can be difficult. If it is accepted, it could alter the resource requirements to cause a complete Project Planning process reevaluation. It could also bring about a major change in the proposed design or schedule.

If it is rejected, the requirement may not disappear. A future upgrade project may be needed to install the request.

Revise project plan (if necessary)

If the change is accepted, the elements of the Project Scheduling process may be required to establish a new schedule. Again, the involved managers, I/S and users, should be kept informed.

Project Evaluating

DEFINITION:

Using the detailed project plan and the project history, this process documents its completion and ensures that all promised deliverables were actually furnished. It compares actual and planned results and identifies reasons for variances.

DESCRIPTION:

The elements of Project Evaluating are:

1. Document the final status of the project and the deliverables.
2. Compare project achievement with the project plans.
3. Identify and report reasons for variances.
4. Obtain approval to terminate the project and report completion.

DATA CLASSES REQUIRED:

Data input to process (data class)	Data output of process (data class)
C2 Project	C2 Project
C3 Change	
R10 Standards/procedures/methods	

Document the final status

The status of completed projects and their deliverables should be reviewed for final closing of the project. Large projects should have a formal postaudit review.

Small problem projects would normally be reviewed as part of a Systems Outage Analysis (SOA) discussed in Chapter 7. Valuable information about the ability to recognize problems, build good solutions, and minimize impact of change can be obtained as well as the definition of resource patterns required to meet the problem resolution. The SOA analysis of closed problems would form a final project evaluation.

Compare project achievement

Larger projects require a review of the actual achievement against the planned results. Factors that should be evaluated include financial performance, timeliness, and personnel utilization. A subset of these projects should be subjected to an outside audit by the overall manager of projects, a separate audit team, or an auditing firm.

Identify and report reasons for variances

These reviews can verify the effectiveness of the planning process, the project control techniques, and the individual project managers. Any variance should be noted and recommended corrective actions listed. One key action would be to update the standards manuals if variances indicate the lack of good control procedures.

Obtain approval to terminate the project

Once completed, the project data is moved into the history files for longer-range analysis of trends. Final approval should verify that no outstanding expenses or charges are pending. As part of the project termination, this element could recommend changes or adjustments in the project standards.

DEVELOPMENT AND MAINTENANCE

Development and maintenance process overview

This group of processes executes required activities in order to create, procure, or modify applications, hardware, networks, software, management systems, facilities, and other resources used in the production and distribution processes.

The six processes will be discussed in the following sequence (Fig. 6–5):

1. Application/Software Development and Upgrade
2. Application/Software Procurement and Upgrade
3. Hardware/Facility Installation and Upgrade
4. Maintenance
5. Tuning and System Balancing
6. Management Systems Development and Upgrade

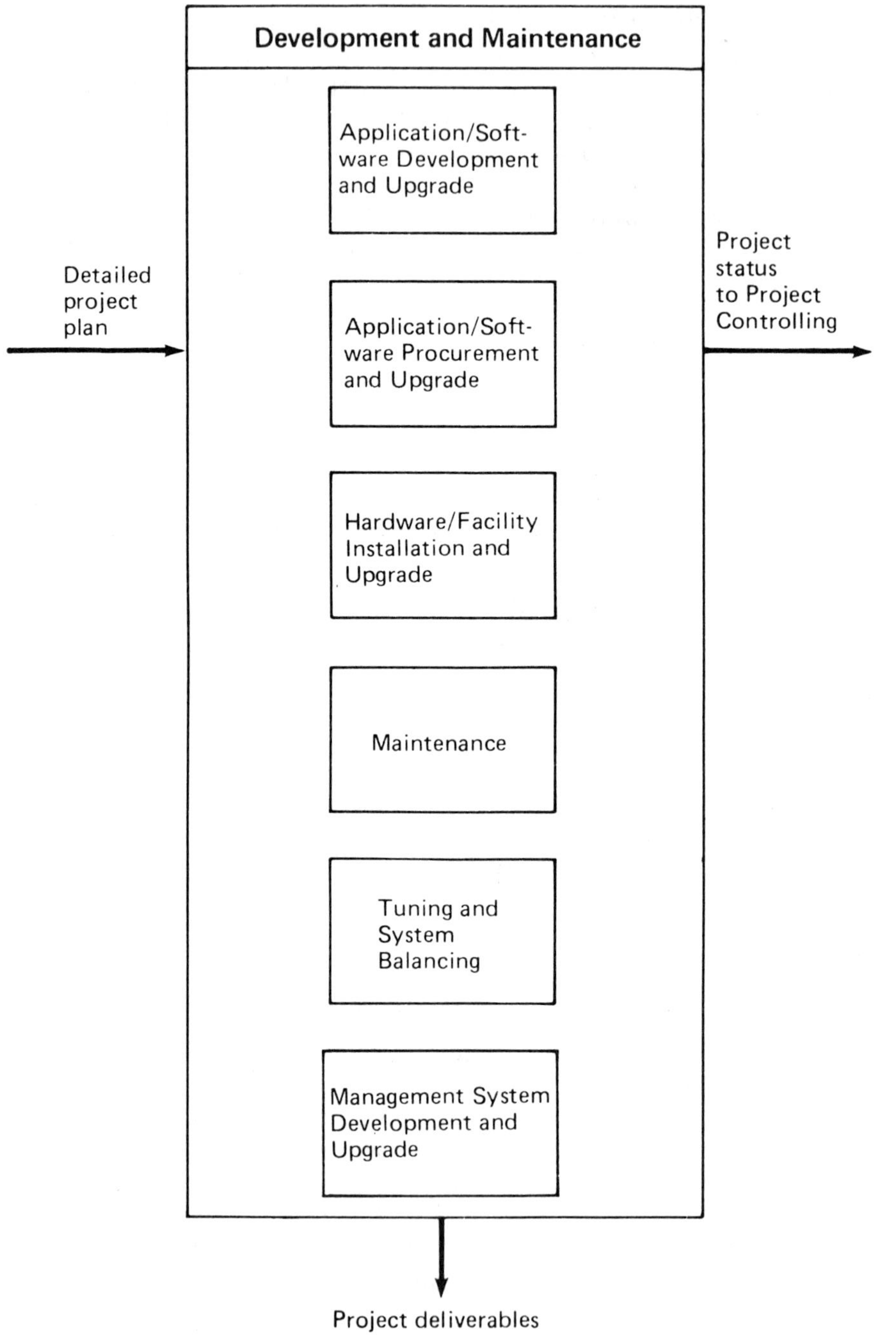

Figure 6–5 Development and maintenance overview.

Each of these processes is a unique project life cycle containing activities to produce the required deliverables. Although each life cycle is discussed separately, it can have interdependencies. For example, a new application may have dependent hardware installation or management systems development projects. The Development and Maintenance Control processes must be aware of these dependencies and track these interrelationships.

The change request should be forwarded to the Resource Control processes at some logical point in each life cycle. The Project Controlling process discussed earlier coordinates this change submittal with the proper life-cycle submittal point.

At the completion of each life cycle, the actual deliverables (for example, processors, programs, documentation, and procedures) are placed in a physical inventory. Status records about these physical inventory items are maintained in the system inventory.

Each life-cycle discussion will specify the logical point for submitting the change request and the placement of the item in the physical inventory. It is assumed that the updating of the system inventory will occur through the management systems interfaces to the Resource and Data Inventory Control process.

Assessing development and maintenance

Questions that could be asked to measure the effectiveness and efficiency of the Development and Maintenance processes include:

- Is there a documented project standards guideline?
- Is that guideline updated regularly?
- Do project managers use that guideline?
- Is the status of the task execution reported on a regular basis?

Application/Software Development and Upgrade

DEFINITION:

Within the framework of a project, this process develops and upgrades applications, operating systems software, other support software, and all the related documentation.

DESCRIPTION:

The elements of Application/Software Development and Upgrade are:

1. Define detailed requirements (including recovery, security, and audit).
2. Design externals of application.
3. Design internals of application.
4. Structure data.
5. Negotiate design compromises with users.

6. Develop and test programs
7. Integrate and test application, including procured modules.
8. Install application/software.

DATA CLASSES REQUIRED:

Data input to process (data class)	Data output of process (data class)
C2 Project	T2 Project updates
R1 Application	
R2 Data	
R3 Software	
R7 Supplies	
R10 Standards/procedures/methods	
R11 Test data	

Define detailed requirements

The major objective of the requirements definition element (or phase) is to establish and obtain formal agreement with users on the business function to be included or excluded in the new application (or software), and any constraints under which the system must be designed.

The products of this element include:

- List of business functions included or excluded
- Overall information requirements
- Interfaces with other systems
- Performance objectives
- Audit and security requirements
- Recovery requirements
- A plan for external design

Overall information requirements include a processing flow through the using departments and the volumes and frequencies of input and output. Interfaces refer to the information flow between user departments and other functional areas.

The information produced in this element is documented in a system requirements report (discussed under the Project Scheduling process) that describes what you are going to do, not how you are going to do it. A common failing is to leap too quickly into the how before what is to be done is known and approved.

Design externals of application

One major objective of the external design element is to define the overall application (or software) from the users' points of view. This provides a picture of what the user can expect. Another objective of this element is to validate that the application, as it is now defined, still meets the business requirements.

The functional information flow in user terms describes:

- Processing flow of data from users to computer, then back to users
- Interfaces with other I/S applications
- Functions performed on the data sent to I/S

The products of this element provide a user view of application (or software) being developed. They are able to review these products with enough information to determine if the products will meet their needs.

Once this effort is completed and approved, the project is on sound ground with respect to a technical plan and approach. Future rework is less likely.

Design internals of application

If the major objective of external design was to present a users' view of the application (or software), internal design must construct an I/S viewpoint of the solution. The major objective of this element is to develop enough detail to provide a precise blueprint.

The products of this element are:

- Program functional specifications
- Hardware/software configuration
- Preliminary system test plan
- Data base/file specifications
- A plan for implementation

Usually, the external and internal design elements are performed and documented in a system design report.

Structure data

In an hour, a large system may process thousands of transactions, make millions of peripheral device accesses, and use billions of computer instructions. The problem of physical data base design is to find a file organization that is close to optimum for periods of days or months, and also consistent with the overall planned logical structures and the data specifications of internal design.

The quality of the data base design depends largely on the expertise of the human designer. Automated methods can assist the designer by identifying problems and design alternatives. They help in identifying homonyms and synonyms, and can detect many types of inconsistencies and incompletely defined requirements. In addition, nonessential (alternate) paths defined between the same pair of data elements can be identified for possible exclusion from the design.

An important by-product of automated methods is the rigor imposed on data gathering. The designer must analyze the requirements of the application functions thoroughly and record the requirements in a precise and consistent format. A significant reduction of errors, omissions, and inconsistencies can be expected.

Negotiate design compromises with users

These external, internal, and data base designs must be reviewed with users to obtain agreement. Any disagreement must be resolved before the next element is started. The result is a binding contract between the user and I/S.

Develop and test programs

The objective of this element is to build and test each component of the application (or software) and ensure that the components fit together into an integrated system.

The products of this element include:

- Program specifications
- Tested, integrated programs
- System test plan
- System test cases and expected results
- System demonstration plan
- Data conversion plan
- User and operator manuals

Early in this activity, the change request should be submitted by the Project Controlling process to the Change Control process. Any later time runs the risk of providing insufficient notice to interested parties.

Since this element typically requires most of the effort of the project, it is critically important to define the external, internal, and data base objectives before actual work starts. This will help keep productivity high.

Integrate and test application

The objective of this element is to test what was developed in the previous elements (to subject it to a variety of stresses and conditions, and verify that the system and documentation meet the design specifications). System test takes time, but it is time well spent.

Products of this element include:

- Operable system
- Tested user and operator manuals
- Plan for installation
- File conversion programs
- Training plan

The application (or software) is operable.

Install application software

The objective is to place the new application (or software) in the physical inventory. Deliverables include:

- Operational system
- Maintenance documentation and plan
- Satisfied and trained users

The application (or software) is now operational.

Application/Software Procurement and Upgrade

DEFINITION:

Within the framework of a project, this process procures and modifies applications, operating systems software, other supporting software, and all the related documentation. It controls the basic buying cycle.

DESCRIPTION:

The elements of Application/Software Procurement and Upgrade are:

1. Define detailed requirements for an ideal system.
2. Review function, integrity, and performance of available offerings, including modifications promised by vendors.
3. Negotiate compromises with users.
4. Confirm or amend buying decisions and select a system.
5. Define system recovery for operating environment.
6. Generate the system and execute provided tests.
7. Publish instructions for integrating the system into the operating environment.
8. Integrate and test application/software, including modules supplied.
9. Install application/software.

DATA CLASSES REQUIRED:

Data input to process (data class)	Data output of process (data class)
E3 I/S industry	T2 Project updates
A1 Vendor	
R1 Applications	
R2 Data	
R3 Software	

Data input to process (data class)	Data output of process (data class)
R7 Supplies	
R10 Standards/procedures/methods	
R11 Test data	

Define detailed requirements for the ideal system

This element is identical to the requirements element discussed under development and upgrade. Since any procured solution will not exactly match these requirements, it is important to define the ideal solution independent of the available offerings. In some cases, an external design may be required to build complete specifications.

Without an adequate statement of requirements, the procurement may become biased in favor of a particular solution rather than the actual needs of the enterprise. This can distort the make/buy decision.

Review function, integrity, and performance

With this ideal system in mind, the available offerings can be examined to determine the best fit of function, integrity, performance, and other relevant factors. If the best fit fails to meet significant requirements, the cost of any modification must be identified or the whole decision to make or buy should be reevaluated.

The required modification should be identified as a dependent development/upgrade project and controlled under the previously described elements. This is also true of any modifications promised by the vendors.

Negotiate compromises with users

Like the development/upgrade project, this element must resolve any differences between the user requirements, the selected offering, and vendor commitments. Since the best fit varies somewhat from the user needs, this element can be slightly more complex than the development/upgrade project.

Confirm or amend buying decisions and select a system

If the modifications are extreme or the fit poor, the user and I/S may wish to open a development/upgrade project and abandon the procurement project. This is a critical decision.

If the decision is firm, then a letter of intent or a purchase order can be released to the vendor. Also, the change request should be submitted by the Project Controlling process to the Change Control process.

Define system recovery for operating environment

Although the vendor should provide an application (or software) that can recover from a failure, the installation must develop recovery procedures and documentation for its specific environment. This should not be left to the vendor by default.

Generate system and execute provided tests

This element is similar to the develop and test element of the development/upgrade project. It differs because the installation is attempting to verify products produced by the vendor.

Often the contract performance is dependent on successfully passing this acceptance test. Once completed, the solution becomes the responsibility of the installation personnel. The terms for any last minute changes and maintenance must be clearly understood.

Publish instructions for integrating

Since the installation has total system responsibility, the instructions for integrating and operating the application (or software) should be produced by the project personnel. Any documentation provided by the vendor should be rewritten or modified to be consistent with installation standards. In all cases, the results should be published for all affected parties.

Integrate and test application/software

This element is similar to the integrate and test element of the development/upgrade project.

Install application/software

This is similar to the element of the same name in the development/upgrade project.

Hardware/Facility Installation and Upgrade

DEFINITION:

Within the framework of a project, this process selects, installs, removes, modifies, and upgrades I/S hardware/facilities.

DESCRIPTION:

The elements of Hardware/Facility Installation and Upgrade are:

1. Define detailed requirements.
2. Select hardware/network/facility.
3. Do physical planning.
4. Define hardware/network/facility recovery.
5. Test new unit.
6. Test complete system.
7. Install hardware/network/facility.

DATA CLASSES REQUIRED:

Data input to process (data class)	Data output of process (data class)
E3 I/S industry	T2 Project updates
C2 Project	
A1 Vendor	
R4 Hardware	
R5 Network	
R6 Facilities	
R7 Supplies	
R10 Standards/procedures/methods	
R11 Test data	

Define detailed requirements

The formalization of the hardware/facility project will vary considerably depending on the size of the unit. The installation of a host processor is almost always set up as a formally controlled project. The installation of a single terminal is often an informal project defined by a change request or purchase order.

In all cases, these projects should be controlled with procedures flexible enough to adjust to variations in size. However, flexibility does not mean skipping an element in the life cycle. This and all other elements should be used to ensure completeness.

Often the hardware/facility project is dependent on some application development or procurement project. In those cases, the detailed requirements must be established with the corresponding project manager.

In most other cases, the detailed requirements must be defined with the users and I/S personnel who are affected (for example, a new terminal on an existing application). The user, responsible application programmer, and operations must concur on the requirements. This effort could be simplified by defining a standard terminal for each application.

Select hardware/network facility

As stated earlier, some preliminary selection may have occurred in the planning processes to overcome long lead times. This selection must be verified and finalized to ensure that proper features are ordered. Any major changes in the original selection should be reviewed by both the project leader and system planners.

In most cases, selection involves analyzing vendor offerings and ordering the unit with the best fit. Hardware/networks are rarely built in-house.

The installation of facilities could involve either procurement or building. Air conditioning units and power supplies are most often procured units that are selected and ordered. A complete remodeling of the computer room or a move to a new location necessitates building.

Under normal conditions, the last selection activity should be the submission of a change request for a formal change review. For larger units, the change request could be delayed. The key is the lead time required for ratification of the pending change.

Do physical planning

Detailed configuration of hardware/facility can be an extremely complex effort that should not be left to chance. A typical installation may have thousands of items connected by cables or communication lines. Physical planning should be done for every hardware/facility project to ensure proper cable ordering and other critical factors. Automation of this element using the system inventory and configuration programs is becoming increasingly attractive because of the large amount of detail that must be maintained.

Define hardware/network/facility recovery

For each unit to be installed, the overall recovery plan should be reviewed and specific procedures documented when required. Clearly, each new terminal of the same type on an existing application requires only a limited review. However, any major change should have well-documented and consistent recovery procedures developed in this element.

Test new unit

The key objective of this element is to ensure that the unit is working correctly before it is inserted into the system. The amount of testing needed depends on the degree of certainty that recovery can be completed (if needed) and the potential service disruption that can be tolerated.

Unit testing will vary widely depending on the type of unit. Many terminals and devices have built-in test procedures to verify that the unit is working correctly. Larger units like a host processor have specially designed tests for that purpose.

Test complete system

Testing the unit in a system environment may be extremely difficult. Drivers can be used to simulate the stress of high-volume on-line transactions. Off hour or weekend testing with selected user terminal personnel is also used to generate a stress loading. The objective is to load test without disrupting the user production environment.

In many cases, it is not feasible to completely test the unit in the final system environment. Testing of the backout and recovery procedures is extremely critical in this situation. Walk-throughs are conducted to train personnel in the exact actions that will be taken if the installation encounters any difficulty. The risk of each potential situation is also evaluated and documented clearly. Communication with all parties concerned and adequate preparation are keys to success. There should be no surprises on the day testing is attempted.

Install hardware/network/facility

The final installation must synchronize with the change control and inventory control procedures of Resource Control. Upon completion of these procedures, the unit becomes an inventory item to be scheduled and used for service.

Maintenance

DEFINITION:

Within the framework of a project, this process corrects defects in hardware, applications, software, and facilities (including engineering changes and program temporary fixes).

DESCRIPTION:

1. Revalidate the cause of the problem.
2. Understand the environment of the suspect component.
3. Diagnose the suspect component.
4. Determine the fix for the failing component.
5. Test the fix.
6. Install the fix.

DATA CLASSES REQUIRED:

Data input to process (data class)	Data output of process (data class)
C2 Project	T2 Project updates
C4 Problem	
R1 Applications	
R2 Data	
R3 Software	
R4 Hardware	
R5 Network	
R6 Facilities	
R7 Supplies	
R10 Standards/procedures/methods	
R11 Test data	

Revalidate cause of the problem

A maintenance project is limited to fixing what is broken. Any addition of new function or modification of old function must be controlled as a development project. These separate project definitions allow management to isolate the resources spent correcting bad implementation and resource failure.

The trigger for maintenance projects is a problem rather than a plan. Normally, service personnel have detected the problem, documented it, and found a temporary bypass action. The problem is assigned to some resolver in a formal manner. The resolver can be an application programmer, systems programmer, hardware specialist, or even a vendor.

That assignment may result from a regular problem meeting, where multiple problems are assigned to various resolvers. With high severity problems, it could be assigned to the resolver prior to the regular meeting.

This element of the project must validate the cause of the problem by examining dumps, performing additional problem determination, or by other available means. In this element, the resolver must begin estimating the resources required to fix the problem. Critical specialists, busy with other activities, may be required. In other cases, the problem may be of such magnitude that management should do additional resource planning.

Understand environment of suspect component

The major objective of this element is to isolate the problem of the failing component. It is assumed that the previous element isolated the suspect component(s). With the system inventory, change history, and a problem log, the resolver can examine the environment for possible sources of difficulty.

- Does the suspect component have a history of problems? How were they fixed? Was a change installed recently?
- Was the installation completed with difficulty? Who was responsible?
- Are there related components in the inventory that could have contributed to the difficulty? What was the impact?

This element should have isolated the source and proposed an action to solve the problem. We now know what failed.

Diagnose suspect component

The objective of this element is to isolate the problem of the specific component (for example, circuit or line of code) that failed. Diagnostic programs can assist this isolation for hardware.

Determine fix for failing component

With the source completely isolated, this element must define a fix to resolve the problem. In some cases, the fix may come from the vendor in the form of an engineering change or a program temporary fix (PTF). In other cases, the problem resolver may have to generate new lines of code or other means to fix the problem.

Once the source and fix have been determined, the Project Controlling process should inform Change Control with a change request.

Test fix

Each fix should be tested on a test system before applying it to the production system. Often, it is difficult to convince a resolver that a small fix requires testing. "Two lines of code will not cause any difficulty . . ." are famous last words before a total systems outage.

One successful approach applies all fixes to a test system. On a cutoff date, that test system is used for developing and testing for a period of time (usually 30 days). If the fixes pass this load test, the new release is moved into the production environment. The cycle is repeated for the next set of fixes including PTFs. This concept minimizes both the resolver's test time and the risk for the production environment.

Install fix

The fix and associated documentation must be installed in the physical inventory.

Tuning and System Balancing

DEFINITION:

Within the framework of a project, this process tunes the I/S resources to ensure proper performance of individual or groups of resources. This includes periodic regression testing to ensure that new changes have not caused undesired performance results in existing resources.

DESCRIPTION:

The elements of Tuning and System Balancing are:

1. Define detailed requirements.
2. Develop a solution.
3. Execute test of the new or modified unit.
4. Test the complete system.
5. Install the new system.

DATA CLASSES REQUIRED:

Data input of process (data class)	Data output of process (data class)
C2 Project	T2 Project updates
C4 Problem	
R1 Application	
R2 Data	
R3 Software	

Data input to process (data class)	Data output of process (data class)
R4 Hardware	
R5 Network	
R6 Facilities	
R7 Supplies	
R10 Standards/procedures/methods	
R11 Test data	

Define detailed requirements

Unlike maintenance, a tuning and system balancing project can be driven by either a plan or a problem. The Capacity Planning process could generate this type project to gather performance data about a proposed new system. It could also use the project to investigate an unexplained variance between the previous plans and the actual results.

In most cases, this project will be driven by some performance problem detected in the Resource and Data Performance Control process. Normally, that process will attempt to resolve the issue within the scope available with service resources (for example, varying devices off-line or changing priorities). If the situation persists or additional resources are required, a tuning and system balancing project would be initiated.

This element would detail the requirements of the planned project or validate the cause of the problem. The results should be an action plan to address the defined situation.

Develop solution

In many cases, the solution will involve using existing or special monitors to capture additional performance data. This can be analyzed to determine the source of difficulty.

In other cases, the installation may choose to build a test data base for regression testing the total system. Using a driver, these tests are run against the system under load to measure the results. Again, performance data is used to identify the source of difficulty.

The results are used to make management decisions about a proper course of correction. If the magnitude of the change is similar to a maintenance fix, this process can install the correction. For more extensive correction, a formal project should be initiated. Both of these solutions require submitting a change request.

Execute test of new or modified unit

Once the solution has been defined, this element executes that test and produces the required data. If the test is unsatisfactory, the previous process element would be reactivated to develop a new or modified solution.

Test complete system

For the fix, the testing is similar to that described for the maintenance project; in fact, the two tests could be combined in the release concept.

Install new system

The installation is similar to the maintenance project.

Management Systems Development and Upgrade

DEFINITION:

Within the framework of a project, this process develops and modifies management standards, procedures, and methods for use within the I/S organization. It also develops methods to measure their effectiveness and efficiency.

DESCRIPTION:

The elements of Management Systems Development and Upgrade are:

1. Define detailed requirements based on enterprise policies.
2. Evaluate alternative standards, procedures, and methodology.
3. Design the solution.
4. Publish instructions for the use of these standards, procedures, and methodology.
5. Test the solution in a limited environment.
6. Install the solution.

DATA CLASSES REQUIRED:

Data input to process (data class)	Data output of process (data class)
E1 Enterprise	T2 Project updates
C2 Projects	
A3 Organization	
R10 Standards/procedures/methods	

Define detailed requirements

This particular project is very similar to the tuning and system balancing project in that it can be either plan or problem driven. The Management Systems Planning process generates planned projects to improve standards, procedures, or methods (for example, a new problem control procedure). This element should expand those preliminary requirements into a clear statement of the need, cost, and benefit. These requirements should be viewed from both the user and I/S perspectives.

For problem situations, this process element must validate the documented problem.

Evaluate alternatives

Alternative standards, procedures, and methodology should be examined to develop a recommendation. The computer industry is rich in books, manuals, and information describing techniques for planning and controlling the I/S business. All these are sources for this analysis. In fact, the document you are reading is a source.

The difficulty is identifying the best alternative, relating it to the specific problems, and developing a business justification for the required resources. This is not unlike the analysis required for the development or procurement of an application. The result is the need for procedures rather than a program.

Design solution

A document similar to the application development system design report should be prepared and reviewed with all affected groups. Upon approval of the design, implementation is largely a matter of developing the standards, procedures, and methods. This effort can be reduced by using a computerized text processing facility.

At the time of approval, the Project Controlling process should issue a change request to the Change Control process.

Publish instructions for use

These documents must pass a document review cycle for clarity of understanding and accuracy of technique. In many ways, this is the unit test. One technique highly effective in this review is a walk-through with the designer attempting to explain the design. The reviewers should include selected personnel in the interested area.

Test solution in limited environment

This test, much like an application system test, must ensure that the results will actually work in the final environment. Education and training are critical to this success. The planned implementation can be tested in a limited situation to measure the effectiveness of the training and the acceptability of the results. Based on this limited test, the documentation and/or training may require modification. The objective is to implement the procedures, not impose them.

Install solution

If the procedures are correct and training has been adequate, the results can be placed in the system inventory. To be placed in the inventory, the procedures must pass the same Change Control process used for other resources. Resources and procedures must work together; procedures tell how the resource is to be used. With common Change Control, this unified result is possible.

RESOURCE CONTROL

Resource control process overview

This group of processes is a mandatory "valve" through which all project deliverables must pass. It ensures a controlled and balanced delivery of changes into the operating environment.

The two processes in this group will be discussed in the following sequence:

1. Change Control
   - Do changes meet sound technical, business, and schedule requirements?
2. Resources and Data Inventory Control
   - How are the service resources controlled?

It is suggested that the reader refer periodically to the flow shown in Figure 6–6.

With this tactical plan for services, development, resources, and management, the I/S development mission and the I/S service missions are given the proper direction and resources required to achieve their goals. They can be held accountable for their results. However, these are not totally independent missions.

The results of the development mission are measured by the ability of the service mission to use the new or modified resources. The service mission will continue to use the resource long after the development project has been completed. The service mission must depend on the development mission to correct any defect in the

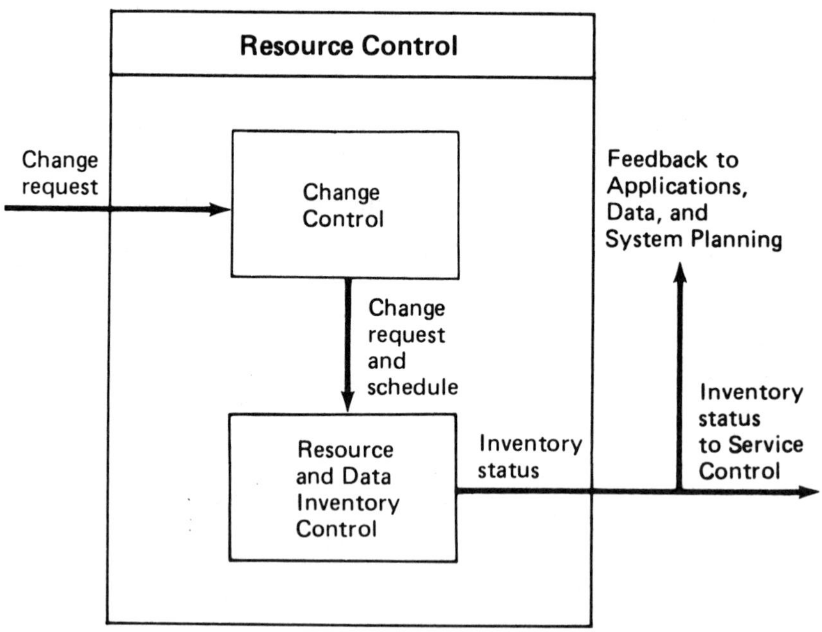

Figure 6–6 Resource control overview.

resource caused by weaknesses in the original design. The development mission can be upgrading a resource already in use in the service mission.

The Resource Control process group has the task of keeping resource information common between those two missions, ensuring the accuracy of that information, and making that information available to all levels of management. This process faces considerable challenges. As the I/S business grows, the quantity, type, and interaction of resources increase substantially, requiring more management attention. Resources ranging from applications to system components are being altered at a high rate to keep pace with user needs and technology.

The people resource becomes a larger share of the budget, necessitating more formal personnel management. User charges for services add the need to control the financial resources. These resources are often distributed geographically to provide security or better user service.

Some of the critical issues to be considered are:

- How does the I/S business prevent this complexity from decreasing the quality of service provided to the I/S customer?
- How does I/S effectively and efficiently manage this vast inventory of resources?
- How are the multiple locations of resources managed?
- How can changes be made while minimizing the impact on existing resources?

Assessing resource control

To assess Change Control and Resource and Data Inventory Control, management could ask the following questions:

- Are all host and network hardware and software changes (including production application changes) subject to change control and tracking?
- Is there a single focal point for all changes?
- Is there a change request document in use that includes, at a minimum, a description of the change, prerequisite/corequisite changes, appropriate management authorization, requested date of implementation, and backout procedures to restore previous conditions?
- Is a change log that reflects current status and history of changes maintained?
- Is a single published schedule or calendar maintained for all changes?
- Is there a formal technical risk evaluation and audit against standards for proposed changes to assess the test and backout procedures and the impact on availability and performance?
- Is management approval required from all appropriate functional areas before implementation of a change?
- Are management reports prepared that include, at a minimum, the number of successful/unsuccessful changes per month by category, by source, and by trends (for example, rate of change)?

- Are all instructions and information required for production jobs and network operations current and complete?
- Is there an established function that controls and monitors the security of these resources?
- Is there a periodic physical audit to ensure that the resource is installed as defined in the inventory?
- Is there a formal method to determine if any more changes can be tolerated, based on the health of the installation?

Change Control

DEFINITION:

Using the change requests, this process selects, coordinates, groups, and monitors all changes to the I/S resources and procedures in such a way that there is either minimal impact on the I/S operations or minimal risk. It triggers resource and data inventory updates.

DESCRIPTION:

The elements of Change Control are:

1. Record change requests.
2. Prioritize and group changes based on a technical assessment.
3. Prioritize and group changes based on a business assessment.
4. Schedule, defer, or reject changes.
5. Monitor test.
6. Monitor install.
7. Report and control the status of all recorded changes.

DATA CLASSES REQUIRED:

Data input to process (data class)	Data output of process (data class)
C2 Project	C3 Change
C3 Change	
C4 Problem	
C6 System performance	
C7 Production and distribution schedule	
R10 Standards/procedures/methods	

Record change requests

Each project in the I/S development mission is given finite resources to produce a specific set of deliverables. Project deliverables include the modified service resource, documentation, and other supporting material. As the project progresses through the normal life cycle, the project manager must request that control of these deliverables be transferred to the final owner. A change request is the formal means of controlling this transfer.

For short-duration maintenance projects, this request must be initiated at the very beginning of the life cycle. With larger development projects, this request would be submitted as early in the life cycle as possible, but no later than the programming and test phase. In either case, the request starts the decision process to transfer the deliverables with a minimum disruption of system stability.

Each change being requested will have a varying degree of complexity, duration, potential impact, dependencies, and ease of recovery. If changes are categorized by these factors, the actions required to ensure successful transfer can be controlled (for example, the following category 1 changes could demand more stringent testing).

- Category 1
  - Possibility of major impact
  - Visible to all users
  - Lengthy install time
- Category 2
  - Possibility of significant impact
  - Visible to multiple users
  - Involved backout procedures
- Category 3
  - Visible change
  - Back out quickly, easily, effectively
- Category 4
  - Minimal impact
  - Day-to-day events
- Category 5
  - Necessary to fix problem
  - Agreement of management required

Changes originate independently, from many different sources inside and outside the computing center, sometimes even from outside the I/S organization. However, there must be someone within the I/S organization who assumes overall coordination and interfaces to all the original change requesters.

Anyone involved in the implementation of a change, whether a problem solver or someone responding to a new requirement, is responsible for the quality of that change. In other words, that person is responsible for making sure that the change is so well planned, prepared, and tested that it causes no unanticipated side effects and therefore no problems.

Unfortunately, this is not enough. If two people are making changes to related modules and neither is aware of the other's actions, the results are unpredictable. No matter how conscientious the people may be, it is likely that the changes will interact with each other and problems will occur.

Therefore, changes must be coordinated. The first step toward successful coordination is the development of a formalized change request procedure and the establishment of a single point of control. The assignment of a person(s) to a change coordinator (Fig. 6–7) role is one means of achieving this single control point.

All change requests are submitted to this person with the pertinent data, that is, a description of the change, the reason for it, any known dependencies (on other changes, or on specific dates), and anticipated effects (on whom, and in what way). This data can be submitted to the change coordinator in a simple manual form (Fig. 6–8) or in a more advanced on-line screen (Fig. 6–9). Either approach will work provided there is central direction on when to enter the data required and the authority required to enter data.

The initial assignment of the change category is the responsibility of the requester and is based on the risks involved. The change process must provide a means to audit that change categories are being properly assigned and to ensure that changes receive the prescribed screening for each category. That audit is often the responsibility of

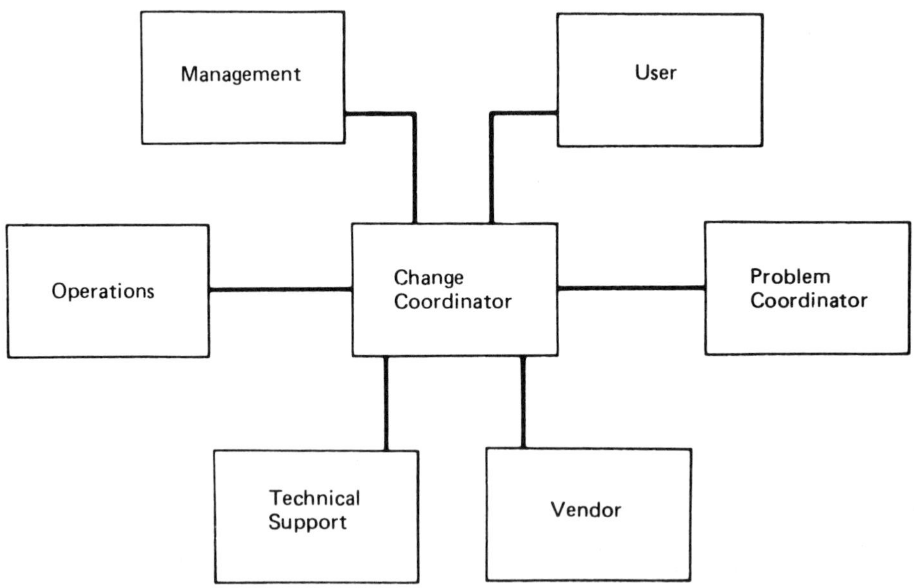

Figure 6–7 Change coordinator dependencies in assessing change.

For Requester: Fill In This Section, Keep Last Copy, and Forward

Change Number ____________ Change Category ____________

Name ____________ Dept ______ Ext ________ Date _____

Affected Element	Type of Change	Description
____________	____________	______________
____________	____________	______________

Reason For Change — Comments

- Solution To Problem ______________________________
- New Requirements ______________________________
- Other ______________________________

Dependencies

This Change Must Be Implemented Before/After/With ____________

____

Supporting Documentation: ______________________________

Who Is Affected?	In What Way?
________________	______________________
________________	______________________

Who Has Budgetary Responsibility?

Name ____________ Dept ____________ ________________
Signature

For Coordinator: Keep Last Copy and Send Rest To Implementer

Agreement Required	Received	Agreement Required	Received
____________	______	____________	______
____________	______	____________	______

Change Scheduled For: ________________ Date: __________

For Change Implementer—Keep Last Copy and Return To Coordinator

Change Implemented On ____________ Signature ____________

Comments ______________________________________

____

____

Figure 6–8 Sample change form.

```
                    CHANGE REQUESTER ENTRY      CHANGE NO.______

 ENTER CHANGE REQUESTER DATA

 1. REQUESTER NAME....(R) KIRBY      11. CHANGE TYPE.........HARDWARE
 2. REQUESTER DEPT....... BILLING    12. CHANGE STATUS....(R)INITIAL
 3. REQUESTER PHONE...... 355-2365   13. USER ID............________
 4. NETWORK NAME......... ________   14. INITIAL PRIORITY....________
 5. SYSTEM NAME.......... ________   15. CHANGE REASON.......WORKLOAD
 6. PROGRAM NAME......... ________   16. PROBLEM FIXED.......________
 7. DEVICE NAME.......... ________   17. USER FORM NUMBER....________
 8. KEY ITEM AFFECTED.... 3277       18. LOCATION CODE.......________
 9. DATE REQUIRED.....(R) 06/13/NN
10. TIME REQUIRED........ ________

19. DESCRIPTION       (R) 3277 TERMINAL FOR BILLING DEPARTMENT

     TO LEAVE THIS PANEL, PRESS ENTER WITHOUT FIELD MODIFICATION
```

Figure 6–9 Example online change screen.

the change coordinator. The Change Control process standards should provide a most likely mapping as a starting point for this consideration (Fig. 6–10).

Each type of change has one or more suggested categories. Although this table provides general guidelines for handling changes, several points should be made about specific changes. These points should be stated in the change standards.

- *Emergency changes.* Before the change is installed, a manager must give approval to the bypassing of normal change procedures. After the emergency is over, documentation of the change must be entered and a management review conducted on the reasons for the situation.
- *Changes to data.* Structure changes or field redefinition must be entered in the change procedures but changes to the content of data fields are excluded.
- *Application changes.* Preproduction changes are tracked as part of the project and are not entered as changes until the formal change request is submitted.

Prioritize and group changes (technical assessment)

Although the change requester and his or her manager must always take responsibility for the equality of each change, some additional quality control audits are required to ensure that the technical standards have been met for more complex changes. A technical assessment provides additional input to the change scheduling element. The extent of a technical assessment will vary with each change.

Type of Change	Suggested Categories 1	2	3	4	E
1. Software					
a. System					
Emergency changes	–	–	–	–	E
Massive temporary fixes	–	2	–	–	–
Specific fix during maintenance	–	–	3	–	–
Enhancements, tools, tuning	–	–	3	4	–
System generations	–	2	–	–	–
Program products	–	2	–	–	–
New releases and conversions	1	2	–	–	–
Service moves	1	2	–	–	–
Data set changes	–	2	–	–	–
Procedural changes	1	2	3	4	–
b. Application					
New releases	1	2	–	–	–
Specific fixes	–	2	3	–	–
Functional enhancements	–	–	3	–	–
Emergency fixes	–	–	–	–	E
Service moves	1	2	–	–	–
Data base change	–	–	3	4	–
Control language changes	–	2	3	4	–
2. Hardware					
Engineering changes	–	–	3	–	–
Microcode changes	–	2	–	–	–
Moves and recabling	–	2	3	4	–
Installation of hardware	1	2	3	–	–
Equipment upgrades	1	2	3	–	–
Terminal moves	–	–	3	4	–
Emergency fixes	–	–	–	–	E
3. Network					
a. Software					
Specific fix during maintenance	–	–	3	4	–
Emergency fixes	–	–	–	–	E
Node name and path changes	–	2	–	–	–
New release and conversions	1	–	–	–	–
b. Hardware					
Path changes	–	2	3	–	–
Spool device changes	–	2	3	–	–

Figure 6-10 Sample change categories.

The technical assessment promotes technical completeness by reviewing the change against a standard or checklist. For example, are test procedures reasonable? Is backout well planned in case something goes wrong? Do changes in related areas produce a high technical risk?

Prioritize and group changes (business assessment)

The business assessment informs management of the risk and potential business impact if this change is made at the requested time. For example, a request to change a financial application during month-end closing could have significant risks. The assessment should define those risks and allow management to alter the change date or put special controls in place to reduce the risk.

Once these assessments are complete, the change is ready for final scheduling and management approval.

Schedule, defer, or reject change

As a point of control, the change coordinator must act as both a "funnel" and a "filter" for all change requests. As a "funnel," the change coordinator must have a broad knowledge of how the system is used and ensure that all changes are scheduled. As a "filter," the change coordinator must be able to negotiate the deferral or rejection of a change request.

A master change schedule must be maintained by the central control point. The change schedule should cover three critical time periods: the changes to occur this week, changes to occur in the next 30 days, and a longer-range schedule for changes with large resource requirements. These schedules are working documents for all managers and implementers.

At a regular meeting, the managers must schedule, defer, and reject changes in such a way as to reduce the number and severity of problems and disruptions caused by changes. The timing of changes is very important.

Several inputs should influence their decisions, including the technical and business assessment, the stability of the installation, and the general "track record" of the person(s) making the change. All people affected should be consulted and agreement reached on when a change can be installed. Changes should not collide or overlap. If later problems are to be solved quickly, they should preferably be spaced in such a way that the effects of a change to a specific element have a chance to manifest themselves before the next change to that element is made.

To provide this period of stability between changes, nonemergency change requests are sometimes combined into a "release" concept. The approved changes are all applied to a release version on or before a fixed cutoff date. This "frozen" release version is used for a test period of 30 to 60 days or until it appears to be stable. At that point, all the changes are released at the same time by replacing the production version with the release version. This approach requires close management attention to the delay caused by releasing changes versus the impact of continuous application of each change request.

Monitor test

Testing proves that a change will perform correctly and will affect other activities or functions only as planned. The project that develops the change is responsible to provide that proof. The monitor test function ensures that the proof exists and is valid for the production environment into which the change is being placed.

Monitor install

A responsibility that still rests with the implements, however, is to notify the central control point that the change has in fact been made. To ensure that the change log actually reflects the planned schedule, the installation tasks must be closely tracked. When a resource is changed, this fact must be recorded, both for later problem resolution and as a means for historical analysis.

One important action that is often overlooked when making a change is to inform parties directly affected (such as operations personnel and users) about the practical details of the change. Informing these people is the responsibility of the project manager or implementer for the change.

Report and control the status

Another major task often overlooked is the historical review of changes and their impact. The goal is to identify factors that can help minimize repetition of errors and encourage replication of success, for example:

- How much personnel was required to plan a change?
- How many changes were backed out?
- How often were changes entered under the wrong category?
- How many unscheduled change meetings were held?
- How many changes caused problems? How much outage occurred? What unit was responsible for preparing the change?

Change control summary

The Change Control process is basically an audit and administrative function. It audits to ensure that changes have been prepared in accordance with prescribed standards. The actual preparation of the change, including testing and installation, is done by other processes in the Development and Maintenance group.

The administrative role generally consists of maintaining the overall change calendar, summarizing the overall change status, and negotiating change plan adjustments to smooth the flow and rate of planned changes. These responsibilities can increase the potential for delivering quality service.

Resource and Data Inventory Control

DEFINITION:

Using change information, this process builds and manages inventories of all the I/S resources (including personnel and financial).

DESCRIPTION:

The elements of Resource and Data Inventory Control are:

1. Identify system, application, data, personnel, supplies, and financial resources.
2. Update inventory status.
3. Maintain security of these resources.
4. Administer access of these resources (including data set space allocation and password administration).
5. Report and control status of inventory.

DATA CLASSES REQUIRED:

Data input to process (data class)	Data output of process (data class)
C1 Service	A1 Vendor
C2 Project	A2 Customer/user/group
C3 Change	A3 Organization
C7 Production and distribution schedule	R1 Applications
A1 Vendor	R2 Data
A2 Customer/user/group	R3 Software
A3 Organization	R4 Hardware
R1 Application	R5 Network
R2 Data	R6 Facilities
R3 Software	R7 Supplies
R4 Hardware	R8 Personnel
R5 Network	R9 Financial
R6 Facilities	R10 Standards/procedures/methods
R7 Supplies	R11 Test data
R8 Personnel	
R9 Financial	
R10 Standards/procedures/methods	
R11 Test data	
T1 Inventory	

Identify resources

The concept of managing an inventory is not new. Manufacturing businesses have formal procedures and organizations to control all forms of inventories: finished goods in a warehouse, in-process items on the production floor, and raw materials ready for production. What is new is the use of these concepts in the I/S business.

The data defining the resources in the I/S inventory is shown in the Resource Data Group (Appendix B). All resources, including personnel and finance, are included in the inventory. The Resource and Data Inventory Control process controls data about these resources and does not normally deal directly with the physical resource. One exception is the data resource required to run the enterprise (including I/S) defined in the "data" data class.

The data base administrator (DBA) has traditionally controlled the definition, allocation, and placement of this data inventory on the physical device. In this context, the data base administrator might be considered a subset of an overall inventory manager role. Very similar techniques and tools are required. For example, the data required to adequately describe the hardware and software resource is shown in Figure 6–11. These data definitions could be stored in the same data dictionary application used to manage the enterprise data.

The Resource and Data Inventory Control process provides information for all three I/S missions: development, service, and consultation.

- The I/S development mission manages the Development and Maintenance processes through the normal project life cycle. The resulting changes must include the definition of the data, information, resources, and their relationships. The information from these engineering processes is stored in the system inventory.
- The I/S service mission uses this information passed from the development mission to schedule and deliver quality service.
- The I/S consultation mission defines the enterprise information and data that these resources are to provide.

In today's complex world, the management of the enterprise data and information resources cannot be considered separately. For example, a petroleum company may have many documents containing information describing exploratory work for drilling operations. It may also have an extensive data base on wells owned in the same exploration area. A drilling engineer must have both forms of information available to do an effective job. Information about documents, publications, and text can be stored in the inventory and retrieved using key words. Both enterprise data and information are included under the "data" data class.

This concept, called the information center, makes enterprise information available to the end user through techniques such as information retrieval or text processing. Complex queries submitted by users are translated using key words to provide a list of possible information and/or texts of the stored information. The heart of this use is a well-maintained inventory.

DATA GROUP	DATA CLASS	SAMPLE DATA ELEMENTS
RES	R3. Software	1. Inventory of installed and in-process software, e.g.: Program name Program type Program status 2. Source/supplier 3. Ownership 4. Security: Access Physical security 5. Recovery rules 6. Auditability 7. Specifications and design characteristics 8. Maintenance requirements 9. Connectivity/prerequisites 10. Object module
RES	R4. Hardware	1. Inventory of installed and in-process hardware, e.g.: Hardware name Hardware type Hardware status 2. Source/supplier 3. Ownership 4. Security: Access Physical security 5. Recovery rules 6. Auditability 7. Specifications and design characteristics 8. Maintenance requirements 9. Connectivity/prerequisites 10. Physical layout

Figure 6–11 Hardware and software data.

Summary data created during normal production can be stored in the inventory to reduce the time required to produce management information. A data base query is used to selectively retrieve and display these results for the executive.

Every enterprise needs an inventory process to manage the resources required to support the enterprise. Since I/S is a business within that business, the same reasoning should hold true for the I/S subset. Once the inventory control point has been established, it should be able to manage any degree of complexity in an I/S installation, consisting of one or more central processing units, a corporate communication network, application and systems software, and storage capability.

A prerequisite to successful Resource and Data Inventory Control is an effective Change Control process. These change procedures and all other process procedures can be stored in the inventory class "standards, procedures, and methods." Management Systems Development and Upgrade projects are used to keep these procedures current.

Another set of procedures in this same data class are those required to operate applications, jobs, or services. These procedures updated as part of any regular project include the normal run-book documentation.

- *Run sequence.* Information of interest includes:

  Operations to be performed

  Workstations to be used (routing), and possible alternatives in case a certain workstation goes down or becomes heavily loaded (alternative routing)

  Conditional routes to be followed in the event of certain specified results or errors

  Dependencies between different applications (jobs) or operations
- *Job frequency.* This specifies how often and when a job has to be processed (for example, daily, weekly, monthly, or quarterly; on which days of the month; or on which dates of the year).
- *Job priority.* This reflects the importance of one job relative to another (as agreed with the user community).
- *User constraints.* These are restrictions imposed by the user; for example, times when input data is due, times before which the job cannot be run, and delivery times.
- *Resource requirements.* These describe the resources needed to process the job at each workstation. Preferably, users should be encouraged and allowed to specify resource requirements in terms natural to them, such as number of transactions to be processed, or number of pages (or lines) to be printed. It then becomes the responsibility of the operations function to translate these user-oriented processing requirements into operations-oriented or machine-oriented resource needs, such as processing time, time to print, and time to burst and bind.

In estimating processing requirements, it may be wise not to rely solely on the users' subjective judgment, but to maintain a history of processing requirements from which the most likely resource needs can be derived. Seasonal variations must also be accounted for.

Update inventory status

Since the inventory is the critical source of data and information, it must be kept current. Enforcement of good change control procedures is a prerequisite to keeping the inventory consistent and accurate.

With the large volumes of data associated with the system inventory, the Resource and Data Inventory Control process should be considered for computerized applications. Applications of this type usually have names such as data dictionary and configuration management.

Maintain security of these resources

It should be clear at this point that these resources are critical to both the enterprise and the I/S business. Security is a necessity. It is assumed that the overall security was planned in the tactical-level process, Security Planning. It is also assumed that the Development and Maintenance projects have built adequate security safeguards into the deliverables.

Enforcing these security rules is the main purpose of this element. This can be statically achieved by procedures that control the update of resources in the inventory. However, the need quickly expands to include the dynamic environment where the second-by-second control of the access and use of these resources is essential, for example, the verification and authorization to use a data base by an application or transaction.

Many installations install software to ensure that time sharing or interactive users cannot destroy or incorrectly use shared data. With this type of software, the users and types of use for critical data bases are defined and administered by the data base administrator. The system automatically verifies security authorization during sign-on procedures. Unauthorized access is prevented and reported. The successful implementation of security depends on this control.

Administer access to these resources

In any advanced I/S business, access control of these resources can be extremely complicated. A user using a terminal in a remote city connected through the distribution network wants access to a transaction and data base.

- Does the user have a right to use that terminal?
- Which distribution facilities can the user access?
- Does the user have the right to use the transaction and/or data base?

Data describing services available to users should be identified and stored in the inventory. To sign on that service, the user must identify the service and security code.

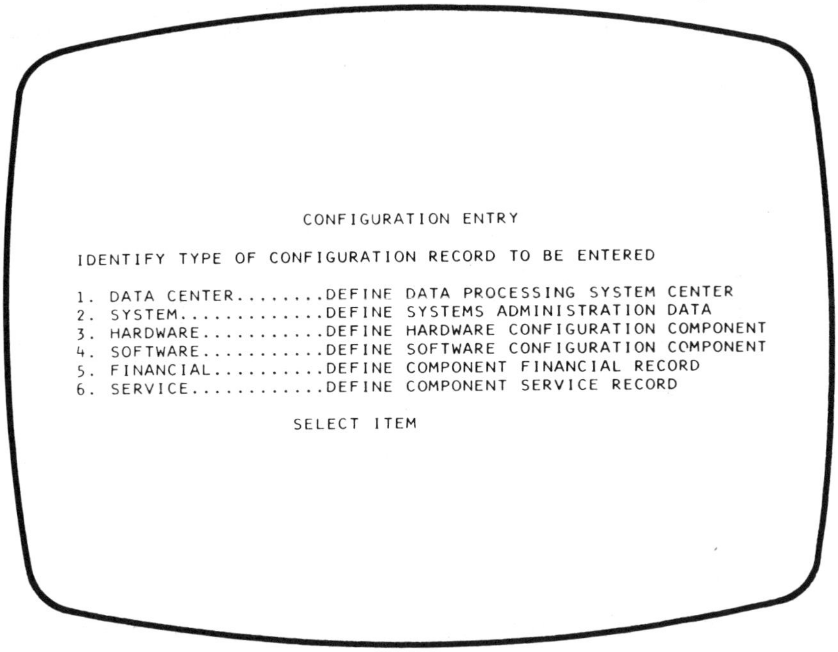

Figure 6–12 Sample menu screen for system inventory.

This process is repeated for each service desired by the user. This user session concept is one example of controlling resource access.

The initial contact point for anyone having problems or difficulty with service is called a user help or a customer service desk. Inventory screens can greatly help. A menu screen identifies the data available (Fig. 6–12). The hardware screen can be used to locate the user terminal in the inventory, including all the important factors such as type, location, and status (Fig. 6–13). With this screen, the parties at both ends of the problem can begin the dialogue required to isolate the difficulty.

The system inventory connectivity screen can be used to better understand the related components in the connection from the terminal to the host processor (Fig. 6–14). Each inventory item will be displayed on separate lines in the sequence that it occurs in the configuration. The help desk person might use this screen to select test procedures to isolate the failing component before seeking technical assistance.

Report and control status of inventory

Since the inventory is critical to the I/S business, its status must be monitored and controlled at both the operational and tactical levels. At the operational level, reports should be developed to allow periodic audits of the accuracy of the inventory. Any deviations must be corrected and reported to management.

Inventory summary information must be passed to three tactical-level Development Planning processes, Application, Data, and Systems Planning. Those processes should monitor trends and the impact of future development.

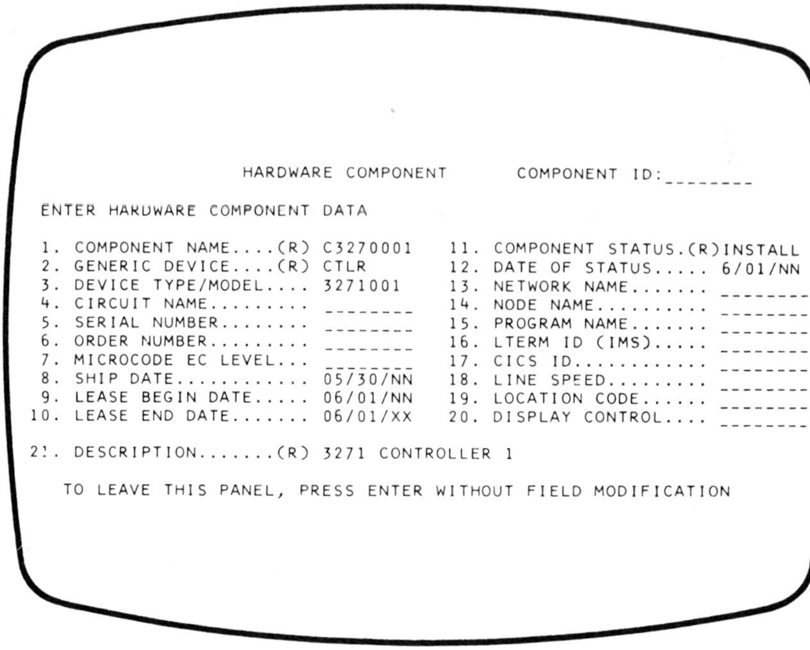

```
                    HARDWARE COMPONENT        COMPONENT ID:________

ENTER HARDWARE COMPONENT DATA

 1. COMPONENT NAME....(R) C3270001    11. COMPONENT STATUS.(R)INSTALL
 2. GENERIC DEVICE....(R) CTLR        12. DATE OF STATUS..... 6/01/NN
 3. DEVICE TYPE/MODEL.... 3271001     13. NETWORK NAME....... ________
 4. CIRCUIT NAME......... ________    14. NODE NAME.......... ________
 5. SERIAL NUMBER........ ________    15. PROGRAM NAME....... ________
 6. ORDER NUMBER......... ________    16. LTERM ID (IMS)..... ________
 7. MICROCODE EC LEVEL... ________    17. CICS ID............ ________
 8. SHIP DATE............ 05/30/NN    18. LINE SPEED......... ________
 9. LEASE BEGIN DATE..... 06/01/NN    19. LOCATION CODE...... ________
10. LEASE END DATE....... 06/01/XX    20. DISPLAY CONTROL.... ________

21. DESCRIPTION.......(R) 3271 CONTROLLER 1

  TO LEAVE THIS PANEL, PRESS ENTER WITHOUT FIELD MODIFICATION
```

Figure 6–13 Sample hardware screen for system inventory.

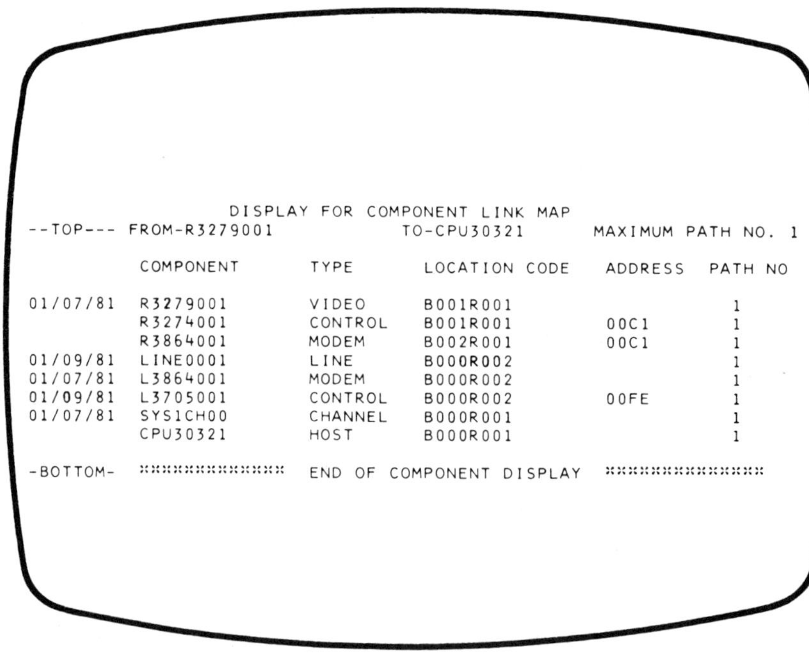

```
                    DISPLAY FOR COMPONENT LINK MAP
--TOP--- FROM-R3279001            TO-CPU30321        MAXIMUM PATH NO. 1

         COMPONENT        TYPE       LOCATION CODE   ADDRESS   PATH NO

01/07/81 R3279001         VIDEO      B001R001                   1
         R3274001         CONTROL    B001R001        00C1       1
         R3864001         MODEM      B002R001        00C1       1
01/09/81 LINE0001         LINE       B000R002                   1
01/07/81 L3864001         MODEM      B000R002                   1
01/09/81 L3705001         CONTROL    B000R002        00FE       1
01/07/81 SYS1CH00         CHANNEL    B000R001                   1
         CPU30321         HOST       B000R001                   1

-BOTTOM- **************** END OF COMPONENT DISPLAY ****************
```

Figure 6–14 Sample system inventory connectivity.

Resource and data inventory control summary

Associated with all resource control is the periodic review of the security access and utilization to protect the corporate assets assigned to the I/S business. Results of this audit could require additional tactical planning to increase overall security.

ADMINISTRATION SERVICES

Administration services process overview

This group of processes administers the finance, personnel, education, and training activities needed to support the total I/S activity.

The three processes in this group will be discussed in the following sequence:

1. Financial Administration
2. Education/Training
3. Staff Performance

It is suggested that the reader refer periodically to the flow shown in Figure 6–15.

Assessing administration services

To assess these processes, management can ask the following questions:

- Are users correctly billed for service changes?
- Is a list of vendors and vendor offerings generally available? Who tracks vendor performance?
- Are the I/S accounting procedures compatible with the enterprise procedures?
- Are purchases ordered correctly? Are the outstanding purchases generally known by all managers?
- Are financial reports adequate to make management decisions?
- Do I/S and user personnel receive adequate training and/or education?
- Are applications installed with inadequate user awareness of the procedures?
- Who is responsible for available education material?
- Are accurate records kept on personnel education/training?
- Who measures the people performance and productivity?

Financial Administration

DEFINITION:

This process applies service rates to I/S resources to determine total costs applicable to individual users (including I/S), accumulates these costs, charges the individual user organization (where appropriate), and matches against the budget. The process

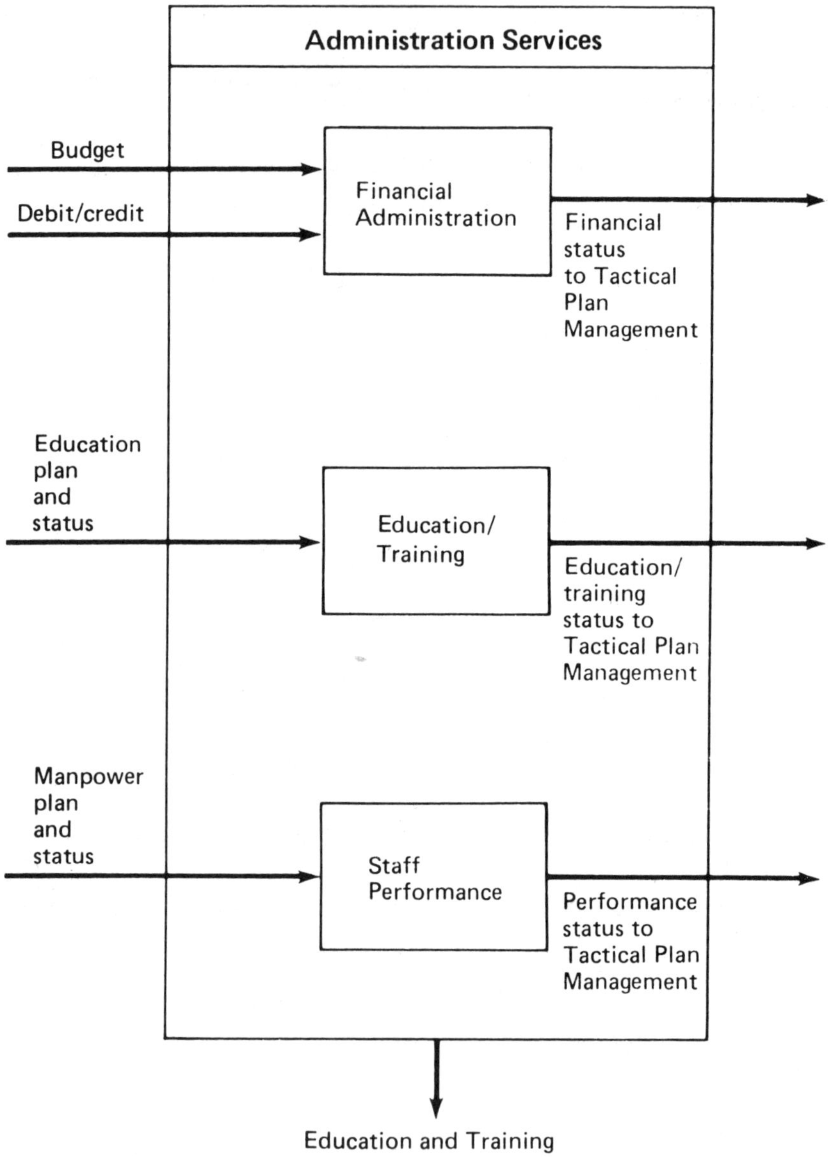

Figure 6–15 Administration services overview.

also includes maintaining contractual agreements for project work, hardware and software leasing, and other supportive efforts.

DESCRIPTION:

The elements of Financial Administration are:

1. Calculate charges due for services when applicable.
2. Administer vendor and other contracts.
3. Execute cost accounting procedures.
4. Purchase equipment, supplies, and services.
5. Report accounting and financial status.
6. Track vendor performance.

DATA CLASSES REQUIRED:

Data input to process (data class)	Data output of process (data class)
C1 Service	C1 Service
C10 Production and distribution logs	T1 Inventory
A1 Vendor	
A2 Customer/user/group	
R9 Financial	
R10 Standards/procedures/methods	

Calculate charges due for services when applicable

The Financial Administration process, like the other processes in this group, provides direct support for the service and development missions. In supporting those missions, it is assumed that charge rates were established in the respective planning processes.

Input for the service mission charges would normally include data produced in the Performance Control process, that is, production and distribution logs. This process element must analyze these logs, apply the proper charge rates against the services rendered, and submit the results to the cost accounting system.

Input for the development mission charges would normally include a time report submitted from each team member on a weekly basis and service charges as described above. The time report would include:

- Task names
- Task identification numbers

- Hours expended on each task during week
- Description of tasks and hours expended on nonproject activities
- Description of tasks and hours expended on project support activities

This data will be used by this element to charge for work performed on projects and to submit the charges to cost accounting. This data will also be used as input to the Staff Performance process for personnel evaluation.

Administer vendor and other contracts

Any contracts negotiated in the development or service missions are controlled by this element. These contracts could include long-term leasing of equipment, vendor programming, and vendor-supplied product agreements.

This control includes the verification of terms, tracking of expiration dates, initiating replacement contracts, and submitting changes to cost accounting for any associated expenses.

Execute cost accounting procedures

I/S cost accounting is generally a subset of the enterprise general ledger system with unique chart of accounts for the I/S expenses. This element must ensure that the accounts are properly set up and that expenses are properly submitted.

In addition, this element should ensure that the financial reports are adequate and understood by the I/S managers.

Purchase equipment, supplies, and services

The purchases of equipment, supplies, and services has become an increasingly important part of the I/S business. Often enterprises buy rather than lease the equipment used in the delivery of service. The use of contract programming services has also increased. This element provides the control for these purchases.

Like other financial administration elements, this function could be a logical subset of the enterprise purchasing process. In other cases, the I/S department might dedicate personnel to this function.

Report accounting and financial status

Output of this element includes reports to service and project managers on the status of associated costs. Summary information about resources would be reported to the Resource Planning processes (for example, actual expenses versus budget).

This element should be aware of the organizational structure and ensure that adequate reports are available. In some cases, the element might submit a requirement for a project to improve this reporting.

Track vendor performance

Vendors support the I/S business in many ways. They may provide help in problem determination and resolution, they may offer services and products, and they may provide consultation to all levels of the I/S organization. This "included value" is critically important to the success of the I/S business.

This element should maintain an accurate list of the vendors, the vendor offerings, and a summary of vendor performance. Vendor performance data about service and development would normally be provided by the organizations using the vendor services. Detailed vendor performance dealing with billing and purchases would be provided by the Financial Administration process.

Education and Training

DEFINITION:

This process educates users and I/S personnel on I/S-related topics through job training or formal education.

DESCRIPTION:

1. Perform training for I/S services and other needs.
2. Perform education for I/S services and other needs.
3. Develop and maintain education documentation (courses, guides, etc.).
4. Maintain education/training profile.

DATA CLASSES REQUIRED:

	Data input to process (data class)	Data output of process (data class)
P4	Personnel plan	T1 Inventory
C10	Production and distribution logs	T2 Project updates
A1	Vendor	
A2	Customer/user/group	
R8	Personnel	
R10	Standards/procedures/methods	

Perform training for I/S services and other needs

Although the words "education" and "training" are often used interchangeably, this document will consider formal classroom learning as education and nonclassroom learning as training. Training by this definition includes teaching terminal operating procedures to an end user and hands-on practice by the computer operator.

Planning for this learning experience could have occurred in the following:

- Skills Planning process for overall I/S training.
- The Development and Maintenance processes for specific application, system, data, or procedure training.
- Direct requests from the Customer Services, Services Marketing, or Production and Distribution Scheduling processes. If insufficient resources are available or the request is extensive, the request would be forwarded to the Skills Planning process.

This element will perform the training as defined in the plan or request. In most cases, this process will draw on other talent in the I/S business to assist the training.

Perform education for I/S services and other needs

This element is identical to the previous training element except that it focuses on classroom learning. Education requires communication skills that are not always found in technically oriented personnel. Therefore, I/S organizations often assign a professional staff of people knowledgeable in these teaching techniques.

This staff can provide in-house education where the demand and cost is beneficial. They can recommend vendor-provided offerings in other cases. The in-house education can be performed with materials developed in the element described next or purchased from a vendor.

Develop and maintain education documentation

Education material is available in text form, videotape, audio cassettes, closed-circuit television, videodiscs, books, periodicals, films, and many other media. This element should maintain a list of the materials available in the industry, the enterprise, and the I/S function. Circulation of this list will inform managers of the potential learning experiences. This can also be used by the Skills Planning process to develop an education plan. Many standard library techniques such as coding and filing also apply.

Although most of this material is acquired from vendors, some of it could be produced internally. For example, a university library that uses a high percentage of part-time help could use a computer-assisted instruction course to educate new personnel about the library system. An insurance company with high turnover positions might do the same for a claims processing application.

This element is responsible for developing that material. Normally, this development would be done in conjunction with an application development project. Therefore, the same Development and Maintenance Control processes would support this effort.

Based on a personnel skills profile, this library could also control the selective dissemination of information throughout the I/S function. For example, as new material enters education, the personnel profiles can be searched to find people with an interest in the topic. A notification can be sent to such people.

Maintain education/training profile

This element adds the education and training profile data to the personnel inventory record. It also periodically distributes reports to individuals and managers about this status information.

Staff Performance

DEFINITION:

This process tracks staff performance and reports productivity.

DESCRIPTION:

1. Collect data on absences, accidents, and attendance.
2. Collect data on job performance.
3. Compare and report productivity.

DATA CLASSES REQUIRED:

Data input to process (data class)	Data output of process (data class)
P4 Personnel plan	T1 Inventory
C6 System performance	C9 Tactical plan
C9 Tactical plan	
C10 Production and distribution logs	
R8 Personnel	
R10 Standards/procedures/methods	

Collect data on absences, accidents, and attendance

With the increased size of I/S organizations and the tendency toward additional remote locations, this element has increased in importance (for example, many remote terminal operators are physically located in plant areas subjected to higher environmental and safety hazards). Once collected, this data is summarized and sent to Skills Planning for analysis.

Collect data on job performance

Many I/S organizations have implemented an objectives-oriented program to formalize the appraisal of individual performance. In this program, an annual evaluation is done by the manager and the employee to measure actual attainment against planned objectives. The objectives were created jointly by the manager and the employee.

This element includes both the objectives setting and appraisal factors of this concept. Even without a formal program, the I/S organization should review its procedures for measuring individual performance.

Compare and report productivity

Throughout this document, we have discussed management of the various I/S resources. This element discusses the productivity of the most critical resource, people. Comparison and reporting of individual productivity were done in the preceding element. This element must consider productivity by I/S organizational units and by I/S compared with the enterprise and the whole I/S industry.

I/S skills are in short supply and cannot be wasted. With these productivity reports, managers can take actions to improve people effectiveness. Skills Planning can measure future sources of people resources. It is generally agreed that the future of I/S will be limited more by people constraints than by technology.

IMPLEMENTATION SUMMARY

Congratulations, both of your projects have been approved by the management steering committee. Separate project teams have been selected and moved to a new working space. Experienced project leaders have been found and trained on the Brazwell project management methodology. You have been chosen as overall coordinator for both projects.

What do you do now? First, you reread the Development and Maintenance process group discussion on managing a Management Systems Development and Upgrade project. Those are the steps that you must accomplish in the next few months. Now, you are ready to read the next chapter.

7

Service-Level Management

Service Mission Definition: Provision of service to the end user, including the collecting, storing, processing, and distributing of data.

SERVICE MISSION OBJECTIVES

The members of *both projects* were given an overview of the service mission processes. The materials in this chapter are the handouts from that session. As overall coordinator, you must make several important decisions, including:

1. Will the processes in your System/Network Control Center look exactly like those in this section?
2. What reports should the Service Quality and Reporting subproject implement? Should they be automated?
3. How will the Customer Assistance subproject interface with this reporting system?
4. How will you implement the tactical-level Service Planning process group?

Before you make those decisions, you should read this chapter to understand the issues more clearly. Readers who are interested only in the operational-level processes might skip the Service Planning section of this chapter. They could read that section as part of Chapter 8.

SERVICE PLANNING*

Service planning process overview

This group of processes is concerned with that part of the strategic plan which shows the services information systems (I/S) will provide to the enterprise within the one to two years of the tactical time horizon. The need for these services may be a result of expanding existing services or introducing new applications. The purpose of this group is to analyze the needs and to define clearly what levels of service are necessary to meet them.

The five processes and their key issues will be discussed in the following sequence:

1. Service Marketing Planning
    - Does I/S have the right service offerings?
    - What are service priorities?
    - What is the proper cost of those services?
2. Service-Level Planning
    - Are the users' service expectations realistic?
    - What is the workload forecast for those services?
3. Recovery Planning
    - What is the recovery plan in the event of a failure?
4. Security Planning
    - What security procedures are required to protect those services?
5. Audit Planning
    - What are the audit requirements of those services?

Figure 7-1 shows the information flow between the processes in the group.

Assessing service planning

Questions that could be asked to measure the effectiveness and efficiency of the Service Planning process group include:

- Does the service plan meet user requirements?
- Is I/S meeting agreed-to service levels and still getting user complaints?
- Do users agree with the service levels and measurement criteria?
- Are the exposures to fraud, loss of data, and inadequate backup being handled properly?

*The remainder of this chapter (with the exception of the "Service Mission Summary") is reproduced from the IBM publication *A Management System for the Information Business,* Volume II—*The I/S Service Mission*, GE20-0749-0 by permission of the IBM Corporation.

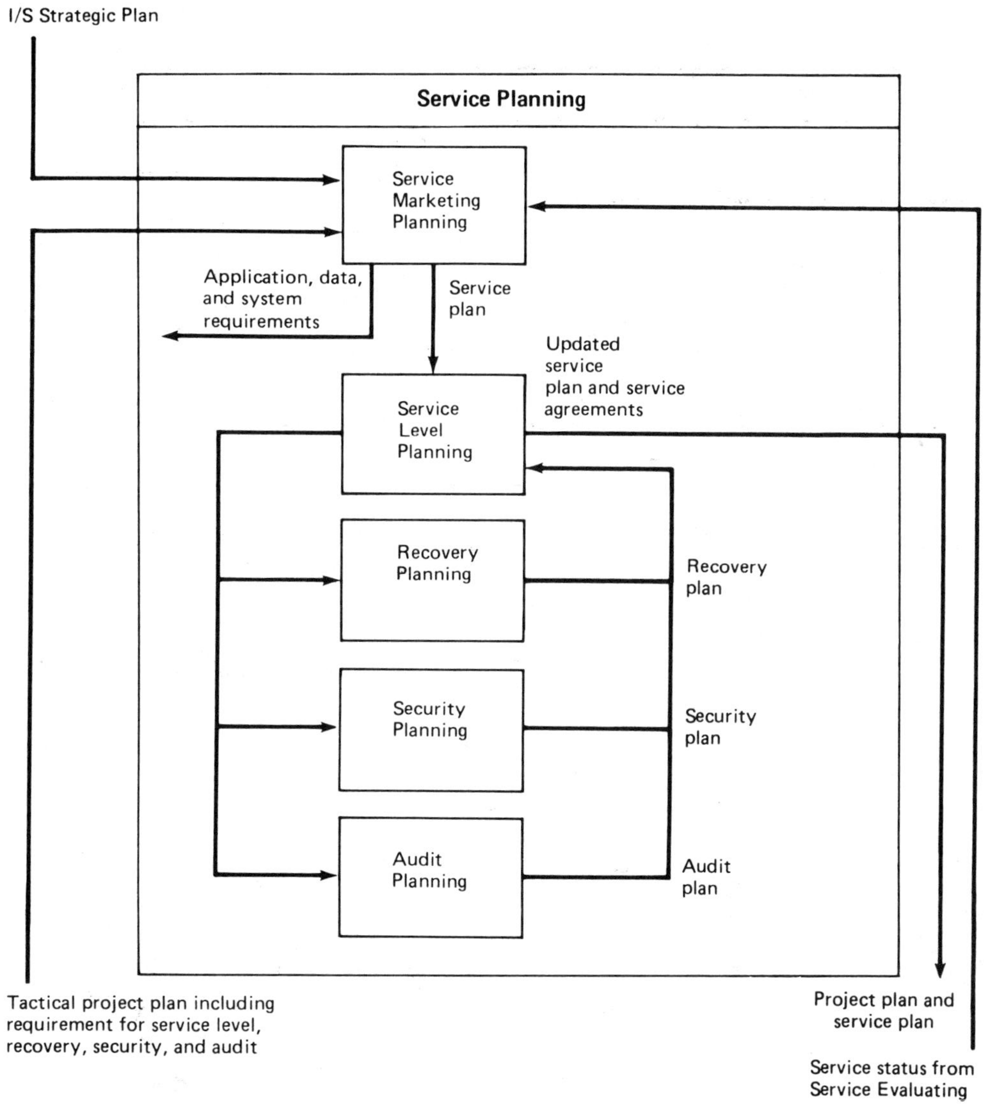

Figure 7–1 Service planning overview.

- Does I/S know what software and hardware are required for each service?
- Does I/S know what data must be available for each service? Is access to the data restricted to the proper persons?
- Does I/S know what actions are required to run applications on different configurations in a recovery or degraded mode?
- Does I/S know which applications have priority in a failure situation?

- Does I/S have documented procedures for rapid restart of those applications or services?
- Does I/S know the business or financial impact of each failure?

Service Marketing Planning

DEFINITION:

Considering the services to be offered during the tactical period, this process evaluates who could use them and forecasts market prices and service volumes. In addition, this process reviews the marketplace for the new services and resources defined under Development Planning and feeds back any additional requirements.

DESCRIPTION:

The elements, key activities and/or decisions, of Service Marketing Planning are:

1. Define the marketplace for all existing and proposed services or applications. This includes any outside service offerings.
2. Identify the services which will be offered.
3. Forecast service volumes by major classes of service.
4. Plan and publish the basis for charging users if this is appropriate.
5. Plan the promotion of services sponsored by I/S.

DATA CLASSES REQUIRED:

Data input to process (data class)	Data output of process (data class)
E2 I/S business	P7 Service plan
P7 Service plan	
P8 Project plan	
C1 Service	
C5 Requirements	
A1 Vendor	
A2 Customer/user/group	
R10 Standards/procedures/methods	

Define the marketplace for all existing and proposed services

The Service Marketing Planning process must define the customers of the I/S business and the services they need. The production and distribution services offered by the I/S business can be extensive and have widely differing purposes. A service might be a single user transaction, an application, or access to a whole subsystem. Some services serve the clerical person attempting to process orders at a terminal. Others serve the business manager in making difficult decisions. Some even serve the I/S business itself, such as personal computing for the application programmer.

As the I/S business becomes more integrated into the enterprise, other types of services can be added. These customer services provide consulting support for information needs and assistance in the development of new applications by the users themselves.

To answer these questions about customers and services, Service Marketing Planning has three major sources of data.

1. The strategic plan defines the long-range direction of the I/S business, including planned service offerings.
2. The development plan defines the application, data, and system changes that are planned over the tactical period.
3. The service plan defines the existing services, the quality of these services, and present consumption by customers.

Using this data and direct contact with customer management, Service Marketing Planning must determine whether the existing and planned services will meet the enterprise's needs.

These I/S service offerings should be described in terms that are understandable to users within the enterprise. These include:

- Description of the service
- Measurements which define the accepted level of service
- Reporting requirements during use of the service

Service measurements or service attributes may be used to determine the level of service required by the user and delivered by I/S:

- *Availability:* a measure of time that defines the interval during which a service offering is fully operational
- *Capacity:* a measure of the potential amount of total workload that could be processed during the period when the service offering is available
- *Utilization:* a measure of the amount of workload actually processed during the availability period
- *Performance:* a measure of the amount of a user's workload that will be processed in a fixed period of time
- *Accessibility:* a measure of how the workload capacity is distributed to the users in a manner that is consistent with the performance commitment
- *Reliability:* a measure of success in processing workload (a function of availability, capacity, and performance)

A similar set of terms which might be called resource attributes have been used within the I/S business to measure and control the individual resources required to deliver service. For example, one major indicator of system availability is host processor availability. However, in an on-line environment, the host processor is only one of many resources that are required to make the service available. At a minimum, the service availability is some combination of total resource availability. A similar comparison could be made for each of the other attributes.

Basically, the user needs to have terminology defined for service. I/S needs terminology for both service and resources. This concept is critically important, not just theoretically interesting. However, the redefinition of such commonly accepted terms could be the source of some confusion. The alternative, creating all new terms, could be equally confusing.

To anyone familiar with the resource terms, several points about the service terms require emphasis.

- Availability is a time period, not a measure of reliability.
- Capacity measures the workload volume that the user needs to have processed.
- Utilization is the amount of capacity of the system that the user actually used.
- Performance measures the speed of processing, that is, the 90th percentile of response time, checks processed per hour, and so on.
- Accessibility is how the user gets access to the system, for example, turnaround times for batch input or number of terminals available.
- Reliability is the probability that capacity, performance, and availability commitments will be met.

Identify services which will be offered

If the existing or planned service offerings cannot meet the customer's needs, Service Marketing Planning must define solutions to fill the gap. One possible solution would be to feed the requirements that cannot be met back to the Development Planning process group. These additional requirements could be included in the next iteration of the application, data, and system plan.

Another solution might be the examination of existing services to determine whether any that already exist could be modified to meet the need. For example, an application currently being used for one user might work for another user if they had separate data bases.

A third possibility would be to examine available services within other I/S functions of the enterprise or those provided by outside vendors. For example, a remote location may have developed a text processing application that could be adapted to meet the new requirement.

It is clear that the interaction of Service Planning and Development Planning can become very complex. Development Planning builds a plan based on its best understanding of the enterprise's needs and the available resources. The changes that result from this plan eventually become the responsibility of the service functions. It is important that the service plan take these changes into consideration and feed back any additional requirements. These, in turn, will cause further changes.

On the other hand, the Service Planning processes cannot become a means to block changes in the development plan. The final decision must be made after the resource needs (capacity, skills, and budget) have been defined in the Resource Planning processes. Only then can management compare the service, development, and resource plans and decide on the correct objectives. The resulting management decisions could require replanning by either Development or Service Planning process groups. To reduce the time necessary for these iterations, these two groups must cooperate closely. The net effect of this interaction should be well-defined service and development objectives over the tactical time period.

Forecast service volumes by major classes of service

The setting of reasonable service objectives is an iterative process, requiring negotiations between I/S and the user of the service. At the beginning of the negotiations, possibly one or two years before the actual use of the service, both parties probably have only a general understanding of the service and the required volumes. Therefore, the initial agreement clarifies what the two parties understand the facts and objectives to be at that point.

Even with this minimal knowledge, it must be assumed that both parties are sufficiently committed to the proposal to begin the tactical planning of resources. With each iteration of the planning process, the increased level of understanding should bring the parties closer to a formal agreement on the service and its measurements. This higher level of understanding should also be coupled with a corresponding increase in commitment. In some cases, the final agreement may even involve a formal, legal document.

During these iterative negotiations of service objectives, it is also important to begin forecasting the volumes associated with the service. In this element of the Service Marketing Planning process, the planner is interested in gross volumes by major service class. These forecasts will accomplish the following objectives:

- Given an early indication of the potential use of a service
- Provide an early justification for new development requirements
- Help determine the basis for charging users

Plan and publish basis for charging users if appropriate

The pricing/costing basis for all current and planned services should be reviewed. Trend analysis using historical data about current services (volume usage, time-of-day usage, usage versus charges) can be used to make projections regarding alterations to the charging approach.

Usage forecasts for planned projects also serve as an input to the proposed plan for charging users. Based on these projections, a preliminary plan is published to begin the negotiation of individual service agreements. The final charging plan must be approved after the total service and resource objectives have been approved in the Tactical Plan Management process.

Plan the promotion of services sponsored by I/S

Many of the traditional business approaches to marketing products can also be applied to I/S. For example, the price of a new service could be temporarily reduced to encourage use and make it profitable in the long term. Demonstration centers could be set up to assist users in the understanding of new on-line services or devices. Also, a customer service function could be established to answer questions and provide overall user support.

For more strategic changes in service, this promotion encourages the user attitude required for successful acceptance. For example, I/S management has decided that an information center is good for the enterprise. Promotion could explain the information center and generate user interest.

These promotional efforts should be planned. The overall service plan with forecasts, pricing, and promotional efforts should be understood and have basic agreement before starting the more formal service-level planning.

Service-Level Planning

DEFINITION:

Using market prices and service volumes, this process negotiates individual service agreements which define respective I/S and user commitments for the tactical time period. The service agreement will identify individual requests for recovery, security, and auditability. The outcome of this process is an overall service plan which incorporates recovery, security, and audit plans.

DESCRIPTION:

The elements of Service Level Planning are:

1. Negotiate service agreements (including recovery, security, audit, and charges).
2. Forecast volumes by service agreements.
3. Develop a preventive maintenance plan.
4. Review agreed-upon service agreements and define the required consultation, help desk, and other support services.
5. Define a total service plan including service levels, recovery, security, and auditability.

DATA CLASSES REQUIRED:

Data input to process (data class)	Data output of process (data class)
P3 System plan	P7 Service plan
P7 Service plan	T1 Inventory
P8 Project plan	

Data input to process (data class)	Data output of process (data class)
C1 Service	
A1 Vendor	
A2 Customer/user/group	
R10 Standards/procedures/methods	

Negotiate service agreements

In any normal business transaction involving a vendor–buyer situation, a business agreement is established by drawing up a contract that clarifies the terms and conditions under which the business transaction will take place. Similarly, a service agreement or document of understanding should be established when a user and I/S agree on a new or changed I/S service to be provided. The purpose of such an agreement is to establish the responsibilities of both parties involved, to clarify and establish expectations on both sides, and to make sure that no surprises arise in the new business relationship.

This service agreement is a documented statement of the service objectives for both I/S and user management. This document contains a description of the service that is to be provided each user and the way to measure whether or not it is meeting the objectives. These service objectives are essential for effective management planning and control.

The definition and acceptance of an agreement require several renegotiations before it is complete. Once an agreement has been accepted, it must be continually monitored for relevance to an ever changing environment. At a minimum, it is assumed that these agreements are reviewed each quarter and revised annually.

To start the negotiations, I/S provides the user with a description of the service being offered and the proposed prices established in the Service Marketing Planning process. For existing services, this would be the previous agreement with updated prices and measurements. A simple agreement might include the parameters shown in Figure 7-2.

I/S and user management can rework the agreement to provide the level of service desired at the appropriate price. After both parties have agreed to all characteristics of the service, the final form of that agreement can range from a simple letter of understanding to a legal document approved by lawyers. In all cases, the result is service objectives committed to by all parties.

To simplify these negotiations, all service offerings of a type (for example, online information, time sharing, remote job entry) may be grouped into a class of service to be offered. Negotiating about classes of service simplifies management control and the corresponding management reporting. Service agreement negotiation improves communication between I/S and the users while establishing I/S costs and constraints.

The implementation of service agreements benefits I/S by providing measures by which I/S management controls the performance of the organization and contrib-

Name of Service	Customer Order Servicing
Host Location	St. Louis
Locations Served	All Sales Offices
Type of Service	On-line Sales Order Entry
Responsible Manager	Ed Van Schaik (214) 555-1212
Availability	7 a.m. – 6 p.m. CST Mon to Fri
Capacity	14,000 Transactions/Day
Performance	Class 2 (90% Less Than 4.1 Sec.) 2000 Transactions/Hour
Accessibility	Type "A" Office 3 Terminals/Office Type "B" Office 1 Terminal/Office
Reliability	95–96.9% at Terminal
Recoverability	Priority 1
Security Level	Class A
Price of Service	$.55 / Transaction

Figure 7–2 Service agreement parameters.

utes significantly to the stabilization of service to users. The I/S function can initiate service agreements most easily by documenting the existing service levels and publishing them as the standard against which I/S will be managed and measured. With experience, I/S can enter into selected negotiations with a few critical users.

However, several points should be emphasized:

- During each iteration of the service negotiation, several other planning processes will be activated. Recovery Planning, Security Planning, and Audit Planning will verify the corresponding factor in the agreement. Capacity Planning, Skills Planning, and Budget Planning will verify the resources required. The agreement is final when all aspects of the planning processes are balanced.

  With both user and I/S involvement in these planning processes, the service agreement will define the objectives and responsibilities of I/S and the users, not just I/S.

- Support from senior management is essential in bringing users and I/S together to develop service agreements. Both enterprise and I/S executives favor the use of service agreements because they provide accountability and measurement on a basis similar to the operation of other functions within the enterprise.

  User management is able to relate to I/S on a more objective, measurable basis and can more effectively relate their usage and cost to their operation. I/S management can measure manager performance in attaining these service levels. Also, essential I/S activities such as capacity planning and project planning can be tied to service levels. This is the focal point of effective management control in organizations that use service agreements.
- Availability of resources (including capacity) is essential to the attainment of service levels. The implementation of service levels requires I/S management to focus on maximizing user satisfaction. To attain committed service levels, capacity to meet the service demands must be available on equipment. A rule used by successful I/S installations is that system upgrades should occur when essential resources (host processor cycles, for example) are utilized 70% of capacity during the shift which processes the most critical work. The figure of 70% is representative, and may vary because of the nature of the work done in a specific installation.

  However, the decision to actually increase or decrease resources is not an activity under this process group. The processes under the Development Planning group define a proposed system solution. This provides input to Service-Level Planning. This system plan and the proposed service plan are passed to the Resource Planning process group to evaluate the balance of resources and service objectives. Several iterations of system and service plans may be required before the resources are adequate. The reader may wish to review this overall ISM flow before progressing through the service mission (Appendix A).

Examples of service agreements and the corresponding measurements of that service will be discussed later under the Service Evaluating process (Figs. 7-21 and 7-22).

Forecast volumes by service agreement

With this clear understanding of the expected services, the user, with assistance from I/S, can forecast and track the volume of information required to meet his or her business needs. In the past, the user has been expected to forecast in I/S terms (for example, host processor hours to be used, amount of connect time). An alternative and more acceptable approach is to forecast the volumes in user-oriented business terms (purchase orders to be processed, employee records to be handled).

These business volumes can be converted into the corresponding service application and/or transactions required to produce the desired information. These service forecasts will eventually be translated into I/S terms in the Resource Planning group process, Capacity Planning.

The accuracy of these forecasts determines the validity of the whole tactical planning exercise. Historical data about the actual delivery of this service can greatly improve the reliability of the forecast. The Service-Level Planning process coupled with the Service Evaluating process must be an ongoing effort to define the services, attributes, and volumes required to satisfy the enterprise's information needs. With this negotiation and compliance evaluation, management can monitor the performance of the I/S service business.

Develop a preventive maintenance plan

In this process element, management must determine what impact the maintenance strategy will have on the availability of the resources. Maintenance Planning is setting basic preventive maintenance objectives of resources required to deliver service. Since this is a critical point in the Service-Level Planning process, a review of all the information gathered would be helpful to understand the planning steps still required.

- The development plan defined the systems, applications, and data which would be available to deliver service. This included an overall preventive maintenance strategy to be applied against these resources.
- The service plan defined the service objectives and the required volumes to be processed by each service type.
- The service plan status defined previous service attainment, resource utilization, and maintenance history against those resources.

The remaining planning elements and processes must make several key management decisions about the ability to meet those service objectives with the planned resources. The resulting service plan with these maintenance objectives will be used by Recovery Planning, Security Planning, and Audit Planning in this process group and subsequently by Capacity Planning in the Resource Planning process group.

The Recovery Planning process uses these maintenance objectives to build an overall plan to ensure the agreed service in case of failure or disaster. If the Recovery Planning process cannot ensure that service, the maintenance plan is one of several factors which could be revised. Therefore, the Service-Level Planning and the Recovery Planning processes function in a closed loop to finalize the service plan (Fig. 7-1).

The hardware and software sections of the maintenance plan require special emphasis. First, consider software preventive service. In today's complex environment, the results of many different programming efforts must coexist in the individual I/S installation. Errors in any one program are compounded by interacting with the many programs making up the total system. When program errors occur, whether in vendor or user-written programs, they often cause disruption in the vital services performed by the I/S facility. Valuable resources must be expended to isolate and correct the errors.

These unscheduled outages can be reduced by applying the concept of preventive service. Under this concept, solutions that have been discovered, reported, and corrected are accumulated and applied on new releases, feature changes, and program modifications. This corrects errors before they occur in the installation and limits the future rediscovery of known problems. Computer programs can be used to track solutions to known problems. These same programs search the history to verify that required conditions exist before applying corrections or installing new features. Effective preventive service requires that solutions must be regularly applied using the service programs.

Hardware preventive maintenance can either be scheduled or predictive. Scheduled maintenance is the periodic inspection of the components of the system based on many factors such as system usage and the performance history of that particular component. The schedule is derived from a maintenance analysis report provided by the service organization.

In today's environment, the need for scheduled preventive maintenance is decreasing and the use of predictive maintenance is increasing. The philosophy of predictive maintenance is to perform needed maintenance on a device before performance drops below acceptable levels. Concurrent maintenance performed during normal shifts lessens the need for standalone time for diagnostics, service, and testing.

As part of the normal maintenance planning, the installation of software preventive fixes and hardware engineering changes should be weighed against the potential loss of available time for scheduled maintenance or outages. The actual testing and installation of these fixes will be discussed as part of the Development and Maintenance Control process group.

Define the required consultation, help desk, and support services

A service agreement implies a commitment between the user and I/S to support the information needs of the enterprise. The need for various support services which can reduce the risk involved in meeting agreements must be weighed against not meeting the committed service levels. These support services, discussed later in the Customer Services and Service Marketing processes, must be staffed at a level consistent with the committed service.

In the sample service agreement (Fig. 7–2), the customer order servicing agreement will require a help function during the prime period to minimize the impact of problems and to achieve 95 to 96.9% reliability. According to this element of Service-Level Planning, I/S must review the existing help function and recommend any additions required to fulfill this and any other agreement.

Define a total service plan

At this point the service plan has defined services, user service agreements, a preventive maintenance plan, and a support plan. Before the service plan can be finalized, the plan must be subjected to a careful analysis of its recoverability, security, and auditability. This is accomplished in the Recovery Planning, Security Planning, and Audit Planning processes, respectively. Several iterations may be required to resolve all these issues.

During these iterations, it may be necessary to redefine services, user service agreements, the maintenance approach, or the support services. The final service plan must be achievable with a reasonable risk for both the I/S and user organizations.

Service-level planning summary

Although the initial installation of this planning process can be a sizable effort, its success depends on making it an ongoing process. Once the basic service plan has been established, it can be controlled and upgraded with much less effort.

Recovery Planning

DEFINITION:

Using individual requests for recovery, this process builds an overall plan to ensure the agreed-upon service for users in case of failure or disaster.

DESCRIPTION:

The elements of Recovery Planning are:

1. Consolidate recovery requirements of all service agreements.
2. Define business and I/S recovery operating environment.
3. Identify variances between operating environment and agreements.
4. Develop overall recovery plan.

DATA CLASSES REQUIRED:

Data input to process (data class)	Data output of process (data class)
P7 Service plan	P7 Service plan
C1 Service	
A2 Customer/user/group	
R10 Standards/procedures/methods	

Consolidate recovery requirements of all service agreements

In a world that depends more and more on the computer to maintain the pace of commerce and to keep the wheels of industry turning, system failures can produce costs far beyond the value of the computer time lost. When failures do occur, it is essential that those concerned know exactly what must be done to recover the lost function in the least possible time. Furthermore, the business impact of each situation must be known to prevent negative impact on the enterprise's customers.

For every service, the business risk, acceptable business standards, and other business factors must be understood to recommend procedures to ensure that the needed recovery can be accomplished. Under ideal conditions, plans should be made to handle all contingencies.

Define business and I/S recovery operating environment

The recovery actions available at the operational level include:

- Bypass
- Backup/backout
- Restart
- Reassignment
    - Data path
    - Personnel
- Reconfiguration
- Isolation/containment
- Circumvention/substitution
- Reconstruction

For every failure situation, actions should have been planned and tested before the operational personnel must use them. The actual testing and implementation of recovery procedures is done in the Development and Maintenance processes.

The recovery planner must have adequate knowledge about the many system resources and their interactions with I/S service offerings. Since this inventory of system resources must be available to all the tactical management processes, the reader will find the following general system inventory concept helpful at this point in the discussion.

To operate a business, there are many entities about which information or data must be kept. These entities range from resources used to deliver service to simple control documents such as a purchase order. Any data classification must keep data about part of a business entity, an entire business entity, or a group of related business entities.

The Resource Group data class (Appendix B) lists the resource entities used by the information systems business. The other data classes define planning, control, and administration entities required to deal with these resources.

The Recovery Planning process uses this system inventory data to measure the impact on the enterprise in various failure situations. Some installations do an excellent job in planning the disaster situation where major resources are lost but almost ignore the day-to-day business impact of the failure of individual resources. Other installations worry only about the immediate problems and are never prepared for the major situation which could put the enterprise out of business. Recovery Planning must address all these situations and ensure that the total business information environment is prepared.

Identify variances between operating environment and agreements

Since recovery issues occur at all planning and control levels, the Recovery Planning process must set the direction and ensure compliance in all situations. This includes attendance at all major project systems assurance meetings to verify that the recovery plans are being implemented.

The available Recovery Planning techniques largely revolve around knowing the services being delivered, knowing the utilization of resources, understanding the business use of information, and using sound business practices in relating all these variables. One technique available for both tactical planning and operational planning is *Component Failure Impact Analysis* (CFIA). CFIA is a systematic approach to help management predict and evaluate the impact of a component failure on those applications thought to be the most critical to the organization, assess current backup and recovery procedures, and consider alternatives designed to improve availability. The basic tool of CFIA is a grid (Fig. 7-3).

Major resources (for example, hardware, software, people) are listed at the top (left to right). Critical applications or services are listed at the left (top to bottom). During the analysis, the impact of a failure on each service by each system component is evaluated and noted on the chart in the form of a symbol explained in an associated legend. Existing capability and bypass procedures are considered in making the evaluation. These and the procedures developed during the analysis are de-

GROUP DESCRIPTION	HARDWARE						SOFTWARE			OTHER
COMPONENT	PROCESSOR	CONSOLE	CHANNEL 1	CHANNEL 2	DISK	TAPE	MVS	JES	TCAM	PEOPLE
NUMBER AVAILABLE	1	1	1	1	6	6	1	1	1	2
APPLICATION/SYSTEM										
PAYROLL CHECKS	X	C	D	D	D	I	X	X		
SALES	X	C	D	D	D	I	X	X	X	
FINANCIAL PLANNING	X	C	D	D	D		X	X		
OTHER										
RECOVERY PROCEDURE STEP NUMBER	1	2	3	4	5	6	7	8		

Figure 7-3 Component failure impact analysis (CFIA) grid.

STEP NUMBER	RECOVERY ACTION	RECOVERY EFFECTS	ALTERNATIVES	NEEDS/ISSUES
5 (disk)	Call C.E. for repair	Assign alternate disk for TSO user	TSO users disabled	Critical disk
6 (tape)	Call C.E. for repair	Sales & A.P. batch proof stopped		Study feasibility of converting
10 (prt)	Call C.E. for repair. Spool A.R. statements to tape	Processing can continue but must stop prior to filling spool disk	Some print can be done on other printer for backup	Develop, test & maintain procedures for offsite usage
11 (display)	Call C.E. for repair	Alternate console is lost. Testing is impacted until repaired		

Figure 7-4 Extract of a full CFIA detail description.

fined in the Step Detail Description chart (Fig. 7-4). The CFIA techniques are well documented.

Develop overall recovery plan

The overall recovery plan must consider the business needs of the enterprise, the technical design, and the management abilities of the I/S organization. CFIA provides a means to accomplish the technical analysis by relating the applications to the critical resources used by each of them. Methods for management analysis were introduced in Chapter 5.

To accomplish the business analysis, it must be possible to predict the possible system failures which could impair the delivery of information services to the business. In many installations, this business impact of each service failure is not clearly defined or tracked.

By using the systems outage analysis data provided from the Service Control processes, the history of component mean time to failure, mean time to repair, and recovery duration can be studied for clear trends and potential failures. In many cases, the user also keeps data about the business impact of each outage and the resultant loss of business opportunity. This data serves to determine the effectiveness and efficiency of the recovery actions.

Recovery planning summary

Predictive data from Service Control processes combined with data provided with the CFIA analysis can be extensive and cover services, resources, and their interactions. Most of this data is already being collected in files in most installations. Recovery Planning makes it useful information.

The difficulty in managing the Recovery Planning process is knowing all the work performed in Service-Level Planning, Project Planning, and the operational levels that have an impact on this effort.

Security Planning

DEFINITION: Using individual requests, this process builds an overall plan to ensure that the agreed-upon levels of security for the systems and services will be met.

DESCRIPTION:

The elements of Security Planning are:

1. Consolidate the security requirements of all service agreements.
2. Define the business and I/S security operating environment.
3. Identify variances between the operating environment and agreements.
4. Develop overall security plan.

DATA CLASSES REQUIRED:

Data input to process (data class)	Data output of process (data class)
P7 Service plan	P7 Service plan
C1 Service	
A2 Customer/user/group	
R10 Standards/procedures/methods	

Consolidate security requirements of all service agreements

Security Planning deals with many of the same issues encountered under Recovery Planning. The service agreement defines the level of security which must be placed on the data and information being produced and distributed under the agreement. It also places security limits on the finite set of resources required to accomplish the results. Each of the many agreements must be examined to understand the total security issue and develop a plan.

Security by definition is the protection of resources from unauthorized destruction, modification, or disclosure, whether accidental or intentional. Studies have shown that the three highest concerns are:

1. Violations caused by errors and omissions
2. Improper management controls to protect resources
3. Inadequate system design

For example, the data resource can be compromised while it is being managed by the system or while it is physically removed from the system. If the data is remote from the system, physical security and control procedures must protect the data. When the data is being managed by the system, software and hardware must identify, authorize, and fix accountability for its use. The lack of either protection can violate the intent of the service commitment.

Define business and I/S security operating environment

The security requirements for I/S services can be derived from the service agreements discussed earlier. In the cases where the specific needs are stated, the security planner must verify their validity and review the current conformity to those standards. For other services with unstated or implied requirements, the planner must define the needs or negotiate them with the customer. This composite of security requirements forms the planner's objectives over the tactical period.

The security planner must review these security requirements against current and planned controls. This is accomplished by understanding the security built into the current system inventory, the planned applications/data/systems, and the planned management system. The magnitude of this effort cannot be underestimated. For example, data security functions are normally implemented through operating systems and data base/data communications products, recommended backup/recovery procedures, application programs, and external control procedures. The application using the data may have several ways of reporting security violations to a security audit trail. Any of these systems or procedures can report attempted or completed security violations. The security planner must be aware of all these combinations.

Identify variances between operating environment and agreements

With these security requirements and the planned environment, the planner must identify where variances need action. Like Recovery Planning, the correction could include redefinition of the service or the service agreement, or refusal to concur with the project and/or management plan.

Develop overall security plan

The security plan must ensure the responsibilities and procedures for protection of the I/S assets, prevent misuse and loss of assets, establish the basis for audits and self-assessments, and preserve management's options and legal remedies in the event of the loss or misuse of assets.

These assets include software, data, equipment, terminals, facilities, and other physical resources. They also include the related application design listings, programs, library functions, and procedures.

Security planning summary

Fulfillment of asset protection responsibilities is mandatory and may be considered a major factor in successful management control.

Audit Planning

DEFINITION:

Using individual requests, this process builds an overall plan to ensure that the agreed levels of auditability for the systems and services will be met.

DESCRIPTION:

The elements of Audit Planning are:

1. Consolidate audit requirements of all service agreements.
2. Define business and I/S audit operating environment.
3. Identify variances between operating environment and agreements.
4. Develop overall audit plan.

DATA CLASSES REQUIRED:

Data input to process (data class)	Data output of process (data class)
P7 Service plan	P7 Service plan
C1 Service	
A2 Customer/user/group	
R10 Standards/procedures/methods	

Consolidate audit requirements of all service agreements

One purpose of Audit Planning is to foster an awareness of auditability requirements in order to avoid developing services or resources which inhibit auditability. Auditability, whether applied to a manual or an automated system, is defined as the characteristics of the system which permit an independent verification of

- The accuracy of the data managed by the system
- The correctness of the function or procedures performed by the system
- The use of good management procedure to control the system

Although this verification deals extensively with the auditing of applications and application design, it must also include the total system environment under which those applications must operate, namely, the whole service mission.

The service agreements define the I/S offerings and the information to be provided. The auditor must examine the existing service agreements and any new ones to establish any auditing requirements that may be necessary; for example, a new on-line application dealing with payroll must have a defined audit procedure.

The purpose of this process element is to understand the business audit needs, the I/S technical resources involved in those needs, and the audit points required to ensure that the needs are being satisfied.

The Audit Planning process must work closely with the Management Planning process group described in Chapter 5. Management Systems Monitoring, a key process in the Management Planning group, audits the effectiveness and efficiency of the I/S management system. The Audit Planning process ensures that the I/S management system actually fulfills the enterprise's needs. I/S resources are common to both functions.

Define business and I/S audit operating environment

The auditor, either an internal auditor or an auditor representing an outside firm, is looking primarily for variances which could have significant material or financial impact on the firm being audited. The integrity of the data is verified by physical counts of items or by mailing confirmations to customers and vendors and then comparing them with what the system purports to have. The correctness of the function being performed is verified by examining the documentation and then independently stimulating the system with input and observing the output. Once it has been verified that the system performs as required, the auditor will observe the management procedures that are used to manage the system and determine if proper controls are being exercised over the day-to-day operation of the system.

Auditability has always been required but has for the most part been the responsibility of the user and the application program. However, as systems become more complex, functions previously in the user domain are being incorporated into the control programs, program products, and other system components outside the application program.

The community of auditors realizes that there is significant potential for increasing the auditability of computer-based systems through the use of the computer. To date, this has meant essentially the use of software for data selection, summarization, comparison, and report writing. This has been provided, for the most part, by the public accounting firms, independent software houses, and the users themselves. However, new requirements are emerging which may impose on hardware and software manufacturers the responsibility for providing enhanced control and audit facilities. Many of these requirements are not specific to auditing and are satisfied by facilities whose primary purposes are to address other needs; for example, the log records of data base changes provide both audit and performance data.

The auditor's objectives for control and review of computer-based systems are almost identical to those of the management assigned to deliver service or develop applications. The significant exception is that the assigned management might have less interest in providing a record of its own activities.

Management controls are exercised to accomplish:

- Prevention and detection of undesirable activity
- Detection of unusual activity

- Correction of deviations
- Measurement and recording of activity
- Substantiation of results

It should be possible to implement, work with, and adjust management controls in a systematic, comprehensive fashion with a minimum of complexity and difficulty.

The audit community has a feeling of inadequacy when confronted by advanced computer-based systems. They have only just become comfortable with batch systems. Now they are confronted by what they conceive to be a far greater magnitude of complexity. Auditors are concerned that the new environment will produce systems to which they will be unable to attest at reasonable cost with reasonable confidence. Some of these concerns may be unfounded. Nevertheless, at this time many questions are being asked and concerns are being expressed.

Identify variances between operating environment and agreements

The individual auditor or a team of auditors must possess a mix of skills that provide a comprehensive understanding of the work that is being reviewed. This includes an understanding of the conceptual design of the application, the description and organization of the data, the processing steps, and the overall environment in which the work is done.

It also requires that the auditor have the capability and not be constrained from performing the following variety of tasks. For purposes of this guideline, we are interested in the auditor's ability to review and prove the entries which affect the corporate books, reports, and data. We are also interested in the ability of the auditor to test and rely on the integrity of the system.

The tasks of the auditor are:

- Verification of adequate controls for user authorization, data collection and entry, processing, output, transmission, error correction, program changes, adjustments, and so on.
- Review of past activities to ensure that current status accurately reflects the historical activity.
- Review of transactions and files for deviation from standards or norms.
- Confirmation of the application with real-world activities and status.
- Review of programmed accounting and other algorithms for compliance with accounting and other standards.
- Review of all changes to programs, control lists, and other system objects.
- Review of exceptions and the methods of handling exceptions. The auditor must be able to prove that all exceptions are properly processed and that correction procedures cannot be used to introduce undetectable errors or commit fraud without great difficulty and collusion.

Develop overall audit plan

The Recovery Planning, Security Planning, and Audit Planning processes require accurate data about the system inventory designed and used by the I/S business. The Audit Planning process must establish rules and guidelines which make the deliverables conform to reasonable standards. The objective is to ensure that services and resources which present significant obstacles to auditability are not built. In addition, they should exploit opportunities to enhance control, audit efficiency, and effectiveness.

For example, is there an opportunity to introduce an auditor exit from application code through use of a special command? It might work like this: The auditor would review the program and determine key points for audit testing, data gathering, and so on; he or she would then ask for insertion of an audit exit in the source program. The exit could then be activated at execution time and branch to an audit subroutine. Activation or cancellation of the audit exit would require audit authorization. Any errors in the audit subroutine would not affect the application.

The system should be designed with the auditor's requirement in mind. The auditor wants to know: who did what, to what, when, from where, using which program, affecting what files, with what inputs, with what outputs, error conditions; he or she wants to apply this information to enhance the auditability of the system.

Since we are addressing the question of auditability for new and advanced systems which currently have incomplete descriptions, it is difficult to identify the unique auditability exposures and opportunities they will create. This is made particularly difficult by the rapid evolution of completely new and complex I/S environments. What we have attempted to do is outline a variety of auditor's thought processes which we hope will enable the designer to play devil's advocate on behalf of the auditor, to raise auditability concerns and address them. Auditability must be a prime design criterion.

Audit planning summary

In the past, the auditor could easily see a separation of responsibility. The separate operating departments, the flow of paper between them, and their separate ledgers were visible and trackable.

Computerization has resulted in a tremendous concentration of data and function. For the most part, computerized data is useful only if subjected to some form of selection and correlation and summarization, which results in a clearly understood report. In a typical computerized environment, a single data entry can update numerous files and leave very little audit trail unless the programs are deliberately designed to do so. The auditor is vitally concerned with accountability. He or she wants to know what has taken place, when, why, and by whom. The auditor also wants to verify that the system is performing as it is supposed to, and that errors can be detected and corrected. These questions can usually be addressed by specific programming efforts. The auditor, however, is not a programming professional and his or her interaction with the machine is, at best, difficult. What the auditor needs is the education, tools, and guidelines to be able to impose his or her requirements on the computerized process to verify data and the existence and operability of controls. What is emerging is a requirement for audit tools and system facilities which provide the auditor with the ability to use the computer as an audit tool.

SERVICE CONTROL

Service control process overview

This group of processes deals with the management of the activities that provide I/S services.

The four processes and their key issues will be discussed in the following sequence:

1. Production and Distribution Scheduling
   - How and when are the committed service levels to be delivered on a daily, weekly, and monthly basis?
   - How are the installed and in-process resources to be used effectively and efficiently over the same time periods?
2. Resource and Data Performance Control
   - How do we measure and control the performance of resources used to deliver the service levels?
   - Do we measure and control the performance of the data resource separately from these resources?
   - How is this resource performance related to evaluating the service performance?
3. Problem Control
   - How do we contain and resolve any problems arising in the delivery of the service levels?
   - What is the role of Problem Control in providing an installation "report card"?
4. Service Evaluating
   - How do we report the planned and actual service attainment to users, user management, and I/S management?
   - How do we correct any variations from the original plans?

Before starting the Service Control process group, the reader should review the overall process flow (Appendix A) to understand the processes that connect to this group. During each Service Control process discussion, the reader should refer periodically to the detailed flowchart shown in Figure 7-5.

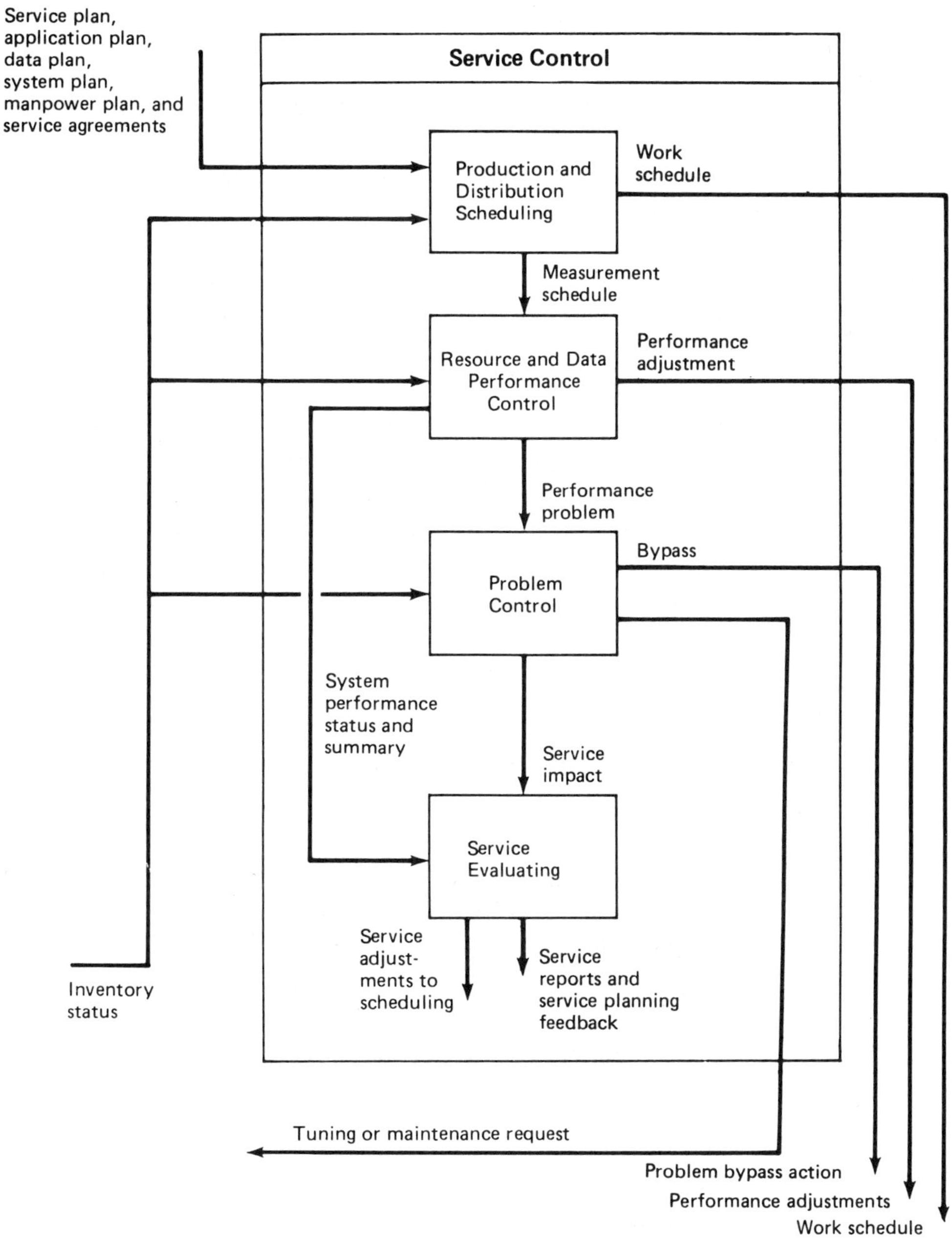

Figure 7-5 Service control process overview.

Assessing service control

Some of the questions that could be asked about the success or failure of the Service Control processes are:

- Are schedules constantly modified? Are a large number of people devoted to scheduling?
- Is work consistently delivered/completed on time?
- Is the achievement of service agreements reported in a way that the user can understand?
- Does the user agree with the reported service-level attainment?
- Is there constant debate between user and I/S on the service achievements?
- Are performance deviations treated as problems?
- Do users know of performance deviations before I/S?
- Do problems bounce from group to group and never get resolved?
- Do problems remain open for a long period of time?
- Does the same problem continually reoccur?
- Are there standards set to determine the time required to resolve different problem types?
- Do certain organizations produce a disproportionate share of problems? Are those organizations identified?
- Can the source of problems be isolated?

Production and Distribution Scheduling

DEFINITION:

Using the tactical plan and the system inventory, this process translates planned service agreements into a 1- to 90-day schedule of work and performance measurement for the Production and Distribution process.

DESCRIPTION:

The elements of the Production and Distribution Scheduling process are:

1. Plan production and distribution service workload.
2. Develop a maintenance and measurement schedule.
3. Develop a current work schedule.
4. Negotiate any deviations from the service agreements with users.
5. Publish work, maintenance, and measurement schedules.
6. Monitor and modify schedules (as necessary).

DATA CLASSES REQUIRED:

Data input to process (data class)	Data output of process (data class)
P7 Service plan	C7 Production/distribution schedule
P9 Capacity plan	T1 Inventory
C3 Change	
C4 Problem	
C7 Production/distribution schedule	
A2 Customer/user/group	
R1 Applications	
R2 Data	
R3 Software	
R4 Hardware	
R5 Network	
R6 Facilities	
R7 Supplies	
R8 Personnel	
R10 Standards/procedures/methods	
R11 Test data	

Plan production and distribution workload

The Production and Distribution Scheduling process has four major sources of information with which to plan the daily, weekly, and monthly service work (Fig.7–5).

1. An operating plan defining the tactical (12- to 24-month) direction for applications, data, systems, personnel and user service agreements. This flows from the Tactical Plan Management process; it sets the basic framework in which the service mission must operate.
2. An inventory of installed and in-process resources. This flows from the Resource and Data Inventory Control process; it defines the basic resources which are available or will be made available by the development mission in the scheduling time horizon.
3. The status and actual attainment of each service. This flows from the Service Evaluating process and provides history on the service mission's ability to meet the operating plan.
4. The status of production and distribution work actually in the I/S installation. This flows from the corresponding Information Services process, Production and Distribution; it allows dynamic rescheduling of existing work.

It should be emphasized that this process has both a static (daily, weekly, and monthly) and a dynamic nature (daily real-time). The static output is a production and distribution schedule showing the work to be performed, performance measurements to be taken, and the maintenance to be performed. The real-time output initiates the transfer of workloads (jobs or transactions) from one site to another or the alteration of priorities on any one site.

The scheduling process should cover the overall flow of work through the entire enterprise from the point at which input is received from the users to the point at which output is delivered to the users. This discussion does not assume any specific organizational approach to the responsibility for overall planning, scheduling, and coordination of work to be performed in all the different work groups. This concept works equally well with a large centralized group or individual work groups performing the detailed scheduling of their own work.

All good scheduling procedures rely heavily on an effective method of forecasting future workload as far in advance as possible. It is obvious that some I/S work can never be predicted a long time in advance and other work may take less or more time to process than originally expected. Nevertheless, it is possible to make a rough plan or schedule, which can be modified later when more information becomes available.

The basic concept involved is shown in Figure 7-6. The full implementation of this information flow is a sizable effort. Using the tactical plan, the service history, and the inventory history, the Production and Distribution Scheduling process functions in each operational time period as follows:

- *Monthly scheduling.* Using the yearly tactical plan as a base, a monthly workload plan is prepared one month in advance. This plan is then modified by additional requests for computer services (on-line work as well as batch work) not known at the time of preparation of the yearly plan. A preliminary monthly schedule is now prepared by adding the dates that jobs are to be processed. This is sent out to the users for review and revision or approval. After negotiation of any changes to run dates that are likely to occur, a final monthly work schedule is developed and sent out. The schedule should cover run dates, due-in and due-out dates, and processing time for all scheduled batch jobs, and hours of operation for on-line services.
- *Weekly scheduling.* Each week, the work to be processed in the next week is scheduled in detail for each workstation, taking into account planned machine downtime and planned availability of workstation operators. This planning work is mainly an internal planning activity for the operations department with little involvement of users, except in cases where it can be seen that agreed services cannot be provided. A good deal of interaction between the production and distribution management, workstation supervisors, and operators can be expected before the weekly work schedule and other associated documents are sent out.

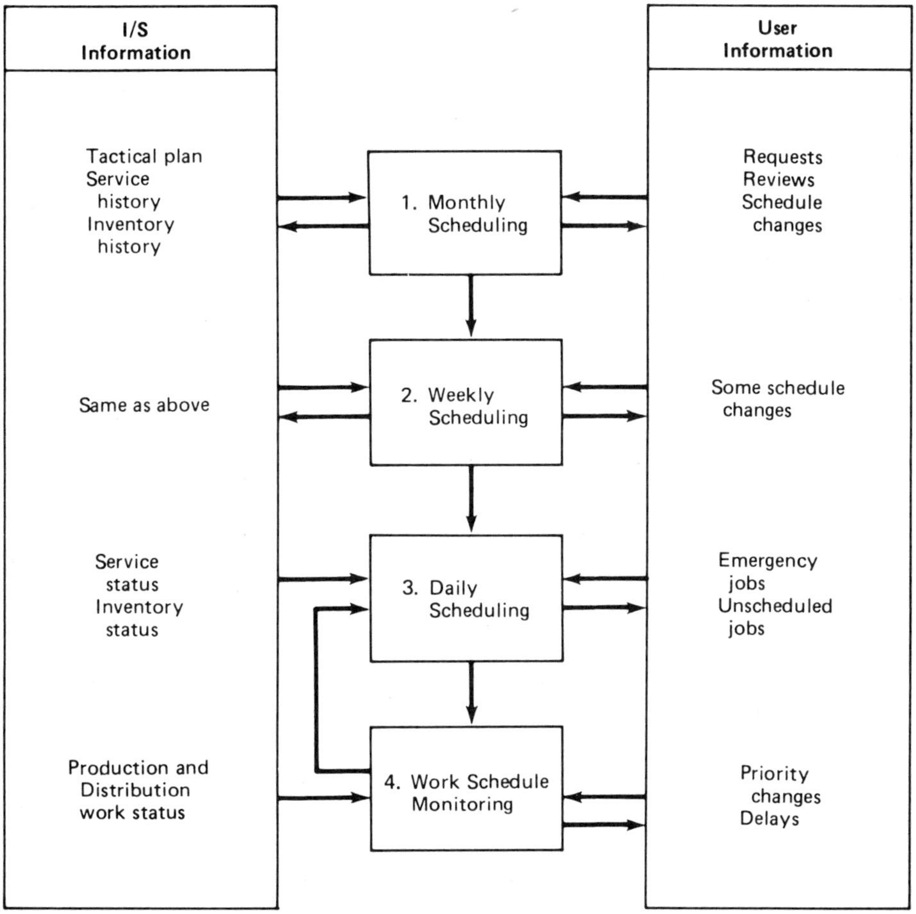

Figure 7–6 Information for production and distribution scheduling.

- *Daily scheduling.* Based on the weekly work schedule, a daily work schedule is prepared one day in advance. The documentation and methodology are the same as that described above for the weekly scheduling cycle. However, additional factors can now be considered, such as the status of previously scheduled jobs (for example, delays that have occurred and reruns needed), operators absent due to sickness, emergency jobs, changed priorities, and last-minute changes in deadlines.

  This daily work schedule does not deal directly with in-process work or work awaiting processing by the system. That type of scheduling is handled by the Production and Distribution process. In most cases, the scheduling of these real jobs, transactions, and data is automatically controlled by the operating system, transaction processor, or other system code. The work schedule is represented to these schedulers by transaction priorities, job classes, and other interfaces with operator control.

- *Work schedule monitoring.* To ensure that the proper level of service is being provided to the users and that the available resources are used efficiently, the actual status of the work in process or waiting must be continuously monitored and posted to the daily work schedule.

  In the event of severe discrepancies between planned and actual schedules, action must be taken to bring the work back on schedule, if at all possible. Any departures from schedule that will jeopardize agreed delivery deadlines must be reported immediately to the affected users. Moreover, delays and reruns that will affect the next day's work schedule must be promptly reported back to production management.

  Other events that also call for a close monitoring of actual work flow are sudden changes in the availability of resources (equipment and personnel) and sudden changes in workload due to unanticipated peaks caused by unscheduled jobs.

As work is processed, relevant operating data should be recorded and passed to Resource and Data Performance Control for analysis. Such analysis serves mainly two purposes:

1. To evaluate adherence to performance objectives. Evaluations should be made on an overall basis covering the total operation activity and, if deemed necessary, on a detail level (for example, by individual user, or by individual workstation and shift).
2. To review utilization summaries for future planning and decision making. Items of interest here are trends (in workload, for instance) over relatively long periods of time that can be used for future planning work. Such information is of great value as input to the yearly tactical plan.

The remainder of this section will explore the operational data which must be added to the service agreements negotiated in the Service-Level Planning process.

Examples of operational data relevant to the original service agreement are:

- General

  Contact points in user and operations departments

  How and when normal contacts should be made

  Daily and weekly schedule variations (particularly in recurring production runs)

  Daily and weekly volume variations (such as number of transactions and expected normal fluctuations)

- User responsibilities

  Latest job arrival times and dates in order to meet agreed delivery deadlines

Advance notification required (if any)
How input data is delivered and identified
Documentation to be provided (mainly run-book material)

- Operations responsibilities
  Job delivery times and dates
  How and when users are notified in case of delays
  How output material is delivered

Develop a maintenance and measurement schedule

While the individual user of computing resources is mainly interested in getting good service as defined by the service agreement, operations management has to make sure that the resources of the computing center are being used economically. Improved service can almost always be obtained by adding more resources, but this always means higher cost and may also mean poorer utilization of resources.

A meaurement schedule must ensure that both service and utilization of resource data will be captured during the execution of work.

- *Service measurements.* All other performance criteria being fixed, the fundamental objective of operations management must be to process as much work through the center as possible. Workload is often measured in terms of job throughput, that is, the average number of jobs processed in the center. However, this measure is not a very precise one, since different jobs generate different amounts of work for the operations function. Also, the jobs may not reflect the true service commitments.

  Today, detailed performance data about jobs and/or transactions can be logged to provide workload analysis. Much of this recording is automatic and does not require special scheduling. However, some recordings can consume a significant share of resources for the logging and should be scheduled. In all cases, the data must be related to the user service commitments.
- *Resource measurements.* I/S is interested in how the resources are being used, and the extent to which they are used. To the extent possible, the service workload measurements should identify the resources consumed by the work. Automated resource measurement facilities should be scheduled to provide both forms of data.

A maintenance schedule, whether it is preventive or concurrent, must consider the service workload impact while the various testing and repair functions are being performed. For example, a disk control unit might be varied off the main system during this maintenance work. The maintenance schedule should define when this work can be done and evaluate any impact on scheduled work. The disk maintenance work could not be done if the disk unit was critical to some on-line application. As stated earlier, predictive maintenance performed during normal shifts lessens the need for standalone time for diagnostics, service, and testing.

Develop current work schedule

It is the task of operations management to strike a balance between the user-oriented performance objectives and the operations-oriented performance objectives. This can only be done by considering the two sets of objectives, not separately, but in conjunction with each other. One way to do this is to treat the user-oriented performance objectives as constraints on the operations-oriented ones.

The scheduling of the work to be processed by the operations function is such a complex task that almost every I/S organization would be well advised to set up formal methods and procedures for handling it. Obviously, many different methods can be used. The methods selected will vary depending on the needs of the particular installation, which, in turn, depend on installation size and the complexity of the workload to be processed. Scheduling an installation where a few, daily, recurring applications dominate the workload is very different from scheduling an installation with a large number of applications, large fluctuations in volume from one run to another, and many unscheduled jobs interspersed between the scheduled, recurring jobs. Scheduling can be totally manual, or it can be partly or fully automated.

A monthly automated schedule showing which applications I/S will process for each user by date is illustrated in Figure 7–7. Each application is listed with the required operations steps and predecessor and successor applications. These dependent applications also list the operations steps and deadlines.

This monthly schedule is expanded into the daily work schedule (Fig. 7–8). Each operations step is scheduled with the following information:

- Input arrival time
- Application identification
- Output deadline time
- Priority (range 1–9)
- Difference (deadline time minus arrival time)
- Owner identification

Your Company
Data Center
Operations Planning

Long Term Plan for 5/2/xx

Occurrence with dependencies				Dependent occurrence (pred. or succ.)					
Appl ID	Input hour	Owner	OP ID	Type	Appl ID	Input	Arr	OP ID	Reason
Jobx	13.00	Smith	CPU1 15	Pred	JOBABCD	xx0425	13.00	CPU1 15	
			RECP 10	Pred	JOBXYZ	xx0430	17.00	RECP 60	Manual entered
			CPU1 15	Succ	JOBABCD	xx0509	13.00	CPU1 15	Weekly runs

Figure 7–7 Monthly production schedule.

Your Company
Data Center
Operations Planning

Daily Operating Plan 5/2/xx-5/3/xx

Appl ID/ OP ID	Priority	Arr/ start	Dur	Defined deadline	Jobname	Appl text Oper text	Owner ID	Predecessor appl ID-OP ID
ICDAY	5	09.00		10.30		Inventory	Buck	
REC 05		09.00	00.05			Cards		
PRP 10		09.15	00.15			Set parms		REC 05
CPU 15		09.40	00.05	09.50	ICJOB1	Update		PRP 10
PRT 20		09.55	00.20	10.35	ICJOB1	Print		CPU 15
HKPDAY	6	07.00		08.00		Housekeep	Thomas	
PRP 10		07.03	00.15			Set parms		
CPU 15		07.28	00.05		HKJOB1	Update		PRP 10
								HKPNGT: CPU 25
PRT 20		07.43	00.10	07.55	HKJOB1	Print		CPU 15

Figure 7–8 Daily production schedule.

- Miscellaneous comments
- Dependency

Regardless of the degree of sophistication of the installation, however, there are four general points to remember:

1. Many managers feel that I/S operations are so unique, and the problems encountered so unusual, that standard production management techniques do not apply at all. This is not true. Despite the indisputable uniqueness in many cases, basic principles of manufacturing job shop production management can be applied directly or with minor modifications to any computing center.
2. In the past, installations using formal methods for scheduling have concentrated on only computer processing. However, computer processing is only one part of the service that operations provides to its users. There is also a preprocessing stage (for example, data input) and a postprocessing stage (for example, bursting). The users see and measure the total service given.

   Consequently, the total flow of work through the entire operations function, from receipt of input to delivery of output, should be scheduled and monitored. While the computer equipment may be the major resource in the computing center, and therefore always a potential trouble spot, many of the problems with level of service are often found in the other workstations that the jobs pass through.
3. The scheduling exercise should address the effective use of personnel. With the personnel costs of many installations approaching 60 to 75% of the I/S budget, the productivity of the service mission has become a major issue. One concept, an operatorless machine room, is being advocated as a means to control these

costs. At a minimum, the scheduling should address the overtime which might be needed to handle the workload and give the users the agreed-upon service.

4. The most important operations-oriented performance criterion for the computing center is probably the cost of the service it provides to the users. Inefficient operations lead to higher costs in the operations function. However, it is not enough just to measure overall costs for the operations department, or even costs of individual workstations, largely because it is impossible to determine how these costs relate to the large variety of services rendered.

   To schedule services accurately, cost must be determined by the type of operation for each service. This includes the unit cost of labor, data that is highly relevant to the concept of standard costs and to the user-oriented accounting units. These costs should be considered during the development of the schedule.

Negotiate any deviations from the service agreement

Once the daily schedule is prepared, it is possible that I/S and/or the user may require a short-term deviation from the agreement. For example, the user may have committed to having input available by 9 A.M. each morning. An unexpected flu outbreak could make that impossible and the user might request a temporary adjustment to the schedule. On an exception basis, the scheduling function should accommodate the request.

However, a regular slippage of deadlines could indicate understaffing to the extent that the agreement is not viable. In that case, renegotiation is called for, rather than continual slippage.

Publish work, maintenance, and measurement schedules

With the use of data bases, the work schedule can be put on-line for operations and user access. For example, a remote workstation operator could use a display to examine pending work and the required times (Fig. 7–9). Using this list, the operator could process each item in the proper sequence. In addition, the workstation operator could report work completion by entering the data into the same display.

Ready List for Work Station: CPU #				Primary 09.45.00		
	Appl ID	Operation text	Due out	Jobname	Duration	PRTY
01	A123	Set parms	21.09.55	A123JOB	00.20	5
02	B456	Input from DE	21.10.00	B456JOB	00.10	6
03	ZZZ	Prod plan	21.10.00	ZZZ1	00.15	4
04	XXX	Inventory	21.10.15	XXX1	00.13	4
05	YYY	Catalog	21.10.28	Y1234	00.08	4

Figure 7–9 Work station ready list example.

Monitor and modify schedule (if necessary)

Once the schedule has been approved, the actual delivery is performed by the Production and Distribution process. Status information about work in-process provides feedback to the Production and Distribution Scheduling process to:

- Maintain a level workload across resources by changing priorities, deactivating initiators, transferring jobs from one installation to another, and other rescheduling methods
- Reschedule resources for short-term maintenance or other corrective actions

This feedback can be automated by having the operating system post work completion directly to the schedule data base. It other cases, the feedback can occur by having operators enter on-line information into the data base.

Production and distribution scheduling summary

In general, the schedule and the measurement of the performance against that schedule are activities requiring constant attention. This is especially true as the users and computers become increasingly separated from each other across multiple locations, for example, data entry in one location and computer processing in another.

The next three processes, Resource and Data Performance Control, Problem Control, and Service Evaluating, provide measurement and control against this schedule.

Resource and Data Performance Control

DEFINITION:

Using the measurement schedule and criteria, this process quantifies, measures, and reports system performance levels to I/S management and the Service Evaluating process. It also triggers performance adjustment activities or performance problem activities.

DESCRIPTION:

The elements of Performance Control are:

1. Measure performance.
2. Analyze trends, deviations, and thresholds.
3. Select predefined corrective actions based on the work and measurement schedule (if necessary).
4. Notify Problem Control of any problem situations that cannot be corrected.
5. Report system, application, and data performance status.

DATA CLASSES REQUIRED:

Data input to process (data class)	Data output of process (data class)
P9 Capacity plan	C4 Problem
C6 System performance	C6 System performance
C7 Production/distribution schedule	C7 Production/distribution schedule
C10 Production/distribution log	T1 Inventory logs
R1 Application	
R2 Data	
R3 Software	
R4 Hardware	
R5 Network	
R6 Facilities	
R7 Supplies	
R10 Standards/procedures/methods	
R11 Test data	

Measure performance

In the discussion on the Production and Distribution Scheduling process, the need for both service workload and resource performance measurements became apparent. While the Resource and Data Performance Control process is primarily interested in the consumption of resources, it must capture the data required to relate that consumption to the services being provided. Those measurements will be used by the Service Evaluating process to be discussed later.

Performance of two critical resources, applications and data, raises unique issues that should be considered. Often, responsibility for data base performance is assigned to a data base administrator in the development organization and the performance of applications remains with the original analyst, programmer, or user. The Resource and Data Performance Control process deals with the performance of all service resources, including applications and data, regardless of the organizational responsibility.

With a system inventory of several hundred thousand items, the initial measurement decision must be where and when to capture the data. Each question can be answered separately.

- Where to monitor the system is the ultimate responsibility of the development mission. As the hardware, software, applications, data, facilities, and procedures are developed, the resource performance attribute must be a major consideration. Each designer must determine where the critical performance data will be captured and how it will measure the anticipated results. Three different approaches could be considered.

1. For example, one on-line transaction processor has a special monitoring tool available to analyze performance. Data about transactions, storage, data files, and so on, is recorded on log files at the option of the installation. These log files can be analyzed to evaluate performance.
2. For the overall system resources, recording points are built into the operating systems and hardware to provide more global data about the system environment. One operating system has separate recording facilities to provide data about job start time, job end time, central processor time used, paging, I/O requests performed, and other system measurements. This data can be reduced to provide the performance information.
3. Another option available for measurement is a probe provided with some form of an external hardware monitoring device to capture and reduce data about the system and its components. This approach has the advantage of not altering the system performance with the measurement tool.

A typical installation will use various combinations of all three of these approaches.

- When to measure is the responsibility of the service mission. An overall measurement schedule is developed in the Production and Distribution Scheduling process. This schedule can address the more general questions such as:

  When do operators switch log files?

  When are special recording means to be started and stopped?

  Who receives the recorded data, and when?

  When is the data to be analyzed and reported?

  During the actual performance monitoring, decisions must be made on the type and quantity of data. Operator functions are generally available to select the desired recordings. In some cases, this static recording and analysis is unsatisfactory to truly measure the service being delivered. For example, an online user with poor response needs immediate assistance to resolve the performance problem.

  One approach available is to have the measurement mechanism constantly compare the recordings against some planned threshold. Any abnormal deviations would signal a performance situation requiring immediate attention and analysis.

Analyze trends, deviations, and thresholds

The volume of data produced in performance monitoring can be extensive, requiring a computer for data reduction and analysis. The threshold concept discussed earlier is one means of isolating the specific data which must be analyzed. In all other situations, the data reduction and analysis should include:

- Combining multiple recording points into some meaningful grouping
- Assimilating the chronological performance record into useful events or incident situations
- Comparing the results against defined standards or objectives
- Defining actions which could be taken
- Informing management on these actions

With a large volume of data, the isolation of good and bad situations is extremely difficult. The performance analyst must have the measurement standards for the critical success factors defined long before starting this analysis. Therefore, this individual needs to understand the service agreements and the scheduling process. In developing the measurement schedule, it is important to review the service history and specify performance monitoring criteria. Therefore, the performance analysis attempts to answer questions that have already been asked.

With these selected criteria, the real-time measurement and analysis becomes a special case where the question is stored in the computer and monitored as a threshold. The ultimate objective of performance control is:

- To reduce the situations where the end user is the first to notice a performance degradation of the on-line system
- To ensure that resources are being used as planned
- To track and report the consumption of resources

Select predefined corrective actions

Once the performance has begun to deviate from expected conditions, a number of procedure-oriented actions are available to return performance to the desired levels. These include:

- Disabling a communication line if the load is too heavy
- Expanding the storage available to a buffer pool
- Increasing the processing regions for on-line transactions
- Changing the priorities of system resources

In some cases, these procedures can be automatically built into the operating system to tune the service request dynamically. In all cases, operational management should be notified of the deviation and the corrective action taken.

Notify problem control of any uncorrectable situations

If the problem persists or indicates a trend, the Problem Control process should be notified. Situations will sometimes arise that indicate performance problems in the system. Performance recording for short durations of time may be required to obtain sufficient data for analysis. On the other hand, overuse of performance monitoring can consume resources and produce excessive data.

Report system, application, and data performance status

The Service Evaluating process uses this data to produce reports on the service attainment measured against the original plan. These service reports must be backed with other reports designed for the measurement of factors related to the I/S operation.

For example, the load on the critical host processor resource can be shown graphically; see Figure 7–10. Examination of the 24-hour period shows loading in the prime time from 70 to 80% and a period from 0:00 to 8:00 hours in which the system was not used. A check of the production schedule would substantiate whether or not this period was unscheduled or no work was available. This report simply

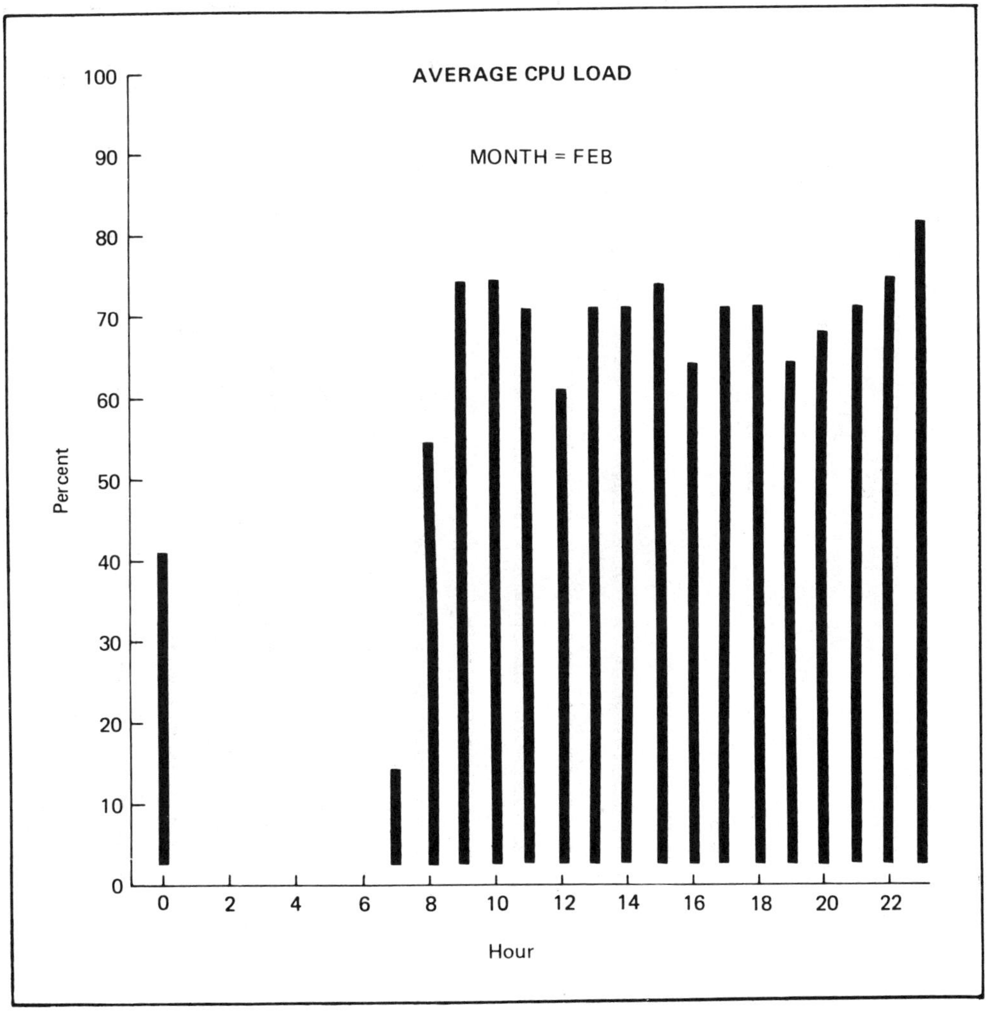

Figure 7–10 Example of daily host processor load.

measures the total consumption and does not reflect the impact on single subsystems like the demand-driven on-line transaction processor. Similar graphs could be produced detailing the subsystem resource consumption.

Another approach to illustrating the subsystem load is shown in Figure 7-11. This graph shows the fluctuation in transactions for the subsystem throughout the day, thus reflecting the change in load. It is clear that the service load between 13:00

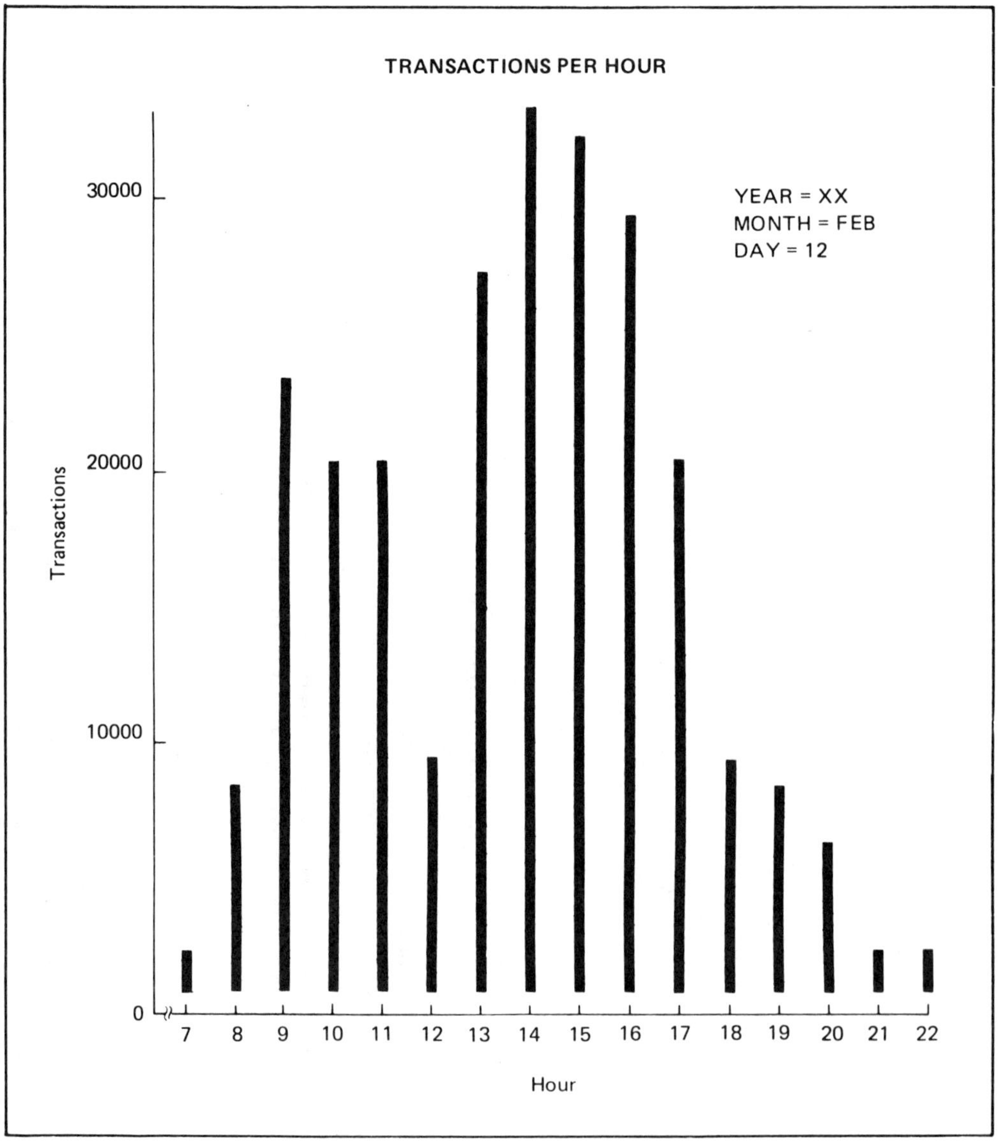

Figure 7-11 Example of daily transaction rate.

and 16:00 hours needs to be monitored to prevent user unhappiness. A corresponding response time is measured at the host processor. Figure 7–12 illustrates the inability of the system to absorb the high transaction rate, causing the response time to ex-

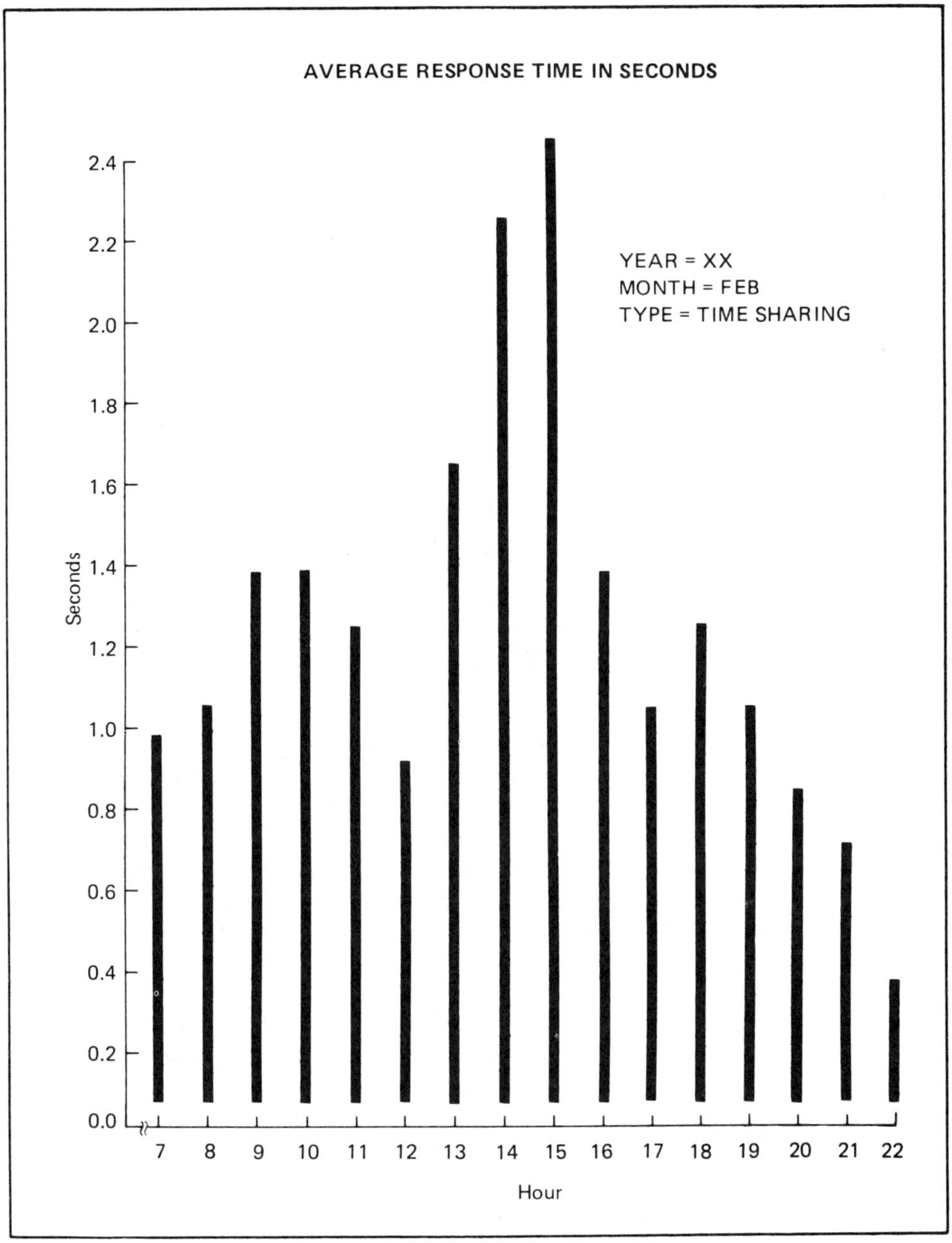

Figure 7–12 Example of daily response time.

ceed 2.4 seconds. If this situation was expected and planned as part of the service-level negotiation, the situation only needs tracking. However, unexpected occurrences of this situation would need management action.

The time-sharing service workload over the same 24-hour period is shown in Figure 7–13. The peak load at 16:00 hours reflects a high host processor and I/O load on the system. Again, response times and user reaction to the service would be required to determine if this is an unsatisfactory situation.

Hour	No trans	Avg CPU sec	Total I/O (no. excp)	Total term I/O	Host hours
7	511	1.89	2755	1167	0.01
8	1209	2.15	6479	2985	0.02
9	735	2.41	3843	1504	0.01
10	2622	2.26	16108	7640	0.04
11	591	2.48	6214	1610	0.01
12	252	1.06	2316	715	0.00
13	667	0.82	5549	2155	0.01
14	973	2.42	5623	2486	0.02
15	2275	3.80	12173	6117	0.04
16	3502	7.67	24577	9775	0.10
17	1618	6.13	11318	3855	0.02
18	829	4.56	10172	2699	0.04
19	346	1.53	4278	927	0.01
20	1023	5.80	13534	2698	0.02
21	1187	3.93	13570	3722	0.02
TOT	18340	3.19	138509	50055	0.38

Figure 7–13 Example of daily time sharing load.

The purpose of monthly summary reports is to develop meaningful pictures of the trends in actual resource usage; these then form a basis for early anticipation of future needs. Early detection of such needs is essential, primarily because of the delivery lead times required by hardware vendors and the installation planning lead time needed in the I/S department itself.

Utilization of equipment resources is measured by three principal variables: (1) overall system utilization, (2) utilization of individual units of equipment, and (3) auxiliary storage space utilization. These reports include:

- *Overall system utilization.* A major problem of reporting is to find a composite measure that adequately describes the overall system utilization, and for which a reliable upper capacity limit can be established. Unfortunately, such a measure depends heavily on the installation. In practice, however, it is often found that overall system utilization is closely related to a simple measure, such as total processing unit usage or total number of lines printed.

  One approach is shown in Figure 7–14, in which the monthly load is examined from the point of view of users of service and the heaviest service demands. Internal application development was one of the largest users, consuming 258.6 host processor minutes of time. The program named Information Management System (IMS) was the heaviest overall consuming function with 1794.2 minutes of host processor time. Using these reports, the service planner can define the future levels of each service and the capacity that will be needed.

- *Utilization of individual units of equipment.* Utilization of individual units of equipment is a measure of the time spent by the various items of computing equipment in performing work. For example, identification of an overly utilized disk drive could allow the data to be spread across multiple units for improved performance.

  However, it is not normally practical to account for each hardware unit separately. They should be grouped by type of device, showing, for example, total and average usage of all printers, all direct-access units of the same type, and all terminals of the same type. In the latter case it may even be useful to separate terminal utilization by type of use, showing, for example, terminals used in interactive programming in one group, terminals used for on-line order entry system in another group, and so on.

  In addition, similar measures should be produced for important noncomputer equipment, such as off-line data entry devices and bursting units, in fact, for all workstations through which the work of the operations activity flows.

Month = Feb.

Service	Tot_CPU min	Lost_CPU min	Lost_CPU %	Avg_CPU min
Appl dev	258.6	7.8	3.0	0.95
Engineer	224.8	8.3	3.7	1.05
Prod run	191.6	33.3	17.5	1.19
Purchase	113.6	15.7	13.8	0.76
Staff	78.4	25.2	32.1	0.07
Custinfo	20.3	0.0	0.0	0.75

Total number of jobs run

Year = XX Month = Feb.

Pgmname	Tot_CPU mins	Nsteps	Avg_CPU mins	Nabend	Lost_CPU %
IMS	1794.2	16335	0.11	553	9.4
APPLX	266.8	645	0.41	5	0.2
APPLY	261.8	363	0.72	67	28.0
FAN3	203.4	698	0.29	15	5.6
PAYROLL	139.1	669	0.21	12	2.1
IEBCOPY	71.5	633	0.11	27	3.3
IEWL	70.0	616	0.11	15	3.3
SWITCH	54.5	427	0.13	60	24.7
AX357S	47.0	418	0.11	25	5.0
AY945	44.7	430	0.10	2	0.0
IEBGENER	35.1	1567	0.02	47	3.5
SHOUT	30.3	1454	0.02	6	1.1

Most CPU consuming programs in prime shift

Figure 7–14 Example of program load.

- *Auxiliary storage space utilization.* Utilization of auxiliary storage media measures the average utilization of disk packs and tape reels. For disk packs it may be necessary to account separately for packs that are always on-line, because when these approach full utilization, it may become necessary to install additional disk drives.

Resource and data performance control summary

It was stated earlier that effective and efficient use of resources should be one of the major objectives of operational management. The Resource and Data Performance Control process provides the management control necessary to achieve that objective.

Problem Control

DEFINITION:

This process receives problems (including performance problems) and monitors their resolution by requesting bypass actions and/or projects (maintenance or tuning). It informs the Service Evaluating process of the service impact of the problems.

DESCRIPTION:

The elements of Problem Control are:

1. Recognize the problem.
2. Report/log the problem.
3. Determine the nature, impact, and true extent of the problem.
4. Select predefined bypass and recovery procedures.
5. Initiate action to resolve the problem.
6. Report and control the status of all problems in hand.

DATA CLASSES REQUIRED:

Data input to process (data class)	Data output of process (data class)
C2 Project	C4 Problem
C3 Change	
C4 Problem	
C7 System performance	
A2 Customer/user/group	
R1 Application	

Data input to process (data class)	Data output of process (data class)
R2 Data	
R3 Software	
R4 Hardware	
R5 Network	
R6 Facilities	
R7 Supplies	
R8 Personnel	
R10 Standards/procedures/methods	
R11 Test data	

Recognize problem

The word *problem* is used in the following sense: In some way, a system does not behave as people affected by it (users, operators, and so on) want it to behave. We know from our experience that problems in this sense occur continually. Run procedures and human intervention to determine and eliminate problems with hardware, operating systems, and application systems are a normal way of life. We also know that the increasing use of larger and more complex systems potentially results in a greater number of problems. Futhermore, many of these problems have a more severe impact on business and on the use of systems than ever before, and they are also in many cases much more difficult to solve.

PROBLEMS INCLUDE:

- Deviations from standards or expectations (whether documented or informal expectations)
- Incidents
- Malfunctions
- Unusual or unexplained occurrences
- Unscheduled IPLs
- Degradations
- Intermittent problems/conditions
- Abnormal situations
- Incomplete or unavailable functions
- Incorrect transaction or program results

AREAS OF PROBLEMS:

- Network
- Hardware and software
- Facilities (power, cooling, for example)

- Applications and data
- Procedures
- Personnel related to the other problem areas

Change is the primary generator of problems; in turn, problem resolution is one of several causes of change. Just as problems and problem solving are part of everyday life in I/S, so are the need for changes and the implementation of changes. All computer installations make changes to their systems; some make these changes very frequently. Essentially, Problem Control must anticipate and react to two sets of underlying reasons for these changes.

First, a need for change occurs because user requirements have changed. This might happen when growth in volume necessitates installation of new or additional hardware, or when a demand for new functional capabilities results in a new application system being put into production. Second, a need for change occurs as a means to correct a detected problem, which is, for example, the case when changes are applied to an operating system in order to improve terminal response times, or when an application program module is modified to correct a detected program error.

Thus, problems cause changes, but changes also cause problems. As a matter of fact, most problems are caused by previous changes. Consequently, there exists an inherent relationship between problems and changes. A problem that lingers, or which leads to a crisis, is expensive and it means dissatisfied users. A change that gives rise to problems is also expensive. Problems and changes cannot be completely eliminated. At best, what one can hope for is that they can be brought under control and handled in an orderly manner. Some installations manage to make changes to resources (equipment, systems, applications) and still keep their users happy. Others seem to live in a permanent mode of crisis.

What accounts for the difference? The answer is not simple. But one part of it, a part often overlooked, is the way in which the problems and changes are handled. The rest of this chapter outlines an approach to the orderly processing of problems and to diminishing their impact on business.

Report and log problem

The first point at which time can be lost or a crisis develop is the point when a problem is first detected. It is, therefore, important that a problem be reported, with all relevant details, as soon as possible after it is detected. Anyone who encounters a problem is responsible for identifying that a problem exists, documenting it as fully as possible, and forwarding the problem description, including supporting data, for problem resolution.

This is especially true of users of terminal systems. Such a user, faced with a problem, may not have any idea what to report, to whom, or how. This development has not created a new need, only given fresh emphasis to what has always been true: Anyone with a computer problem, from the newest terminal user to the most experienced programmer or computer operator, needs a clear and accessible reporting procedure. Some of the properties of such a procedure are:

- A well-designed problem reporting document or on-line screen. In any advanced I/S business, an on-line application to report problems is a necessity. A sample screen for that application shows the data that the original problem reporter and subsequent problem solvers could enter (Fig. 7–15).

  In the earlier phases of growth, a manual document is often used to report problems (Fig. 7–16). Similar data is provided.
- Clear instructions as to what information is needed and what supporting documentation is desirable.
- Only one reporting point. The problem reporter should never be forced to diagnose the problem (is it a hardware or a software fault?) before the report can be made.

It is important to realize that the majority of user problems arise from unclear procedures or lack of understanding about the system complex. A user help desk has been used successfully by many installations to serve this customer service function. Personnel with good communication skills and overall knowledge staff the help desk during hours when the critical services are to be available. With this help, the user can normally solve the minor problems and properly document the more difficult ones.

Backing up this help function is a full- or part-time problem coordinator. When the incident (problem) has been documented, the problem has to be followed through to its solution. Thus, the role of the problem coordinator is to ensure that problems

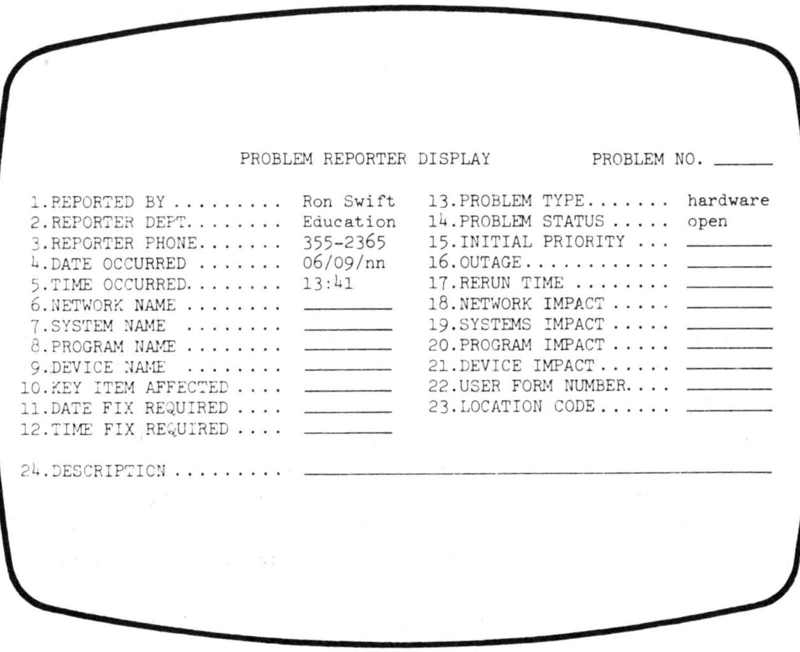
PROBLEM REPORTER DISPLAY PROBLEM NO. ______

1.REPORTED BY	Ron Swift	13.PROBLEM TYPE.......	hardware
2.REPORTER DEPT........	Education	14.PROBLEM STATUS	open
3.REPORTER PHONE.......	355-2365	15.INITIAL PRIORITY ...	______
4.DATE OCCURRED	06/09/nn	16.OUTAGE............	______
5.TIME OCCURRED........	13:41	17.RERUN TIME	______
6.NETWORK NAME	______	18.NETWORK IMPACT	______
7.SYSTEM NAME	______	19.SYSTEMS IMPACT	______
8.PROGRAM NAME	______	20.PROGRAM IMPACT	______
9.DEVICE NAME	______	21.DEVICE IMPACT	______
10.KEY ITEM AFFECTED	______	22.USER FORM NUMBER....	______
11.DATE FIX REQUIRED	______	23.LOCATION CODE......	______
12.TIME FIX REQUIRED	______		

24.DESCRIPTION .... ________________________

Figure 7–15 On-line problem screen.

Reporting Section: Completed By: ____________
Reported By:
Name: ____________ Location: ____________ Phone: ____________
Date: ____________ Time: ____ : ____
Area: ____________ User ID: ____________
Job No.: ____________ Network Name: ____________
System ID: ____________ Terminal Type: ____________
System/User Impact: ____________
Description of Problem: ____________

Problem Determination Section: Completed By: ____________
Problem Area:
___ Hardware ___ System Software Application Name: ____________
___ Environment ___ Procedure Other ____________
Describe Supporting Documentation (must be attached)

Failing Component: ____________ Responsible Resolver: ____________

Coordinator Section: Completed By: ____________
Problem Already Reported: Yes/No Report #: ______ Priority: ______
Assigned To:
Dept/Name: ____________ Date: ____________ Priority: ____________
Status: ________ Start Time: ______ : ______ Completed ___/___/___ ___:___
Dept/Name: ____________ Date: ____________ Priority: ____________
Status: ________ Start Time: ______ : ______ Completed ___/___/___ ___:___
Bypass Action Taken: ____________

Description of Resolution: ____________

Change Request No.: ____________ Date: ____________ Time: ____________
Approved Date/Time: ___/___/___ ___:___
Completed Date: ___/___/___ Time: ___:___
Total Outage (HH:MM): ___:___

Figure 7–16 Sample problem reporting form.

are funneled to the right person for resolution, to monitor the status of outstanding problems, and to enforce priorities and schedules of problem resolution.

The problem coordinator is key to the success of solving problems. The establishment of this function, its placement within the organization, and the influence it has are subjects that should be carefully considered before the function is created.

Following the problem systematically is largely a matter of communication: communication between reporters, other users potentially affected, problem solvers. Here, there is plenty of scope for misunderstanding and delay, such as:

- Is the real problem described in the problem report?
- How severe is the problem? Is it holding up a project? Or, even worse, is it affecting regular business activities of the company?

- Has a similar problem been reported before? Perhaps a bypass is already available.
- What is the deadline for problem resolution?
- Who is the right person to solve the problem?
- How much time is needed?
- Is there a major discrepancy between time to solve and the required deadline? If so, should management be involved?

If the problem coordinator is actually setting priorities and assigning problems to problem solvers, rather than just doing the clerical work of documentation gathering and logging, then a professionally qualified person is needed in this position. The position should be filled by someone able to relate to other people's problems, a self-starter who can and does follow up when necessary, a person who communicates well with technicians, users, and outside consultants. It would be ideal for the problem coordinator to have a broad I/S background in order to understand the sequence of events needed for effective problem handling.

The maintenance of a problem log is essential. Such a log should contain information which describes the problem, gives the source and priority, and tells the status. Several key points are:

- As the status changes, the entry in the problem log should be updated. For high priority problems, the status should be monitored daily, for example, through critical situation meetings with concerned parties. For problems with lesser priorities, less frequent updates are sufficient, and these can be done during periodic, perhaps weekly, meetings with problem solvers. The actual frequency of meetings will depend on the level of activity, but they should be held at least twice weekly.
- Alert thresholds should be built into the log or record-keeping system to inform management of critical or recurring situations.
- A review of the system error statistics should be used to predict problems and make log entries.
- In all cases, the originator of the problem should be kept informed on the status and final resolution of the problem.

Determine the nature, impact, and true extent of the problem

Once the problem has been reported, the report must be analyzed for completeness, source of the problem, and resolution possibilities. Problem Determination can be defined at four levels and routed to the appropriate skill level based on the type of problem.

- *First Level* Problems in procedures, applications, or user terminal operations; usually recognized by end user of the system; usually short time to resolve, possibly even as problem is being described; handled by user interface or help desk personnel

- *Second level* Problems related to easily detectable broken system components (hardware, software, applications); resolution can be medium to long; handled by master terminal operator or system console operator
- *Third Level* Problems that cross multiple technical specializations or are intermittent and not easily isolated; resolution typically long; handled by system programmers and host or network technicians
- *Fourth Level* Problems that require management notification or involvement and reallocation of personnel due to critical nature of application or length of time that the problem has remained unsolved.

In all cases, the problem coordinator must ensure that the source is determined and resolution or bypass has started.

Select predefined bypass and recovery procedures

Many problems can be solved with procedural solutions such as re-IPL of the system, restart of a program, and equipment reconfiguration/switching. In most cases, the procedures required have been planned and approved in advance of the situation which has arisen and are executed in cooperation with the Production and Distribution processes. In unusual cases, emergency procedures may have to be generated to overcome the situation temporarily. These situations should be reviewed to establish more permanent procedures in case the cause or problem is repetitive.

Initiate action to resolve the problem

Problem solvers provide or obtain solutions to problems the fastest way possible. The solvers might be the system programmers, application programmers, technical support personnel (such as the data base administrator), or vendor personnel (hardware, software, communications).

Time can be gained and productivity improved for the problem solver in various ways. Several have already been mentioned: The problem coordinator sees to it that the solver gets only the right problems, not someone else's, and ensures that the information supplied is complete, accurate, and at the right level of detail. Getting the problem to the right person requires a predefined and clear division of responsibilities among potential problem solvers.

Few tools or procedures will actually solve a problem, or even tell how to do it. The human brain is unbeatable in that respect. However, much of the time of the problem solver is taken up by overhead: digging for background information, deciding whether this is really his or her problem, tracing possible causes, documenting progress, keeping an historical file, obtaining approval of the solution, and deciding when to install it. Valuable problem solving time can therefore be gained by designing good tools and procedures to help speed up this administrative work.

Since problems are often caused by changes, the solver, having isolated the fault to a particular element of the installation, needs to know what changes have recently been made to that element. With an adequate listing of the system resource inventory and the recent changes, the history leading to this incident can be traced. This change tracking was discussed in Chapter 6.

Report and control status of all problems

Management reporting of system incidents is complementary to the user service level reports. They should be used to monitor some of the underlying probable causes of operational inefficiencies, which ultimately lead to poor user service.

These reports provide management with factual information about the internal aspects of service delivery. Based on this information, the Management Planning processes could allocate resources to processes that can prevent or better appraise the causes of failures.

System incidents and change activities are measured by three factors: rerun time, system failures and unscheduled downtime, and status of reported problems. Reports are issued weekly or monthly depending on the level of management for which they are intended.

- Rerun time measures the total amount of rerun time and the reasons for reruns. Reported items include, for example, the total number of rerun hours, and individual rerun items expressed in hours and as a percentage by cause (such as incorrect or incomplete input material, improper run procedures or setup procedures, software or hardware problems, and operator mistakes).
- The category of system failures and unscheduled downtime measures the total number of system failures and the unscheduled downtime and gives the reason for the breakdowns. In addition, the number of failures and the downtime should be reported by individual hardware devices, such as processing units, printers, direct-access devices, magnetic tape units, terminals, and control units for peripherals. The performance of off-line equipment (data entry, bursting) is important to the productivity of the operations function and could also be included in the reports. A typical abend report is shown in Figure 7–17.
- Status of reported problems could, for example, include the number of problems outstanding at the beginning of the period, number of problems reported, number of problems solved, and the age and number of problems still outstanding. Reporting could be done by problem area, and by severity level with problems at the highest severity level described and listed individually, together with target dates for their solutions. A sample problem status report is shown in Figure 7–18.

One control technique available to the problem manager is Systems Outage Analysis (SOA). The SOA technique categorizes the cause of all outages over a period of time. The frequency of this analysis will depend on the stability of the system and

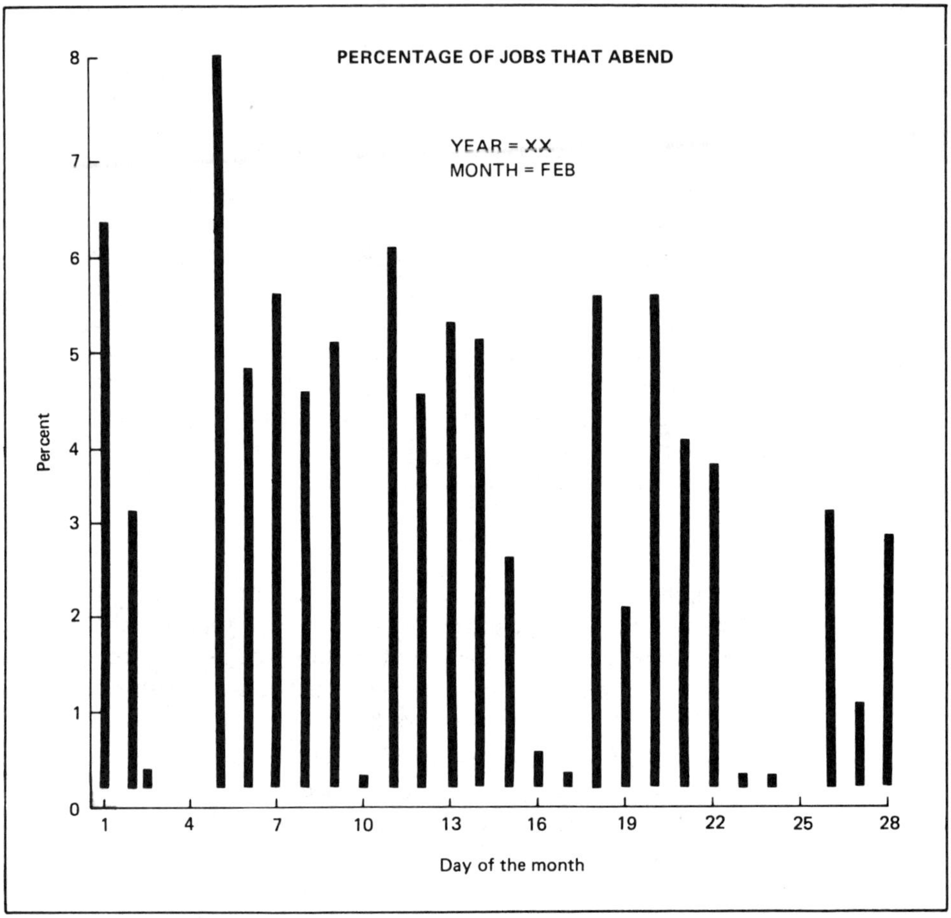

Figure 7-17 Abnormal end report.

Date: 05/14/xx Problem Management Calendar Report Page 001
Time: 11:08:15

Date occurred	Problem number	Component affected	Current status	Prty	Date entered	Assignee	Date assigned
01/23/xx	0000048	tso	closed	02	01/23/nn		
02/18/xx	0000065	cpu1	closed	01	02/18/nn		
02/26/xx	0000068	line1	closed	02	02/26/nn		
03/13/xx	0000094	modem1	closed	06	03/13/nn		
03/18/xx	0000101	display	closed	01	03/18/nn		
05/01/xx	0000135	display	closed	02	05/01/nn		
05/08/xx	0000138	line1	closed	06	05/08/nn		
05/11/xx	0000141	mvs	open	01	05/11/nn	sysprog	05/11/nn
05/12/xx	0000142	tcam	init	02	05/12/nn	psrjoe	05/12/nn

Figure 7-18 Status of problems report.

the effectiveness of Problem Control. This is done regularly to detect emerging, unfavorable problem trends and to focus management on correcting the situation.

The causes of systems outages include:

- Scheduled outages
    - Hardware: Preventive Maintenance
    - Hardware: Scheduled Maintenance
    - Software: Scheduled Maintenance
    - Other
- Unscheduled outages
    - Hardware failures
    - Software failures
    - Environmental problems
    - Unknown

The technique consists of plotting the systems outage hours and individual incidents over the analysis time period to understand the impact of the outages better (see Fig. 7–19 on page 208). Through careful analysis of each incident, the study team can verify that the problem was reported correctly and that correct recovery actions minimized the lost time. In many cases, a series of problems indicates a rapidly degrading system leading to eventual total systems outage and lost time. A good problem control implementation will recognize this situation and begin early correction. The SOA technique can measure the effectiveness of this correction and recommend improvement in the tracking and resolution of problems.

Problem control summary

The containment of problems is critical to the effective and efficient delivery of service. Any weaknesses in this control mechanism must be addressed early in the phases of growth.

Service Evaluating

DEFINITION:

Using performance status and data on the impact of problems, this process translates them into user terms and compares them with service agreements for the purpose of identifying and reporting any variances to users and management.

DESCRIPTION:

The elements of Service Evaluating are:

1. Translate operational data (production/distribution performance and problem) into service level terms.

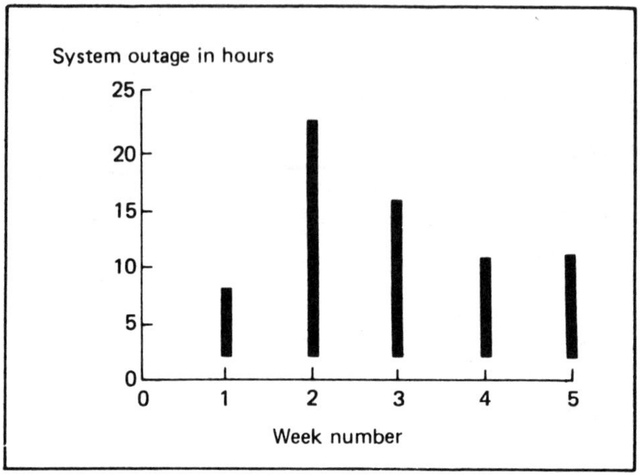

Key problem analysis

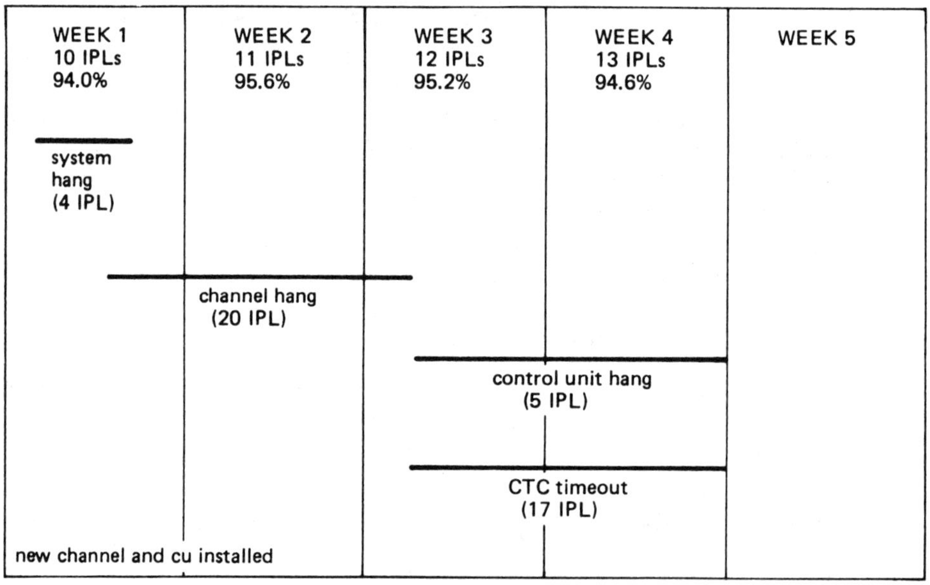

Figure 7–19 Systems outage analysis example.

2. Assess user rating of service.
3. Evaluate compliance with service agreements.
4. Identify and report reasons for variance.
5. Report service status and new service requests.

DATA CLASSES REQUIRED:

Data input to process (data class)	Data output of process (data class)
C1 Service	C1 Service
C4 Problem	T1 Inventory
C6 System performance	
C7 Production/distribution schedule	
A2 Customer/user/group	
R10 Standards/procedures/methods	

Translate operational data into service level terms

A service rating is one approach to the measurement of service agreements. If a service rating is defined as a single number to report the service level delivered, the results can be easily understood, tailored by service, and evolutionary according to experience. Figure 7–20 illustrates this service rating approach. All service offerings are reported with this rating.

Each time the service levels are negotiated, I/S and user management jointly agree on the measurement factors that produce the ratings for each offering. Two examples illustrate measurement factors that might be used.

In the first example (Fig. 7–21), the user management wanted to focus on the reliability of the service and user response time. The target service rating (7) measured by a 95 to 96.9% service reliability reflects an acceptable attainment of the objective. A service rating of 0 to 4 measured by a 84.9% or less service reliability indicates an unacceptable level of service. The remaining ratings are used to provide consistency from exceptionally good (10) to exceptionally bad (0) service.

Response-time characteristics are used as the second measurement factor in the service rating. To facilitate this measurement of service levels, transactions are placed in classes; the fastest response applications are class 2; the slowest are class 5.

For each transaction class, a range of response measurements must be established based on the user acceptability. Only the class 2 transactions are shown in Figure 7–21. With these spreads, a measured transaction response for that class can be converted into a rating of 0 to 10. In addition, a weighing factor must be established based on the relative importance of each class. The illustration uses a range of four for class 2 through a one for class 5. The overall response achieved is the sum of the each class rating multiplied by its weighing factor divided by the total weight factor (10).

This response factor is combined with the reliability factor based on user needs of 70% reliability and 30% response.

	Rating	Service
↑ Better than target	10	Excellent service
	9	Same
	8	Good service
Target	7	Acceptable (production schedules met)
Lower than target ↓	6	Functional (production impact, minor lates and inconvenience)
	5	Same
Target missed ↓	4	Unacceptable service (major impact)
	3	Same
	2	Same
	1	Same
	0	Same

Figure 7-20 Service rating targets.

In the second example (Fig. 7-22) the remote job entry (RJE) users are interested only in service reliability and the number of interrupts to the service. Separate factors are considered for prime shift and total period of availability. The RJE service is converted to a rating for each day's actual delivery of service.

The service rating is an excellent management reporting tool. It is understandable by all levels of management, flexible enough to be applied to all categories of service, and improves communication with senior management.

Assess user rating of service

To verify the objective measurements of service, key users can be asked for a more subjective rating. Selected users and user management are called daily and asked to report their perception of the quality of service. In a large installation, this is usually a statistical sample of the users. These subjective ratings ranging from 1 to 10 are listed in Figure 7-23 next to the objective measurements obtained in the two previous agreement examples.

The service attainment for each class of service is listed vertically with the days of each month listed horizontally. The results of the daily computer summarization

Agreement 1–On-line Services

Factor 1: Reliability of Committed Service Availability Measured at the Host

Reliability	Rating	Reliability	Rating
100%	10	78–84.9	4
99–99.9	9	69–77.9	3
97–98.9	8	59–68.9	2
95–96.9	7	50–58.9	1
91–94.9	6	less than 50	0
85–90.9	5		

Factor 2: Transaction Response Time

(Example for a class 2 transaction only)

Response Time (sec)	Rating	Response Time (sec)	Rating
under 2	10	7.0–7.9	4
2.1–2.9	9	8.0–8.9	3
3.0–3.9	8	9.0–9.9	2
4.0–4.9	7	10.0–10.1	1
5.0–5.9	6	over 10	0
6.0–6.9	5		

Weighing of transactions = class rating times weight factor

Class 2 – weight of 4
Class 3 – weight of 3
Class 4 – weight of 2
Class 5 – weight of 1

Total response rating = sum of weighted rating divided by total weight (10)

Overall Rating: 70% host reliability rating
30% total response rating

Figure 7-21 Example service rating 1.

Agreement 2 — Remote Job Entry			
	Factor	Measurement	Rating Points
Prime Shift	A. Reliability of committed availability (20%)	over 97%	4
		96–96.9	3
		95–95.9	2
		94–94.9	1
	B. Number of interrupts (40%)	0	8
		1	6
		2	4
		3	2
All Shifts	C. Reliability of committed availability (20%)	over 97%	4
		94–96.9	3
		91–93.9	2
	D. Number of interrupts (20%)	over 3	4
		4	3
		5	2
Overall Rating = A+B+C+D/2			

Figure 7–22 Example service rating 2.

are recorded in the column for the I/S rating. User calls for subjective measurements are recorded in the column designated as the user rating. The results of each day are added before the new version of the report is distributed.

Evaluate compliance with service agreements

By comparing the I/S objective measurements at the central processor with the user's subjective measurements at the terminal, I/S management is able to obtain information about how well they are meeting user needs.

Consider two examples in Figure 7–23. On the fourth day, the actual service attainment for the on-line service was only 5, compared with 10 for the previous two days. Management quickly corrected the situation and was back to a 9 level by the next reporting day. Both user and I/S were aware of the poor level.

On the seventeenth day, the user perceived that the service was only 3, whereas I/S measured a level of 10. It was apparent that something was wrong. In analyzing the situation, I/S management learned that the user had a high absentee rate on that day. This prevented the completion of the on-line data entry that was perceived by user management as bad service. Since this was not addressed in the original agreement, I/S negotiated a new agreement under which the data entry could be accomplished in an alternate manner when these unusual conditions occurred. Both I/S and the users were satisfied with the resolution.

SERVICE LEVEL RATING				
	ON-LINE SERVICE		REMOTE JOB ENTRY SERVICE	
DAY	USER RATING	I/S RATING	USER RATING	I/S RATING
1	9	9	9	10
2	10	10	10	10
3	10	10	7	9
→ 4	5	5	8	10
7	9	9	8	10
8	8	9	8	10
9	7	7	9	10
10	9	9	10	9
11	10	10	10	10
14	10	10	10	10
15	9	9	10	10
16	8	8	10	10
→ 17	3	10	10	10
18	8	7	10	10
nn				

Figure 7–23 Daily service level reporting.

Identify and report reasons for variance

Periodic reviews of performance data can determine whether the service as negotiated and forecasted actually meets the user's needs. This data allows a management review of the effectiveness of the service delivery. It is possible that the service needs to be renegotiated, the volumes reforecast, or the delivery mechanism improved.

Report service status and new service requests

In addition to reporting the status of individual services, this process should also report trends and new service requirements. One service trend over a longer period of time is shown in Figure 7–24.

Two important trends are shown in this illustration:

1. The overall rating has been improving over the three-year period and greatly exceeds the negotiated 7 level. After a period of time, the user will assume a

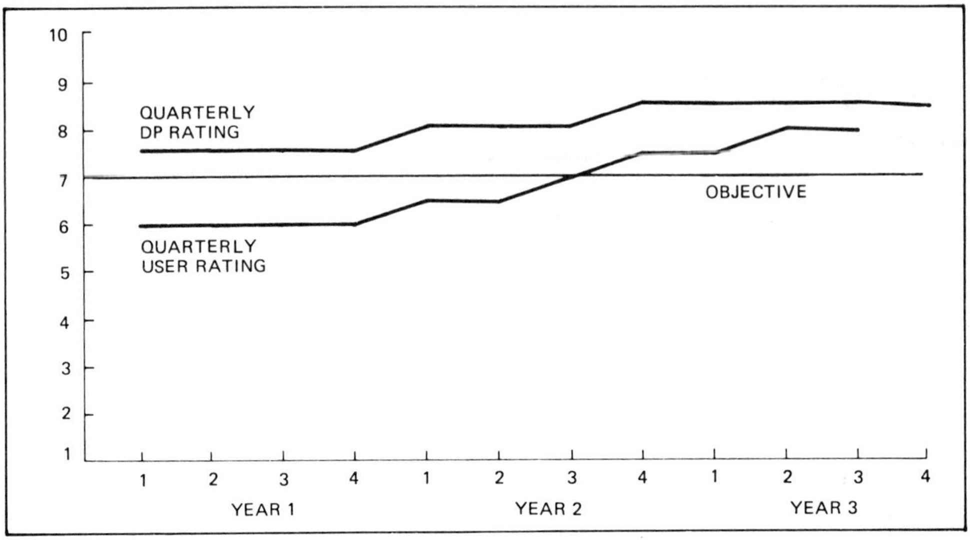

Figure 7–24 Service level trends.

normal level of 8 or above. If I/S management is prepared for future delivery at the 8 level, the situation is acceptable. However, management attention is required if new services will bring the normal back to the 7 level at some future date.

2. The user and I/S ratings are converging; this indicates a better understanding of the rating mechanism.

Service evaluating summary

Service agreements provide a practical way to plan, measure, and control the operation of an I/S installation. They are the foundation of a management system that delivers stable, acceptable service to users and provides the basis for improved communication between I/S and user management.

INFORMATION SERVICES

Information services process overview

Since many decisions have been made at the strategic, tactical, and operational planning levels, these processes tend to define activities or tasks required to accomplish those decisions. This group of processes executes required activities in order to deliver production, distribution, and supporting services.

The four processes and their key issues will be discussed in the following sequence (see Fig. 7–25):

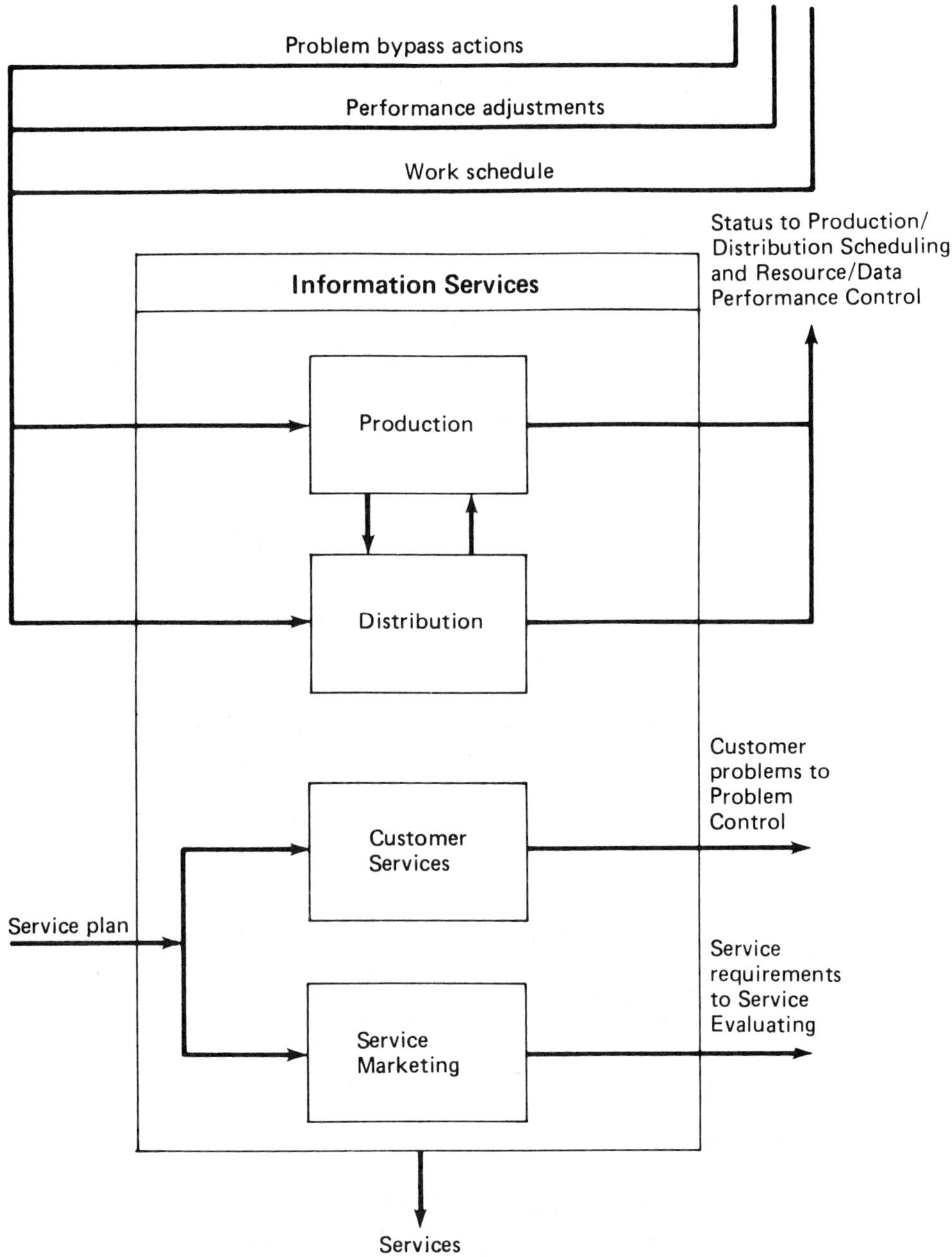

Figure 7–25 Information services process overview.

1. Production
    - What are the tasks required to deliver production services?
2. Distribution
    - What are the tasks required to deliver distribution services?
3. Customer Services
    - How does I/S support user interfaces to those services?
4. Service Marketing
    - Does I/S need to market those services to meet user needs effectively?

Also, these tasks are much more familiar to most readers than those previously discussed and will not require the same level of discussion. Therefore, each process will have only limited coverage.

Assessing information services

Questions which could be asked to measure the effectiveness and efficiency of the Information Services processes include:

- Are the instructions and information required for production jobs and network operations current and complete?
- Do the Production and Distribution processes report the status of work completed or in process?
- Is there a user help desk?
- Is there a clearly identified master terminal operator?
- Is a system inventory listing available for operations?

Production

DEFINITION:

This process schedules and executes jobs, transactions, and data through the hardware/software on a minute-to-minute basis to meet the agreed-upon service levels. It monitors the progress of work against the schedule and takes corrective actions (based on the 1- to 90-day schedule defined in production and distribution scheduling).

DESCRIPTION:

The elements of this process are:

1. Receive jobs, transaction, and input data from distribution.
2. Set up, initiate, and run jobs and transactions.
3. Make jobs, transactions, and output data available to distribution.
4. Monitor the progress of production work against the production and distribution schedules and, if necessary, take action (scheduling or performance).

5. Execute predefined or emergency production procedures for bypass, recovery, security, and/or performance.
6. Record and report information on status, incidents, actions taken, and results.

DATA CLASSES REQUIRED:

Data input to process (data class)	Data output of process (data class)
C7 Production/distribution schedule	C10 Production/distribution logs
C10 Production/distribution logs	
R1 Applications	
R2 Data	
R3 Software	
R4 Hardware	
R5 Network	
R6 Facilities	
R7 Supplies	
R8 Personnel	
R10 Standards/procedures/methods	
R11 Test data	

Receive jobs, transactions, and input data from distribution

This element describes the responsibility for receiving the real work (jobs, transactions, and data) into the production facility. Upon receipt, it is considered to be in-process work until the results are again returned to the distribution facility.

In an automated distribution facility such as a communication network, these interfaces of production and distribution are accomplished with various queues. For a manual distribution facility, the work is transferred to a queue by a device like a reader.

Up to this time, these basic definitions have never been a major concern and may appear to be somewhat trivial. However, the advent of large multihost and distributed systems allows work to pass through many queues during the distribution and production processes. To ensure accountability and service control, the management of these processes must be examined as carefully as all the other processes.

Set up, initiate, and run jobs and transactions

This in-process job or transaction scheduling differs from work scheduling. The routing of the jobs and transactions, much like that in a manufacturing shop floor control, is determined by the planned work schedule defined previously in the Production and Distribution Scheduling process and operator control.

The work schedule is normally implemented through job classes and transaction processors built into the system and subsystems. The operator can override these built-in controls to alter this sequence, that is, change the transaction class to a higher-priority class.

This in-process work is scheduled through the various resources (central processor, disk drives, tape drives, etc.) required to complete the production of information.

Make jobs, transactions, and output data available to distribution

The production and distribution interface is a queue of output (for example, print files, messages). The actual physical printing of output occurs in the Distribution process. In a remote batch or on-line system, this is easy to visualize since the output device is physically separated from the production facility. For local output, the Production and Distribution processes share the same physical resource, that is, the host processor to which the printer or output device is attached.

This production and distribution resource sharing is not unique within the I/S business, for example, the distribution message queues are often controlled by an access method which resides on the same host processor. This resource sharing requires careful management control to prevent conflicts and to ensure quality service.

Monitor progress of production work

This in-process job or transaction schedule monitoring is often limited to progress messages (logs) as each job or transaction is routed through the production facility. The operator can supplement these logs by initiating displays of in-process work queues.

With an automated work schedule, the job or transaction schedule status can be posted directly to the work schedule by the operating system. Work scheduling personnel can look at both the planned work and its current status.

Execute predefined or emergency production procedures

The tasks in this process can range from reinitializing the whole system to varying the status of a device. Once the operator is informed of the situation, the person must locate and execute the correct procedure.

Record and report information

All of these required tasks are critical to the final completion of the service mission. Therefore, each action should be accompanied by logs to allow managers and auditors to trace the event history. These production logs provide a major feedback to the various planning and control processes.

Production summary

This process provides the actual production delivery mechanism for information services and should be a key focus of management attention. The success of this process is a direct measure of the overall planning and control success.

Distribution

DEFINITION:

This process schedules jobs, transactions, information, and data through the distribution network on a minute-to-minute basis to meet the agreed service levels. It monitors the progress of information movements against the schedule and takes corrective actions based on the 1- to 90-day schedule established in production and distribution scheduling. It also includes the receiving, storing, and shipping of data and information through the distribution network.

DESCRIPTION:

The elements of this process are:

1. Translate data into machine-readable form.
2. Receive, register, and validate input from all sources.
3. Package, distribute, check, and register outputs.
4. Monitor the progress of distribution work against the production and distribution schedules and take corrective action (if necessary).
5. Execute predefined or emergency distribution procedures for bypass, recovery, security, and/or performance.
6. Report distribution status, incidents, actions taken, and results.

DATA CLASSES REQUIRED:

Data input to process (data class)	Data output of process (data class)
C7 Production/distritution schedule	C10 Production/distribution logs
C10 Production/distribution logs	
R10 Standards/procedures/methods	

Translate data into machine-readable form

This element is responsible for receiving the real work (jobs, transactions, and data) from the user or from a production facility, and translating it into a form required for the final destination. If the final destination is a production processor, this translation would convert the terminal coding to the machine-readable processor form. From the time the work is received until it is transferred to another user or production facility, it will be considered as distribution in-process work.

In a distribution facility such as a communication network, this element is automated with communication lines, controllers, and modems. For a manual distribution facility, the work must be transferred through some device, such as a reader.

Receive, register, and validate input from all sources

The distribution inventory of in-process work must be available to management to ensure that work is not lost, that the security procedures are followed, and that the final destination is actually reached. This element describes those functions.

In an automated distribution facility, this element is supported with system function to manage these queues and verify passwords or other security control methods.

Package, distribute, check, and register outputs

Required parts of the distribution in-process work queue can be moved to the final user, another distribution queue, or to a production queue according to this element. As stated earlier, this would include the actual physical printing of output.

Monitor progress of distribution work

This element is similar to the job or transaction schedule monitoring described under Production. Progress messages (logs) are produced as each job or transaction is routed through the distribution facility. The operator can supplement these logs by initiating displays of in-process work queues.

With an automated work schedule, the job or transaction schedule status can be updated directly to the work schedule by the operating system. Work scheduling personnel can look at both the planned work and its current status.

Execute predefined or emergency distribution procedures

The tasks in this process can range from reinitializing the whole network to varying the status of a terminal. Once the operator is informed of the situation, the person must locate the correct procedure and execute it.

Record and report information

All of these required tasks are critical to the final completion of the service mission. Therefore each action should be accompanied by logs to allow managers and auditors to trace the event history. These distribution logs provide a major feedback to the various planning and control processes.

Distribution summary

Since the Distribution process provides the link from the user to the Production process, it also requires management attention. Often, the user cannot differentiate between the two processes and only knows that they are related to overall service.

Customer Services

DEFINITION:

This process provides the interface with users, helping them to arrive at reasonable expectations and guiding them in realizing these expectations.

DESCRIPTION:

The elements of this process are:

1. Publish support service offerings, including a contact person and a telephone number.
2. Provide user help offerings for appropriate services, for example, information center, development center, and user help desk.
3. Forward all problems to the appropriate function.

DATA CLASSES REQUIRED:

Data input to process (data class)	Data output of process (data class)
P7 Service plan	C4 Problem
C1 Service	
C4 Problem	
C7 Production/distribution schedule	
A2 Customer/user/group	
A3 Organization	
R10 Standards/procedures/methods	

Publish support service offerings

Any customer services function focuses on the questions and problems that customers have with the business offerings. Its purpose is to improve customer satisfaction. For example, most utility companies have customer services functions to answer questions about energy consumption, billing, and so on. If the call indicates a problem with the facilities provided by the utility, a service representative can be dispatched to the customer's home.

Any user of the I/S business should have a similar path to answer questions and solve problems with I/S services. Studies indicate that 85% of all problems encountered by the I/S user involve procedures or simple misunderstandings of the facilities, for example, an unplugged terminal or unclear transaction input.

This element of Customer Services should publish a support plan, including the phone number and person to be contacted in case of difficulty.

Provide user help offerings

To meet services agreements, a desire to satisfy the needs of the users must permeate the operations function and its staff. In a large installation, this may well justify a special staff function for user relations being established within the computing center. This function would be the primary point of contact for users and have the explicit responsibility of addressing user needs.

At a minimum, the customer services function should interface to the Problem Control process to

- Log all problems
- Resolve minor problems
- Report resolutions of all problems

This function is often called a "user help desk."

This function can be far more comprehensive where the customer or user is actually doing some of the I/S business processes, for example, developing an application using personal computing services or using a general query service.

A Development Center customer services could answer questions or solve problems associated with developing a program or application. An Information Center customer services could answer questions or solve problems associated with use of a particular data base or query language.

Forward all problems to the appropriate function

These customer services functions make customers more productive in their use of the I/S services. Questions and problems not resolvable at the customer services desk can be forwarded to the I/S personnel most likely to assist the customer. By minimizing the obstacles the customer must face, the I/S image and effectiveness can be improved.

Although these functions are normally associated with short-term solutions to problems, they also form a natural interface to many of the tactical planning processes. For example, the customer concern could require consultation to establish requirements for data. The Data Planner (called a Data Administrator) would be notified by the customer services function and provide customer assistance.

Customer services summary

This productivity issue is not limited to the customer. Without a customer services function, the customer will often use a scattershot approach, that is, going to many I/S personnel with the same problem, hoping at least one will solve it. With customer contact and proper assistance, the I/S personnel will see only the critical problems directly related to their area. Therefore, they can be more productive.

The customer services function is one of the best public relations investments that I/S management can make.

Service Marketing

DEFINITION:

This process markets services to users and identifies needs for future services. This includes the sale of any product, resource, or service developed and/or owned by the I/S organization.

DESCRIPTION:

The elements of this process are:

1. Select service offerings to fit client needs.
2. Market these offerings appropriately.
3. Report user needs for new services.
4. Initiate actions to provide services.
5. Execute public relations activities on behalf of the I/S organization.

DATA CLASSES REQUIRED:

Data input to process (data class)	Data output of process (data class)
P7 Service plan	C1 Service
C1 Service	C5 Requirements
C5 Requirements	
A2 Customer/user/group	
R10 Standards/procedures/methods	

Select service offerings to fit client needs

With the increased variety and complexity of I/S services, the marketing function traditional to other businesses could be added to the I/S business. One key responsibility of any marketing function is to match the needs of potential, new, and current customers with the available services. By consulting with the customer, the marketing person can ensure that the customer and I/S are working together and maximizing the productive use of the I/S business.

This function should work closely with the Service Level Planning function to establish service objectives and possibly agreements.

Market these offerings appropriately

In environments with large application development backlogs and high customer demand for service, why should I/S market its offerings? The answer lies in the productivity of people. The I/S business is often given 1 to 2% of the enterprise's resources to provide information for 100% of the enterprise. If I/S can encourage personnel in the other 98% to become involved in the I/S business, the overall productivity of the enterprise will benefit.

The Development Center and Information Center can provide this marketing function in addition to the customer services function described previously. Marketing personnel or consultants can work with each customer to understand immediate needs and propose a solution. The solution could be as simple as adding a personal computing terminal, providing some basic education, or directing him to the customer services function.

Report user needs for new services

During these marketing efforts, customer needs will arise which cannot be easily met with existing services. These needs must be forwarded to the Service Marketing Planning process to be included in future development or new services.

Initiate actions to provide services

Reporting these needs to the planning functions does not relieve Service Marketing of the responsibility of follow-up. The marketing person should follow the progress of the request and constantly search for other solutions to the customer's needs.

Execute public relations activities

Although the Service Marketing process concentrates on the relations between the customer and the I/S organization, it must also be concerned with the I/S image in the enterprise and community. A good public relations effort can greatly improve this image.

Periodic tours of the I/S facilities can break down the false image of the computer as a mysterious black box. Internal newsletters improve the overall awareness of the work being performed by the I/S function. Participation in user groups and community projects are all ways to create a good public image.

Service marketing summary

If I/S is a true business, it should not ignore any idea that has proven successful in other businesses without a careful evaluation. Marketing of information services opens many new avenues of user and I/S communication.

SERVICE MISSION SUMMARY

After 18 months and much hard work; the order entry application, System/Network Control Center, and associated technology are working beautifully. Users are getting responsive answers to their questions. Service quality has significantly improved. You have been promoted to an executive position in the marketing organization.

However, one part of the overall effort was deferrred temporarily pending the availability of resources. That was the implementation of the tactical-level Service Planning processes. You objected to the decision by the executive committee. They did agree to start a new project immediately upon completion of the System/Network Control Center project.

In the next chapter we will explore this progress toward phase IV.

8

Long-Range Planning of a Management System

Development Mission Definition: Development of new services and applications for other departments in the enterprise.

Service Mission Definition: Provision of service to the end user, including the collecting, storing, processing, and distributing of data.

Consultation Mission Definition: Consultation with other departments on the need for and use of information.

ALEX CALLS AGAIN!

The vice-president of marketing asked you an interesting question. "How long will the new service quality last if we don't start long-range planning?" Before you could answer, there was an urgent phone call from Alex Brazwell's office. Alex has called a meeting to discuss the possible merger with two other companies in nonrelated industries. Alex is concerned about the impact on I/S and wants your input. The meeting, which includes Ms. Allen, is scheduled for next week. Alex is clearly driving I/S toward a phase V environment, yet we are barely out of phase III.

During the week, you and Ms. Allen held several meetings to examine possible recommendations for Alex. Your lack of experience in both tactical and strategic planning proved to be an obstacle. Ms. Allen was very concerned about this shift from phase III to phase V without passing through phase IV. She proposed two recommendations for Alex.

1. The first recommendation was a top-down Business Systems Planning study of the three companies. The entrepreneur study team could focus on critical questions such as:
   - Do the three companies have compatible shared values, strategy, structure, staff, skills, and style?
   - Where is each company in its phases of growth?
   - What processes and data are implemented in each company?
   - What are their information needs?
   - What is the I/S organization for each company?

   She suggested that Alex would be the executive sponsor and you would be the project leader. She would assist as a participant.
2. The second recommendation was a Management Planning study to be conducted after your Business Systems Planning study is completed. She suggested that you should be the executive sponsor and she would be the study leader. The study would focus on the tactical I/S processes needed for Brazweli and the other companies.

Alex liked your recommendations and implemented them.

We will first focus on the Business Systems Planning issues in the section entitled "Strategic Planning and Control." We will assume that study is completed before we examine the tactical-level issues.

STRATEGIC PLANNING AND CONTROL*

Strategic planning and control process overview

This group of processes is concerned with adjusting I/S over time to meet the changing conditions and requirements of the environment (for example, society, the market, and advances in technology). It involves setting long-range objectives, establishing overall priorities, and selecting strategies to be used to meet the objectives.

The three processes in this group will be discussed in the following sequence:

1. Business Strategic Planning
   - How does the enterprise develop a strategic plan?
   - How is this plan translated into an I/S mission, policies, and information needs?
   - What is the I/S strategy for organization (for example, centralized or decentralized), user relationships, technology use, and resource growth?

*The remainder of this chapter (with the exception of "Long-Range Planning Summary," "Another Management Planning Study," and "Another Success") is reproduced from the IBM publication *A Management System for the Information Business,* Volume III—*The I/S Development Mission*, GE20-0750-0, and Volume IV—*Managing I/S Resources*, GE20-0751-0, by permission of the IBM Corporation.

2. Architecture Definition
    - What structure of applications, data, and technology is required to support the enterprise's strategic plan?
    - How do these structures relate to existing applications, data, and technology?
3. I/S Strategic Planning and Control
    - How does I/S plan to meet these enterprise information needs?
    - What approvals are required for this long-range plan?

It is suggested that the reader refer to Figure 8–1.

Assessing strategic planning and control

Several questions can be asked to define a good or bad performance of strategic planning.

- Does an enterprise strategic plan exist?
- Does an I/S strategic plan document exist?
- Does the I/S strategic plan support the enterprise strategic plan?
- Does the I/S strategy document include enterprise information needs, office systems, communications, or is it limited to host processor growth over the next few years?
- Has I/S consistently met the information needs of the users and the business in the past?
- Is I/S noted for its short-term methods in meeting day-to-day user needs and problems? This often results in wasted effort and loss of revenue.
- Are the planning processes getting too involved in the future and ignoring the present?
- Is the planning too centralized, ignoring most of the company?
- Have the planning processes developed suitable goals for measuring their effectiveness?
- Is planning too formal, to the exclusion of creativity and flexibility?
- Has planning deteriorated to projections of the future rather than rethinking true needs?
- Is planning done only periodically when there is a crisis?
- Are the plans attempting to do too much too soon?
- Are the plans reviewed regularly with departmental and divisional managers?
- Are the plans used too rigidly?
- Are the plans ignored and replaced by intuition?
- Is performance measured against the planned volumes and costs?

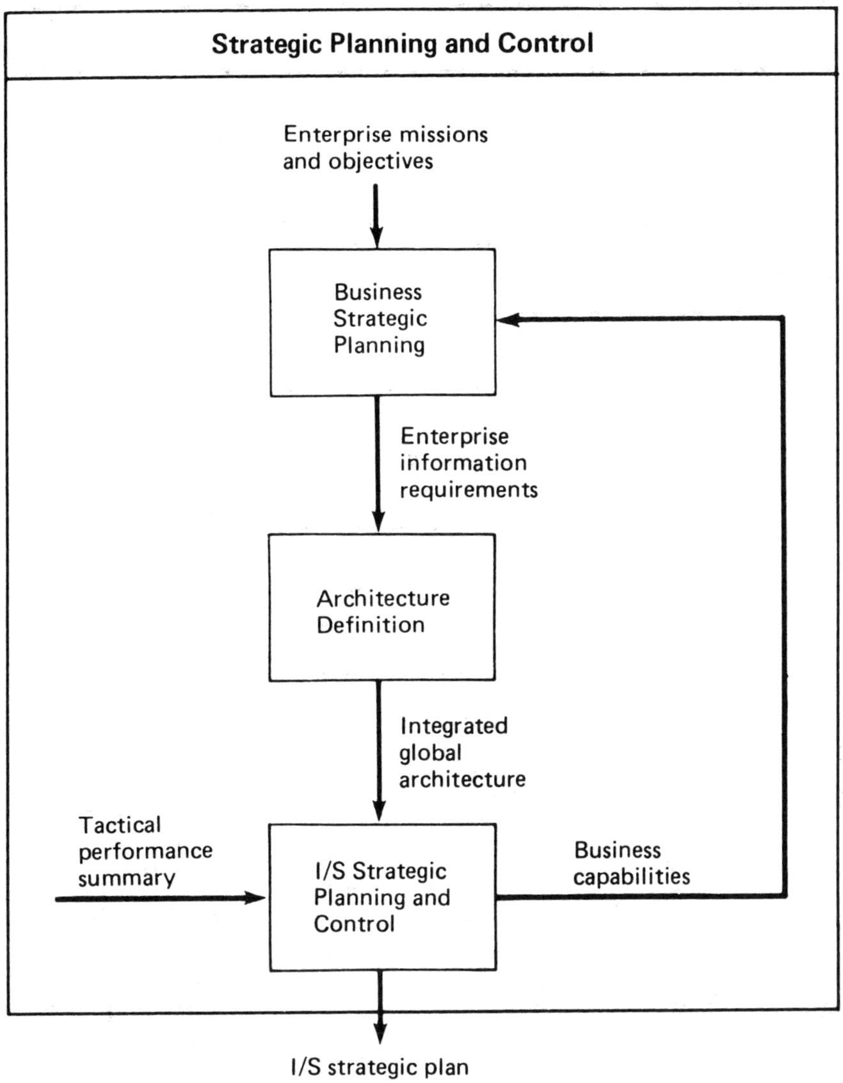

Figure 8–1 Strategic planning and control overview.

Business Strategic Planning

DEFINITION:

Using all available inputs from the enterprise (formal and informal), this process defines what the enterprise asks of its I/S function through the strategic plan period, normally five years.

DESCRIPTION:

The elements of Business Strategic Planning are:

1. Define I/S mission based on enterprise mission and objectives.
2. Define I/S policies.
3. Define business processes, information, and information flow of the enterprise (including I/S).
4. Define enterprise requirements for information (including I/S) through the strategic time period.

DATA CLASSES REQUIRED:

Data input to process (data class)	Data output of process (data class)
E1 Enterprise	E1 Enterprise
E2 I/S business	E2 I/S business
E3 I/S industry	
C8 Management systems performance	
R9 Financial	
R10 Standards/procedures/methods	

Define the I/S mission

There are many reasons for creating strategic plans. First, the current business environment is much more complex and unsettled than it has ever been. This trend will probably continue. A strategic plan enables a company to project the future of the enterprise and take the necessary steps to ensure that the projected business path can be followed. It can also enable examination of areas that may cause problems and decide to eliminate, bypass, or accept them, recognizing the risk. Also, the increasing number and complexity of government regulations place new information needs on the enterprise.

From an I/S perspective, the strategic plan must anticipate the information needs required to make the enterprise strategy successful. This information must allow the planning and control of both the enterprise and I/S functions, while accommodating a rapid change in technology and business conditions.

Therefore, it is critically important that the enterprise have a clear strategy that is well documented. A significant study was done to analyze the performance, over five years, of companies with formal strategic plans and those without. A comparison was also done with the former organizations for the five-year period before the introduction of strategic planning. Results were measured against sales, earnings per share, stock price, earnings on total capital, and earnings on common equity. In every case those companies with strategic plans in place did considerably better than those who had none. Within those same organizations, there was also a significant improvement in the five-year period compared with results in the previous five years when formal plans did not exist.

The aim of this section is to provide a better understanding of Strategic Planning and Control processes as they relate to the information needs of the enterprise and the corresponding I/S strategy. Key questions are:

- What business are we really in?
- What are our long-range objectives?
- What products will become obsolete and when?
- How and when should we replace such products?
- What and where are our markets?
- What market share should we aim at?
- How will we achieve that?
- What are our capital needs?
- What will be our cash flow over the next years?

Dealing with these issues requires the participation not only of management but of all levels of the organization. Involvement in this process will facilitate acceptance of change. The issues above were formulated in the context of the corporate strategic process. However, they are just as relevant in an I/S context. The techniques to formulate and implement an I/S strategic plan are comparable to those required in general business planning.

The I/S function within the enterprise must provide the information to make the enterprise successful, taking advantage of available information technology. Success or failure is often dependent on these I/S services. It is thus vital that I/S have a clearly defined mission backed with documented policies.

The three primary missions of the I/S function are:

1. Provision of service to the end user including collecting, storing, processing, and distributing data
2. Development of new services and applications for other departments in the enterprise
3. Consultation with the other departments on the need for and use of information

The concepts and procedures associated with the first two missions were discussed in previous chapters. These two missions provide the traditional role where the user is responsible for the consumption of information and I/S is responsible for the production of information. In later phases of management systems development, the critical dependence of the user on this information creates the need for the third mission.

In the consultation mission, the I/S function must be aware of information use and help guide the enterprise in the proper strategic planning of its information needs.

To accomplish this, the I/S objectives must be set by the enterprise objectives. The I/S function must also be fully aware of the overall enterprise strategic direction.

From the user perspective, the consultation mission involves the user as a joint beneficiary of the I/S resources. The user and I/S equally develop strategies, plans, and objectives in the Business Strategic Planning process.

Define I/S policies

Enterprise executive management should address the following policy questions and establish I/S strategic objectives:

- How is the I/S function to be organized across the enterprise? Should it be centralized within one corporate organization, decentralized into separate profit centers, or distributed across several organizations?
- How should I/S management practices differ from those of the enterprise?
- How does I/S impact the overall business strategy?
- What is the corporate policy on the use of advanced technology?
- What is the corporate policy for resource growth (people, facilities, computers, data, etc.)?
- What is the corporate policy on charges for I/S services and development? Should the consumer of information carry the burden or should these costs be capitalized across the enterprise?
- What methods will be used for setting projects and services priorities among the many information needs?

This policy setting is often done by a steering committee of senior executives with the participation of the I/S executive. I/S executive involvement helps to ensure that the policies can be achieved.

Define business processes and information flow

The techniques used for the Business Strategic Planning process will vary from enterprise to enterprise. There is no right solution and no single approach. However, one approach that has been successful is called BSP, Business Systems Planning. The desire to support business needs underlies the top-down philosophy of the BSP methodology. The BSP methodology is shown in Figure 8–2.

Step 1, defining business objectives, was discussed above. Step 2, defining business processes, establishes the prime long-term basis for I/S support in the business. Step 3, defining data classes, can be done on the basis of the processes to be supported. Step 4 will be discussed in the Architecture Definition process.

In order to achieve the overall long- and short-term objectives of any business, a variety of related functions are carried out on a day-to-day basis. These functions or processes relate to the decisions or activities that are critical to the success of the business. These processes are often interdependent, leading to their grouping into logical blocks.

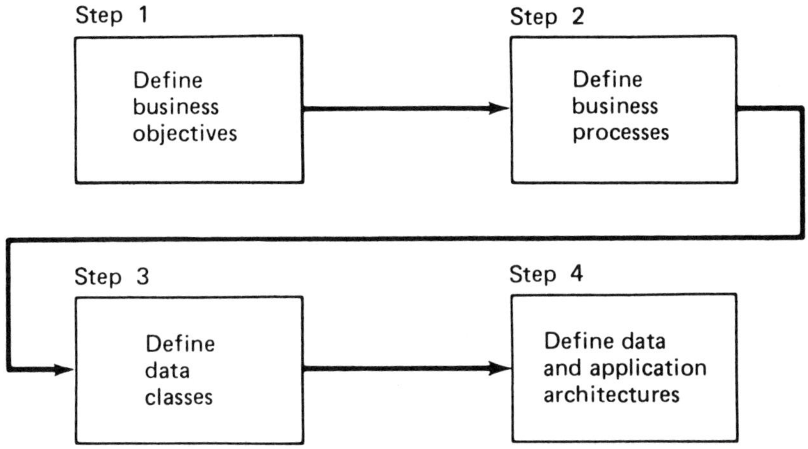

Figure 8–2 General BSP planning approach.

In a mature business environment, the processes are independent of the people who may perform them, that is, the people may change but the processes remain. When a business acquires a new venture, a new set of processes need to be added to support this new area (for example, a steel company acquiring a petroleum business would have new processes for the refining and distribution of crude oil).

The processes ensure that the right information is in the right place at the right time. A data class, as the name implies, is a major category of data needed to support one or more business processes. For example, customer information is a data class needed in several process areas, such as order entry, billing, and distribution. This step results in a definition of all the data required to make the process successful.

It is essential that an organization be willing and able to express its long-term goals and objectives. For some organizations, this can be done principally through the business plan. For others, where a business plan is not available or current, it can be done as a part of the BSP methodology. In either case, senior management must recognize this need to ensure their involvement and commitment to a meaningful BSP study.

There are some major considerations at each level of the plan that will help or destroy its aim. In the formulation of planning processes, the following factors should be considered:

- Top management cannot delegate planning. A staff or planning organization can drive the planning processes, but the plan must be built by the managers.
- If the enterprise is achieving success without planning, there is often a question as to why it is needed now. Planning should begin during this period of success, not under problem conditions.
- Ignoring the power structure of a company can result in plans that cannot be implemented. All involved managers should participate in the planning processes.

- The enterprise planning must be at a high-enough level in the organization to obtain concurrence and executive support.
- Assuming that it is unnecessary to plan since the future is unpredictable can seriously reduce the value of the exercise.
- Assuming that it is too hard or too easy can also produce an undesired result.
- It is invalid to assume that long-range planning will solve current problems.

Since rapid change is inherent to I/S, architectures can be used to provide structure, to evaluate priorities, and to reduce the impact of change on the enterprise.

The word "architecture" can have multiple meanings when used in the context of a management system. Chapter 1 defined the horizontal axis, the business processes and related data, as the ISM Architecture (Fig. 8–3). The Business Strategic Planning process defines a process architecture to provide structure for the business to be supported by I/S.

The process architecture can be used to examine organizational alternatives or develop an understanding of the application systems that could support the enterprise. The latter concept will be explored in more detail under the Architecture Definition process.

Define enterprise requirements for information

The BSP methodology uses an interview technique to define and plan the information requirements of the enterprise. In the interview, the managers are asked questions similar to the following:

- Job responsibilities and objectives

  What do you perceive as your specific area of responsibility?

  What are the objectives that guide you in meeting your responsibilities?

  What are the major decisions you must make that affect your specific objectives?

  What are the major problems you encounter in meeting your objectives?

  How is your performance in meeting your responsibilities and objectives measured?

  How do you measure the performance of your subordinates?
- Current information needs

  What type of internally generated information do you use to meet your objectives?

  Which of these information needs do you find most useful? How is it used?

  Which do you find least useful?

  Is the information you currently use in meeting your objectives accurate? Is it consistent? Is it timely?

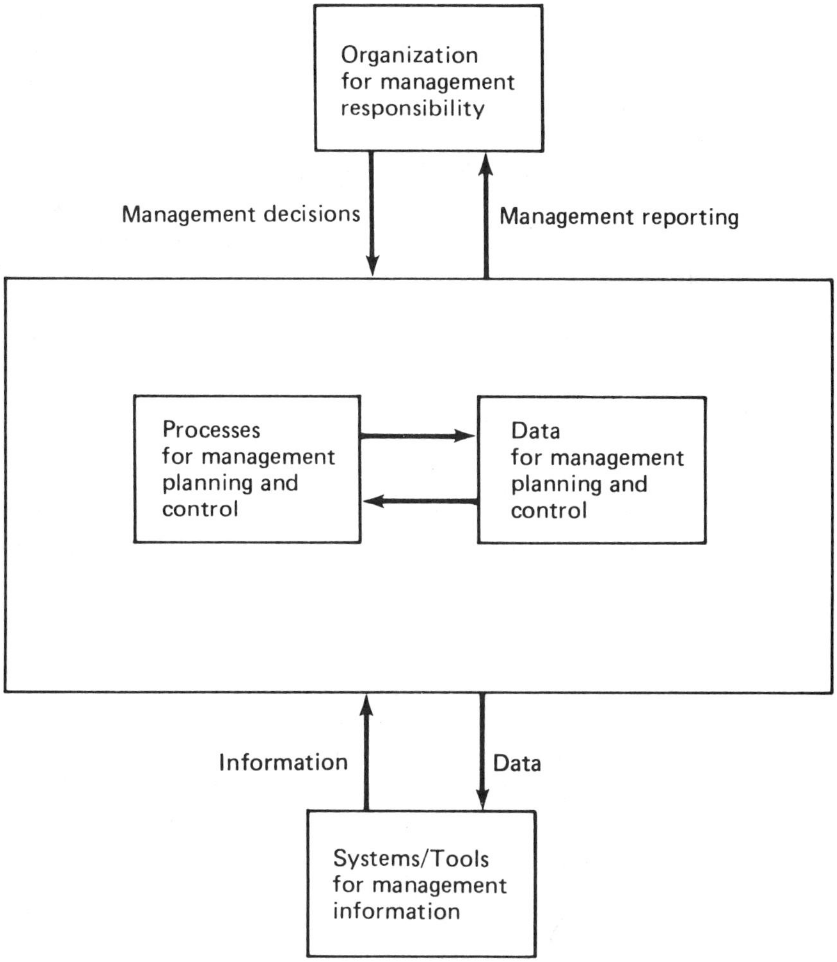

Figure 8–3 Components of a management system.

Are there areas in which additional information would help you meet your objectives? What are these areas? What type of information would be useful?

Compared with existing information sources, what value would you place on this additional information?

- Projection of information needs

  Within the next five years, do you anticipate emerging technologies or changing business practices that will change the nature of your responsibilities and managerial objectives?

If you do, what changes in your informational needs do you project these changes will necessitate?

These information requirements are consolidated into a statement of needs.

Business strategic planning summary

This planning process has attempted to understand the enterprise by defining the business mission, objectives, strategies, policies, and basic business processes. It has defined the information to run the business in terms of data classes and information requirements.

The next process will attempt to build a structure to provide this information.

Architecture Definition

DEFINITION:

Using the information obtained in the Business Strategic Planning process and considering the whole enterprise, this process defines in I/S terms the goals towards which all future action should move.

DESCRIPTION:

The elements of Architecture Definition are:

1. Define data architecture for the enterprise.
2. Define application architecture for the enterprise.
3. Define I/S technology architecture for the enterprise.
4. Integrate architectures.

DATA CLASSES REQUIRED:

Data input to process (data class)	Data output of process (data class)
E1 Enterprise	E2 I/S business
E2 I/S business	
R10 Standards/procedures/methods	

Define data architecture for the enterprise

The process architecture can to some extent be looked on as the path(s) by which data and information are passed around the business to make decisions and/or perform tasks. The data, application, and technology architectures define potentially automated means for moving this information.

The data architecture is a logical grouping of the most important and frequently used data in the enterprise and I/S. The data architecture contains both the current and future data needs of the business and I/S. The need for an understandable data architecture has become more important with new technologies to store, produce, and distribute information.

Like business processes, the data can be defined into a natural hierarchy of data groups, data classes, and data elements. This hierarchy of data for the I/S business is presented in Appendix B. For each group, the data classes and data elements are described to build a structure to support the I/S business. Since I/S is a subset of the overall enterprise, this data concept should apply equally to the total data needs of the enterprise. The content of the data groups depends on several factors, including the amount of data necessary to achieve the best results for each group and the interdependency of the use of each group.

These logical groupings of business data can be structured into an I/S conceptual model for later data planning. Implementation of this data structure and projection of size requirements will be discussed under the Data Planning process.

Define application architecture for the enterprise

Since I/S applications can be an integral part of a business and be critical to its overall effectiveness, it is essential that they support the organization's true business needs. And since applications represent major investments of time and money, they must be defined with a structure to limit duplication and redundancy.

The application architecture is dependent on the processes and the data required to support those processes. They are in reality the means by which the data requirements are to be brought together as required for individual processes or groups of processes. Although the exact application architecture will be unique for each enterprise, the model shown in Figure 8–4 illustrates some of the key concepts:

- The systems in this example are grouped into five major application groups: Environment and Planning, Engineering, Administration, Production, and Marketing.
- These application groupings are based on the data and processes required by the business rather than the organizations to be supported (Fig. 8–3). Although similar names are sometimes used for the organizational component, the application groupings do not relate to any specific organizational structure or even to the prime using organization.
- The application model should cover the complete range of systems that could be developed for the enterprise even though resources or justification may not be currently available. Often, changes in the business environment will necessitate a new priority of systems to meet that change. With a complete model, it will be easier to set new priorities.
- This application model provides a road map for all development and maintenance work within the enterprise. Each conceptual subsystem must have

Environment and Planning System Group

Plan management
Engineering planning
Manufacturing planning
Marketing planning
Resource planning

Engineering System Group

Task definition and authority
Project definition
Task planning and reporting
Data transfer
Documentation and procedures
Selection
Quality control
Technical

Administration System Group

Personnel
Finance
I/S support

Production System Group

Engineering and production data control
Customer order servicing
Forecasting
Master production schedule planning
Inventory management
Manufacturing activity planning
Order release
Plant monitoring and control
Plant maintenance
Purchasing and receiving
Stores control
Cost planning and control

Marketing System Group

Consumer goods distribution
Sales analysis

Figure 8-4 Sample enterprise application model.

sufficient definition that will allow eventual development of an application system.

- Many of these application systems may already exist in the I/S inventory, either as a complete system or in part. With this model, each existing system can be evaluated for improvement or total replacement. One major effort of Application Planning should be to anticipate when an application will become obsolete.
- The applications to support the I/S business within the enterprise should also be included.

To define the application architecture, it is important to understand in some depth the processes of the business and the data required to carry out those processes. The technique used by BSP to build this architecture includes:

1. Building a process-to-data matrix that designates which process creates, updates, and accesses the various data classes

2. Rearranging the processes and data to have the creation of data cluster along the diagonal of the matrix
3. Grouping applications or systems around this creation diagonal to balance the impact of both processes and data on the conceptual system
4. Documenting these groups for later classification into subsystems at the tactical level

To show the interdependencies of data, a general flow diagram is often drawn for both the processes and the applications (see Appendix A). With this structure and flow, there should be less need for a "forced" fit or dramatic changes in individual applications. The overall picture allows a framework for evaluating each piece.

Define technology architecture for the enterprise

The technology architecture provides the means by which the application and data architectures are to be delivered. Without it, it would be difficult and probably inefficient to provide the right information to the right location at the right time. The technology architecture includes each hardware, software, network, and facility element. Its structure should consider the impact on the existing elements and provide the right links to fit additional elements. Each element can be improved or replaced individually.

However, within that structure is an increasing number of options by which the information requirements can be achieved. Technology is advancing so rapidly that the best available technological solution today may not be the ideal tomorrow. The technology architecture must be updated to plan for these changes.

The I/S technology architecture should provide structure, functions, and interfaces which are transparent to implementation. This architecture should not require updates of any significant interfaces, except when new technology becomes available. Essential advanced system interfaces should be anticipated, whenever possible.

Integrate architectures

The data, application, and technology architectures are interdependent and must be integrated into a total structure on which an I/S plan can be built. This will normally require several iterations through various combinations before a final recommendation can be derived. The final recommendation could include options based on defined requirements (for example, performance, availability, workload).

Architecture definition summary

This process has translated the information requirements into a structure to support those needs. The next step must make decisions about the best course to achieve the results.

I/S Strategic Planning and Control

DEFINITION:

Based on the goals of I/S and the constraints of the enterprise, this process provides, in an I/S strategic plan, the general direction on how to attain these goals. It specifies the sequence in which the key activities of the enterprise will be addressed and how the existing services provided will evolve. It also ensures coherence and consistency of this direction against the tactical achievements.

DESCRIPTION:

The elements of I/S Strategic Planning and Control are:

1. Evaluate alternate implementation of services, applications, and data, including business justification and risk assessment.
2. Define and prioritize the strategic objectives within the I/S policies.
3. Obtain approval for the I/S strategic plan.
4. Control the I/S strategic plan against the tactical performance.

DATA CLASSES REQUIRED:

Data input to process (data class)	Data output of process (data class)
E1 Enterprise	E2 I/S business
E2 I/S business	
E3 I/S industry	
C8 Management systems performance	
C9 Financial	
R10 Standards/procedures/methods	

Evaluate alternate implementation

To ensure that the I/S plan matches the enterprise strategy, the previous two processes established the environment (mission, strategy, objectives, policies, etc.) and the structure (data, application, and technology architectures) required to support the business. Using this base, the I/S strategic plan must set the direction for the three missions (service, development, and consultation) and establish the resource limits for those missions. The substrategies must be mutually compatible.

The service strategy establishes the services to be offered:

- What will they be?
- How will they be delivered?

- When, approximately, will they happen?
- How much personnel will be required?

The development strategy establishes the new services and resources to be offered based on the various architectures:

- What applications are to be developed and when?
- What data bases are to be developed and when?
- What technology is to be used and when?
- What will be the approximate personnel requirements?
- What will be the investment in purchased software?

The consultation strategy establishes direction for redefining the enterprise information requirements.

- Will the BSP methodology be used? When?
- What studies are to be conducted?
- Will a BSP be required in the I/S area?
- Who will manage these activities? User? I/S?

The resource strategy sets limits on the other strategies and eventually provides the overall optimization of the strategies.

- Have the strategies taken advantage of new technologies?
- What are the strategic personnel requirements by skill type?
- What personnel policies will be required to obtain these skills?
- What organization will be required to manage the personnel?
- How is service, development, and consultation to be funded?
- Are new sources of funding required?
- How are the substrategies to be measured?
- Who will do the measurement?

These questions are not easy to answer and in some cases may not be answerable. If the course is not understood or predictable, it may be as important to understand where the I/S functions have the potential for high risk. Executives should constantly monitor the progress on all paths with emphasis on these high-risk paths.

Define and prioritize the strategic objectives

In every organization, great competitive benefits can be gained by planning the strategic direction. Probably one of the most difficult questions facing an executive is how best to apply the fast-changing I/S technology to competitive advantage. This requires a real knowledge and awareness of the direction of the technology, then carefully planning its use.

An example of this strategic direction and its consequences can be seen in such industries as banking and insurance. The companies with foresight and I/S direction were prepared to install consumer terminals much earlier than those who had failed to foresee the future. They had the basic technology in place at the right time.

There are some basic ground rules required for an I/S strategic plan:

1. It should be in harmony with the strategic plans of the enterprise. This does not mean that if the enterprise does not have a strategic plan I/S will be unable to produce one. There are many ways of getting the information needed:
   - Discussions with user executive management.
   - Formalized reports from users on their future I/S needs.
   - If all else fails, an I/S strategic plan should be drawn up and circulated to the chief executive and all user management. It should state the "assumed" overall business strategy and the "assumed" individual departmental strategy. Unless otherwise directed by the chief executive, this becomes the published direction of I/S.
2. I/S strategic planning is the responsibility of the highest level of management within the I/S organization. The top I/S manager for practical reasons may appoint a senior staff member to actually draw up the document. In large organizations, this may even be a plans and controls group that guides both the strategic and tactical plan formulation. In others, this could include an architecture group.
3. The I/S strategic plan should cover a minimum of three to five years.
4. The I/S strategic plan must be updated and controlled using one of two approaches:
   - At the same time every year, each manager is required to report attainment and required changes.
   - Based on the feedback of the tactical plan's significant events (acquisitions or divestments in the organization, major technical changes, etc.), the strategic plan is reviewed and updated. A major detailed review is held every two or three years.
5. The I/S strategic plan should be started at such an organizational level that it covers the present business direction but is flexible enough to expand with business changes.
6. The I/S strategic plan should not only be in harmony with the strategic plans of the enterprise but also act as an input to the enterprise plans. This ensures that the plan accounts for technological changes that in themselves can open up new areas of potential business growth.

   The I/S strategic plan must suggest additions, deletions, or changes to the business plan that ensures that the future course of I/S is a positive contribution to the enterprise.
7. The I/S strategic plan should be simple, easily understood, readable, and use a good format. Preparation flexibility through use of computer terminals should also be considered.

Many strategic plans are developed as a paper document. However, great benefit can be gained through developing any plan using the computer and terminals. This allows for easy update and access, as well as close exchange with other departmental strategies.

8. Resource forecasts should be in reasonably gross terms and be based on historical data and trends. By collecting historical data, the computer can also be used to show the trends in business and technology. More important, steps can be taken to correct undesirable trends by adjusting the strategic plan.
9. Both users and I/S should be involved throughout the planning process. The results should lead to a successful attainment of the business objectives and strategies.

Obtain approval for the I/S strategic plan

As stated earlier, it is important that someone (preferably the top I/S manager) have responsibility for the I/S strategic plan. This person must interface with the enterprise executives and user management to ensure acceptance for the I/S strategic plan. This manager must also maintain overall credibility, not only of the plan itself but also of the control of the plan. Control includes handling any concerns, issues, and problems that arise as the plan is being implemented.

Whether manual or computerized, the strategic plan document contains many needed factors and must be easily understandable. It should provide flexibility in making changes and take management style into account.

This document might contain these sections:

- Executive summary
- Planned goals in logical categories
- Strategies, including outlines of alternatives and reasons for selecting the recommended approach
- Assumptions
    - Policy
    - Technology
    - Environment
    - Constraints and issues
- Resource summary (usage and planned)
- Project summary for long-range projects
- Architecture summary (existing and planned)
    - Data
    - Application
    - Hardware
    - Software
    - Facilities
    - Network

It may be necessary to add supplementary sections that cover goals and strategies in more detail (for example, major long-range project plans with resource estimates and schedules).

Control the I/S strategic plan against the tactical performance

This process element receives information from the Tactical Plan Management process in the Resource Planning process group to measure the actual attainment of the strategic plans. Based on these measurements, this process can study trends and make recommendations to control the strategic direction.

I/S strategic planning and control summary

In conclusion, the I/S strategic plan should be simple, easily understood, and readable. Resource forecasts should be in reasonably gross terms. Both users and I/S should be involved throughout the planning process. The results should lead to a successful attainment of the business objectives and strategies.

The strategic plan will be the starting point for more detailed tactical service, development, and management planning. The more detailed resource forecasts will be discussed in the Resource Planning process group.

LONG-RANGE PLANNING SUMMARY

Your study team attended a class which explained these concepts in more depth. With your limited planning experience, you hired a consultant to assist in the methodology. The study was completed on time and presented to Alex. Alex was pleased.

ANOTHER MANAGEMENT PLANNING STUDY

You were given approval to initiate the study of the tactical-level processes. As the executive sponsor, you ask Ms. Allen to call a meeting to plan the study implementation. At the meeting, everyone agreed to use the Management Planning methodology that worked successfully for the System/Network Control Center.

The key processes to be studied are in four groups: Development Planning, Resource Planning, Service Planning, and Management Planning. The latter two groups have already been discussed in this book. You might review Chapter 5 and "Service Planning" in Chapter 7. Development Planning and Resource Planning are introduced in this chapter.

DEVELOPMENT PLANNING

Development planning process overview

This group of processes concentrates on the part of the strategic plan outlining the technical development that I/S has to undertake within the tactical time horizon. It defines manageable projects that can be implemented.

The four processes in this group will be discussed in the following sequence:

1. Application Planning
   - What applications are required in the tactical time period (that is, one to two years) to meet the strategic information needs of the enterprise?
   - What applications are required to meet new tactical needs?
   - Are these new applications or are they upgrades of existing applications?
2. Data Planning
   - What data is required in the tactical time period to meet the strategic information needs of the enterprise?
   - What data is required to meet new tactical needs?
   - Are these new data or are they upgrades of existing data?
3. Systems Planning
   - What systems (hardware, software, network, and facilities) are required in the tactical time period to meet the strategic information needs of the enterprise?
   - What systems are required to meet new tactical needs?
   - Are these new systems or are they upgrades of existing systems?
4. Project Planning
   - What is a reasonable set of projects to achieve these results?
   - What are the costs and benefits resulting from these projects?
   - What is the relative priority of these projects?

It might be helpful for the reader to refer from time to time to the flow shown in Figure 8–5.

Assessing development planning

Questions that might be used to measure the effectiveness and efficiency of the Development Planning process group include:

- Does enterprise and I/S management understand that any significant loss of data could create severe financial impact or even total failure of the enterprise?
- Does the chief executive understand that he or she could be held criminally responsible for the misuse of the data resource?
- Is a total loss of information control possible with the distributed use of new, less expensive means to process and store data?
- Does the tactical project plan match the strategic objectives?
- Does this project plan include all resources required during implementation?
- Does the application plan define the required data and system needs?
- Has all responsible management agreed on the prioritization of projects?

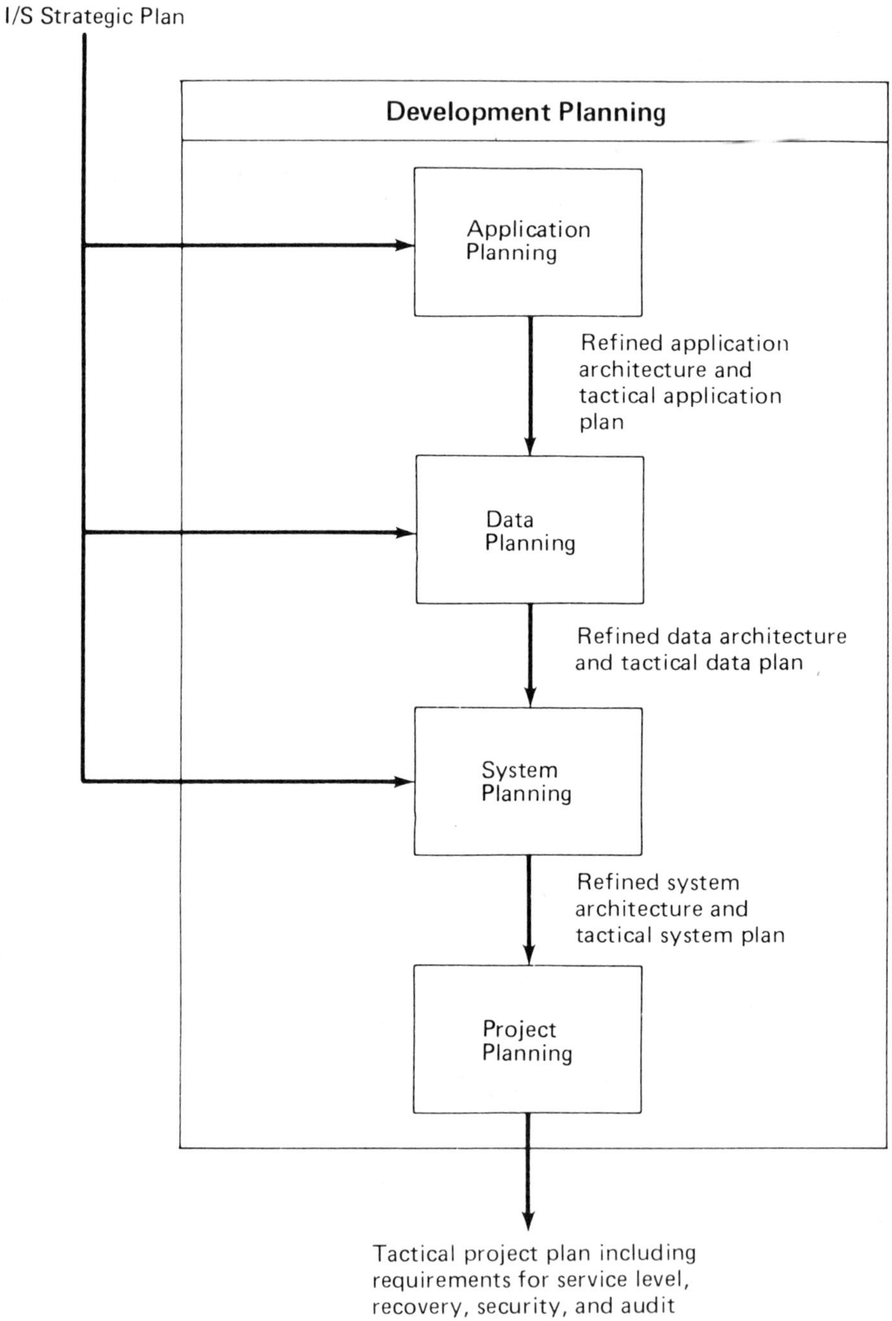

Figure 8–5 Development planning overview.

- Is the user satisfied that the tactical time period is long enough to plan his or her activities?
- Does the development plan include I/S needs for supporting the I/S business?
- Has the development plan considered the possible use of existing applications, data, and systems?
- Are the projects technically feasible?
- What risks are associated with the projects? How will these risks be managed?
- Has the actual time and resource expended on previous projects matched the plans with reasonable variances?
- Are new or unplanned projects constantly added to the project plan late in the tactical period?
- Is there a large backlog of user needs that cannot be met?
- Does the development plan address the needs of all levels of management?
- Has the plan sufficiently identified and quantified all necessary criteria to judge the benefits and priority of projects, for example, the financial benefits and regulatory constraints?

Application Planning

DEFINITION:

Considering each key function of the enterprise that has to be addressed during the tactical period and the existing applications, this process translates strategic goals into an application plan.

DESCRIPTION:

1. Expand the application architecture for each area where service is to be developed and/or supplied.
2. Develop or update the application plan for the tactical time period.

DATA CLASSES REQUIRED:

Data input to process (data class)	Data output of process (data class)
E2 I/S business	P1 Application plan
E3 I/S industry	
P1 Application plan	
C5 Requirements	
A1 Vendor	
A2 Customer/user/group	
R1 Applications	

Expand the application architecture for each area

The word "architecture" can have multiple meanings when used in the context of a management system. Figure 8–6 shows the components of a management system. This document defined the horizontal axis, the business processes, and the related data as the process architecture. The systems/tools component of the management system provides information to support both the information business and the overall enterprise.

The terms "data architecture," "application architecture," and "technology architecture" are used to describe conceptual models of the systems/tools component. Three processes in the Development Planning process group, Application Plan-

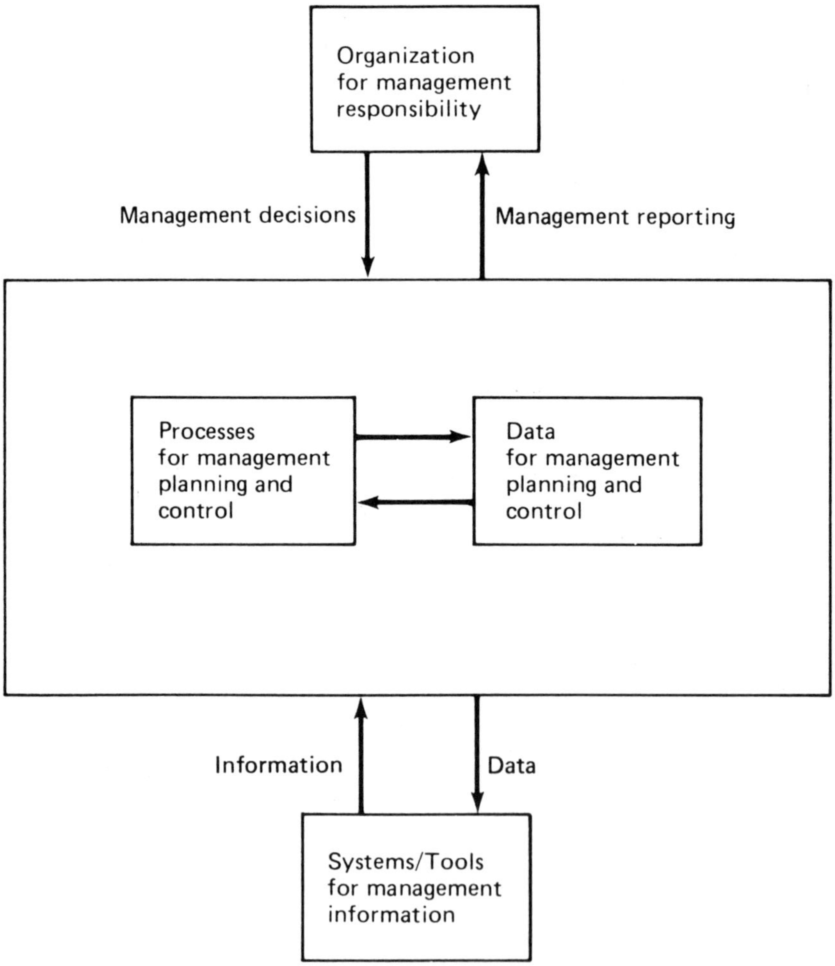

Figure 8–6 Components of a management system.

ning, Data Planning, and Systems Planning, expand the model of each respective architecture.

The Application Planning process has three major sources of data. Each of these sources will be explored to understand the alternatives available within this process.

One major input to Application Planning is an enterprise application architecture developed in the Strategic Planning and Control process, Architecture Definition. Although the exact application architecture will be unique for each enterprise, Figure 8-7 illustrates some of the key concepts:

- The systems in this example are grouped into five major application groups: Environment and Planning, Engineering, Administration, Production, and Marketing.
- These application groupings are based on the data and processes required by the business rather than the organizations to be supported (Fig. 8-6). Although

Environment and Planning System Group
- Plan management
- Engineering planning
- Manufacturing planning
- Marketing planning
- Resource planning

Engineering System Group
- Task definition and authority
- Project definition
- Task planning and reporting
- Data transfer
- Documentation and procedures
- Selection
- Quality control
- Technical

Administration System Group
- Personnel
- Finance
- I/S support

Production System Group
- Engineering and production data control
- Customer order servicing
- Forecasting
- Master production schedule planning
- Inventory management
- Manufacturing activity planning
- Order release
- Plant monitoring and control
- Plant maintenance
- Purchasing and receiving
- Stores control
- Cost planning and control

Marketing System Group
- Consumer goods distribution
- Sales analysis

Figure 8-7 Enterprise application model.

similar names are sometimes used for the organizational component, the application groupings do not relate to any specific organizational structure or even to the prime using organization.

- The application model should cover the complete range of systems that could be developed for the enterprise even though resources or justification may not be currently available. Often, changes in the business environment will necessitate a new priority of systems to meet that change. With a complete model, it will be easier to set new priorities.
- This application model provides a road map for all Development and Maintenance work within the enterprise. Each conceptual subsystem must have sufficient definition that will allow eventual development of an application system.
- Many of these application systems may already exist in the I/S inventory, either as a complete system or in part. With this model, each existing system can be evaluated for improvement or total replacement. One major effort of Application Planning should be to anticipate when an application will become obsolete.
- The applications to support the I/S business within the enterprise should also be included.

The user requirements uncovered in the I/S service processes offer a second source of data. The tactical-level process, Service Marketing Planning, constantly reviews the service marketplace with the available or planned services in mind to ensure that they are meeting the enterprise needs. Any user requirements for new services that require development will be passed to Application Planning.

Although many of these user requirements originated in the operational level service processes, Service Evaluating and Service Marketing, they are consolidated in Service Marketing Planning. These operational needs could range from new fields in a report to whole new applications.

The system inventory of installed or in-process applications provides the third source of data. In-process indicates that some change is being implemented by the Development and Maintenance processes. Application Planning is charged with the responsibility of constantly being aware of all applications and development activity being carried out in relation to them, including maintenance.

The status of application in the system inventory can be any of the following:

- Planned for some future development
- Under development
- Operational with enhancements being developed
- Operational with outstanding problems being fixed
- Operational and being used regularly
- Operational but rarely used

With this application model, the user requirements, and the existing system inventory status, the Application Planning process must define any additional requirements to be met over the tactical time period. This is a critical step in the whole planning process.

In all cases, user involvement is required to obtain reasonable and complete information requirements. The user who clearly understands the enterprise processes must somehow state the information needs in a way that I/S personnel can understand. On the other hand, I/S personnel must probe to verify that the requirements are related to the job being performed by the user and not simply meeting the user's personal needs.

When there is a time lag between requirements definition and actual use of the application, the user may have been transferred or promoted. If the requirements do not truly reflect the user's job, the solution will not be usable by the new personnel. To reduce the sensitivity of applications to changes in organization and personnel, techniques for defining information requirements should be given high priority.

One technique, Business Systems Planning Implementation (BSPI), provides a methodology that allows the user and I/S to define applications based on business processes. Although the BSPI methodology is normally used with the strategic planning processes, it is equally applicable to Application Planning. The difference is not in the methodology but in the scope and level of detail to be studied.

With this use of BSPI, general business processes defined in the business strategic plan are developed in more detail for each business area. These enterprise business processes define the functions to be managed or performed by the enterprise's personnel. These processes would be similar to those defined in the ISM Architecture for the I/S business subset.

The geographic location of these business processes and data has a significant impact on the application plan. For example, an enterprise with several manufacturing locations will have many of the processes duplicated at each location. The application plan must consider this distribution of enterprise business functions before defining a technical solution.

To capitalize on the knowledge of both the I/S and users involved in the business area, BSPI uses a study team approach in requirements definition. The study team is staffed with user and I/S personnel who have some knowledge of the business area to be studied. Generally, the study is chaired by a key user manager.

Interviews are conducted with users and user management involved in these business processes to define the required information needs. These requirements are used to detail the subsystems in the global application model.

This BSPI approach of building an application model based on a comprehensive definition of requirements is time consuming and requires the close cooperation of I/S and users. However, alternative approaches have many more serious problems. One alternative assumes each application should be individually planned for the specific set of requirements in the various enterprise organizations. This leads to an application inventory filled with duplicate or overlapping solutions creating redundant or conflicting reports. Eventually, the Application Planning process is forced to overcome this duplication by complete resystemization of applications. If Application Planning starts with an application plan based on a consistent application architecture, the needs of all enterprise organizations (including I/S itself) can be met.

With the ever-increasing complexity of the I/S business, the need for an application architecture supporting I/S has become more important. In fact, some of the critical application programmer talent may be required to develop systems to improve the overall management of the I/S installation.

On-line systems for handling I/S problem, change, and configuration applications are already available to meet some of these needs. These applications have a remarkable similarity to those used to support the total enterprise. Throughout this volume, it should be remembered that application architectures for both the enterprise and the I/S subset must be planned and developed.

The I/S support system described in the previous application model could include the following subsystems (Fig. 8–8) but, like the enterprise model, this example should be used only as an illustration to define a unique model for each I/S business. Several points about the example are important:

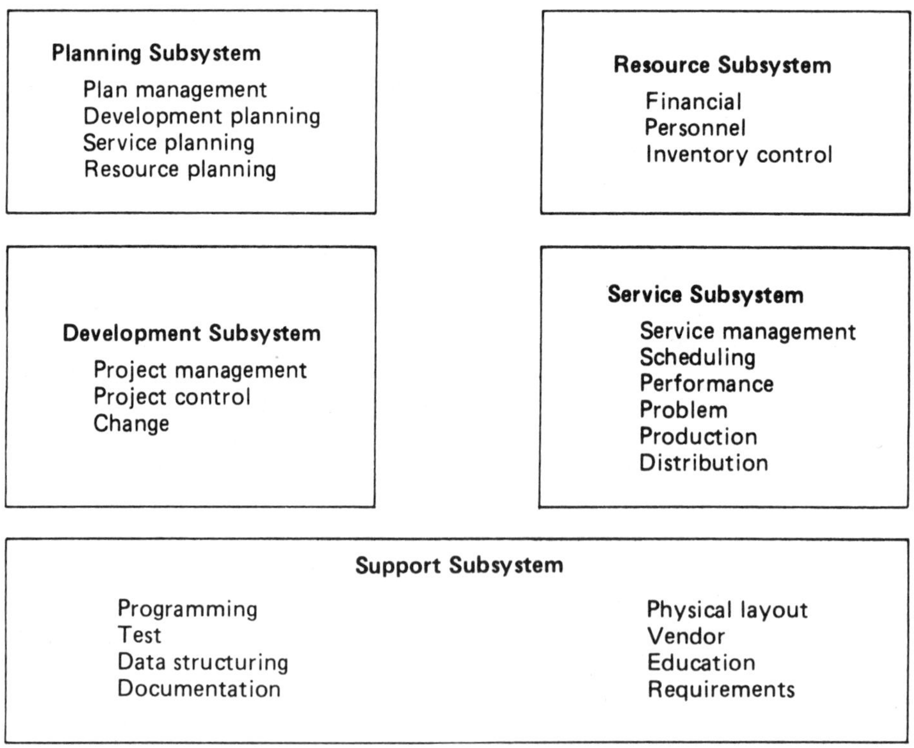

Figure 8–8 I/S application model.

- The development and service subsystems support the corresponding missions in the I/S business.
- The planning and resource subsystems provide support across these missions to manage the I/S resources.
- The support subsystem provides more technically oriented systems to service the operational level execution tasks.

Develop or update the application plan

The Application Planning process can now consider the generation of project proposals to modify or improve the flow of information in the enterprise or the I/S business (Fig. 8–9). In most cases, the initial application plan will be revised by the Data and Systems Planning processes to give a complete recommendation. This project objectives document becomes the major source for obtaining approval for the project effort and the required resources. At the operational level, the project objectives document is supplemented by a formal project control document.

From the tactical to the operational levels, the project must be defined, approved, and implemented using the following flow:

- The Application Planning process must determine whether the information requirement can be satisfied with existing applications in the inventory. If not, this process must define new or modified applications to achieve the desired results. The project objectives for one or more solutions must be developed and documented.

  Key factors in the system overview are the planned service levels and the recovery, security, and audit criteria required by the application. These are used in the Service Planning process group once the application plan is defined.

2. The Data Planning and Systems Planning processes (discussed later) add additional project details.
3. The Project Planning process (described later in this chapter) estimates the time and resources for the proposed solutions with reasonable accuracy. These estimates must allow management to understand the potential savings and costs. The accuracy of these numbers can be improved as the various phases of the project are developed and constantly reviewed by management.
4. At this stage, management must be given sufficient details to allow further work to be performed based on reasonable risks. These project plans are accepted or rejected in the Resource Planning process group. Before this acceptance, these plans are used as one factor in Service Planning.
5. Once the project objectives are approved, the actual development is controlled using project data to ensure that the final application meets the original conceptual design and that resources are expended according to the approved plan. The resulting deliverables become part of the system inventory used by the service function.

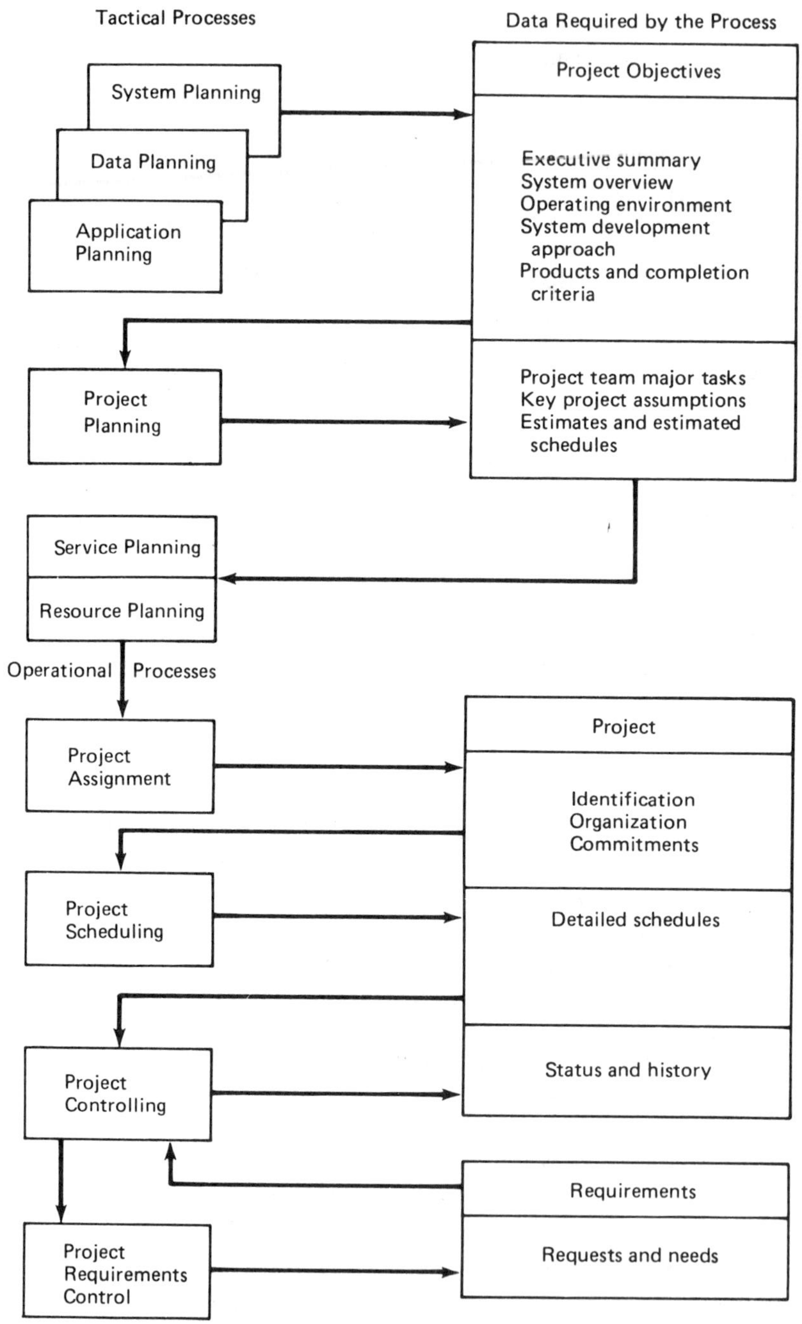

Figure 8-9 Project flow through the ISM architecture.

It is important to remember that the flow through each planning and control level allows the final application to satisfy the specific information and service requirements while maintaining a consistency with the application architecture.

By devoting personnel to this Application Planning process, the information needs of the enterprise can be defined and projects can be started with sufficient resources to be completed successfully. Often this flow starts too late in the application cycle. The result is "crash" efforts to satisfy information needs. Projects become uncontrollable and resources are consumed without satisfying the user's needs. Although many of the Application Planning techniques are still state of the art, some basic methodologies can be applied.

Consider the example of planning for applications in a distributed environment. In this environment, the application can take advantage of hardware that is physically placed at multiple locations: an intelligent terminal physically separated from the host processor but logically connected through communication lines; two host processors networked together with communication lines.

In planning these solutions, some application functions with high user interactions may be best situated on the intelligent terminal to maximize user productivity. Other functions may be best suited to the larger capacity of the host processor or could be either remote or central without affecting the user interactions. In many cases, the final location of this function will be based on the relative costs of each solution, on the need for data sharing, and on control requirements for security and audit.

Application Planning in this environment must work closely with Systems Planning to reduce the possible combinations to some manageable set. One approach is to have Systems Planning define the acceptable hardware guidelines for the enterprise with enough combinations to provide several alternatives. These combinations must be manageable and controllable within the enterprise and I/S management abilities. These prototype solutions can be applied to each possible application to ensure that future system changes will not make the applications obsolete or require extensive rework.

In selecting a solution, the first application design might consider only the host–terminal relationship with little or no function distributed in the network. This could be considered the base case using the advantages of the large central complex. In the second design, any application function could be distributed to a remote location if it has any reasonable justification. Each function can be evaluated on the feasibility and benefit of moving it to the remote location. This solution creates a base case for maximum distribution of function.

The best design for the application is somewhere between these two extremes. The functions can be evaluated individually to define a recommended solution for this application. One factor which cannot be overlooked in this exercise is the impact on data of each solution. The proposed solution may force data to be separated or duplicated between each location. The cost, security, and recoverability of this data become major factors in the final solutions.

Application planning summary

It should be apparent that the success of Application Planning is highly dependent on a clear strategic direction and an accurate system inventory. With these application proposals, the next two processes will add a data and system perspective.

Data Planning

DEFINITION:

Using the application plan and the present status of data, this process translates the strategic goals and direction into a data plan.

DESCRIPTION:

1. Expand data architecture in relation to the updated application architecture.
2. Develop/update data plan for the tactical time period.

DATA CLASSES REQUIRED:

Data input to process (data class)	Data output of process (data class)
E2 I/S business	P1 Application plan
E3 I/S industry	P2 Data plan
P1 Application plan	
P2 Data plan	
C5 Requirements	
A1 Vendor	
A2 Customer/user/group	
R2 Data	

Expand data architecture

The Data Planning process has three major data sources:

- The Strategic Planning and Control process, Architecture Definition, provides the global application, data, and technological architectures or models for the total enterprise. The data model for the I/S business subset illustrates this data framework (Appendix B).
- The Application Planning process provides an expanded application model and project objectives for new or modified applications.
- The status of the system inventory (installed and in-process data bases) is provided by the Resource and Data Inventory Control process.

Before discussing the expansion of the data architecture, it might be helpful to review some basic concepts about the data resource. In Chapter 3 data was presented as an enterprise resource that needs management attention like any other resource. This concept is indeed true, but data does have some unusual factors not common to all other enterprise resources.

- Ownership of the data resource is shared jointly by the enterprise and the I/S business. During the gathering of data, the using group owns the data until it is recorded and submitted for processing into information. This raw form of data continues to exist on documents in the using organization. In many cases, preliminary decisions are made on this raw form of the data, for example, the initial customer order can be used to give the customer a possible ship date.

  When the data arrives in the I/S business area, it is processed into useful information by application programs that place the data on disk or tape. The final form of information returned to the user is determined by the steps built into those production programs. During this production of information, the data is duplicated and stored in vaults for audit and security.

  After processing the data, the information form of data is distributed to many organizations in the enterprise where it is used to make business decisions. The reports are also maintained for historical purposes by many of these groups.

  The obvious question is: Who owns the data in its many forms and ensures that it has consistency? In many installations, each independent group owns its copy of the data and may not be aware of the other copies. At a minimum, the Data Planning process should record this joint ownership and resolve any conflicts. To the other extreme, one person with a title such as Data Administrator could have the prime or sole responsibility.
- The data resource should have a standard classification and identification mechanism. We classify personnel by skills, physical characteristics, and work location. The personnel resource is identified by the person's name or employee number. We classify inventory items by purchased, manufactured, and consumable. These items are identified by a part number or name.

  The data resource is often recognized by the document name, the data base, or the report. With this lack of clear definition and ownership, the data elements become duplicated and redundant. In many cases, the users of the final information are not even aware of this redundancy or overlap. The Data Planning process must build this identification and classification of the data resource.
- The data resource changes form through the gathering, processing, and reporting functions. The value and scaling factors at each stage must be known to the person designing the application. In many cases, the person using the final results was never involved in these original definitions and may not know the limitations or design constraints. Again, ownership of data becomes a major concern.

All user organizations who own this data must develop a desire to identify, plan, and control the overall data resource of the enterprise. Since the data is used in so many places, I/S must be at least heavily involved in these activities. The identification and classification of data can use techniques similar to those used in the management of other enterprise resources.

- Each unique data element can be given a name for recognition as a raw material (input documents), in-process assembly (data bases), or finished goods (reports). A data dictionary or an inventory control program can be used to define and track these data elements and their uses.
- Since the number of elements in the enterprise (including I/S) can be extensive, they may be combined into data groups and data classes. For example, the data associated with the I/S business is shown in Appendix B. This group, class, and element arrangement forms a classification system for data to assist in the search for similar data elements or to assign the name for a new element. This is accomplished with a series of key words, concatenated to permit a key word search for the element, that define the major and minor groupings of data like account codes used for financial control of funds. The unique identification and classification of data form the base for managing the data resource within the total enterprise.
- The Data Planning process must go through the difficult and time-consuming task of isolating the data resources existing in the enterprise. Anyone who has automated an enterprise inventory will appreciate the magnitude of this effort. Since many of the data items already exist in computer form as program and data file definitions, this is perhaps an obvious starting place. Unclear documentation, intermediate totals, and other lack of standards will complicate this effort.
- The next step must be to relate these data elements to the documents, data files, data bases, reports, and business processes that use them. The "where used" lists must resolve the data form translation problem and determine whether it is the same or different element and the scale factors and similar characteristics must be recorded.

Once these elements are recorded, it is the responsibility of all parties to ensure that the inventory of data is kept current and accurate, an effort requiring constant management attention. Is the exercise worth the effort? This is a question asked with the automation of any inventory or similar resource. The answer lies in the value of that resource to the enterprise.

The translation of a conceptual data model into usable data bases is accomplished through logical and physical structuring. Logical structures define the data as it would appear to the application program. Physical structures define the data as it would appear on the disk or other storage media.

The Data Planning process logically structures data bases using the application requirements and data definitions available in the data inventory. These logical structures will be refined and physical structures produced in the operational level development and maintenance processes.

Designing an integrated data base is currently a costly and time-consuming activity. An integrated data base exists to serve many application functions and its design must consider the requirements of these functions. When inconsistencies and redundancies are present in these requirements, design trade-offs must be made. Once the data requirements have been identified and recorded for all the application functions that use the data base, the designer must subject these requirements to examination and analysis that can be tedious and time consuming.

The goal is to devise a data base having a controlled number of redundant data elements connected only by those relationships required to support each application function with reasonable performance. It should minimize interfaces, reduce duplication, and still be extendable without restructuring to new functions. Automatic computations can assist this analysis, helping the designer produce a better data base in a shorter period of time.

Develop update data plan

Data requirements can come from two sources. Those requirements for planned applications should have been defined as part of the Application Planning process. With integrated data bases crossing both business process and application boundaries, additional data requirements can come from the total business use of data. Data Planning must ensure that both sets of requirements are complete and compatible with the data architecture.

In the case of Data Planning extending a planned application, the resulting data plan is added to the already existing project objectives statement. In other cases, Data Planning could create the project objectives statement. For example, restructuring an already existing data base to accommodate a higher transaction volume must be defined as a project and be allocated resources.

The data controls at the operational level ensure that the data is properly used to deliver service to the enterprise. Data Planning must constantly review these controls for efficiency and effectiveness. Specific controls are generally covered under the organizational group known as the Data Base Administrator and are the prime responsibility of the Resource and Data Inventory Control process.

Data planning summary

The Data Planning process has extended the application plan with a careful look at the data resource. The next process, Systems Planning, will apply hardware, software, network, and other resources to this plan.

Systems Planning

DEFINITION:

Using the application and data plans, the present status of hardware, software, and network and the request for modification of existing services, this process translates the strategic goals and direction into a systems plan for hardware, software, network, and facilities.

DESCRIPTION:

1. Expand systems architecture in relation to the updated application and data architectures. This architecture will be used for later capacity planning.
2. Develop proposed and updated systems plan for the tactical time period to include current/planned resources (hardware, software, network, and facilities) and those for scheduled maintenance.

DATA CLASSES REQUIRED:

Data input to process (data class)	Data output of process (data class)
E2 I/S business	P1 Application plan
E3 I/S industry	P2 Data plan
P1 Application plan	P3 Systems plan
P2 Data plan	
P3 Systems plan	
C5 Requirements	
A1 Vendor	
A2 Customer/user/group	
R3 Software	
R4 Hardware	
R5 Network	
R6 Facilities	
R7 Supplies	
R10 Standards/procedures/methods	

Expand systems architecture

Like Application and Data Planning, this process has three major data sources:

- It receives an application, data, and technology architecture from the strategic planning and control processes.
- It receives expanded architectures and plans from the Application and Data Planning processes.
- It receives an inventory status from the operational processes.

The Systems Planning process performs technology selection of systems resources (hardware, software, network, and facilities) for the Application and Data Planning processes. "Technology selection" by this process should not be confused with "hardware and software acquisition" discussed in the Development and Maintenance processes. The Systems Planning process examines various technology alternatives and builds a plan based on these results. This recommendation should be by basic technology type and/or available vendors. The final selection of vendor, type, and features should occur as part of the project which might be 12 to 18 months after the tactical planning.

In cases where the vendor or technology type has long lead times for delivery, the Systems Planning process might make a preliminary selection and place a letter of intent with the vendor. This decision must be verified during Capacity Planning and reevaluated at project time. Clearly, this long lead time suggests early selection of the project leader to prevent conflicts between long-range planning and project control.

The Application Planning, Data Planning, and Systems Planning processes are highly interrelated: applications and data drive systems, systems drive applications, and data. All are required. However, the organizational responsibility for these processes is sometimes unclear and leads to a discontinuity in the tactical planning flow.

Consider the following typical example:

1. The application development organization develops an application plan that concentrates on the user requirements, the proposed application solution, and the project schedule. The specific system requirements (hardware, software, network, and facilities) are not clearly identified. Its main focus is the personnel resources required to develop projects.
2. The systems programming organization develops a systems plan without the identification of specific applications and data needs.
3. Any subsequent service or capacity planning work will find that the two plans cannot be directly related. The planner must make some high-risk assumptions or forget the planning exercise.

Regardless of organizational assignment, the Systems Planning process must ensure that all resources are clearly identified for application and data projects. These systems resources (hardware, software, network, and facilities) must also be compatible with the strategic technology architecture.

The tactical planning processes are highly iterative and require several verification steps before the final plan is accepted. For example, the combined systems, data, and application plan must pass the recovery and security planning of the Service Planning process group. It must also be verified for sufficient capacity in the Resource Planning process group.

In these iterations, the Systems Planning process actually sets the system framework for both application and data planning. This becomes critical in the multilocation environment referred to under Application Planning. For example, the proposed applications could run on a single host or on multiple hosts.

In the first case, the application plan has an impact on the systems plan for only one host. In the other cases, the application plan has an impact on the systems plan for both hosts. The systems planner must have a clear picture of the interaction of these solutions. Since the combinations could become unmanageable, the planner must build the plan on reasonable assumptions of what the installation can manage effectively and efficiently.

Develop proposed and updated systems plan

In addition to the host area, the Systems Planning process must include:

- In a multihost environment, the applications are often completely within one host or the other with information exchanged between them. With distributed data processsing, the application functions can access either host or be performed within the distribution network. The systems planner must work closely with the application planner to devise a satisfactory solution for the end user.

  One approach discussed previously requires the systems planner to set reasonable standards for the design of applications based on the ability of the installation to manage the technology. Once the project proposal is documented, the systems planner must review the design and offer an evaluation of other approaches. The final proposal is presented to the end user after this negotiation is completed between the planning processes.
- In the single host, multihost, and distributed data processing environments, the distribution network to move information between nodes adds a new dimension to the Systems Planning process. Information can move on private communication lines, communication utilities, and satellites. Systems Planning must define a network to handle the desired information flow at optimum cost.

  With computerized approaches to network planning, the planner can study many combinations for capability and cost before deciding on a final proposal. The application plans provide details on terminal location, message types, message traffic, and other design factors. The system inventory provides data on the devices and interconnections in the current network.
- Systems Planning of the I/O devices (tapes, disks, mass storage, and printers) is perhaps one of the most difficult planning efforts. All devices have design capabilities that offer some approximation of the potential use. The actual rates are based on the total system environment. For example, most large systems share devices across channels and through switching devices. The I/O pool must be studied carefully to decide on the exact components to meet the enterprise needs.

  Perhaps the best planning effort for I/O is a careful analysis of the use of each inventory item based on data captured by the system. The planner can find devices (for example, disk drives and printers) with excessive utilization or limitations and propose alternative devices to address the problem. Many installations conduct regular I/O studies to analyze the use of data and the storage media required. Often a hierarchical approach to various levels of costs and speeds can meet user needs while maintaining operational efficiency. Systems are available that will assist the movement from one device to another to automate the actual implementation of this plan.

The proposed system changes could update an application or data project objectives document. In other cases, it could require a new project objectives document (for example, a change in the host processor to utilize new technology). It is important to realize that the systems planner is not expected to have all the skills to build this plan but must be able to negotiate those skills when required; the planner must have a system perspective and understand how all the system resources fit together.

Systems planning summary

In earlier phases of growth, the Systems Planning process is sometimes combined with many of those in the Service Planning and Resource Planning process groups. Although one person may be doing multiple functions, this process is unique and has a specific purpose.

Project Planning

DEFINITION:

Using application, data, and systems plans, this process translates them into manageable, clearly defined, and documented projects.

DESCRIPTION:

1. Define technically feasible and manageable projects.
2. Define project resources and time and service-level requirements (including recovery, security, and audit requirements).
3. Define any unique control requirements for each project.
4. Financially justify and prioritize the project plan.

DATA CLASSES REQUIRED:

Data input to process (data class)	Data output of process (data class)
P1 Application plan	P8 Project plan
P2 Data plan	
P3 Systems plan	
P8 Project plan	
R10 Standards/procedures/methods	

Define technically feasible and manageable projects

Every I/S organization should develop a standard project structure and apply it to all new development projects. It may not matter what the details of the structure look like if the list of activities and tasks is reasonably complete, each task is well defined with respect to the results that are expected, and the project has well-defined phases.

Each project phase is a self-contained, manageable piece of work. A project cannot proceed to the next phase of development until it has successfully completed the existing phase. If problems occur in a phase, work can be restarted in that phase without returning to previous phases.

Chapter 6 presented a discussion of the phase activities for the project types shown in Figure 8-10.

The creation of any new resource or procedure is considered development. Adding new features or functions to an existing resource or procedure is considered upgrade. Repairing incorrect implementation or broken resources is considered maintenance.

Efforts to research the potential use of applications, data, or systems can be considered as special cases of these projects and planned with the same processes. The major difference in a research project lies not in the project but in the use of the project results. Pure development projects generally have a known requirement and result. Research projects generally define the requirement and need during the study. In both cases, management must be given the anticipated results and resource expenditure.

The advantages of using a standard project structure are:

- The risk that important tasks are forgotten is minimized, especially with inexperienced project managers.

Project type	Processes Creating Project Type
Application/software development and upgrade	Application, Data, and Systems Planning
Application/software procurement and upgrade	Application, Data, and Systems Planning
Hardware/facility installation and upgrade	Systems Planning
Maintenance	Problem Control
Tuning and system balancing	Systems Planning and Problem Control
Management system development and upgrade	Management Systems Planning

Figure 8-10 Project types.

- Project planning time is reduced because project managers need not go through the process of inventing their own list of activities.
- Each task has a precise meaning and well-defined output. Everyone involved, therefore, speaks the same language; this simplifies follow-up and review.

All ongoing development projects should be formally tracked by higher management through regular progress reports. The daily or weekly reports were discussed under Development and Maintenance Control. At the tactical level, each project should be reviewed on a monthly or quarterly basis. In all cases, the project report lists the latest accomplishments for each project; states whether it is on target, ahead of, or behind the planning completion date; and indicates any problems encountered and/or solved since the last report.

Define the project resources and time

The standard project structure should contain major, predefined milestones at which point the following meetings should occur:

- I/S managers, involved personnel, and outside technical experts should review the technical and operational feasibility of the project deliverables.
- Informal technical walk-throughs should be held with user personnel.
- I/S management, the steering committee, and users should formally review and evaluate the economics of the project.

Each milestone represents a decision point to allow the project to continue to the next scheduled milestone, to cancel it altogether, or to request revision. The logical times for external reviews to occur are at the end of each project phase.

These milestone tasks become part of the project objectives document (Fig. 8–11). For each of these tasks, the resources and time must be estimated to allow managers to make reasonable decisions on the results and the associated risks. The precision of these estimates will vary with the project's size and complexity. These estimates will be refined as the project passes the many phases of its normal life cycle. If the initial estimates are incorrect beyond reasonable limits, the project must be reevaluated at the tactical level. Other projects may have a better return when the estimate is corrected.

At the tactical level, management must have sufficient information to allocate resources to various feasible projects. Clearly, any estimate could be improved, given sufficient time and effort. In some larger efforts, the risk may be so large that a feasibility project, committing only resources to better size the effort, may be required. The final project can be estimated using these results.

In larger, phased projects the estimates of later phases can be improved as more specific requirements are defined in the requirements phase. On most projects, these estimates can be based on the history of similar projects within the enterprise. The productivity of various groups can vary depending on the experience level and kind of effort. Historical information can be used to isolate these factors and provide standards.

Executive Summary-
This section contains information that can be used to present the proposal to executive management. It contains a short description of the present system, the need for a new method, the objectives of the new system, and a summary of costs and schedule.

System Overview-
Each function of the new system is discussed separately; business functions to be included and those being specifically excluded are clearly indicated.

Operating Environment-
This section describes the operating conditions for the system.

System Development Approach-
This section describes the approach taken to solve the problem, including a list of the products of the design phase and the project guidelines and standards to be used.

Products and Completion Criteria-
This section discusses the reviews and approvals for the intermediate and final products to be produced, as well as the completion criteria for each product and for the entire project.

Project Team Major Tasks-
This section lists the major milestone activities in the project for both the I/S and user departments.

Key Project Assumptions-
This section defines any assumptions made in the problem definition, solution, or solution approach. The key assumptions used to develop the estimates and schedules are extremely critical.

Estimates and Estimated Schedule-
This section estimates the manpower and other resources required for the project.

Appendices-
Appendices to the project objectives document contain the following information: change control plan, status reporting plan, financial justification, special deliverables, or project guidelines.

Figure 8–11 Project objectives document.

Define any unique control requirements for each project

Although the standard project control methodology will handle most projects, there are always unusual situations where exceptions will be required. These exceptions should be documented in the project objectives for management approval. All exceptions should be periodically reviewed by management for possible additions to the standard methodology.

Financially justify and prioritize the project plan

The development plan is a proposal to invest resources to improve the applications, data, and systems available to deliver service. The project plan developed in the previous processes has all the factors required to make this investment analysis.

Investment evaluations as such are not new. Most enterprises would find it unthinkable to invest in new, more productive manufacturing equipment without a thorough investment evaluation. The investments in the development plan may be of the same order of magnitude. The purpose of formal procedures for cost/benefit analysis of development investments is:

- To provide uniform treatment of all investment proposals by establishing criteria for making judgments, recommendations, and decisions about them, and by making certain that a minimum amount of information at some level of quality is available.
- To determine economic feasibility of a proposed application, data, or system in terms of profitability and the effect on the capital needs of the company.
- To rank the various investments in order of importance not only relative to each other, but in relation to other investment alternatives outside I/S.
- To evaluate the relative cost of acquiring the solution from outside the company rather than developing it in-house.
- To highlight any uncertainty in the data used as input to the investment evaluations, and the sensitivity of these evaluations to errors.
- To create a firm basis for postinstallation cost/benefit control and to pinpoint unrealized expectations. For example, this year, user operational costs were $150,000 higher than anticipated; I/S production costs for the application were 15% lower than projected.

The purpose of any investment evaluation is to estimate the costs and benefits resulting from the implementation and use of applications, data, and systems. These investment evaluations will be used in the Resource Planning process group to make management decisions on the expected benefits versus the anticipated costs. Ideally, these costs and benefits should be expressed in monetary terms. This is not always possible in I/S because of many intangible factors.

In general, the economic feasibility of any proposed application, data, or system project should include this step-by-step procedure (Fig. 8–12):

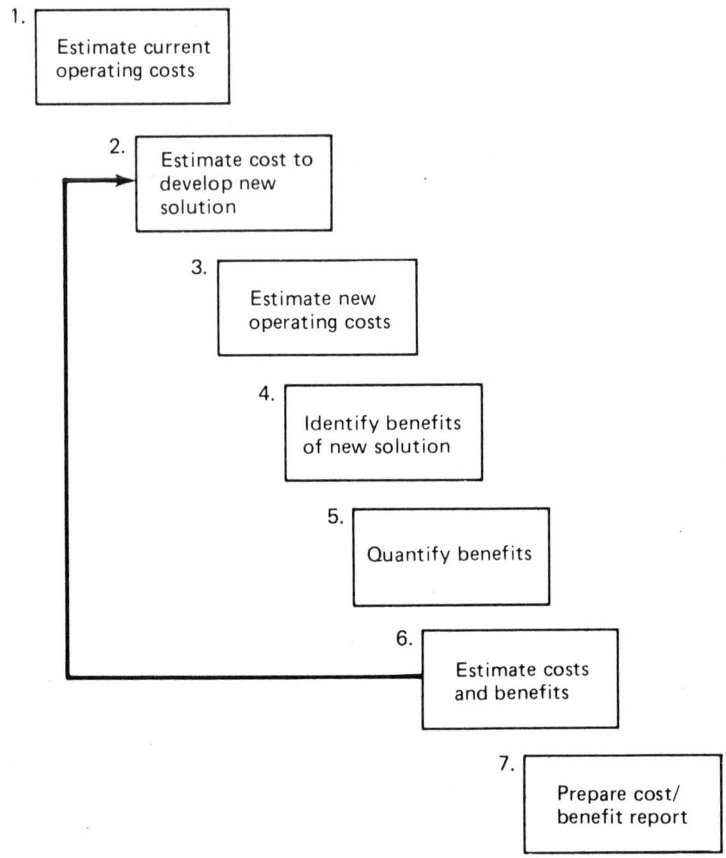

Figure 8–12 A step-by-step procedure for cost/benefit analysis.

1. Estimate the annual operating costs involved in perpetuating existing working methods. If the old system is a manual one, only user department operating costs are involved; if the new system is to replace one already automated, I/S department costs to operate the existing system in the future should also be estimated. Users should agree that the estimated user department costs are accurate.
2. Estimate the costs to develop (or acquire) and install the new proposed solution. A good project plan will provide all the background information needed to develop these costs by major development phase.
3. Estimate the annual operating costs of the proposed solution. These operating costs are composed of two parts:
    a. User department operating costs. The cost estimate produced under step 1 above is modified to include the user's assessment of the effect of introducing the proposed new solution.

b. I/S operating costs, which include both running costs and maintenance costs.

4. Identify the expected benefits to be gained from the proposed solution. At this stage, itemize only the benefits; quantification will follow next. One possible benefit, for example, is the reduced operating costs in the user department.
5. Quantify the benefits to determine the economic value of each of the benefits established. Benefits whose values cannot be quantified in monetary terms should be quantified using other measures whenever possible.
6. Evaluate the combination of tangible costs and returns using appropriate quantitative investment evaluation techniques.

   At this stage, the proposed solution may seem economically infeasible or the alternative approaches may be more attractive. Therefore, iteration of steps 2 through 6 may be required until a feasible alternative is found, or until a number of feasible alternatives have been explored.
7. Document the cost/benefit report as a supplement to the project objectives, giving consideration to tangible savings and intangible factors such as adherence to the enterprise's strategic plan.

Although the effort involved in bringing out all the true costs associated with the development, implementation, and operation of a new solution should not be underestimated, the problem of listing and quantifying the potential benefits is probably more time consuming and difficult.

The monetary value of a benefit is determined by its contribution to the net income or profit of the company. This contribution can occur as a reduction in outflow (reduced costs) or as an increase in cash inflow. However, benefits in the form of increased cash inflow are not necessarily the same as increased revenue. Assume that a user states that a proposed application will increase sales revenue by $100,000 per year due to increased sales volumes. If the increased revenue is accompanied by extra production and marketing expenses of $90,000 to manufacture and sell the additional goods, the real value of this benefit is not $100,000 but $10,000. However obvious this may seem in this trivial example, it is nevertheless a mistake often made in benefit assessments.

A computer application aimed principally at reducing operating costs by automating routine tasks (such as payroll administration and bookkeeping) is a straightforward investment with benefits fairly easy to evaluate. The operational savings, in this case, are the difference between the total projected operating cost using the present working methods and procedures, and the total projected operating cost using the proposed application, accounting for both user department costs and I/S costs. Mostly, savings arise from reduction in personnel due to displacement of people, but they may also come from reduced costs due to less use of floor space, equipment, and materials in the user department.

However, the significant contributions to the performance of a company come from applications that provide better quality of information, completely new information, more accurate and reliable information, information that is available faster, new ways to increase revenues, and ways to provide new services.

Some of the benefits here may be very obvious but are not always easy to quantify. What is the value of better information in decision processes, for instance? How do you quantify the improved service obtained with better information? In order to throw some light on the factors that need to be taken into account and the problems involved in quantifying benefits, consider a few examples.

The most obvious benefit of an automated accounts receivable system is probably the reduced operating cost. However, a much more important benefit is perhaps that the improved turnaround in invoicing reduces the cash requirements of the company (assuming that the delay between receipt of an invoice by the customer and receipt of payment by the company stays the same). With proper assumptions, the value of this benefit can be quantified in terms of reduced cost of capital (which affects the net income) and improved liquidity.

In this instance, quantification of the benefits in monetary terms is relatively straightforward. The corresponding analysis for an inventory management system, however, is a little more difficult. Again, some cost reduction is achieved by simplified administration of the inventory and purchasing activities. And if we estimate that the average inventory level is reduced by a certain amount, the benefits of that can be quantified in terms of the impact on net profit and tied-up capital. But what is the monetary value of fewer stockouts? It may be possible to state that the probability of stockout is reduced from 10% to 5% as a result of the new inventory management system, but what is the monetary value of having fewer stockouts that result in improved service to customers?

Quantification becomes even more difficult in evaluating the effects of improved management information on strategic and tactical decision making. This intangible benefit comes in the form of better decisions by human decision makers that finally lead to certain desired effects. Any attempts to attach a credible cash value will probably be futile.

Successful development of a reliable cost/benefit analysis depends very much on the ability of the analyst to quantify the benefits to be derived from the proposed solution. When the benefits are difficult to quantify, the analyst might consider the following:

- It is the users who can best determine and quantify the benefits of a proposed solution. They know how the solution is to be used and what business activities will be affected. On the other hand, users often have only vague ideas about what the cost of obtaining the desired information would be. Extensive cooperation between users and I/S analysts is a good starting point in the difficult task of assessing benefits and determining a reasonable trade-off between value and cost of information.
- If a benefit is not likely to have any major impact on the outcome of the final decision regarding a proposed solution, quantification is not necessary.

- Quantification through probability is one approach to reducing the risk of inaccurate benefit analysis (Fig. 8–13). Consider the following example:

  A small motor freight company wants to estimate the value of a vehicle-scheduling application to improve the utilization of its fleet of distribution trucks. Company management choose to account for the benefit in terms of reduced operating costs because fewer vehicles will be needed to do the same amount of transportation work. The total annual variable operating cost for the distribution activity is $1 million. The exact cost reduction expected is unknown, but experiences throughout the industry indicate normal gains to be in the range of 5 to 25%, depending on how efficient the manual scheduling is and the type of distribution activity.

  The company uses the following strategy to estimate the monetary value. First, probable ranges of cost reduction are established (column 1 of Fig. 8–13). Next, a subjective assessment of the probability of the cost reduction falling into each of these established ranges is made (column 2). By means of the calculations shown in columns 3 through 5, a dollar saving for each of the possible ranges of cost reduction is determined, and these savings are added together to give a total probable saving that represents the value of the benefit of improved utilization of distribution vehicles.
- The development plan will become a major input to the Budget Planning process. The value of a benefit as a line item in a budget makes it much more concrete and meaningful. Therefore, quantification becomes easier. If a benefit has a value, it should either reduce costs (line items of expense in the user's budget), or increase revenues (additional units sold).
- Quantification through pricing the value that the user is willing to pay for the benefits is another consideration. The user could be asked: How much are you

1 Possible Cost Reduction (%)	2 Probability of Occurrence (%)	3 Midpoint of Possible Cost Reduction (%)	4 Cost Reduction ($) Col. 3 x Total Cost	5 Probable Saving ($) Col. 2 x Col. 4
0 – 5	10	2.5	25,000	2,500
5 – 10	50	7.5	75,000	37,500
10 – 15	30	12.5	125,000	37,500
15 – 25	10	20.0	200,000	20,000
	0	–		
Total Probable Savings				97,000

Figure 8–13 Quantification of benefits through probability.

willing to pay for this benefit? One dollar? Ten thousand dollars? Five dollars? One thousand dollars? And so on. At some point an agreement on a reasonable price (and, therefore, value) is usually reached.

Once the cash flows have been determined for a proposed solution (initial investment, operating costs, and returns), the Project Planning process must combine the effects of these cash flows into a single measurable project proposal.

For the company, the project proposal is a common, standard measure that will tell us whether the anticipated future returns make the investment worthwhile, not only in itself, but also in relation to other potential investments.

Project planning summary

At the beginning of this section, we stated that the evaluation and selection of new I/S application, data, and systems is an important management task, possibly the most important one in I/S. The project proposal document deserves careful attention. It represents the concrete basis for management's evaluation and decision making; it establishes the financial, technical, and operational feasibility of the proposed application itself; and it establishes priority and significance relative to other investment opportunities, inside and outside the I/S area.

RESOURCE PLANNING

Resource planning overview

The strategic plan becomes a major source of information for the tactical-level process groups, Development Planning, Service Planning, and Management Planning (discussed in other chapters).

Another tactical process group, Resource Planning, receives requirements from Development Planning, Service Planning, and Management Planning and resolves them into a sensible, achievable, and coordinated tactical plan for the total I/S function (see Appendix A information flow). These processes compare the available and alternative resources against the identified resource requirements, identify imbalances, recommend corrective action, and publish an approved plan. This function also tracks achievements and triggers all tactical processes needed to react to deviations.

The processes in this group will be discussed in the following sequence (see Fig. 8–14):

1. Capacity Planning
    - Is the capacity of hardware, software, network, and facilities adequate to meet the service and development plans?
    - Is the plan for supplies adequate?
2. Skills Planning
    - How much staff at what level of education is required to meet the service and development plans?

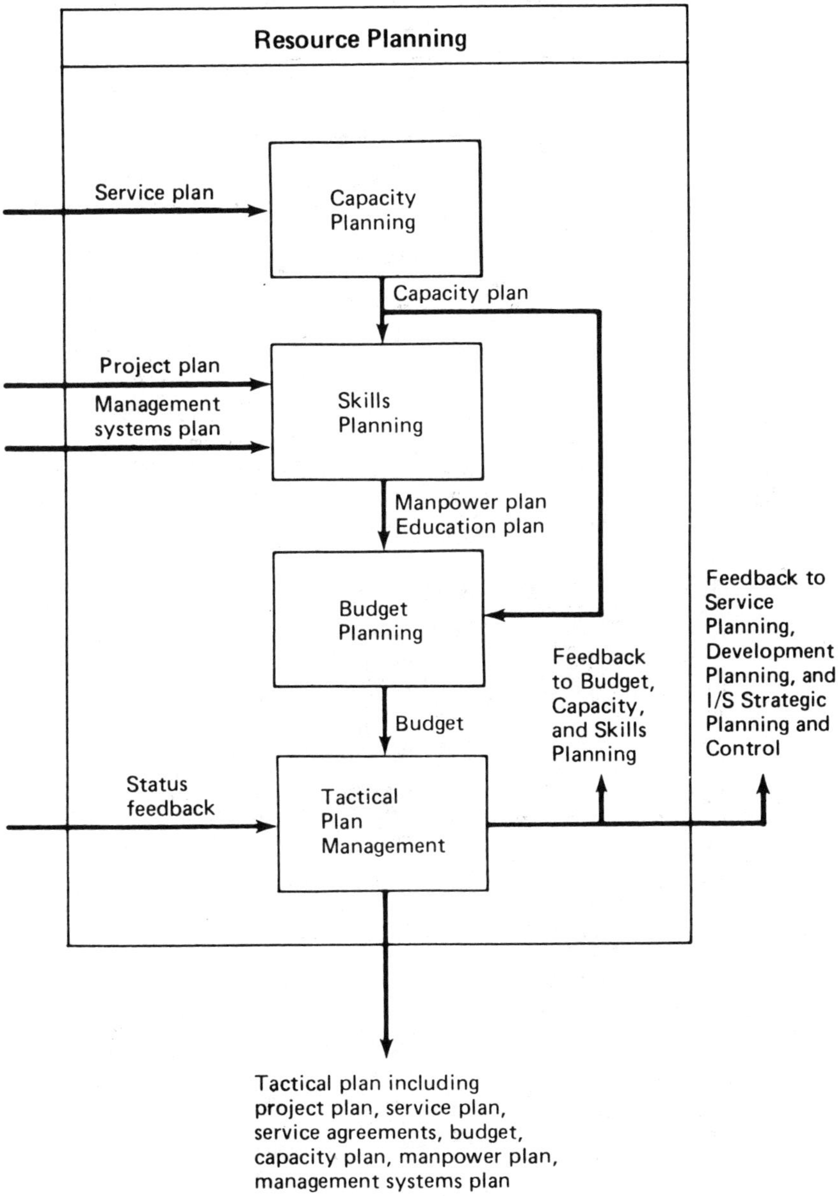

Figure 8–14 Resource planning overview.

- What job classifications are required for this personnel?

3. Budget Planning
   - What financial resources are required to meet the service and development plans?
   - What budgeting procedures are required?
4. Tactical Plan Management
   - Are the tactical resources balanced?
   - How does management approve the tactical plans for service, development, resources, and management?
   - How are the tactical plans tracked?

The tactical plan that results from the four processes listed above provides the framework for the day-to-day operational level processes of the I/S business and is often called the operating plan. At a minimum, this plan should be an operating budget for the various organizations involved in the I/S business.

A more complete operating plan would contain the service, development, management, and resource objectives defined in the Service Planning, Development Planning, Management Planning, and Resource Planning process groups, respectively. This includes among other things:

- Service agreements defining the service, measurements of that service, and requirements for resources
- Development projects defining the scope, basic tasks, and resources required
- Management projects defining procedure changes and the required resources

The key issue in Resource Planning is combining the resource needs for these objectives into an overall plan for capacity (hardware, software, facilities, and network), skills (people), and budget (finances). Once combined, management must make decisions that may require rethinking these objectives and priorities, or acquiring new resources. This is an iterative process.

These key resource issues are often not examined sufficiently until the project or service has begun. Projects without adequate resources cause the project team to overwork and quickly become frustrated. Requirements get dropped or schedules slip, creating dissatisfaction. Once the project has started, it is difficult to stop and wait for resources to become available even though there is no hope of completion. Under time pressures, the resulting resources are sometimes placed into service without adequate testing, resulting in service disruption and problems.

Resource Planning combined with Resource Control and Administrative Service process groups allow the management of I/S resources. As the I/S function grows and matures, this is increasingly critical. Some factors that contribute to this are:

- The I/S resources may not be under the direct control of the I/S organization. In some businesses, the development mission is performed by personnel working directly for the using departments. The traditional I/S organization may provide services ranging from consultation on development such as the Development Center to providing development production services.

- Terminals and some of the related equipment may be acquired, owned, and even operated by the user department.
- The production and distribution resources may be distributed around the enterprise with ownership by either the I/S department or user department.

Therefore, the resource plan must cover the whole I/S business regardless of distribution or ownership.

Assessing resource planning

The effectiveness and efficiency of the Resource Planning processes can be measured by the following questions:

- Are there processes in place that compare the available and alternative resources against identified requirements?
- Is there a capacity plan that is updated on a regular basis?
- Is there a facilities plan?
- Is management given proposal alternatives for meeting resource needs?
- Are the personnel and education plans documented?
- Are career paths documented and enforced?
- Is there a documented budget that is updated regularly?
- Are management reports available that include analysis of planned versus actual resource consumption?

Capacity Planning

DEFINITION:

Using the forecast load from new projects or from the evolution of existing services, this process defines in a capacity plan how I/S resources will cover the demand. It also proposes alternatives to management (for example, number of shifts, decreased services, changes in systems plan).

DESCRIPTION:

The elements of Capacity Planning are:

1. Translate service requirements into a load forecast of hardware, network, software, facilities, and supplies.
2. Define capacity of existing and planned resources (hardware, network, software, facilities, and supplies).

3. Compare load forecast against this defined capacity.
4. Identify, evaluate, and propose alternate load forecasts and capacity.
5. Document capacity plan.

DATA CLASSES REQUIRED:

Data input to process (data class)	Data output of process (data class)
P3 Systems plan	P9 Capacity plan
P7 Service plan	
P9 Capacity plan	
C6 System performance	
R2 Data	
R3 Software	
R4 Hardware	
R5 Network	
R6 Facilities	
R7 Supplies	
R10 Standards/procedures/methods	
R11 Test data	

Translate service requirements into a load forecast

The workload forecasts from Service Planning serve as a measure of the user demand for service. These service demands must be translated into resource demands needed to meet that load. Therefore, the historical or projected capacity requirement for each transaction, application, or service must be tracked and used to extend user demand to capacity demand. For example, a transaction type may historically take 0.25 second of host processor time and 100 input/output calls to complete. Using this data, the planner can project the effect of 1000 transactions per hour. Much of this data can be summarized from service and performance data captured in the Service Control process group.

It should be emphasized that Capacity Planning, like all other tactical processes, requires ongoing attention and is not limited to the planning of major installation changes. Too often this process is equated only with the actions required to plan the new central processor installation.

Trend reports showing the previous forecasts against the actual consumption can also be used (Fig. 8–15). For example, the capacity installed in the third quarter of year 1 was not adequate to cover the demands for the planning period, causing a shortage in the first quarter of year 2. The capacity planner failed to react to this situation and underestimated the following year by an even larger amount.

In year 3, the situation was finally corrected by bringing the capacity to the demand capacity level for the whole year. This self-correcting part of Capacity Planning should have been more responsive to prevent user dissatisfaction when enter-

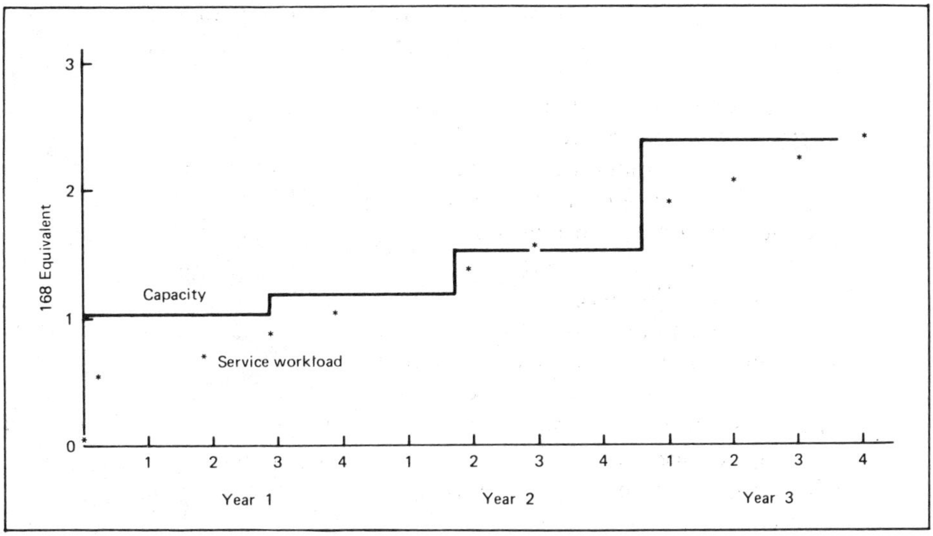

Figure 8–15 Capacity planning trend report.

prise demands were not met. A quarterly review of demand, planned capacity, and the capacity consumption would have increased this awareness.

Define capacity of existing and planned resources

Capacity planning of future equipment needs cannot normally be based only on extrapolations of historical data. Major changes in resource requirements (for example, new applications being installed) must also be considered. When evaluating the need for additional capacity, it is important to understand that the net capacity available for productive use is not the same as gross capacity installed. Losses in productive capacity due to scheduled preventive maintenance, unscheduled downtime, and maintenance and installation of new software releases must be considered.

Before the various techniques are discussed, it should be emphasized that Capacity Planning requires more than a highly skilled mathematician programming algorithms and models. Much of the work centers on defining long-range plans, tracking those plans, and making difficult business decisions for the installation. These management skills can be complemented by technical skills, but can never be replaced.

It should also be remembered that Capacity Planning does not have the responsibility to actually design the application, data, and system solution to be evaluated. The solution to be studied is based on three sources:

1. The overall application, data, and technology architectures were defined in the Strategic Planning and Control process group.
2. This strategy was expanded into a planned application, data, and system solution in the Development Planning process group.

3. The existing system inventory defines the applications, data, and systems already in existence or being altered by the Development and Maintenance process group.

In some cases, the planned resources may have such long lead times that the Systems Planning process placed a letter of intent or order to ensure delivery. At the operational planning and control level, this on-order resource becomes part of a formal project and must be actually ordered. Any significant variation between the tactical and operational planning levels may require a recycle of the Capacity Planning process. It is assumed that these existing and planned resources are the basis for Capacity Planning.

The techniques available for the projection of capacity are extensive and too complex to discuss in this chapter. However, some basic concepts should be reviewed.

Usage techniques. Tracking the usage of resources against services is essential to any technique and requires data capture and reduction in Service Control. Initially, critical resource measurements center around the host processor, storage, channels, communication lines, and high-response applications. Eventually all resources should be tracked.

Usage rules from other installations have been documented and made available so that customer data can be compared with situations elsewhere. The simplest of these is a system selection guide that provides performance and technical guidelines for products and systems. It has a number of specifications and rules of thumb to assist in sizing and capacity decisions.

U.S.A.G.E. (Understanding Your System and Application Growth Environment) is an IBM methodology used to forecast growth in host processor capacity requirements over a period of one to two years. It is based on customer recording of system data. U.S.A.G.E. consists of rules of thumb, tables, formulas, and calculations to allow the management team to make a capacity decision. U.S.A.G.E. statistics offer a simple and inexpensive method to handle the regular planning cycle requirements dealing with Capacity Planning.

The following techniques are designed for situations in which a major change is occurring and history does not provide an adequate method of projection:

Capacity modeling. An analytical model or mathematical formulas can be created to predict the system or subsystem required under the new conditions. Using this model, the planner can use estimates or current data on similar situations to project the results of the desired conditions. This approach is far more time consuming and expensive. Unless a model is already available, a highly trained, mathematically oriented person is needed to generate the formulas. In some cases, the lead time is too short to permit this approach. Even if a model is available, the results may be difficult to verify with real data.

Innumerable models have been developed to project computer performance, perform analytic queuing for on-line systems, and estimate performance of data base systems. The on-line queuing models can estimate transaction response for applications and resource utilization of resources such as host processor and disk storage. The data base models assist in the design of data bases and the related application.

Simulation techniques. Rather than a mathematical representation of the unknown situation, the capacity planner might use simulation techniques to project performance of the application or resources. An IBM model or simulator, System Network Analysis Program/Systems Host Overview Technique (SNAP/SHOT), will illustrate this approach.

Built into the simulator are performance characteristics of resources such as host processors, terminals, and communication lines. These are used to calculate the anticipated results of the situation to be simulated. It is difficult and expensive to keep these factors current in the rapidly changing computer environment.

The person requesting results from simulations must have some idea of the desired answer and uses the technique to prove or disprove the case. In most situations, the techniques are used for a specific set of conditions such as a new application, a new host processor type, or expanded terminals on the communication facilities. For example, SNAP/SHOT could simulate:

- A single line with intelligent controllers
- A major new on-line application
- The whole system

It should be remembered that complexity increases with each new variable, requiring more data and time for analysis.

To define the requirements to the simulator, the planner builds control information describing the application, message rate and types, configuration, and other factors. The simulator provides flexibility in analyzing the host, the network, or the communication system. This includes the ability to analyze multihost or distributed environments. The planner receives information on line utilization, transaction throughput response times, queue statistics, and other factors to identify critical resources.

Synthetic benchmarking. The most expensive and complex method is testing with actual resources under simulated conditions. Tools are available to store terminal messages in a script and present them to the on-line application as though many users were at real terminals. Typical uses include time sharing and information systems applications.

Since this is a real simulated environment, the test results can measure loading and response times for the conditions being tested. With the high cost of the run and resources, normally only a subset of resources and conditions can be analyzed. Unless the planner has ready access to test equipment, the time duration can be long.

The success of this technique depends on careful planning of the expected results and the simulated environment. In many cases, the test does not truly represent the real situation; it often provides inconclusive results. This technique is frequently used in conjunction with modeling or discrete simulation to generate resource data or verify model results. In all cases, this method should be used sparingly.

With these techniques, the Capacity Planning process can be used to project capacity growth for the installation and make recommendations to management. These must be merged with other resource recommendations in Tactical Plan Management.

Compare load forecast against this defined capacity

The development of a capacity plan generally requires that a large number of combinations be examined to investigate alternatives and to understand the sensitivity to critical variables. Critical variables such as transaction rates can be increased or decreased in the analysis to determine the effect of small errors in the estimates and to study the shape of the response curve. Sometimes the response deteriorates rapidly as the load is increased. The capacity requirements must be planned with these factors of anticipated growth in mind and with sensitivity to variables.

Identify, evaluate, and propose alternatives

Once the alternatives are examined, a recommendation must be made to management, including any imbalances between load and planned capacity. These imbalances must be studied and resolved in the Tactical Plan Management process. Available options include:

- Altering the load by having Service Planning, Development Planning, and/or Management Planning review the planned objectives on which the resource plan was built
- Altering the available resources by having Development Planning define an expanded system design to be used for the resource plan
- Combining these alternatives

Document capacity plan

The assumptions and rationale for the final selection must be documented in the tactical plan. This should include a brief overview of the alternatives studied in the planning process. The final plan is passed to Skills Planning and Budget Planning for completion of the resource plan.

Capacity planning summary

Capacity Planning is perhaps one of the most critical processes in the ISM Architecture. It must ensure that sufficient hardware, software, applications, networks, facilities, and other critical resources are adequate to provide quality service. A resource shortage will cause poor service. A resource excess could cause inefficient and costly operations or an increased price for the service. This balance must be established and agreed upon by management.

The next two processes ensure that adequate personnel and finances are available to meet this plan.

Skills Planning

DEFINITION:

Using the requirements identified in the project plan (including management systems) and in the service plan, this process defines in the personnel and education plans how the existing and planned skills will meet the demand.

DESCRIPTION:

The elements of Skills Planning are:

1. Define the personnel required to support the service plan.
2. Consolidate the personnel required for the project plan, service plan, and career paths.
3. Identify existing and planned personnel.
4. Establish and evaluate alternative personnel plans.
5. Define the education plan.
6. Document the personnel and education plans.

DATA CLASSES REQUIRED:

Data input to process (data class)	Data output of process (data class)
E3 I/S industry	P4 Personnel plan
P4 Personnel plan	
P7 Service plan	
P8 Project plan	
P9 Capacity plan	
A1 Vendor	
A3 Organization	
R8 Personnel	
R10 Standards/procedures/methods	

Define the personnel required to support the service plan

Investments in new I/S services have provided major contributions to the enterprise productivity and have traditionally been a means to control costs while increasing services. In today's environment, the same productivity issues are appearing in the I/S business itself. Considering that 50 to 75% of I/S budgets are personnel costs, this observation should not come as a surprise.

Henry Ford once defined productivity not as a measure of how hard we work but as how we use our intelligence, our imagination, and our tools. Since I/S has historically been staffed with young, highly intelligent personnel, it would appear that it has all the ingredients to address these productivity issues. Unfortunately, the emphasis has been on solving complex technical problems rather than on I/S productivity.

Management positions have traditionally been filled with persons well versed in this technical environment. Managers have not always balanced technical skill with sound business judgment on dealing with the productivity of the I/S functions.

To define the personnel needs for the service mission, one has to understand some of the basic trends of the industry. In general, the I/S workload increases at a rate ranging from as low as 13% to as high as 35% compound growth rate (CGR). At the same time, the cost of labor is increasing at rates that exceed 8 to 18% (CGR).

If this increased workload must be met with any significant growth in the staff required, the personnel costs will absorb an increasing share of the I/S budget. In many installations, the personnel budget already exceeds 50% of the budget. Some of this increased cost is offset by increased price/performance of the technology.

Combine this personnel growth with the problem of the shortage of skilled personnel in the industry and the conclusion is obvious. The I/S managers and technicians must become interested in both productivity and technology.

One approach to service staff productivity is to use techniques previously used in industrial engineering for other production operations. This approach includes:

- The classification and description of every job in the service function
- Comparison of each job against standards for the workload volumes to be achieved. In the specific area of tape mounts, a study showed that across 20 similar installations, significant differences were noted in the tape mounts per person per month. In fact, one center had 8000 and another had 800, a ratio of 10:1. This discrepancy can be explained by different working methods or physical circumstances in each center. Productivity methods in the best center could be applied to the worst, resulting in a better overall use of personnel.
- Applying techniques that improve the productivity of each job. One approach already discussed is the use of better techniques or methods. A second approach is computerized techniques to manage the resources and the tasks to use the resources. In the section on Resource Control, the possibility of computerized management of the I/S resource inventory (tapes, data bases, terminals, software, etc.) provides a clear productivity solution. New technology such as mass storage can even reduce or eliminate the need for some I/S job positions.

  To use these productivity techniques, Skills Planning must monitor the development and management plans for weaknesses that would cause an unnecessary staffing burden. Likewise, management should make the productivity issues a key factor in those plans.
- Monitor productivity and define new standards based on these measurements. Productivity reporting was discussed in the Administration Services section.

Consolidate personnel required

The Development and Maintenance processes have a similar productivity issue. Since this area is normally staffed with even more highly skilled personnel, the results can be more critical. Labor saved can be used to reduce the application backlog or to apply computerized support for the service functions.

The combined service and project needs must be analyzed relative to the available personnel and planned career paths. The importance of building adequate skill levels cannot be overemphasized. The lead time to hire and train people combined with the general shortage of experienced personnel makes this process extremely critical. In enterprises with mature Skills Planning, I/S managers are being trained in the skills associated with good counseling and career setting. Many enterprises have regular management training programs that can be used for this purpose. The transition of good technical personnel into managers is something that will not always occur without formal training.

Identify existing and planned personnel

One approach to expanding the career path of I/S personnel is to concentrate on creating skills that can be used throughout the enterprise. In most enterprises, I/S constitutes less than 1% of the total enterprise personnel needs. One technique to open the other 99% of the enterprise for I/S personnel can be incorporated into the Development and Maintenance processes. User department personnel are brought into the I/S organization on a temporary basis to help design the requirements for the new information system and to develop a test plan for it. When the system becomes operational, these persons become responsible for the use and integrity of the system. This flow of people in and out of the I/S business allows the analyst to understand better the total enterprise and to develop skills required for careers in user areas.

To meet the extensive personnel needs for I/S, the roles of the user and I/S must be evaluated and planned. Limited, critical I/S resources can be supplemented with user resources as described. In other approaches such as the information center, the user may even be required to assume the role of analyst and programmer for certain requirements.

Establish and evaluate personnel plans

In some installations, a transfer of management talent has been used to increase the effectiveness of personnel planning. I/S manager positions, including the top I/S executive, are being filled with persons having an outstanding record as a good manager elsewhere in the enterprise. These people face the challenge of learning to control a highly technical business. The concepts in this document assist that effort.

If I/S can be considered a business, many general management concepts can be applied to its effective planning and control. This does not eliminate the need for highly technical managers in certain areas, but allows traditional skills to be used at the top and middle management levels.

Define education plan

In this changing personnel environment, the need for education is more and more critical. As part of the personnel plan, this factor should be documented and stated as a financial requirement.

Skills planning summary

Skills Planning is no less essential than Capacity Planning. Together, they define the resources to make the service and project plan work. The next process will examine the financial needs of the resource plan.

Budget Planning

DESCRIPTION:

This process converts individual plans into financial terms and identifies how funds will be obtained and allocated.

DESCRIPTION:

The elements of Budget Planning are:

1. Translate plans (system, service, project, capacity, personnel, and education) into financial terms.
2. Reconcile sources of funds.
3. Establish and evaluate alternative budgets.
4. Document departmental budgets.

DATA CLASSES REQUIRED:

Data input to process (data class)	Data output of process (data class)
E2 I/S business	P5 Financial plan
P3 Systems plan	
P4 Personnel plan	
P5 Financial plan	
P7 Service plan	
P8 Project plan	
P9 Capacity plan	
A3 Organization	
R9 Financial	
R10 Standards/procedures/methods	

Translate plans into financial terms

Assuming all the planning processes leading to Budget Planning have been done properly, this element need only combine all the results. Too often, this work is not accomplished and the budget cycle is substituted for tactical planning. Assumptions about the strategic, development, service, and resource objectives are based more on the budget than on true user needs. An I/S business responsive to the enterprise must place these planning processes in their proper sequence.

The first step is to examine each plan produced by the previous processes:

- The service plan defines the services, their costs, and the means of charging customers for that service.
- The development plan defines the projects to be accomplished, the cost of those projects, and the means of charging customers for that development.
- The personnel plan defines the skills required, their costs, and the education required to maintain skill levels, and relates those skills to the respective service and development plans.
- The system and capacity plans provide detailed information about the resources included in the service and development plans. This includes historical data about the usage of these resources.

There is considerable diversity of budgeting practices among both enterprises and their I/S subset. A typical budget consists of three types of budgets: an operating budget showing operations for the forthcoming planning period, a cash budget showing the anticipated sources of cash and use of cash, and a capital budget showing planned acquisitions of fixed assets. Each of the plans must be translated into these budgets.

- The operating budget is prepared for each organization in terms of revenues and expenses. It presents financial plans in a meaningful form to the people responsible for carrying out the I/S business. Within I/S, the costs of each organizational unit are shown separately to serve as a control of the expected performance.

  Costs and expenses are also prepared for each product (such as an application). The product-oriented cost budget is less useful for control purposes unless the organizational structure responsible for the development cost is clearly defined.

  The organizational and product budgets are based on the same operating budget total.
- For cash management, the revenues and expenses of the operating budget must be translated into cash receipts and cash disbursements. The result of this translation is the cash budget, which is used to ensure that the enterprise will have enough cash during the period covered by the budget.
- The capital budget is essentially a list of what management considers to be worth-

while acquisitions of new fixed assets. The most important fixed asset is the computing equipment in the I/S environment. If the enterprise purchases equipment, the capital demand can be appreciable.

Most enterprises prepare their budgets once a year. Responsible managers should participate in the budgeting process and should agree that the budgeting goals are reasonable. The budget is of little value unless it is supported with sufficient details to clearly pinpoint the manager's role.

Reconcile sources of funds

While the savings or benefits of computers are realized primarily by the users, most of the costs are generated in the I/S organization. The Budget Planning process must review the proposed budget and establish the source of funds. In most cases, these funds will be an internal transfer between the user and I/S departments. In other cases, the I/S function may be a true profit center with funds coming as revenues from outside sources. All these must be examined in this process.

Establish and evaluate alternative budgets

As I/S accounts for a larger and larger share of the company's financial resources, the demand increases for I/S to control costs and to show that it is cost-justified. Correct decisions regarding new applications can be made only if the cost estimates for development, production, and maintenance are accurate. Moreover, after completing a development project, actual costs incurred need to be totaled and compared with initial projected costs. When an application has been put into production, the actual costs must be continually monitored.

Effective budgeting and cost accounting of I/S services is becoming more and more important, regardless of the cost allocation approach used for user departments. There are valid reasons to manage the I/S function by the same strict standards used in other business units. This implies two factors:

1. Cost must be managed from an organizational viewpoint. Each manager within the I/S function should be held responsible for all authorized costs.
2. Cost must be managed by product. Costs for a product (directly or indirectly) must be accumulated and evaluated over the entire product life cycle.

The cost data that an enterprise develops, collects, and maintains is used for two purposes: financial accounting and management control. Financial accounting mainly provides financial information to parties outside the business, such as stockholders and government agencies. It is only concerned with historical information. Management control is concerned with information that helps managers do their jobs effectively; consequently, it is not only concerned with historical data but also with estimates of what will happen in the future.

Document departmental budgets

Budget Planning should have the following capabilities:

- To provide for complete budgeting of the I/S business, including all its subunits, application systems, projects, and activities.
- To provide for continual and systematic accounting of costs by organizational unit, application system, project, and activity.
- By close coordination with the Administration Services process group, to permit monitoring of actual costs versus projected costs for organizational unit, application system, project, and activity. This includes the capability of making postactivity cost analysis and tracking the results of new working techniques.
- To provide a basis for equitable distribution of costs for the I/S services to users (where the enterprise has decided to charge out costs).
- To provide a historical basis for improving planning and budgeting methods in the future as experience is accumulated.

Budget planning summary

Cost overruns have been so common in I/S that many people assume they are inevitable. This situation is unacceptable in any true business environment. I/S expenditures have often reached proportions where they affect the profit picture of the entire enterprise. All managers are expected to make plans and commit to them. A budget is really only a plan expressed in financial terms. Moreover, a budget can be used for control and coordination.

Tactical Plan Management

DEFINITION:

This process merges individual plans and resolves any imbalances. It monitors performance against the total plan and determines any corrective action that is necessary.

DESCRIPTION:

The elements of Tactical Plan Management are:

1. Balance the plans (service, project, capacity, personnel, education, budget, system, application, and data) and obtain management approval.
2. Publish the plans (service, project, capacity, personnel, education, budget, system, application, and data).
3. Compare actual attainment with the plan and analyze variances.
4. Rebalance the plans and obtain management approval (if necessary).
5. Republish the approved plan (if necessary).

DATA CLASSES REQUIRED:

Data input to process (data class)	Data output of process (data class)
E1 Enterprise	C9 Tactical plan
E2 I/S business	
P1 Application plan	
P2 Data plan	
P3 Systems plan	
P4 Personnel plan	
P5 Financial plan	
P6 Management systems plan	
P7 Service plan	
P8 Project plan	
P9 Capacity plan	
C1 Service	
C2 Project	
C6 System performance	
C7 Production and distribution schedule	
C8 Management systems performance	
C9 Tactical plan	
R8 Personnel	
R9 Financial	
R10 Standards/procedures/methods	

Balance plans

Managers participating in the Tactical Plan Management process must make the final decision on the acceptability of all the proposed plans (service, project, capacity, personnel, education, budget, system, application, and data). Each plan must be evaluated individually and collectively to understand the total planned results over the planning horizon, normally two years. Imbalances must be documented and studied for possible corrective actions. Finally, recommendations must be made to alter specific plan proposals or accept the combined results.

Using these recommendations, the original planning processes can create a new proposal or build more justification for the original proposal. Therefore, this process is the end of the iterative loop, which must be cycled until all issues are resolved and a plan finalized. The effectiveness of the tactical planning process will be measured by the ability of the operational level processes to achieve the results. The efficiency of these processes is dependent on the frequency of planning and the length of time required to resolve these iterations.

In some installations, this cycle is performed annually unless some major event forces a reevaluation; for example, some major technological announcement or new business direction will reopen the planning cycle. In other installations, the plan is updated on a quarterly basis to keep the plan more current and reflect changes in the business environment. With this rolling plan approach, a new quarter is added as the oldest quarter is dropped from the planning horizon. The second approach is feasible only if the tactical planning process iteration time is short and the processes are driven by a formal planning organization.

All plans must be based on certain assumptions about the future. To arrive at valid assumptions, a large amount of supporting background information must be collected and analyzed. Whenever possible, such information should be expressed in quantitative as well as qualitative terms.

Publish plans

Dissemination of the plan to the many managers and operating personnel is a challenge, especially if the plan is to be a true working document. All too often such plans are like a treasured trophy, only to gather dust on the manager's shelf. A simple hard-cover notebook that can be easily updated makes the document more useful. A simple checklist summary is useful as a working addendum.

In cases in which the rolling plan approach is used, the plan can even be placed on-line to make it more accessible. The time for each planning iteration is reduced and managers have immediate access to the latest version of the plan, as well as to all previous versions for trend analysis.

Compare actual attainment with the plan and analyze variance

These plans are a major input to the operating level process groups: Service Control, Development and Maintenance Control, and Resource Control. Those process groups control the day-to-day tasks to achieve the desired results.

Data generated at the operational control level must be accessible to the planning processes to track the actual attainment and replan if necessary. At monthly intervals, this control loop examines quarterly trends and the magnitude of daily fluctuations. This analysis measures the effectiveness of the tactical planning processes.

Rebalance the plans

Based on the foregoing analysis, management must make several difficult decisions to correct any variance:

- Hold any management decision and wait for more trend data.
- Make recommendations based on the available information to the Capacity Planning, Skills Planning, and Budget Planning processes to alter the resource plan, including facilities.
- Make recommendations based on the available information to the Service Planning, Development Planning, Management Planning, or Strategic Planning and Control processes to alter the objectives and the subsequent resource plan.
- Decide on a combination of the above choices.

All involved managers should participate in this decision-making exercise, normally in a monthly staff meeting. Although the actual replanning is done by the responsible manager, the staff meeting encourages cooperation and minimizes the chance that different managers will unilaterally correct the variance. These manager actions sometimes conflict, increasing the variance rather than solving it.

Republish the approved plan

The importance of keeping every involved manager current with the plan cannot be overemphasized. This area requires close management attention.

Tactical plan management summary

The Tactical Plan Management process is the critical bridge to the day-to-day operational time horizon. By looking ahead over the 12- to 24-month time horizon, this process can give the "doers" a solid framework for doing their daily tasks. They can then concentrate on doing their tasks in the most efficient manner.

ANOTHER SUCCESS

Your Management Planning study made recommendations that greatly improved the planning of I/S resources in the merged companies. Alex was again happy.

Success seems to breed success. You have been promoted to corporate vice-president of planning and administration for the new merger. Ms. Allen has become the vice-president of information systems.

The moral of this book is: The three windows (phases of growth, the 7-S factors, and the ISM Architecture) can give you a clear view to the top of the organization.

Appendix A:
*Detailed ISM Process Model**

SERVICE MISSION PROCESSES

Service Planning Group

Service marketing planning (1)

Considering the services to be offered during the tactical period, this process evaluates who could use them and forecasts market prices and service volumes for the tactical time horizon. In addition, this process reviews the marketplace for the new services and resources defined under Development Planning and feeds back any additional requirements.

1. Define the marketplace for all existing and proposed services/applications. This includes any outside service offerings.
2. Define service offerings.
3. Forecast service volumes by major classes of service.
4. Plan and publish basis for charging users if appropriate.
5. Plan the promotion of services sponsored by I/S.

*Entire appendix is reproduced from *A Management System for the Information Business,* Vol. I—*Management Overview,* GE20-0662-1, by permission of the IBM Corporation.

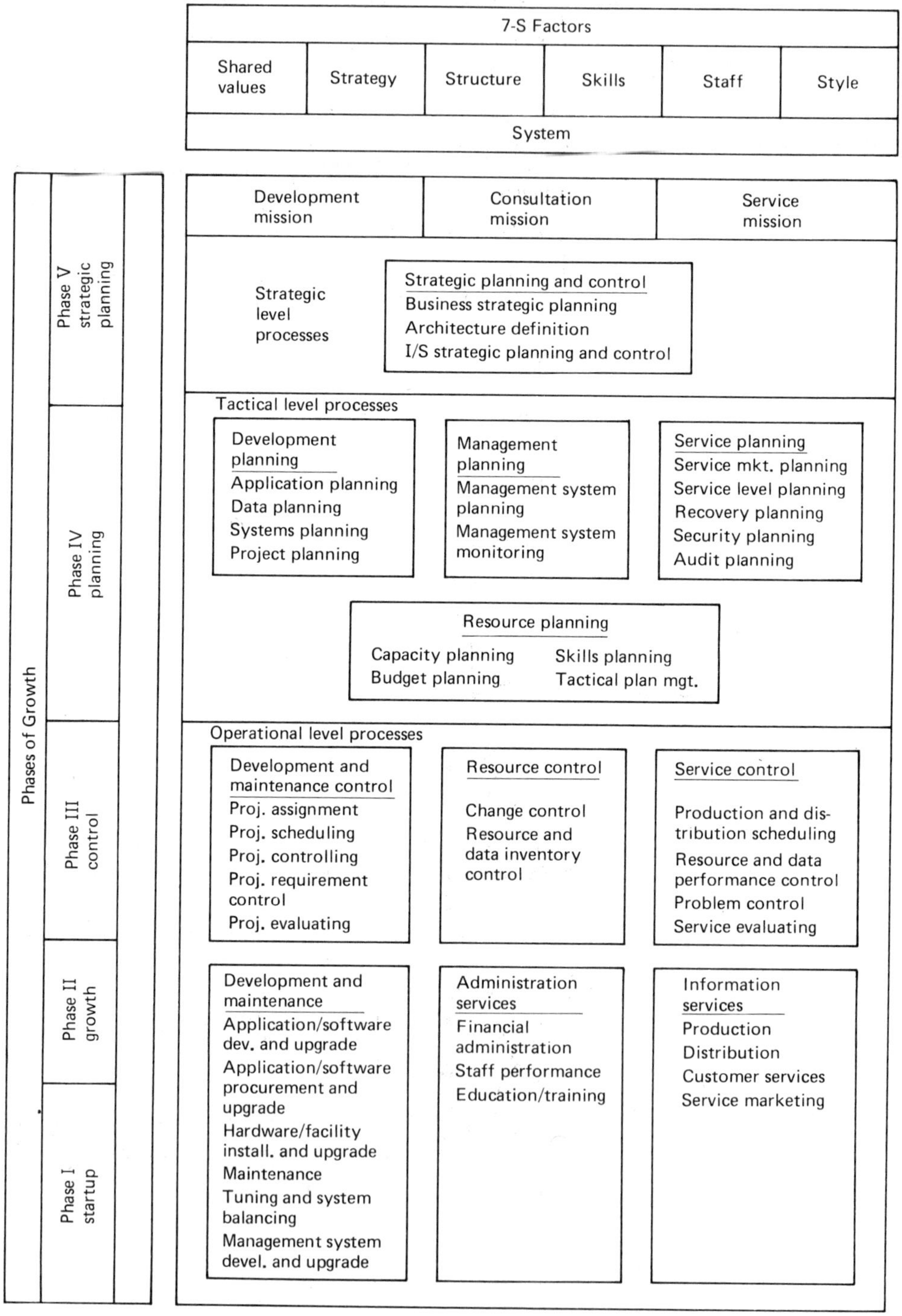

Figure A–1 ISM process overview. Reproduced by permission of the IBM Corporation.

Service-level planning (2)

Using the service volume forecasts and service charge rates, this process negotiates individual service agreements which define respective I/S and user commitments for the tactical time period. It also identifies individual requests for recovery, security, and auditability and creates an overall service plan which incorporates consolidated recovery, security, and audit plans.

1. Negotiate service agreements (including recovery, security, audit, and charges).
2. Forecast volumes by service agreements.
3. Develop a preventive maintenance plan.
4. Review agreed service agreements and define the required consultation, help desk, and other support services.
5. Define a total service plan including service levels, recovery, security, and auditability.

Recovery planning (3)

Using individual requests for recovery, this process builds an overall plan to ensure the agreed-upon service for users in case of failure or disaster.

1. Consolidate recovery requirements of all service agreements.
2. Define business and I/S recovery operating environment.
3. Identify variances between operating environment and agreements.
4. Develop overall recovery plan.

Security planning (4)

Using individual requests, this process builds an overall plan to ensure the agreed-upon levels of security for the systems and services will be met.

1. Consolidate security requirements of all service agreements.
2. Define business and I/S security operating environment.
3. Identify variances between operating environment and agreements.
4. Develop overall security plan.

Audit planning (5)

Using individual requests, this process builds an overall plan to ensure that the agreed-upon levels of auditability for the systems and services will be met.

1. Consolidate audit requirements of all service agreements.
2. Define business and I/S audit operating environment.
3. Identify variances between operating environment and agreements.
4. Develop overall audit plan.

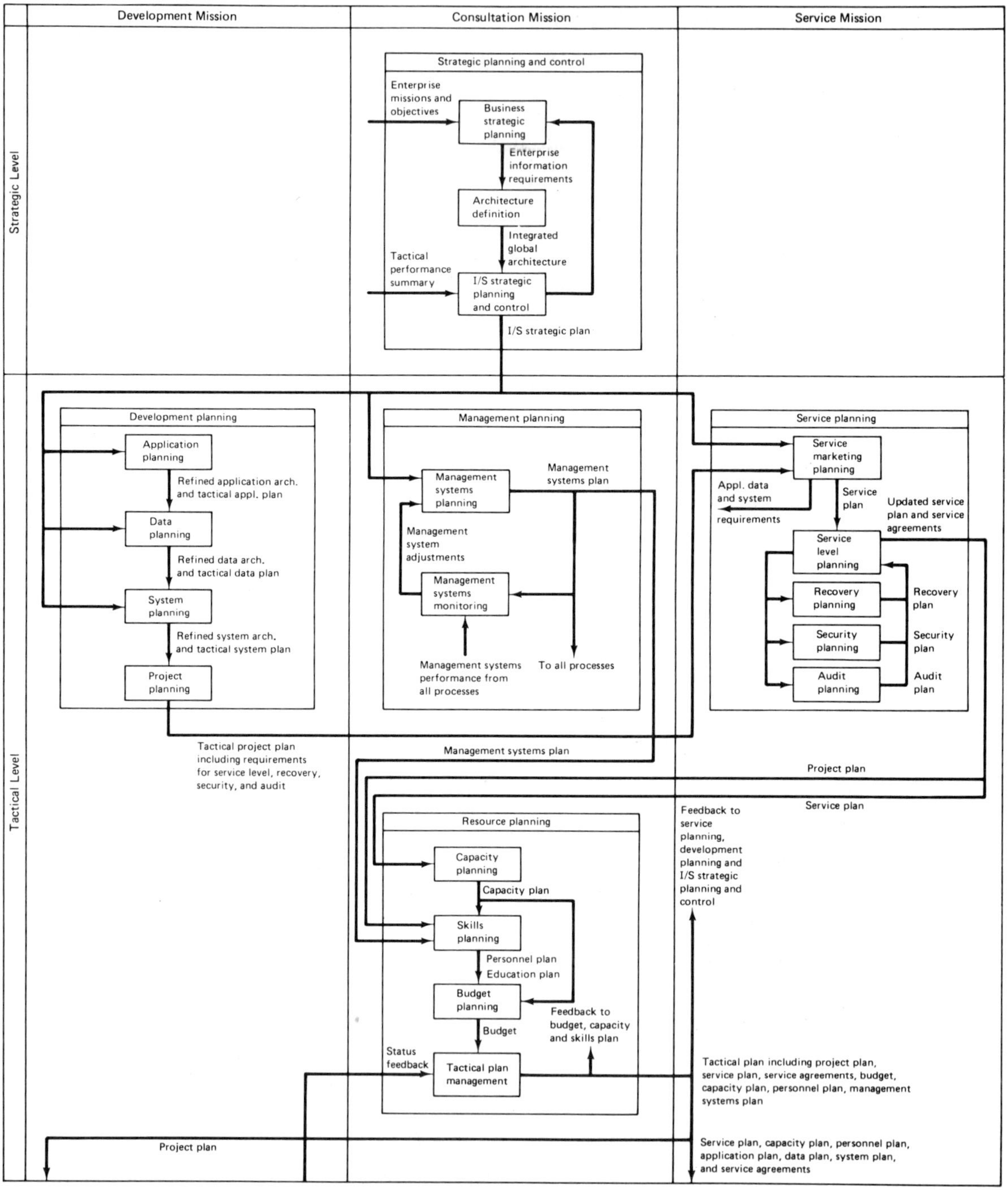

Figure A–2 Information systems management architecture. Reproduced by permission of the IBM Corporation.

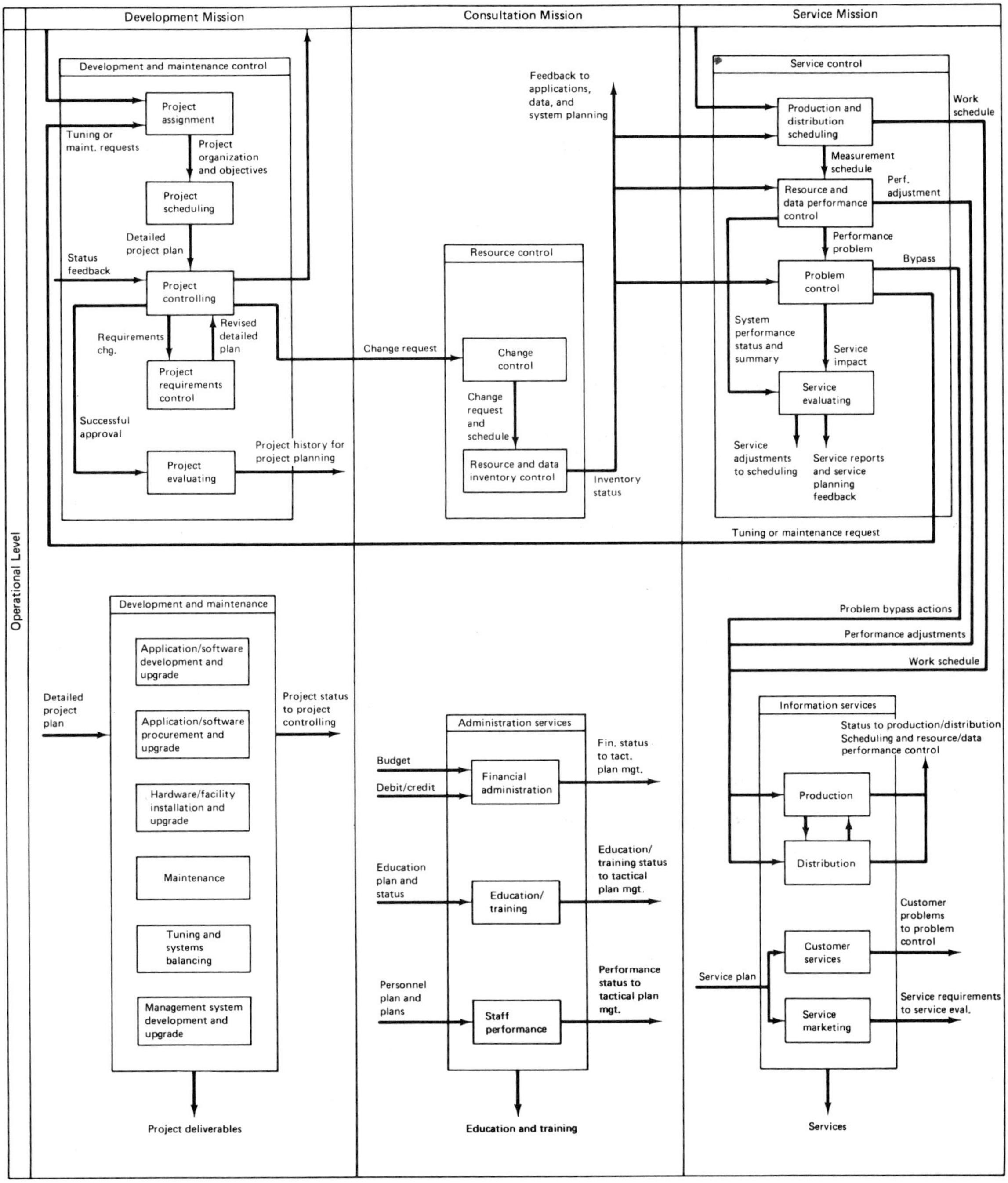

Figure A–2 *(cont.)*

Service Control Group

Production and distribution scheduling (6)

Using the tactical plan and the inventory, this process translates planned service agreements into a 1- to 90-day schedule of work and performance measurement for Production and Distribution.

1. Plan production and distribution service workload.
2. Develop a maintenance and measurement schedule.
3. Develop current work schedule.
4. Negotiate any deviations from the service agreements with users.
5. Publish work, maintenance, and measurement schedules.
6. Monitor and modify schedule (as necessary).

Resource and data performance control (7)

Using the measurement schedule and criteria, this process quantifies, measures, and reports system performance levels to I/S management and service evaluation process. It also triggers performance adjustment activities or performance problem activities.

1. Measure performance.
2. Analyze trends, deviations, and thresholds.
3. Select predefined corrective actions based on the work and measurement schedule (if necessary).
4. Notify Problem Control of any uncorrectable situations.
5. Report system, application, and data status.

Problem control (8)

This process receives problems (including performance problems) and monitors their resolution by requesting bypass actions and/or projects (maintenance or tuning). It informs the service evaluating process of the service impact of the problems.

1. Recognize problem.
2. Report and log problem.
3. Determine nature, impact, and true extent of the problem.
4. Select predefined bypass and recovery procedures.
5. Initiate action to resolve the problem.
6. Report and control status of all problems in hand.

Service evaluating (9)

Using the performance status and the problem impacts, this process translates them into user terms and compares them with service agreements. It also identifies and reports any variances to users and management.

1. Translate operational data (production, distribution, performance, and problem) into service-level terms.
2. Assess user rating of service.
3. Evaluate compliance to service agreements.
4. Identify and report reasons for variance.
5. Report service status and new service requests.

Information Services Group

Production (10)

This process schedules and executes jobs, transactions, and data through the hardware/software on a minute-to-minute basis to meet the agreed-upon service levels. It monitors the progress of work against the schedule and takes corrective actions (based on the 1- to 90-day schedule defined in production and distribution scheduling).

1. Receive jobs, transactions, and input data from distribution.
2. Set up, initiate, and run jobs and transactions.
3. Make jobs, transactions, and output data available to distribution.
4. Monitor progress of production work against the production and distribution schedules and take corrective action (if necessary).
5. Execute predefined or emergency production precedures for bypass, recovery, security, and/or performance.
6. Record and report information on status, incidents, actions taken, and results.

Distribution (11)

This process schedules jobs, transactions, information, and data through the distribution network on a minute-to-minute basis to meet the agreed-upon service levels. It monitors the progress of information movements against the schedule and takes corrective actions (based on the 1- to 90-day schedule established in production and distribution scheduling). It also includes the receiving, storing, and shipping of data and information through the distribution network.

1. Translate data into machine-readable form.
2. Receive, register, and validate input from all sources.
3. Package, distribute, check, and register outputs.
4. Monitor progress of distribution work against the production and distribution schedules and take corrective action (if necessary).
5. Execute predefined or emergency distribution procedures for bypass, recovery, security, and/or performance.
6. Report distribution status, incidents, actions taken, and results.

Customer services (12)

This process provides an interface with the user to understand their expectations and to help and guide them in realizing these expectations.

1. Publish support service offerings including contact person and telephone number.
2. Provide user help offerings for appropriate services (e.g., information center, development center, and user help desk).
3. Forward all problems to the appropriate function.

Service marketing (13)

This process markets services to users and identifies needs for future services. This includes the sale of any product, resource, or service developed and/or owned by the I/S organization.

1. Select service offerings to fit client needs.
2. Market these offerings appropriately.
3. Report user needs for new services.
4. Initiate actions to provide services.
5. Execute public relations activities on behalf of the I/S organization.

DEVELOPMENT MISSION PROCESSES

Development Planning Group

Application planning (14)

Considering each key function of the enterprise which has to be addressed during the tactical period and the existing applications, this process translates the strategic goals and direction into an application plan.

1. Expand the application architecture for each area where service is to be developed and/or supplied.
2. Develop/update application plan for the tactical time period.

Data planning (15)

Using the application plan and the present status of data, this process translates the strategic goals and direction into a data plan.

1. Expand data architecture in relation to the updated application architecture.
2. Develop a proposed updated data plan for the tactical time period.

Systems planning (16)

Using the application and data plans, the present status of hardware, software, and network, and the request for modification of existing services, this process translates the strategic goals and direction into a systems plan for hardware, software, and network.

1. Expand systems architecture in relation to the updated application and data architectures. This architecture will be used for later capacity planning.
2. Develop proposed and updated system plan for the tactical time period. The systems plan includes current/planned resources (hardware, software, and facilities) and those for scheduled maintenance.

Project planning (17)

Using application, data, and systems plans, this process translates them into manageable, clearly defined, and documented projects.

1. Define technically feasible and manageable projects.
2. Define project resources, time, and service-level requirements (including recovery, security, and audit requirements).
3. Define any unique control requirements for each project.
4. Financially justify and prioritize the project plan.

Development and Maintenance Control Group

Project assignment (18)

Using the tactical plan, this process defines, in a project organization and objectives document, the project scope, leadership, and user involvement necessary to ensure successful accomplishment.

1. Select project leader.
2. Define I/S and user involvement.
3. Obtain management commitment.

Project scheduling (19)

Using the plans and the documentation of the project, this process prepares a detailed project plan including objectives, resources, time scale, tasks, organization, and deliverables. This process also obtains approval from the project team, sponsor, and I/S.

1. Define deliverables.
2. Define tasks.

3. Estimate project.
4. Schedule resources.
5. Finalize detailed project plan.

Project controlling (20)

Using the detailed project plan, this process monitors the project through its phases, conducting reviews, resolving any development problems, and documenting its life. This also includes submitting the change request to move the deliverables to the system inventory.

1. Track progress against plan.
2. Report status.
3. Conduct project reviews, resolve development problems, and review any make/buy decision.
4. Submit change request.

Project requirements control (21)

This process accepts or rejects requests for changes and adjusts the detailed project plan to incorporate the approved ones. These changes result from modified objectives, new procedures, new technology, or errors in the original project scope.

1. Receive requests for requirements changes from users and other sources.
2. Analyze specifications of new request, including the impact on the project.
3. Accept or reject request.
4. Revise project plan (if necessary).

Project evaluating (22)

Using the detailed project plan and the project history, this process documents its completion and ensures that all promised deliverables were actually furnished. It compares actual and planned results and identifies reasons for variances.

1. Document the final status of the project and of the deliverables.
2. Compare project achievement with the project plans.
3. Identify and report reasons for variances.
4. Obtain approval to terminate the project and report completion.

Development and Maintenance Group

Application/software development and upgrade (23)

Within the framework of a project, this process develops and upgrades applications, operating systems software, other support software, and all the related documentation.

1. Define detailed requirements (including recovery, security, and audit).
2. Design externals of application.
3. Design internals of the application.
4. Structure data.
5. Negotiate design compromises with users.
6. Develop and test programs.
7. Integrate and test application, including modules procured.
8. Install application/software.

Application/software procurement and upgrade (24)

Within the framework of a project, this process procures and modifies applications, operating systems software, with supporting software, and all the related documentation. It controls the basic "buy" cycle.

1. Define detailed requirements for ideal system.
2. Review function, integrity, and performance of available offerings, including vendor modifications promised.
3. Negotiate compromises with users.
4. Confirm or amend "buy" decision and select system.
5. Define system recovery for operating environment.
6. Generate system and execute provided tests.
7. Publish instructions for integrating into operating environment.
8. Integrate and test application/software, including modules supplied.
9. Install application/software.

Hardware/facility installation and upgrade (25)

Within the framework of a project, this process selects, installs, removes, modifies, and upgrades I/S hardware/facilities.

1. Define detailed requirements.
2. Select hardware/network/facility.
3. Lay out physical planning.
4. Define hardware/network/facility recovery.
5. Test new unit.
6. Test complete system.
7. Install hardware/network/facility.

Maintenance (26)

Within the framework of a project, this process corrects defects in hardware, applications, software, and facilities (including engineering changes and program temporary fixes).

1. Revalidate cause of problem.
2. Understand environment of suspect component.
3. Diagnose suspect component.
4. Determine fix for failing component.
5. Test fix.
6. Install fix.

Tuning and system balancing (27)

Within the framework of a project, this process tunes the I/S resources to ensure proper performance of individual or groups of resources. This includes periodic regression testing to ensure that new changes have not caused undesired performance results in existing resources.

1. Define detailed requirements.
2. Develop solution.
3. Execute test of new or modified unit.
4. Test complete system.
5. Install new system.

Management systems development and upgrade (28)

Within the framework of a project, this process develops and modifies management standards, procedures, and methods for use within the I/S organization. It also develops methods to measure their effectiveness and efficiency.

1. Define detailed requirements based on enterprise policies.
2. Evaluate alternative standards, procedures, and methodology.
3. Design solution.
4. Publish instructions for use of these standards, procedures, and methodology.
5. Test solution in limited environment.
6. Install solution.

CONSULTATION MISSION PROCESSES

Strategic Planning and Control Group

Business strategic planning (29)

Using all available inputs from the enterprise (formal and informal), this process defines what the enterprise demands of its I/S function through the strategic plan period and what freedom I/S has in meeting these demands.

1. Define I/S mission based on enterprise mission and objectives.

2. Define I/S policies.
3. Define business processes, information, and information flow of the enterprise.
4. Define enterprise requirements for information through the strategic time period.

Architecture definition (30)

Using the information obtained in Business Strategic Planning process and considering the whole enterprise, this process defines in I/S terms the goals toward which all further action should be undertaken.

1. Define data architecture for the enterprise.
2. Define application architecture for the enterprise.
3. Define I/S technology architecture for the enterprise.
4. Integrate architectures.

I/S strategic planning and control (31)

Based on the goals of I/S and the constraints of the enterprise, this process provides, in an I/S strategic plan, the general direction on how to attain these goals. It specifies the sequence in which the key activities of the enterprise will be addressed and how the existing services provided will evolve. It also ensures coherence and consistency of this direction against the tactical achievements.

1. Evaluate alternate implementation of services, applications, and data, including business justification and risk assessment.
2. Define and prioritize the strategic objectives within the I/S policies.
3. Obtain approval for the I/S strategic plan.
4. Control the I/S strategic plan against the tactical performance.

Management Planning Group

Management systems planning (32)

Using strategic guidance and an assessment of the existing management system, this process defines a prioritized management plan to improve the management system through a project approach.

1. Relate this I/S process model to the local situation.
2. Define I/S organization and its objectives.
3. Relate organizational responsibility to the I/S processes.
4. Define the requirements for standards, procedures, and methodology to enhance the management system and thus increase the effectiveness and efficiency of the I/S processes (including financial and personnel performance/productivity improvements).

5. Define technically feasible and manageable projects to support the management system.
6. Define project resources and time.
7. Justify and prioritize the management systems plan.

Management systems monitoring (33)

Using feedback from all the I/S processes, this process assesses the effectiveness of the management system and makes sure that it will be enhanced, if necessary.

1. Collect and summarize organization performance data.
2. Compare to the organizational objectives and standards.
3. Diagnose deviation or substandard performance.
4. Analyze variance and initiate effectiveness/efficiency improvements in the organization, standards, procedures, or methods.

Resource Planning Group

Capacity planning (34)

Using the forecast load from new projects or from the evolution of existing services, this process defines in a capacity plan how I/S resources will cover the demand. It also proposes alternatives to management (number of shifts, decreased services, changes in systems plan, etc.).

1. Translate service requirements into a load forecast of hardware, network, software, facilities, and supplies.
2. Define capacity of existing and planned resources (hardware, network, software, facilities, and supplies).
3. Compare load forecast against this defined capacity.
4. Identify, evaluate, and propose alternate load forecasts and capacity.
5. Document capacity plan.

Skills planning (35)

Using the requirements identified in the project plan (including management systems) and in the service plan, this process defines in the personnel and the education plans how the existing and planned skills will meet the demand.

1. Define the personnel required to support the service plan.
2. Consolidate personnel required for the project plan, service plan, and career paths.
3. Identify existing and planned personnel.
4. Establish and evaluate alternative personnel plans.
5. Define education plan.
6. Document personnel and education plans.

Budget planning (36)

This process converts individual plans into financial terms and identifies how funds will be obtained and allocated.

1. Translate plans (system, service, project, capacity, personnel, and education) into financial terms.
2. Reconcile sources of funds.
3. Establish and evaluate alternative budgets.
4. Document departmental budgets.

Tactical plan management (37)

This process merges individual plans and resolves any imbalances. It monitors performance against the total plan and determines any corrective action that is necessary.

1. Balance the plans (service, project, capacity, personnel, education, budget, system, application, and data) and obtain management approval.
2. Publish the plans (service, project, capacity, personnel, education, budget, system, application, and data).
3. Compare actual attainment with the plan and analyze variances.
4. Rebalance the plans and obtain management approval (if necessary).
5. Republish the approved plan (if necessary).

Resource Control Group

Change control (38)

Using the change requests, this process selects, coordinates, groups, and monitors all changes to the I/S resources and procedures in such a way that there is either minimal impact on the I/S operations or minimal risk. It triggers resource and data inventory updates.

1. Record change requests.
2. Prioritize and group changes based on a technical assessment.
3. Prioritize and group changes based on a business assessment.
4. Schedule, defer, or reject changes.
5. Monitor testing.
6. Monitor installing.
7. Report and control the status of all recorded changes.

Resource and data inventory control (39)

Using change information, this process builds and manages inventories of all the I/S resources (including personnel and financial).

1. Identify system, application, data, personnel, supplies, and financial resources.
2. Update inventory status.
3. Maintain security of these resources.
4. Administer access of these resources (including data set space allocation and password administration).
5. Report and control status of inventory.

Administration Services Group

Financial administration (40)

This process applies service rates to I/S resources to determine total costs applicable to individual users (including I/S), accumulates these costs, charges the individual user organization (where appropriate), and matches against the budget. The process also includes maintaining contractual agreements for project work, hardware and software leasing, and other supportive efforts.

1. Calculate charges due for services when applicable.
2. Administer vendor and other contracts.
3. Execute cost accounting procedures.
4. Purchase equipment, supplies, and services.
5. Report accounting and financial status.
6. Track vendor performance.

Education and training (41)

This process educates users and I/S personnel on I/S-related topics through job training or formal education.

1. Perform training for I/S services and other needs.
2. Perform education for I/S services and other needs.
3. Develop and maintain education documentation (courses, guides, etc.).
4. Maintain education/training profile.

Staff performance (42)

This process tracks staff performance and reports productivity.

1. Collect data on absences, accidents, and attendance.
2. Collect data on job performance.
3. Compare and report productivity.

Appendix B: Data Class Definitions*

DATA GROUPS

Administration Group (A)

A1. Vendor
A2. Customer/user/group
A3. Organization

Controls Group (C)

C1. Service
C2. Project
C3. Change
C4. Problem
C5. Requirements
C6. System performance
C7. Production and distribution schedule
C8. Management systems performance
C9. Tactical plan
C10. Production and distribution logs

*Entire appendix is reproduced from *A Management System for the Information Business,* Vol. 1—*Management Overview,* GE20-0662-1, by permission of the IBM Corporation.

Environment Group (E)

E1. Enterprise
E2. I/S business
E3. I/S industry

Plans Group (P)

P1. Applications plan
P2. Data plan
P3. Systems plan
P4. Personnel plan
P5. Financial plan
P6. Management systems plan
P7. Service plan
P8. Project plan
P9. Capacity plan

Resource Group (R)

R1. Applications
R2. Data
R3. Software
R4. Hardware
R5. Network
R6. Facilities
R7. Supplies
R8. Personnel
R9. Financial
R10. Standards/procedures/methods
R11. Test data

Transaction Group (T)

T1. Inventory
T2. Project updates

DETAILED DATA CLASS DEFINITIONS

Data group	Data class	Sample data elements
ADM	A1. Vendor	1. Vendor records 2. Offerings a. Products

Data group	Data class	Sample data elements
		b. Financial conditions c. Maintenance conditions d. Etc. 3. Performance 4. History 5. Contracts
ADM	A2. Customer/user/group	1. Customer records 2. Capabilities 3. Relationship assessment 4. History 5. Requirements/needs 6. Service agreement a. Workload forecast b. Agreement performance c. Etc.
ADM	A3. Organization	1. Organization description (Identification codes, mission, charter, objectives) 2. Planned and existing organization structure and quantity of skills 3. Job descriptions/skills/cost 4. Career paths 5. History
CONT	C1. Service	1. Service offering a. Security b. Recoverability c. Auditability d. Etc. 2. Pricing 3. Service performance a. Usage b. Financial 4. History 5. Orders for service
CONT	C2. Project	1. Identification 2. Organization a. I/S b. User 3. Commitments a. Deliverables b. Cost c. Time d. Resources e. Etc. 4. Schedule a. Tasks b. Dependencies c. Resources d. Etc.

Data group	Data class	Sample data elements
		5. Requirement changes 6. Status a. Project b. Deliverables c. Etc. 7. History
CONT	C3. Change	1. Definition of request 2. Dependencies 3. Schedules 4. Status 5. History/trends 6. Inventory update request
CONT	C4. Problem	1. Definition of problem 2. Dependencies 3. Status 4. History/trends 5. Maintenance/tuning request
CONT	C5. Requirements	1. Type of requirement a. Application, data, hardware, facility, network, etc. b. Etc. 2. Business case 3. Requesting organization 4. History/trends
CONT	C6. System performance	1. Measurements 2. Standards 3. Variance
CONT	C7. Production and distribution schedule	1. Production schedule 2. Distribution schedule 3. Maintenance schedule 4. Measurement schedule 5. Service agreement deviations 6. Performance summary
CONT	C8. Management systems performance	1. Organizational assessment 2. Standards/procedures/methods assessment 3. Performance data summary
ENVIR	E1. Enterprise	1. Enterprise mission and objectives 2. Enterprise business processes and information flow 3. Enterprise plans 4. Environmental factors a. Government regulations b. Competition c. Market changes d. Economic trends e. Etc. 5. Enterprise profile/history 6. Enterprise information requirements 7. Enterprise policies

Data group	Data class	Sample data elements
ENVIR	E2. I/S business	1. I/S mission and objectives 2. Global I/S business processes and information flow 3. I/S strategic plans 4. Environmental factors a. Governmental regulations affecting I/S b. Enterprise factors affecting I/S c. Etc. 5. I/S profile/history 6. I/S policies 7. Global architecture for application, data, and technology 8. I/S information requirements 9. Tactical performance summary
ENVIR	E3. I/S industry	1. Technology trends 2. Vendor offerings 3. Environmental factors affecting the industry a. Government attitude b. Etc. 4. Methods and courses available 5. Industry profile/history
PLAN	P1. Application plan	1. Description a. Architecture b. Identification c. Etc. 2. Dependencies 3. Benefits 4. Priorities 5. Preliminary cost estimate 6. Gross design and service requirements to be satisfied in tactical period 7. Planned usage
PLAN	P2. Data plan	1. Description a. Architecture b. Identification c. Etc. 2. Dependencies 3. Benefits 4. Priorities 5. Preliminary cost estimate 6. Gross design and service requirements to be satisfied in tactical period 7. Planned usage
PLAN	P3. Systems plan	1. Description a. Architecture b. Identification c. Etc. 2. Dependencies 3. Benefits

Data group	Data class	Sample data elements
		4. Priorities 5. Preliminary cost estimate 6. Gross design and service requirements to be satisfied in tactical period 7. Planned usage 8. Preventive maintenance plan
PLAN	P4. Personnel plan	1. Skills type by organization 2. Quantity required and when 3. Productivity factors 4. Cost rates 5. Education plan 6. Identification
PLAN	P5. Financial plan	1. Funding 2. Expense budget 3. Capital budget 4. Consolidated budget 5. Identification
PLAN	P6. Management systems plan	1. Description of processes a. Architecture b. Identification c. Etc. 2. Dependencies 3. Benefits 4. Priorities 5. Preliminary cost estimate 6. Gross design and service requirements to be satisfied in tactical period 7. Planned usage 8. Planned organization
PLAN	P7. Service plan	1. Service offering 2. Service forecast a. Volumes b. Manpower c. Revenue d. Cost e. Etc. 3. Service promotion plan 4. Marketplace 5. Recovery plan 6. Security plan 7. Audit plan
PLAN	P8. Project plan	1. Identification 2. Dependencies 3. Resources 4. Priority of projects 5. Project profiles
PLAN	P9. Capacity plan	1. Load forecast 2. Existing and planned capacity by system group or unit

Data group	Data class	Sample data elements
		3. Imbalances 4. Performance summary 5. Identification
RES	R1. Applications	1. Inventory of installed and in-process applications a. Program name b. Program specifications c. Status d. Etc. 2. Source/supplier 3. Ownership 4. Security a. Access b. Physical security 5. Recovery rules 6. Auditability 7. Specifications and design characteristics 8. Maintenance requirements 9. Connectivity/prerequisites 10. Objective module
RES	R2. Data	1. Inventory of installed and in-process data sets a. Data set name b. Assigned library c. Data base name d. Status e. Etc. 2. Source/supplier 3. Ownership 4. Security a. Access b. Physical security 5. Recovery rules 6. Auditability 7. Specifications and design characteristics 8. Maintenance requirements
RES	R3. Software	1. Inventory of installed and in-process software a. Program name b. Program type c. Status d. Etc. 2. Source/supplier 3. Ownership 4. Security a. Access b. Physical security 5. Recovery rules 6. Auditability 7. Specifications and design characteristics

Data group	Data class	Sample data elements
		8. Maintenance requirements 9. Connectivity/prerequisites 10. Object module
RES	R4. Hardware	1. Inventory of installed and in-process hardware a. Hardware name b. Hardware type c. Status d. Etc. 2. Source/supplier 3. Ownership 4. Security a. Access b. Physical security 5. Recovery rules 6. Auditability 7. Specifications and design characteristics 8. Maintenance requirements 9. Connectivity/prerequisites 10. Physical layout
RES	R5. Network	1. Inventory of installed and in-process network a. Name b. Type c. Status d. Etc. 2. Source/supplier 3. Ownership 4. Security a. Access b. Physical security 5. Recovery rules 6. Auditability 7. Specifications and design characteristics 8. Maintenance requirements 9. Connectivity/prerequisites 10. Geographical distribution
RES	R6. Facilities	1. Inventory of installed and in-process facilities a. Facility name b. Facility type c. Location d. Status e. Etc. 2. Source/supplier 3. Ownership 4. Security a. Access b. Physical security

Data group	Data class	Sample data elements
		5. Recovery rules 6. Auditability 7. Specifications and design characteristics 8. Maintenance requirements 9. Connectivity/prerequisites 10. Physical layout
RES	R7. Supplies	1. Inventory of supplies a. Supply name b. Supply type c. Usage/reordering d. Status e. Etc. 2. Source/supplier 3. Ownership 4. Security a. Access b. Physical security 5. Recovery rules 6. Auditability 7. Specifications and design characteristics 8. Storage requirements 9. Connectivity/prerequisites
RES	R8. Personnel	1. Personnel records a. Employee identification b. Employee organization c. Employee skills d. Employee location e. Date of hire/termination f. Promotions g. Education h. Status i. Etc. 2. Education records 3. Performance 4. History 5. Compensation records
RES	R9. Financial	1. Accounting codes (chart of accounts) a. Account number b. Invoice number c. User charge codes d. Contract number e. Order number f. Status g. Etc. 2. Budget performance 3. History a. Accounting codes b. Transactions

Data group	Data class	Sample data elements
		4. Debit/credit transactions 5. Purchase order
RES	R10. Standards/procedures/methods	1. Inventory a. Definition b. Ownership c. Security d. Status e. Etc. 2. History 3. Documentation
RES	R11. Test data	1. Inventory of installed data sets a. Data set name b. Assigned library c. Data base name d. Status e. Etc. 2. Source/supplier 3. Ownership 4. Security a. Access b. Physical security 5. Recovery rules 6. Auditability 7. Specifications and design characteristics 8. Maintenance requirements

References

1. Peter F. Drucker, *Management: Tasks, Responsibilities, Practices* (New York: Harper & Row, 1974).
2. Philip B. Crosby, *Quality Is Free* (New York: McGraw-Hill, 1979).
3. Peter F. Drucker, *The Effective Executive* (New York: Harper & Row, 1967).
4. *A Management System for the Information Business,* Vol. I—*Management Overview,* GE20-0662-1, IBM Corp., Armonk, N.Y., 1981.
5. Richard L. Nolan, *Managing the Data Resource Function* (St. Paul, Minn.: West, 1974).
6. Richard L. Nolan, "Managing the Crises in Data Processing," *Harvard Business Review,* March-April, 1979.
7. Richard Tanner Pascale and Anthony G. Athos, *The Art of Japanese Management* (New York: Simon and Schuster, 1981).
8. Thomas J. Peters and Robert H. Waterman, Jr. *In Search of Excellence* (New York: Harper & Row, 1982).
9. Stanley M. Davis and Paul R. Lawrence, *Matrix* (Reading, Mass.: Addison-Wesley, 1977).
10. Robert N. Anthony, "Planning and Control Systems: A Framework for Analysis," Division of Research, Graduate School of Business Administration, Harvard University, Boston 1965.
11. *Business Systems Planning: Information Systems Planning Guide,* GE20-0527-3, IBM Corp., Armonk, N.Y., 1981.
12. *Managing the Application Development Process, Part 2,* SR20-7246-1, IBM Corp., Armonk, N.Y., 1978.
13. *A Management System for the Information Business,* Vol. II: *The I/S Service Mission,* GE20-0749-0, IBM Corp., Armonk, N.Y., 1983.

14. *A Management System for the Information Business,* Vol. III: *The I/S Development Mission,* GE20–0750–0, IBM Corp., Armonk, N.Y., 1983.

15. *A Management System for the Information Business,* Vol. IV: *Managing the I/S Resources,* GE20–0751–0, IBM Corp., Armonk, N.Y., 1983.

Index